ESSAYS ON NEW YORK COLONIAL LEGAL HISTORY

Contributions in Legal Studies
Series Editor: *Paul L. Murphy*

They Have No Rights: Dred Scott's Struggle for Freedom
Walter Ehrlich

Popular Influence Upon Public Policy: Petitioning in Eighteenth-Century Virginia
Raymond C. Bailey

Fathers to Daughters: The Legal Foundations of Female Emancipation
Peggy A. Rabkin

In Honor of Justice Douglas: A Symposium on Individual Freedom
Robert H. Keller, Jr., editor

A Constitutional History of Habeas Corpus
William F. Duker

The American Codification Movement: A Study of Antebellum Legal Reform
Charles M. Cook

Crime and Punishment in Revolutionary Paris
Antoinette Wills

American Legal Culture, 1908-1940
John W. Johnson

Governmental Secrecy and the Founding Fathers
Daniel N. Hoffman

Torture and English Law: An Administrative and Legal History from the Plantagenets to the Stewarts
James Heath

The Origins of the American Business Corporation, 1784-1855
Ronald E. Seavoy

Prologue to Nuremberg: The Politics and Diplomacy of Punishing War Criminals of the First World War
James F. Willis

ESSAYS ON NEW YORK COLONIAL LEGAL HISTORY

Herbert A. Johnson

Contributions in Legal Studies, Number 21

GREENWOOD PRESS
WESTPORT, CONNECTICUT • LONDON, ENGLAND

Library of Congress Cataloging in Publication Data

Johnson, Herbert Alan.
Essays on New York colonial legal history.

(Contributions in legal studies, ISSN 0147-1074; no. 21)
Bibliography: p.
Includes index.
Contents: The advent of common law in colonial New York—The prerogative court of New York, 1686-1776—Some nice sharp quillets of the Customs Law—[etc.]
1. Law—New York (State)—History and criticism. I. Title. II. Series: Contributions in legal studies; no. 21.
KFN5078.J63 349.747'09 81-6204
347.4709 AACR2
ISBN 0-313-20874-3 (lib. bdg.)

Library of Congress Catalog Card Number: 81-6204
ISBN: 0-313-20874-3
ISSN: 0147-1074

First published in 1981

Greenwood Press
A division of Congressional Information Service, Inc.
88 Post Road West, Westport, Connecticut 06881

Printed in the United States of America

10 9 8 7 6 5 4 3 2 1

Contents

Preface

A quarter century has been stored in memory since Julius Goebel introduced me to legal history in his first-year Columbia Law School course on the Development of Legal Institutions. Since that time I have been fortunate to be able to call on him for advice and counsel at various phases in my career, but his greatest contribution to my training has been the awakening in me of an enthusiasm for legal history that has grown with the passing of time. No one who has worked with Professor Goebel, even as a student in a large law school, can fail to profit from his sterling example of accuracy in research and writing, and precision in the analysis of evidence.

When financial considerations compelled me to transfer to the evening division of New York Law School, I found another distinguished legal historian teaching constitutional law. Paul Hamlin by that time had been cruelly crippled by arthritic disease, but his mind was alert and he had just completed his editorial work on the earliest minutes of the New York Supreme Court of Judicature. His good counsel and encouragement convinced me that it was possible to begin a career in legal history, and that I should persist in my inclination to enter graduate school rather than embarking upon the practice of law. Of course the step could not have been taken without the full concurrence of my wife, Barbara, who agreed to invest our life's savings in tuition fees, and who continued to provide financial support while I pursued the elusive goal of a doctoral degree in history. In the years before large governmental programs for the support of graduate studies came into existence, and teaching assistantships were virtually nonexistent, many wives assumed similar responsibilities, but none did so with more grace and patient understanding than Barbara.

Graduate faculties have traditionally suffered a drain of qualified legal historians to the law schools, where talented men all too often languish in a miasma of student indifference to legal history and faculty bemusement or hostility. Consequently, in 1960 it was my good fortune that Richard B. Morris was teaching graduate courses and seminars at Columbia, and that he agreed to accept me as a student. For five years thereafter we were associated, first as teacher and student, and subsequently as fellow laborers on the Papers of John Jay. Not only did he provide thorough training in research, writing, and editorial methods, but he also taught me to view legal history in a broader societal and intellectual context. Catherine Crary claimed that most of her good ideas for articles and monographs came, either directly or indirectly, from conversations with Professor Morris.

I suspect that many of the essays that follow, developing as they did from my unpublished doctoral dissertation, were sparked by one or more of his suggestions.

When the opportunity to work on John Marshall's papers caused me to move to Virginia in 1967, only three of these essays had been written. I learned then what I had always suspected—that legal history research demands being within a reasonable proximity to the original sources. Manuscript grubbing is time consuming when one is on permanent station; it can be impoverishing when one is one temporary duty. The passage of years has convinced me that my active work on New York colonial legal history must be brought to completion, and the appearance of this collection of essays seems an appropriate coda to an exciting period in my research activities. Since 1960 a burgeoning interest in colonial legal history has produced numerous significant articles and books that have supplemented my contributions to the history of New York law. The preparation of the following bibliography on American colonial legal history has led me to realize how rich the scholarship of the past twenty years has been, and how much my work has been enhanced by that of others.

The essays are arranged in a rough chronological order, but not necessarily as they were written. The last, on English statutes and their reception, draws heavily upon evidence submitted in other essays, hence its posterior position in the collection.

Herbert A. Johnson
Columbia, South Carolina
October 2, 1980

Acknowledgments

For permission to reprint materials in this collection I am indebted to Dover Publications, Inc., Harper and Row, the *American Journal of Legal History*, *New York History*, the *William and Mary Quarterly*, and the *University of Pennsylvania Law Review*. For the release of republication rights I am indebted to Fred B. Rothman & Company. David Syrett of Queens College (City University of New York) has graciously consented to the inclusion of our joint article on customs law.

Over the years my work on these subjects has been sustained by the encouragement and support of my wife Barbara. Despite serious illness she has continued to bring to our marriage the gifts of knowledge, wisdom, and understanding; without her self-sacrifice the bibliographical work would not have been possible.

H. A. J.

American Colonial Legal History: A Historiographical Interpretation

Introduction

NEARLY THIRTY YEARS AGO Professor Julius Goebel commented that "American legal history is in its infancy, and if it is to be reared in accord with the high standards which have prevailed in the writing of English legal history, the matter of tutelage is critical."[1] Although the past three decades have witnessed considerable maturity in the field, there is still a persistent need to give careful attention to the education of a new and larger group of young legal historians. Historiography, one of the most effective pedagogical tools, has been and remains "the foster child of legal history,"[2] in spite of a revived interest in the history of law and the establishment of graduate-level programs at the University of Virginia and Harvard University. To condemn neophytes to wander aimlessly through the maze of American colonial legal history without the aid of historiography is to frustrate them and to elicit from them harsh words of criticism for their elders. One can easily imagine them rephrasing the lament of Peter Van Schaack, one of the many pre-Revolutionary law clerks trained in New York before the advent of the blessed Blackstone, "How many hours have I hunted, how many books turned up, for what three

1. Julius Goebel, Jr., and T. Raymond Naughton, *Law Enforcement in Colonial New York: A Study in Criminal Procedure (1664–1776)* (New York, 1944), xxxiv.

2. The phrase is that of John P. Reid, in *1962 Annual Survey of American Law* (New York, 1963), 742.

minutes of explanation from any tolerable lawyer would have made evident to me."[3] In training legal historians, as in educating colonial law clerks, there is a time for complication through the contemplation of variables, and there is also a time for simplification through the consideration of general principles. Generalization is fostered and facilitated by historiographic analysis and criticism. Thus, if American colonial legal history is to remain a viable academic discipline in the present and to flourish in the future, we must make the initial effort necessary to understand the subject as it has been studied and presented in the past. Based upon the insights gained from considering past writings in the field, we might determine what approaches might prove fruitful for future explorations.

The history of colonial American law came to scholarly attention around the turn of the century when the "frontier thesis" of Frederick Jackson Turner occupied the focal point of historical debate.[4] Not surprisingly, the work of certain legal historians reflected Turnerian influences. The work of Paul S. Reinsch, in particular, was notable for its emphasis on the unique qualities of seventeenth-century American colonial law, and the relationship which the relatively civilized frontier communities in the New World had with the development of legal rules and procedures that differed from Old World models.[5] Although

3. Henry C. Van Schaack, *Life of Peter Van Schaack* (New York, 1842), 9.

4. Turner's exposition of his "frontier thesis," originally delivered as a paper before the American Historical Association annual meeting in 1893, is printed in Frederick J. Turner, *The Frontier in American History* (New York, 1920), 1–38; an excellent critical and historiographic study of the Turner thesis is Ray A. Billington, *The American Frontier* (Washington, 1959), particularly 14–17. John Higham indicated that Turner's was a "divided heritage" encouraging both the use of the frontier and section theses, as well as stressing the importance of western history, *Writing American History* (Bloomington, 1970), 121. In the legal history field it is, of course, the frontier thesis which has the broadest applicability. Richard Hofstadter pointed to a basic contradiction in Turner's work; while Turner was a theorist of historical causation, he was nevertheless opposed to "one idea systems" in the interpretation of historical events and development, *The Progressive Historians* (New York, 1968), 120.

5. Reinsch's doctoral dissertation at the University of Wisconsin was first published in 1899, and is his principal work in American colonial legal history. Its republication in "The English Common Law in the Early American Colonies," in *Select Essays in Anglo-American Legal History*, 3 vols. (Boston, 1907–9), I, 367–415, has made it a classic exposition of Turnerian interpreta-

Reinsch's emphasis on the influence of primitive conditions upon legal development for the most part has been discredited; there were, nevertheless, a number of valid interpretive insights gained from the Turnerian analysis. First and foremost, it was recognized that geographical factors were vitally important considerations to the student of early American law.

This influence of geography on the development of colonial law was profound, indeed. As a rule, colonial court jurisdictions were territorially larger than those in the mother country. Moreover, the cruder systems of transportation made actual distances in the colonies vastly greater than they were in England. Within any given American colony the court systems served both isolated frontier communities in which no trained lawyers practiced, as well as large provincial capitals and trading centers where the bar flourished. Here colonial practitioners equaled in knowledge and skill all but outstanding among their English contemporaries.[6]

---

tion. In a later work, *Colonial Government* (New York, 1902), 244, Reinsch rather inconsistently found that British institutions were successfully adopted by nineteenth-century British colonial possessions; however, Reinsch also discovered these same colonists to be making "decidedly novel experiments" with British forms of government. *Ibid.*, 244–246.

6. The Massachusetts General Court exercised relatively limited jurisdiction over the western counties of the province, and the local courts were initially endowed with powers far in excess of those authorized by the charter. Those same local courts were content with a six-man rather than a twelve-man jury. Joseph H. Smith, ed., *Colonial Justice in Western Massachusetts (1639–1702): The Pynchon Court Record* (Cambridge, Mass., 1961), 66, 90–91. Smith's conclusion is that the court structure and practice was not responding to "frontier" influence, but rather "in shaping the jurisdiction of the lower courts of the judicial hierarchy the General Court [i.e., legislature] followed an eclectic policy grounded upon expediency and pragmatism." *Ibid.*, 198. Clearly one of the practical considerations was the physical impossibility of close supervision over the distant courts of the western counties.

A somewhat similar situation existed in remote Albemarle County, North Carolina, where the local county courts followed their own mode of procedure in spite of proprietary orders to the contrary. Mattie E. W. Parker, ed., *North Carolina Higher-Court Records: 1670–1696,* 3 vols. to date (Raleigh, N.C., 1961–), II, lxxiii–lxxiv. Among the manuscript records of the Tryon County (New York) Court of Common Pleas, I have found unusual motions in arrest of judgment and for a new trial; the routine method of correcting error in counties nearer to the provincial capital at New York City was to take an appeal by writ of error to the Supreme Court of Judicature.

Density of population and landholding patterns, as well as familial relationships, likewise created the need for new principles of law and altered procedures in the courts. We have only begun to appreciate the impact that population density can have on legal development. Clearly, as the number of individuals in a given jurisdiction increases, the number of their legally cognizable controversies also begins to rise. Necessarily the law must exercise an increasing amount of social control as men and communities change from independent, relatively isolated agrarians, into interdependent urbanites.[7]

An emerging school of historical demographers, although primarily concerned with the political and social aspects of statistical studies, has begun to provide the basis for a reevaluation of the connection between population density, family structure, and the law. Philip Greven, for example, has noted the gradual abandonment of a community-wide preference for equal portions being given to all sons under wills and inter vivos deeds of gift in early Andover. This rejection of what is inaccurately termed "partible inheritance" coincided with a growing scarcity of land that persisted in the later years of settlement. By way of contrast, the town of Dedham held fast to the customary rule of equal division of agricultural lands among all the sons of the testator or grantor, according to Kenneth Lockridge, leading to severe economic hardship by the time the fourth generation reached maturity.[8] In a sense the legal rule in Massachusetts Bay remained static—partible inheritance applied to intestate succession in both Andover and Dedham—but in actual practice, those who took positive steps to arrange their estates in those two communities were

7. The legal consequences of population density can best be seen through the experiences of colonial city administrations. As settlement became more dense, the need for greater protection against fire became apparent and water supply became a matter of public concern, as did the increase of crime, violence, and vice. Carl Bridenbaugh, *Cities in the Wilderness* (New York, 1955), 55–93, 206–248. "Townspeople tended to greater violence in their behavior toward one another." *Ibid.*, 222.

8. Philip J. Greven, Jr., *Four Generations: Population, Land and Family in Colonial Andover, Massachusetts* (Ithaca, 1970), 37, 4–78, 83. Kenneth A. Lockridge, *A New England Town: The First Hundred Years* (New York, 1970), 157–159.

guided by sharply different attitudes toward the proper distribution of land.

The Greven and Lockridge studies also demonstrate the conservatism followed by the town proprietors of Andover and Dedham in their initial distribution of land among the original settlers. Lockridge suggests that the preference for small land grants, revolving around the future town common, was for the purpose of achieving social and economic cohesion, and to advance the religious and utopian purposes which formed the basis for the township enterprise. Greven stresses the originally strong preference for an open-field system of agriculture, which made it necessary to maintain land in small tracts reasonably proximate to the town commons and house lots. As an alternative, Greven suggests that the lack of grown children in the new settlement may have limited the supply of labor which each family could devote to its lands; consequently, smaller grants were necessary to avoid waste or inefficient cultivation.[9]

Scarcity of labor is, of course, just another aspect of population density; the sparse population of colonial America had an impact on all phases of community activity, including the formation of the law. As an example of this phenomenon, Sung Bok Kim's study of New York tenants and their jural relationship to their landlords shows that the economic reality of labor scarcity forced the magnates to waive whatever may have remained of their ancient legal privileges and immunities. They provided their prospective tenants instead with substantial advantages in their leases, before adequate settlement of manorial lands could be obtained.[10]

It may be argued that these influences did not alter the law as it existed in the statute books, or as practiced in the courts, but such an interpretation is undoubtedly too narrow a conception of what the law is. Customary usages have always played an important role in the development and modification of the law, and colonial America was

9. Greven, *Four Generations,* 49; Lockridge, *New England Town,* 12, 13.

10. "A New Look at the Great Landlords of Eighteenth-Century New York," *William and Mary Quarterly,* 3d ser., XXVII (1970), 599–610; attempts to regulate labor in colonial America are discussed in Richard B. Morris, *Government and Labor in Early America* (New York, 1946).

forced to utilize custom when New World conditions dictated alterations from the English pattern. As settlements aged, their economic and social circumstances began to approximate those of the mother country, and early variations from English practice undoubtedly began to fall into disuse as a consequence. However, variations built into the American situation—large tracts of land on the western frontier and an undersupply of labor in the older sections of the colonies—continued to make their inroads into the monolithic adoption of English common law throughout the colonial period.

Few students of American colonial history have failed to marvel at the appetite for litigation displayed by the early Americans. Historical demographer John Demos has examined the architecture of Plymouth Colony homes in the seventeenth century. When the limited space, and hence small opportunity for privacy, is compared with the large size of the individual family units, it becomes obvious that the living arrangements of Plymouth residents were fraught with possibilities for intrafamilial conflict. Some of these arguments actually reached the courts of law, where Demos discovered them along with a strikingly large number of law cases between neighboring families. Demos advances a "germ of a hypothesis" which should cause legal historians to pause and contemplate: that these colonists redirected their feelings of anger and aggression, aroused by overcrowding, by arguing with and suing their neighbors.[11] Certainly this is as plausible an explanation as has ever been given for the multitude of small and inconsequential matters which came before many of the seventeenth-century colonial courts.

While these historical demographers are not Turnerians in the narrow sense of the term, they, and indeed most modern historical writers, share in the rich heritage that Turner left to the profession. Turner was the first to break with the old institutional school which attempted to trace the gradual and unilateral historical development of sharply segregated portions of human and community life. In legal

11. John Demos, *A Little Commonwealth: Family Life in Plymouth Colony* (Oxford, 1970), 46–51. This volume is filled with insights that will be helpful to all colonial legal historians.

history, as Roscoe Pound has argued persuasively, this approach resulted in a severe categorization and a compartmentalization of historical study which eliminated the need to consider the overall impact of formative influences upon the law derived from all sorts of human experience and thought.[12] By way of contrast, the "Turnerverein" returned to the historian's task of assessing *all* causative factors and of isolating those which appeared to be most determinative in shaping the new American nation.[13] In that sense their history was more catholic than that of the old institutional school they intended to replace. While Turnerianism has come into disrepute because of the emergence of internationalism and intellectual history,[14] the revisionism has been directed primarily at the western provincialism of the school and its tendency toward overemphasis of environmental determinism. American history in general partook of this revisionism, as did American colonial history, but both have preserved the most valuable of Turner's lessons concerning the influence of environment on human life and thought, and particularly on the development of legal institutions and principles. The Turnerians anticipated the use of social science methods in historical analysis and writing, and it is in this context that the school has the most to offer to the study of American legal history.[15]

12. Pound rejected the historical jurisprudence of the nineteenth century, and found its interpretations of legal history too narrow and compartmentalized. As far as he was concerned, the dynamic nature of the law was not taken into account in institutional studies which stressed gradual legal development along experiential lines. Roscoe Pound, *Interpretations of Legal History* (Cambridge, 1923), 12, 52, 74, 85–88, 92–93, 103, 188. He counseled, "'Physical environment may not be ignored by jurist or legal historian." *Ibid.*, 117.

13. Higham, *Writing American History*, 118; Hofstadter, *Progressive Historians*, 66–67.

14. Higham, *Writing American History*, 122.

15. *Ibid.*, 125. Higham attributes the revival of Turnerian emphasis in the years 1941 to 1946 to the contributions of the social scientists. It is this period which I have, for convenience, termed "neo-Turnerianism." There is undoubtedly a great deal of Turnerian influence in the work of James Willard Hurst and his disciples, who stress the interaction between law and society in nineteenth-century America, but I have not discussed this school because its techniques are not generally applicable to the materials for colonial legal history.

Turnerianism undoubtedly has meant a variety of things to different historians, and it was only within the narrow circle of his disciples that Turner was followed with any semblance of orthodoxy. Among the true Turnerian colonial legal historians, Reinsch stands alone. But Richard B. Morris in his *Studies in the History of American Law,* first published in 1930, can be said to be one of the earliest legal historians in the "neo-Turnerian" school which stressed the social sciences and multiple causation. There is a paradox in all this. For Morris by virtue of his place of birth and training, as well as by intellectual inclination, was a more fit candidate for inclusion in the "asphalt flowers" school of historical writing, which because of its international sentiments and urban inclinations attacked the midwestern provincialism of Turner. Morris's dissertation, written under the direction of Evarts B. Greene—an institutionalist of the Osgood school—exhibited striking parallels to Turnerian thought and method in legal history. For example, Morris noted that it was the topography and barren soil of New England that forced the abandonment of the English inheritance system of primogeniture, and the concentration of landholdings into freehold tenements arranged in compact settlements.[16] Following Reinsch's example, Morris examined all of the colonies, rather than the experience of only one jurisdiction, and found among them certain common characteristics which seemed to justify the use of the term "American law" in pre-Revolutionary America.[17] His hypothesis, that "profound changes in social outlook can be traced to conditions on the frontier and to a changed intellectual and theological equipment," was to be tested by a comparative study of three topics of substantive law that would show "social engineering evolving out of the frontier."[18] Morris's inclusion of intellectual and theological factors undoubtedly represents an alteration of, or even a departure from, the Turnerian pattern, and it is in this sense that his disclaimer of membership in the "indigenous law"

16. Richard B. Morris, *Studies in the History of American Law,* 2d ed. (Philadelphia, 1959), 75–77.
17. *Ibid.,* 11.
18. *Ibid.,* 10–11, 20–21.

camp of the Turnerians must be understood.[19] In the larger sense that we have viewed the writings of the "Turnerverein," there was much in *Studies* that entitled it to be included within the Turnerian or, perhaps more accurately, the "neo-Turnerian" school.

The controversial and pioneering approach of *Studies* was evident in two aspects of the work. First, it was a pilot work which attempted to study, in a comparative way, certain principles of law as they evolved in the American colonies. Second, it treated three topics of substantive law—the distribution of land, the rules of tort liability, and the legal rights of women—which were most susceptible to social, intellectual, and environmental influences. In retrospect it might be said that there were two inherent limitations to Morris's approach. His selection of topics was not at all representative of a valid cross section of colonial law; moreover, his attempt to employ the comparative method across jurisdictional lines utilized a scholarly format which encouraged disregard for the subtle differences between the colonies with respect to their institutions, environment, social structure, and their constitutional position within the British Empire.

But we must realize that Morris considered his monograph only a pilot study to point the way toward a new approach in American colonial legal history. The important thing was not that he chose topics which were most likely to reflect alterations because of American conditions, but rather that he was willing to come to grips with the substantive law. Limitations in source materials made it extremely difficult to study such subjects, and vast preliminary searching was required to develop the necessary documentation for analysis. The value of a multijurisdictional approach to substantive law materials might be justified on these grounds alone. Morris's aim was not to trace the detailed evolution of legal principles and institutions, but rather to identify those factors of environment, society, and intellectual activity which influenced the development of law in colonial

19. Significantly, Morris did not expressly repudiate the "frontier thesis," of an indigenous form of law developing in America, in his 1959 introduction, but rather asserted that its impact should be closely evaluated, region by region. *Ibid.*, vi, viii.

America. While writing in the framework of a traditional institutional historian, heavily influenced by Turnerian analysis, he transcended the methodology of both fields, and throughout *Studies* there were thoughtful commentaries that can still lead scholars down new and unexplored investigatory paths.

Morris noted, for example, the seventeenth-century New England policy for the wide distribution of the ownership of real property and the consequent evolution of rules of descent and distribution of intestate estates to encourage that policy. The work of Greven and Lockridge, discussed above, continues this exploration through a more detailed analysis of the history of given New England localities. Morris commented on the Kentish origins of New England settlers, and surmised a connection between partible inheritance and Kentish gavelkind. While the connection has been disproved in a later article by George L. Haskins, the examination of English customary law and its impact on American colonial legal institutions has become an important part of the analytical tools of all historians, including those working in legal history.[20]

The section in *Studies* dealing with tort law in colonial America remains unique in the subtlety of its analysis and the scope of its coverage. Since the various forms of modern liability had not evolved by the end of the eighteenth century, it was extremely difficult to determine precisely what English common law was at any given point during the American colonial period.[21] Naturally the lack of any colonial law reports before the end of the eighteenth century prevented other than the most general surmises concerning the principles

20. *Ibid.*, 69–125; the material on gavelkind is in *ibid.*, 103–111. Haskins, "The Beginnings of Partible Inheritance in the American Colonies," *Yale Law Journal*, LI (1941–42), 1280–1315, as reprinted in David H. Flaherty, *Essays in the History of Early American Law* (Chapel Hill, 1969), 204–244. For studies stressing the influence of English customary law on colonial legal institutions see Julius Goebel, Jr., "King's Law and Local Custom in Seventeenth Century New England," *Columbia Law Review*, XXXI (1931), 416–448, as reprinted in Flaherty, ed., *Essays*, 83–120; and Sumner Chilton Powell, *Puritan Village: The Formation of a New England Town* (Middletown, 1963).

21. For a general discussion covering developments from Anglo-Saxon times to 1850, see John H. Wigmore, "Responsibility for Tortious Acts: Its History," in *Select Essays in Anglo-American Legal History*, III, 474–537.

of tort liability which the colonists considered applicable to their peculiar circumstances. In regard to trespasses of animals, Morris noted that the English colonies universally imposed a duty on landowners to fence their fields against wandering livestock, while English law required that cattle and other animals be "fenced in."[22] American colonists in the seventeenth century did not resort to the futility of the deodand—a procedure for inflicting punishment upon animals, or even inanimate objects, which caused tortious injuries. However, Morris pointed out that as English common law rules gained greater acceptance during the eighteenth century, American courts began to utilize the deodand with increasing frequency.[23] By way of contrast, American colonials preceded their English contemporaries in passing laws for the prevention of cruelty to animals.[24] These and other divergences from English common law rules of tort liability demonstrate invaluable insights into the social conscience and value systems of colonial America. They reveal, moreover, the extent to which legal history studies in this area can advance our general understanding of colonial civilization.

Significant though these discoveries were, it was Morris's comparative method which made *Studies* a classic in the field, and one worthy of careful attention by the present generation of legal historians. Although the colonies differed markedly from one another, each was more like its sister provinces than it was like the mother country. Colonials were as troubled by the variations between provincial legal systems as they were by the uncertain adoption of English case law and statutes by the courts of colonial America. The New York Moot, meeting during the last decade of the colonial period to debate points of law, found that most of its sessions dealt with con-

22. *Studies,* 208–217; see also "Statutory Modifications of the Common Law Trespassing Cattle Rule," in Young B. Smith and William L. Prosser, eds., *Cases and Materials on Torts* (Brooklyn, 1951), 662–665; and William L. Prosser, *Handbook of the Law of Torts* (St. Paul, 1941), 434.

23. *Studies,* 225–230; a more detailed consideration of colonial deodands is in Cyrus H. Karraker, "Deodands in Colonial Virginia and Maryland," *American Historical Review,* XXXVII (1932), 712–717.

24. *Studies,* 231, 232.

flict of laws between the province of New York and the precedents and statutes of her sister colonies.[25] Morris suggested the connection between the New England codes, the Duke's Law of New York, and the Pennsylvania "Great Law" of 1682. This phenomenon of intercolonial statutory borrowing was later more fully explored by George L. Haskins and Samuel E. Ewing.[26]

In retrospect it becomes apparent that Morris was far in advance of his time when *Studies in the History of American Law* was published. The work of succeeding generations of legal historians has benefited immensely from these early scholarly explorations. Although more recent and detailed monographs have modified certain of Morris's conclusions, his overall approach in his *Studies* has successfully met the test of time. It has been unfortunate that more of the topics he explored were not reconsidered and expanded as new materials became available. Perhaps even more significant in a historiographic sense is the fact that Morris's grand design for the study of colonial legal history has not been given its proper due; as a result much remains to be accomplished before the fullest potentialities of his creative pioneering work can be fulfilled.

While Turner's influence predominated in the early twentieth-century writing of colonial legal history and, as we have seen, was carried to new levels of utility by the work of Morris, the older institutional school of history had by no means surrendered its place to the exponents of the frontier thesis. Nor, for that matter, had all legal historians embraced the "indigenous law" principle. Throughout these early years, the flow of institutional monographs continued. The work of German-trained institutional historians, particularly that

25. For a discussion of the Moot, see Herbert A. Johnson, "John Jay: Colonial Lawyer" (unpubl. doctoral dissertation, Columbia University, 1965), 177–181.

26. "The Spread of Massachusetts Law in the Seventeenth Century," *University of Pennsylvania Law Review,* CVI (1957–58), 413–418, as reprinted in Flaherty, ed., *Essays,* 186–191. An interesting general article on statutory borrowing is Stefan A. Riesenfeld, "Law-making and Legislative Precedent in American Legal History," *Minnesota Law Review,* XXXIII (1948), 103–144.

of Herbert B. Adams, stressed the remote European heritage of colonial American law, thereby promoting an exaggerated sense of continuity across the ages.[27] It was monographic studies such as these which drew the sharpest criticism from Turner and his students. However, we should note that Adams's studies of colonial legal institutions *predated* Turner's "frontier" speech by more than ten years. The leading institutional historian of American colonial history, Herbert L. Osgood, wrote *after* Turner had come to public attention and redirected the historiographical thought of the profession. Osgood was emphatic about showing the use of English institutions in the New World. But he was also careful to point out that these applications of English antecedents were not mere slavish imitations, but a conscious selection of Old World forms and rules in which the colonists resorted to "natural selection" to choose those that seemed suitable to meet the needs of their frontier conditions.[28]

Osgood was the first professional historian to treat the American colonies and the colonial period in totality, and his monumental works remain essential basic reading for students in the field.[29] Unquestion-

27. Adams's principal works in legal history are "The Germanic Origin of New England Towns," in *Johns Hopkins Studies in History and Political Science*, ser. 1, no. 2 (1882), 5–38; "Saxon Tithing-men in America," *ibid.*, ser. 1, no. 4; and "Norman Constables in America," *ibid.*, ser. 1, no. 8 (1883). His contemporaries John W. Burgess and Albert B. Hart were more active in political history and political science.

28. *The American Colonies in the Seventeenth Century*, 3 vols. (New York, 1904–7), I, 426; II, 437; III, 14–15. In an earlier address Osgood had also stressed the need for a study of the colonies as a group, from the viewpoint of a general American colonial history, as well as forming a part of the British Empire. "The Study of American Colonial History," in *Annual Report of the American Historical Association for the Year 1898* (Washington, 1899), 65–66, 70. In the same article he stressed the need to study colonial political and constitutional institutions, for "it is only through law and political institutions that social forces become in a large sense operative." *Ibid.*, 68.

29. Totality in the sense that quantitatively Osgood covered the chronology of colonial America with a thoroughness not previously achieved, and at the same time qualitatively "total" in the sense that while his focus was on political developments, he was quite sensitive to economic influences on history, as well as certain religious and intellectual considerations. In a sense my use of the term "totality" for Osgood's work seems similar to the "unity" which Avery Craven discovered in the work of Turner. Compare Avery Craven, "Frederick Jackson Turner," and E. C. O. Beatty, "Herbert Levi Osgood,"

ably his close analysis of institutional development and his expertise in the presentation of a highly objective and factual narrative place him in the front rank of those historians in the institutional school. Yet his work also exhibits familiarity with the methodology of the Turnerians as well as a certain sensitivity to the use of social science methods. Indeed, as we have indicated, there are passages which contain so much environmental determinism that they could, if taken out of context, be assumed to have been written by Turner himself.

While tracing colonial legal historiography it is essential that one recognize the pervasive impact of Frederick Jackson Turner upon even the institutionalists, and particularly upon Osgood. It is only by tracing the institutional school backward in time to the essays written by Herbert B. Adams on colonial legal institutions that we can uncover a pure institutional approach. Adams's work by modern standards is somewhat cumbersome in its reasoning, and unpersuasive in its treatment of the problems of causation. The abundance of doctoral dissertations and narrow monographs in the institutional school which follow Turner in time, but reject his influence, have not made any perceptible impact on the history of American colonial law.[30] Osgood's great work on colonial America, however, outshines the efforts of his contemporaries, simply because he was willing to

---

both in William T. Hutchinson, ed., *The Marcus W. Jernegan Essays in American Historiography* (Chicago, 1937), 259, 279–283. Beatty comments, "With all his attention to minutiae, Osgood possessed the power of clear and forceful generalization." *Ibid.*, p. 289.

Osgood's volumes on the eighteenth century were published posthumously as *The American Colonies in the Eighteenth Century*, 3 vols. (New York, 1924). His studies of the land system of the seventeenth-century colonies and the court system of the later proprietary colonies are particularly valuable for legal historians. Osgood, *Seventeenth Century*, I, 424–467; II, 16–57, 277–308.

30. Many of these monographs provide valuable descriptions of legal systems and institutions; however, their failure to deal with the problems which are fundamental to colonial legal history is unfortunate. See Arthur P. Scott, *Criminal Law in Colonial Virginia* (Chicago, 1930); Elmer B. Russell, *The Review of American Colonial Legislation by the King in Council* (New York, 1915); Edwin L. Page, *Judicial Beginnings in New Hampshire, 1640–1700* (Concord, N.H., 1959); Charles J. Hilkey, *Legal Development in Early Massachusetts* (New York, 1910); and Oliver P. Chitwood, *Justice in Colonial Virginia* (Baltimore, 1905).

adapt what was best in the institutional methods and to accommodate that substantial residue to what he deemed valid in the Turnerian historiography.

While Osgood's work bears the mark of Turner's pervasive influence, it remains nevertheless one of the outstanding contributions of the institutional school to American colonial history. In countless graduate schools throughout the nation, students turned their attention to the study of the evolution of institutions. Those interested in legal history examined with increasing care the legislative acts and court records of colonial America. Supposedly following Leopold von Ranke's dictum "to tell history as it really was," they aimed for objective truth by remaining free from any preconceived ideas. For American colonial legal history this meant placing major emphasis on institutional developments rather than on the evolution of legal thought. Indeed the inheritance of the institutional school is at once the greatest glory, and the most stultifying influence, on the writing of legal history at the present time.

An institutionalist attempts to avoid any amount of speculation or interpretation of the meaning of his primary sources. This approach requires that his subjects be those which can be explained through the examination of substantial amounts of primary source material—not only for information and explanation, but also for verification of one's findings. Before writing institutional history in the classical manner, one must first be certain that the sources are adequate, lest research lead the scholar down paths where his evidence will become too sparse to provide the definite information and gratifying verification which is essential to the objective institutionalist. In other words, the accidents and vagaries of documentary preservation become inherent limitations upon the scope of the work which any institutional historian may undertake.

One result of this archival determinism has been that little has been written about the substantive law of colonial America. Practically no serious institutional work has been done on the legal history of the southern colonies other than Maryland. Procedural matters, on the other hand, are well documented in the many surviving court records of the seventeenth century, and the less informative, but nevertheless useful, court minute books of the eighteenth century. While southern court records, and indeed all court archives other than those of New England, were in serious disarray during the nineteenth century, and for most of the present century, Massachusetts documentation has been preserved in great bulk, and has served to feed the note cards of countless graduate students working in American colonial legal history. One can safely venture the assumption that the legal history written about seventeenth-century Massachusetts Bay and Plymouth exceeds in sheer volume the history of all of the other colonies put together.[31]

Despite the narrowness and conservatism of institutional legal history, it should be abundantly clear that an understanding of legal procedure is absolutely essential to telling the overall story of legal development. The law now is, and has always been, predicated upon certain preordained systems of adjective law which dominate not only the substance of the law but also the very manner in which lawyers and laymen customarily think about their courts and the law administered therein. Because procedural law is the best-documented area of early American law, it offers to the legal historian his best hope to understand the fundamental assumptions upon which all of colonial jurisprudence was founded. Yet those who write upon procedural matters tend to consider them the alpha and the omega of colonial legal history, which only leads to interpretive difficulties.

Matters of procedure are generally isolated from public interest and concern; as professional topics they fall entirely within the expertise of lawyers and judges. For centuries adjective law was virtually immune to legislative alteration, and evolved through court

31. For the lack of southern studies see Flaherty, ed., *Essays,* 12–13. Pennsylvania has suffered neglect despite the presence of a strong history department at the University of Pennsylvania throughout this century. Massachusetts' preeminence may be attributable to the location of Harvard University, but a substantial number of the Massachusetts articles and monographs are by non-Harvard-related scholars. Columbia University, by way of contrast, seems to have sent its students and faculty members to concentrate their efforts on the relatively meager and inaccessible source material for New York colonial history.

rulings and customs of the profession. Thus procedural law is something very special in the spectrum of legal knowledge, and it is unwise to inflate it beyond the limits of its importance. To consider procedural law a bellwether of legal development is highly misleading, for by doing so scholars—like the blind man grasping the tail of the elephant—may wind up accounting the characteristics of but one part of the beast. It is true that Maitland admonished his hearers, "The forms of action we have buried, but they still rule us from our graves," but earlier in the same speech, he had noted that his preference for procedural matters was not shared by all, and many felt that "substantive law should come first—adjective law, procedural law, afterwards." In the shadow of Maitland, we have perhaps fallen victim to an overemphasis on the very topics which were most neglected in his day. It is time that the pendulum of historical study swung back in the direction of substantive law topics, for as Maitland also pointed out, it is through greater knowledge of procedure that we are enabled to better understand the substantive law.[32]

Among the institutional historians of early American law, none has equaled the stature of Julius Goebel, Jr. Trained at Columbia's Faculty of Political Science under John Bassett Moore, Goebel completed his doctoral dissertation in diplomatic history in 1915,[33] and then moved on to study and teach at Columbia Law School until his retirement in 1968. After several years studying medieval English criminal procedure, Goebel turned his scholarly talents toward the study of criminal procedure in colonial New York. In collaboration with T. Raymond Naughton he published the definitive monograph on this subject in 1944.[34] The work shows all of the insights to be

32. The oft-quoted expression is from a lecture Maitland delivered in London which was published posthumously in 1909. Frederic W. Maitland, *The Forms of Action at Common Law,* ed. by A. H. Chaytor and W. J. Whittaker (Cambridge, Eng., 1968), 1.

33. Julius Goebel, Jr., *The Recognition Policy of the United States* (New York, 1915), 8.

34. *Law Enforcement in Colonial New York: A Study of Criminal Procedure (1664–1776).* Goebel's earlier study was *Felony and Misdemeanor: A Study in the History of English Criminal Procedure* (New York, 1937); earlier he wrote an exploratory article on the New York manorial system, which re-

gained from an encyclopedic knowledge of English criminal procedure and its application to colonial adaptations. Crisp and precise in its discussion of details, *Law Enforcement* is an outstanding example of institutional history at its best.

Goebel, following the more expansive tradition of Osgood, clearly recognized the limitations of the earlier and more orthodox institutional legal history. His introductory remarks to *Law Enforcement* leave little doubt that he was interested in the influences and social forces which shape the law. "The legislation of another age has meaning only if examined in connection with the social, economic and political factors which conditioned its enactment," he counseled.[35] There were certain differences between American colonial law and its English precedents, but Goebel stressed the cultural background of the settlers, which he believed was most responsible for determining the nature of the legal rules they wished to apply in their American settlements.

Aware of the separateness of the American colonies from the mother country, as well as from one another, he commented on the variations in intellectual "pull" which English tradition exerted on each colony. Goebel denied, in general, both Turner's "frontier theory" in the development of American law and Roscoe Pound's rejection of colonial legal history as irrelevant to the subsequent development of American law and legal institutions.[36] According to Goebel, the study of American colonial legal history was concerned with "the problem . . . of accounting for historical reality and it is

---

mains one of the best legal history studies of these remnants of feudalism. "Some Legal and Political Aspects of Manors in New York," Order of Lords of Colonial Manors in America, *Publications*, no. 19 (1928).

35. *Law Enforcement*, xxix. The close analysis of statutory materials per se is of course important to the legal historian's craft. See the works of Mark DeWolfe Howe, "The Sources and Nature of Law in Colonial Massachusetts," in George A. Billias, ed., *Law and Authority in Colonial America* (Barre, Mass., 1965), 1–16; "The Recording of Deeds in the Colony of Massachusetts Bay," *Boston University Law Review*, XXVIII (1948), 1–6; and "The Process of Outlawry in New York: A Study of the Selective Reception of English Law," *Cornell Law Quarterly*, XXIII (1937–38), 559–573, as reprinted in Flaherty, *Essays*, 433–450.

36. *Law Enforcement*, xix, xx, xxi.

more profitably approached as one in the mutations of a transplanted culture. Like every bit of Old World civilization brought overseas, the law underwent a process of indenization, of acquiring a New World identity."[37] In other words, the legal historian had to understand all of the forms of English law, both common and local, in order to be able to accurately trace their growth and adaptations in the alien soil of the American colonies. Goebel concluded that there were only slight variations between colonial New York's criminal procedure and that utilized in the mother country. The degree to which English procedural standards had been transplanted was what governed the proficiency of New York lawyers, and not any influence of the "frontier."[38]

Goebel restored the importance of institutional studies as much by the excellence of his work as by his allowance for the influence of nonlegal factors. Although he cannot in any way be said to have advocated a "social science" approach to legal history, he was very much concerned with the impact of the total human experience upon the development of American law. When viewed within this context, the law was not a subject isolated from general historical development in the American colonies as a whole.

Legal historians view Goebel and Morris as representatives of two different "schools" of colonial legal history, yet the foregoing discussion blurs many of the most facile distinctions which have been made between them. Clearly Morris searched for general rules in the development of colonial law, and was intent upon those changes from English practice which might demonstrate the existence of an indigenous law in seventeenth-century America. Equally obvious is the fact that Goebel worked in a more restricted jurisdictional framework, with a primary interest in examining the growing professional expertise of colonial lawyers and their relationship to the gradual acceptance of English rules. As we have indicated, substantive law subjects lend themselves to broad and general treatment, and the absence of adequate sources for each colony might frustrate or discourage institutional historians. Conversely, criminal procedure is so well docu-

37. *Ibid.*, xx.
38. *Ibid.*, xxi, xxviii–xxix, 760.

mented in each of the provincial systems that a comparative approach to all the colonies would lead to mountains of detail that would engulf the reader, if not the would-be author.

Part of the distinction between the two men is thus inherent in their subject matter, but in terms of thematic interpretation of their materials they differ even more markedly. Simply stated, the two legal historians differed in their allocation of importance to the law itself. Morris used legal history to provide a body of evidence for an extended commentary on colonial Americans and their society. Goebel treated legal history as the central focus of his study, subordinating all other considerations, and considering only those other historical forces and events which were directly relevant to legal development. Goebel's work was "legal-centered" while that of Morris was "society-centered."[39] These differences in scholarly viewpoint are what account for the variety in their legal history, but essentially both men were products of the institutional school as altered by Turner. Being younger, Morris was more profoundly influenced by the social sciences and their impact on historical analysis. However, the distinctions do not seem sufficiently large to justify the differentiation of a "Goebel" school and a "Morris" school of American colonial legal history.

A variety of viewpoints, rather than true historiographic distinctions, has typified the writing of American colonial legal history since the publication of *Studies* and *Law Enforcement.* Joseph H. Smith, a former student of Julius Goebel who assisted in the preparation of *Law Enforcement,* turned to the paths developed by the imperial school of colonial history and wrote a superb monograph covering the legal and constitutional aspects of Privy Council appeals from the colonies.[40] Conforming to the "imperialist" format, Smith included

39. See Richard B. Morris, "The Sources of Early American Law: Colonial Period," *West Virginia Law Quarterly,* XL (1933–34), 215–216, for the clearest statement of this viewpoint which underlies much of Morris's work in legal history. A similar statement stressing the social history possibilities for legal history sources is George L. Haskins, "Court Records and History," *William and Mary Quarterly,* 3d ser., V (1948), 550, 551.

40. Joseph H. Smith, *Appeals to the Privy Council from the American Plantations* (New York, 1950); see also his article "Administrative Control of the Courts of the American Plantations," *Columbia Law Review,* LXI

Jamaica and the British West Indies within his area of study; he thereby became the first American legal historian to consider imperial law as it had been understood and administered at Whitehall during the seventeenth and eighteenth centuries.

There was a wealth of local detail in Smith's *Appeals* volume, but his focus never shifted far from the Privy Council chamber. The reader was given an excellent overview of the legal development of each colony as it appeared to the bureaucrats in London. At the same time he was instructed in the intricacies of Privy Council procedural and substantive law. What was especially noteworthy in Smith's study was the care with which he delineated the impact of political pressures and the influence of the royal prerogative upon the Council's legal decisions. Smith found that the members of the Council were extremely ignorant of colonial conditions, and quite condescending in their evaluation of the legal accomplishments of colonial lawyers and judges. This official attitude, he concluded, prevented the Council from ever becoming an effective supreme court for the plantations; it tended, on the contrary, to encourage a spirit of independence on the part of the colonists.[41]

With an eye toward the advent of the American Revolution, however, Smith cautioned against placing an undue emphasis on the Council's actions in constitutional appeals from the North American plantations. Similar legal matters arising in the Channel Islands were treated as routine judicial business, he noted. The Privy Council did not manage its appellate business as if it were the supreme court of the empire, but rather as if it were the highest appellate court in each colonial jurisdiction. Moreover, colonial conditions and the internal

---

(1961), 1210–1253, as reprinted in Flaherty, ed., *Essays,* 281–335. For discussions of the imperial school see Michael Kraus, *The Writing of American History* (Norman, 1953), 242–270; Lawrence H. Gipson, "The Imperial Approach to Early American History," in Ray A. Billington, ed., *The Reinterpretation of Early American History* (San Marino, Calif., 1960), 185–199. Charles M. Andrews drew attention to the imperial approach in an early paper, published as "American Colonial History, 1690–1750," *Annual Report of the American Historical Association for the Year 1898* (Washington, 1899), 49–60.

41. Smith, *Appeals,* 654–664.

appellate systems within each colony resulted in large variations in the number and types of appeals which the Privy Council heard from each of the overseas possessions. The Council thus emerged in *Appeals* to be a tribunal charged with the overall review of legal business within each colony, rather than an instrument of the royal prerogative utilized to consolidate and unify the legal development of Britain's far-flung colonial empire.[42]

Smith's *Appeals* is as significant in constitutional history as it is in legal history. It helped to fill a substantial void in the general history of the American colonies, for little work of such careful detail had been done on the constitutional relationship of the colonial governments with the mother country and with one another. Just as a study of the present-day Supreme Court of the United States places one at the nexus of law and politics, so the study of the Privy Council placed one at a similar advantage in understanding the British Empire before 1783.

While Professor Smith's excursion into the broad world of imperial judicial activity was under way, another legal historian, George L. Haskins, emerged from his earlier studies of English parliamentary institutions to commence a reinterpretation of the legal and constitutional history of the Bay Colony. After establishing his credentials by writing a number of provocative articles on property law and decedent estates in Massachusetts and Plymouth,[43] Haskins undertook the task of rewriting the legal and constitutional history of Massachusetts for the first two decades of its existence. Like Goebel he sought, and usually found, in the background of the settlers adequate basis for the

42. *Ibid.*, 655.

43. Haskins's earlier books on English legal history were *The Statute of York and the Interest of the Commons* (Cambridge, Mass., 1935) and *The Growth of English Representative Government* (Philadelphia, 1948). Among Haskins's early articles are "The Beginnings of Partible Inheritance in the American Colonies," *Yale Law Journal*, LI (1941–42), 1280–1315, as reprinted in Flaherty, ed., *Essays*, 204–244; and "A Problem in the Reception of the Common Law in the Colonial Period," *University of Pennsylvania Law Review*, XCVII (1949), 842–853, which was revised and published as "Reception of the Common Law in Seventeenth-Century Massachusetts: A Case Study," in Billias, ed., *Law and Authority in Colonial America*, 17–31.

legal principles which developed in the colonies in North America. However, in writing his major work, *Law and Authority in Early Massachusetts,*[44] he focused not only on the legal institutions which the Bay Colonists had known, but also on the religious and philosophical ideals upon which they based their New World experiment in self-government. In this way Haskins brought intellectual history to bear on the problems of colonial legal history.

The years from 1630 to 1650 were crucial to the future development of law and authority in Massachusetts, for these were "the formative years during which, under the pervasive influence of Puritan doctrine, and with virtually no outside interference, the structure of civil government took shape and was completed."[45] Dealing with the evolution of both public and private law, Haskins emphasized the impact of tradition—social, political, legal, religious, and intellectual—as well as the dynamic pressures requiring a restructuring of the law, both public and private, to make it more suitable to the overall goals for which the colony was founded. Such conscious efforts toward change he denominated "design," hence the subtitle of the word, "a study in tradition and design."[46]

Rather than dealing with the detailed development of private law in the second section of his book, Professor Haskins chose to examine certain of those subjects to demonstrate the process of the reception and adaptation of English legal traditions into the law of Massachusetts. His discussion emphasized the diverse sources upon which the colonists drew to construct their early legal system. *Law and Authority* thus provides a blueprint of the manner in which a new government was erected in Massachusetts. Yet in explaining these developments even to 1650, Haskins was required to touch on nearly every aspect of the totality of life within the colony. The central theme dealt with causation—those cultural forces which made Massachusetts law different from the law of England and, at the same time, a recognizable subsystem of English law.

44. George L. Haskins, *Law and Authority in Early Massachusetts: A Study in Tradition and Design* (New York, 1960).
45. *Ibid.*, ix.
46. *Ibid.*, 228–231.

What emerged from *Law and Authority* was a particularly complex story of the convolutions of these various cultural forms and their ultimate amalgamation into a coherent system of public and private regulations for the governance of life by the Puritans within the "City upon a Hill." Yet it is not because of its institutional findings that the book is entitled to careful study by legal historians, but rather because of its inclusion of intellectual factors among those forces which shape and condition the development of law. Following the paths blazed in intellectual history by Samuel Eliot Morison and Perry Miller, Haskins made their methods an integral part of his study of Massachusetts legal development in the seventeenth century.[47] Except for a few article-length treatments,[48] no legal historian has so far been inspired to follow Haskins's example in utilizing intellectual history as a key to causation in American colonial law. Nevertheless, it is unquestionable that law responds as much to ideas which are current in society as it does to factors such as land availability, population density, and economic development. American colonial legal history can learn from Michael Kraus's perceptive teachings that the Atlantic Ocean, far from being a barrier to interchange of ideas and customs, actually served as an efficient bridge of communications and transportation, linking together the portions of Britain's colonial empire washed by its waters.[49]

We know that English lawbooks were used extensively in the colo-

47. "Religious doctrine," asserts Haskins, was one of the "principal strands which held together the web of government." *Ibid.*, 43. His fourth chapter, "A Due Form of Government," examines Massachusetts civil government in the light of Puritan political thought. *Ibid.*, 43–65. The sixth chapter, "Communities of Visible Saints," deals with public and private law ramifications of Puritan religious practices and ethical standards. *Ibid.*, 85–93. On the connection between religion and law, see Simeon L. Guterman, "The Interaction of Religion, Law and Politics in Western Society: Its Historical Character and Influence," *University of Miami Law Review*, XVII (1963), 439–468.

48. Haskins's student Ralph H. Clover published an excellent study along these lines entitled "The Rule of Law in Colonial Massachusetts," *University of Pennsylvania Law Review*, CVIII (1960), 1001–1036. Another useful study is David Fellman, "Property in Colonial Political Theory," *Temple Law Quarterly*, XVI (1942), 388–406.

49. Michael Kraus, *Intercolonial Aspects of American Culture on the Eve of the Revolution* (New York, 1928), particularly 210; *The Atlantic Civilization: Eighteenth Century Origins* (Ithaca, 1949).

nies, but we have not begun to study the extent to which they became "American" lawbooks through their influence in colonial courts and in training American lawyers.[50] There is no comprehensive list of English lawbook holdings in colonial libraries, something which would provide an invaluable guide to the number of copies of each title and its geographic distribution in North America. This would be a handy method for determining the most widely-circulated English legal literature, and make possible a much more sophisticated answer to the difficult question of how much of American law followed English precedent in the eighteenth century.

Another continuing intellectual influence on colonial legal development can be found in those members of the colonial bar who received their legal training at either the Inns of Court or some English country law office. Sending young men to England for their professional training was not a popular practice in every colony, by any means, but even those provinces which sent a token number of students were rarely without at least one English-trained attorney or barrister in their midst.[51]

Recently Joseph Smith has published a thoughtful article considering the theory of judicial precedent as it was followed in the American colonies.[52] Carefully examining the printed records of the American colonies, as well as many manuscript sources, Smith found a strong

50. Eldon R. James, "A List of Legal Treatises Printed in the British Colonies and the American States Before 1801," in *Harvard Legal Essays Written in Honor of and Presented to Joseph Henry Beale and Samuel Williston* (Cambridge, Mass., 1934), 159–211, particularly 159–179. Although James's list is an impressive one, anyone familiar with colonial law practice can readily see that a substantial number of English lawbooks were imported, since they were not locally printed. Some bibliographic work on colonial law libraries has been done. Paul M. Hamlin, *Legal Education in Colonial New York* (New York, 1939), 73–94, 171–196; Johnson, "John Jay," 168–175, 265–272; Edwin Wolf 2d, "Historical Development of the American Lawyer's Library," *Law Library Journal,* LXI (1968), 440–450.

51. Hamlin, *Legal Education,* 12–23; Johnson, "John Jay," 10–12, 17–20; Edward A. Jones, *American Members of the Inns of Court* (London, 1924).

52. "New Light on the Doctrine of Judicial Precedent in Early America: 1607–1776," in John N. Hazard and Wenceslas J. Wagner, eds., *Legal Thought in the United States of America under Contemporary Pressures* (Brussels, 1970), 9–39.

tendency in eighteenth-century American courts to follow English precedent unless their own legislature or some prior decision by their provincial courts indicated that English law did not apply. He concluded that the doctrine of judicial precedent, just beginning to develop in England, took strong root in the American provinces. In directing scholarly attention to the possibilities inherent in a multijurisdictional study of a doctrine of law, Smith reaffirmed the underlying validity of Richard Morris's multijurisdictional approach in *Studies*. At the same time, by stressing a jurisprudential aspect of colonial law, he brought into play the analysis of legal philosophy as it was practiced, if not fully articulated, in the American colonies. The materials are scarce, as Smith's article shows, but similar studies might be undertaken concerning the colonial attitude toward the statute of frauds, the principle of res judicata, or such aspects of the law of evidence as the hearsay rule, the best evidence rule, or exclusion of privileged communications.[53]

Every so often, each legal historian should take a busman's holiday into comparative studies. In a certain sense every legal historian resorts to the comparative method, for as Maitland noted in his inaugural lecture, true legal history cannot exist without comparisons between variations in the law and between one legal system and another. George Haskins's comparative study of codification—drawing parallels between the experiences, both social and legal, in early New England and similar phenomena in the Greek colonies at isolated points on the shores of the ancient Mediterranean sea—stands as a model of imaginative comparative history.[54] We have studied revolutions in a comparative way, and we are beginning to analyze imperial expansion and administration in a comparative framework.[55] Is it not

53. Morris, *Studies,* treats the privileged communication between spouses in a cursory way, 199, 200.

54. George L. Haskins, "Codification of the Law in Colonial Massachusetts: A Study of Comparative Law," *Indiana Law Journal,* XXX (1954–55), 1–17.

55. For a discussion of comparative revolutions, including a useful bibliography, see Robert R. Palmer, "The Revolution," in C. Vann Woodward, ed., *The Comparative Approach to American History* (New York, 1968), 46–61; on imperalism in the nineteenth century see Robin W. Winks, "Imperialism," in *ibid.,* 253–270; comparative colonial empires in the seventeenth and

time that men who know the law utilize one of legal education's greatest gifts to the social sciences? The more widely dispersed in time the comparisons may be, the less utility the conclusions may have for "hard-core" legal history; yet the insights into causation are enhanced by similar responses made throughout the ages to nearly identical circumstances. And increasingly what legal historians must seek is not merely factual knowledge of the past, but also a more sophisticated understanding of the nature of law and its part in the broad spectrum of human experience in society.

Within the scope of American legal history it is important to consider the effects of periodization and categorization upon the writing of legal history. Many years ago Professor Daniel Boorstin drew attention to the fact that legal historians tend to categorize and classify their topics according to subjects recognized in modern American law.[56] He criticized this tendency in terms of its propensity toward anachronism as well as its hobbling effect on historical analysis. Boorstin wished to have legal history broadened in scope, and at the same time have it recognized that the law itself was an integral part of historical development. He concluded that legal historians should concern themselves more actively with the relationship between the history of law and the growth of society and its institutions. More recently, Stanley N. Katz has suggested that another problem is one of periodization: that by adopting overly shortened time periods, legal historians do not permit themselves proper freedom to examine long-range developments in the history of law.[57] If, for example, the study of eighteenth-century colonial law were continued through the Jacksonian period, certain patterns might emerge that would not be discernible if the analysis had been terminated in 1776 or even 1800. There are, of course, vast differences between the research methods of colonial legal history and the history of later decades when the

---

eighteenth centuries are treated in John J. Tepaske, ed., *Three American Empires* (New York, 1967).

56. Daniel J. Boorstin, "Tradition and Method in Legal History," *Harvard Law Review*, LIV (1941), 424–436.

57. "Looking Backward: The Early History of American Law," *University of Chicago Law Review*, XXXIII (1966), 867–884.

number of printed reports of cases facilitates the work of the scholar in his search for rules of law. Yet the variation in research technique should not prove overly inconvenient, for most colonial legal historians have a basic acquaintance with the system of legal research necessary to gain access to the printed law reports.

In a general way, we must realize that what Professors Boorstin and Katz have suggested is that legal historians must be willing to abandon some of the conventions which they have established in the past. What they need is to strike out for a broadly conceived legal history that seeks to explain colonial law, not in contemporary legal context, but as it was conceived in the seventeenth and eighteenth centuries. The constructive criticism of these two scholars is entitled to great weight, and will no doubt receive the compliment of scholarly adoption within the next few years. As a group, colonial legal historians have adapted slowly to changing trends in historiography. But as we have seen, there is a close correlation between the writing of American colonial history in general and the interpretive and historiographic methods which have altered the writing of colonial legal history.

A major development which has made American colonial legal history a more promising field in recent years has been the slow but steady increase in the number of court records which have appeared in print.[58] This assures future generations of legal historians a readily available source of materials for conducting comparative studies among colonial jurisdictions. Coupled with the new methodological approaches, this multiplication of printed sources makes the subject at once less narrow in its research techniques, and promises to liberate the legal historian from the drudgery of scanning countless volumes and file boxes of manuscript court records, seeking one or two bits of evidence among the dirty and crumbling documents. The time conserved could well be used for more extensive evaluation of causation than has been customary in the past.

Complementing the publication of American colonial court records

58. For a survey see Michael G. Kammen, "Colonial Court Records and the Study of Early American History: A Bibliographical Review," *American Historical Review*, LXX (1964–65), 732–739.

has been the appearance of the legal papers of colonial practitioners. The most significant of these, of course, were the *Legal Papers of John Adams,*[59] which hopefully will set a standard for future publications of this nature. Law practice in the colonies was not specialized, but general in nature, and thus the legal papers of an active attorney provide a superb "lawyer's eye" view of the law as integrated in his practice. Practitioners are not permitted the academic legal scholar's leisure to view law as a large topic, divided into several distinct categories, such as contracts, torts, equity, property law, constitutional law, or domestic relations. Any given case might well involve several of these subjects, as well as the usual problems of the law of evidence and rules of practice, which can shape the issues presented to the judge or jury. The distortions of legal history caused by categorization, particularly those mentioned by Boorstin, can be neutralized by looking at the legal system through the extant law office files of a colonial lawyer. While the appearance of lawyers' papers has not as yet been sufficiently large to make a cumulative impact in this direction, we can anticipate some historiographic trend as new legal papers appear in print.

American colonial legal history has grown considerably in the past forty years, and its indebtedness to the interpreters of the general history of colonial America is readily apparent. At this time it seems abundantly clear that there is room for greater expansion of the study as well as a need for new and altered viewpoints toward the proper subjects for legal history study. Legal historians owe it to themselves as well as to the historical profession in general to undertake work in topics for which the documentation is slender and conclusions can be only tentative in nature. Problems of causation must be analyzed with care, bringing to bear upon legal development and its history all of the current discoveries in the social sciences. There is a need for

59. L. Kinvin Wroth and Hiller B. Zobel, eds., *Legal Papers of John Adams,* 3 vols. (Cambridge, Mass., 1965). For a comment on the legal aspects of the major historical publication projects, see Richard B. Morris, "The Current Statesmen's Papers Publication Program: An Appraisal from the Point of View of the Legal Historian," *American Journal of Legal History,* XI (1967), 95–106.

comparative studies, as well as expansion into the field of legal philosophy and its history in colonial America. There have been, and will continue to be, finite limits to the information which legal historians can obtain from colonial materials. Much documentary evidence has already been destroyed, and that which remains does not always contain the information which the researcher would like to have. Faced with discouragement over this state of affairs, legal historians need not despair, for the example of students of Roman law, struggling with their fragmentary and scattered collections of rescripts and monumental inscriptions, should serve to breed a sense of documentary abundance. The lack, we must admit, lies not as much within the documentary record as within ourselves—we are unimaginative and poorly-motivated.

Much has been written about the relationship between legal studies, historical scholarship, and the profession of legal history.[60] The perennial interest in this topic is, no doubt, directly proportional to the number of legal historians seeking placement in their field, either in history faculties or in the law schools. For clearly there is little need for legal history unless it be considered pertinent to one or the other of the disciplines—at least as far as job placement of legal historians is concerned. Yet the subject is a valid professional subdivision which draws upon both law and history for its techniques of study and for the training of its professionals. It can do much for both law schools and graduate schools in advancing their pedagogical purposes. To historians legal history brings a specialized knowledge of the law and the development of legal institutions. The degree to which historians of the law can broaden their perspectives to include in their works a proper consideration for the interrelationship between law and so-

60. Among the more helpful articles are Charles F. Mullett, "The Value of Law to Historians," *Missouri Law Review,* IX (1944), 144–164; Ben W. Palmer, "The Historian and the Lawyer," *American Bar Association Journal,* XXXII (1946), 530–536; Charles E. Wyzanski, Jr., "History and Law," *University of Chicago Law Review,* XXVI (1959), 237–244; Frederick B. Wiener, *Uses and Abuses of Legal History: A Practitioner's View* (London, 1962); and Calvin Woodard, "History, Legal History and Legal Education," *Virginia Law Review,* LIII (1967), 89–121.

ciety will help to determine how far legal history can lead the way toward a better understanding of the nature of man and his social activities. To legal educators and law students, legal history explains the law as it was in the past, thereby throwing light on the state of the law at the present. It has been said that the current development of legal studies places undue emphasis on "presentism," leaving students and professors without a sense of the past and consequently with an unreal view of the law and its place in the social framework.[61] Legal history can provide a useful antidote to such a tendency. It can provide lawyers and law students with a sensitivity toward the evolutionary characteristics of legal development—a kind of guide to the achievements and failures of the past in the attempts made to use legal methods to improve the state of man, his institutions, and his way of life.

In the final analysis, the history of law in colonial America, or any other field of legal history, is basically historical in its approach and methods. History as the study of human life and experience within recorded time includes within its broad commission the study of men's laws and the institutions they have erected to enforce their laws. To deny the primary historical foundation of legal history, and to make it relevant to today's problems, is to confuse the purpose of legal history and to debase its practice. Simply put, legal history is the memory bank of the legal profession; it serves lawyers best when it remains independent of their preoccupation with the present, as well as their desire to shape the progress of the future through the guiding hand of reforming legislation and court decisions. At the same time, however, legal history must communicate its findings in such a way as to make its lessons clear and meaningful to men of the law. Legal history should be expected to explain the importance of purely technical studies to the general history of the law as well as the overall history of the American people.

The challenge to legal history in the years ahead—particularly to American colonial legal history—is one of redefining its own identity.

61. *Ibid.*, 109, 112.

It must move forward to examine the history of law within a broader context than ever before, and to exhibit in its writings and its teaching the vitally important role that law has always played in our society. As we have seen, the leading scholars in the field of American colonial history have already pointed the way that must be traveled; it is for the legal historians of the present, and those who are being trained to write and teach in the future, to fulfill the great expectations and dreams of those who have so rapidly advanced the study in the past seventy years.

The Legal History of Colonial New York

The Advent of Common Law in Colonial New York

ONE OF the most perplexing questions in the legal history of the American colonies is posed in determining the reasons underlying the transition from a seventeenth-century system of local law to an eighteenth-century legal system in which English common law became the established mean. While historians and lawyers have generally approached the problem seeking continuity and evolutionary development, it is here contended that this change, at least as far as the Province of New York was concerned, was abrupt, calculated, and dictated by the legal development which had occurred during the proprietary period from 1664 to 1685.

To understand the wholesale acceptance of English common law after 1691, it is necessary to review the legal institutions of New York as they developed during the relative calm of the years 1664 to 1685. During the period of the Dominion of New England and the military tribunals of Leisler's revolt, the political turmoil was such as to discourage normal legal development. Hence those years are excluded from this study. A further limitation on the scope of this essay is imposed by the need to compare the disparate legal systems of proprietary New York without becoming involved in the intricacies of minute differences in substantive or procedural law. For these reasons, this essay will consider the jurisdiction of courts to be the basis upon which the New York legal systems may be compared, and shall restrict its analysis to the colonial courts in the New York counties as far north as Westchester.

The mode of settlement of New York determined the manner in which its laws were to be formed during the seventeenth century. Dutch traders at New Amsterdam brought with them the highly developed civil law system of their homeland, and this Roman-Dutch law continued to govern the relations between the people of New York City long after the flag of the Dutch West India Company was lowered at the fort on the Battery.[1] Migration of settlers from Connecticut across Long Island Sound and overland from western Connecticut, resulted in the introduction of "Bible Codes" in the areas of their settlement in Westchester and Suffolk Counties.[2] Superimposed on these two indigenous systems of law was the English common law, preferred by the proprietor and the Crown. These three disparate legal systems supplied law to the inhabitants of proprietary New York. Considering the large elements of the population who owed loyalty to the two indigenous systems, it is remarkable that the institution that survived into the eighteenth century was English common law.

How did it happen that New Yorkers permitted twenty-seven years of precedent under the proprietary government to be discarded in exchange for the wholesale importation of English common law? What had so weakened the indigenous legal systems that they fell easy victims to the externally imposed institution? Where are the vestiges of Roman-Dutch civil law and the "Bible Codes" in the eighteenth century? What, in short, worked this remarkable transformation in such a short period of time?

One of the most striking characteristics of New York law during the proprietary period was its complexity. The complexity resulted not only from the attempt to apply three systems of law within one political subdivision, but also from the very confused situation concerning the jurisdiction of courts. Both the complicated nature of the law and the conflicting court jurisdictions, in turn, may be attributed to the precarious hold of the English conquerors over the Dutch and Puritan province. Faced with the problem of governing a colony where the majority of the population was non-English and non-Anglican, English governors refrained from making sudden changes; rule by diplomacy rather than by force resulted in the continued application of Dutch and Puritan law in the proprietary province of New York.

After the conquest of New Netherland, the English governor, Richard Nicolls, was faced with the formidable task of ruling a population composed of Dutch-speaking inhabitants and Puritan dissenters. Both groups had evolved their own legal systems, and promised to offer strong resistance to the imposition of English common law. Consequently the Duke's Laws, promulgated in the spring of 1665 did not apply to the Dutch settlers, and appeased the Puritans of Long Island by substantially restating their town laws, which were based upon the Bible Codes of New England. Representatives of the Westchester and Long Island towns met at Hempstead, in March of 1665, and gave reluctant approval to this new code of laws. One major reason behind the resistance to the Duke's Laws at the meeting was that the governor's approval was required for the election of townsmen to serve as constable and overseers in local communities. The institution of a system of courts based upon the local justice of the peace and triennial Courts of Sessions, also was unpopular. Such restrictions upon the previous self-government of the towns were bound to cause resentment.[3]

Surprisingly the delegates to the Hempstead assembly did not realize that the Duke's Laws, despite their ostensible reaffirmation of the Long Island Bible Codes, actually provided procedural devices whereby the extinction of Puritan law was guaranteed. There is no question that the jurisdiction of the Courts of Constable and Overseers, the successors to the independent town courts of Long Island, was sharply restricted. Hitherto such courts had general jurisdiction to try all matters; now their authority was reduced to where they could try only small causes where the amount in controversy did not exceed £5. Furthermore, appeals from the Courts of Constable and Overseers, were to be heard by the Courts of Sessions. The Sessions Courts, composed of justices of the peace appointed by Nicolls, reviewed the decisions of the local courts and also confirmed the appointment of the constable and overseers of the towns on behalf of the governor.[4] In this way, the Duke's Laws guaranteed not only the close local supervision of the town courts in their judicial capacity, but also enabled the governor to verify the political reliability of a town official before his election was confirmed. It seems clear that a continuance of some vestige of the New England codes was being tolerated, but only under close supervision. Nicolls had begun to lay the foundation for a centralized judicial system based upon the authority of the governor.

Despite the efforts of Nicolls and his advisers, the system of courts established in Long Island and Westchester proved to be a cumbersome arrangement. The lower courts were to have jurisdiction only over those areas within town limits. Town boundaries in the seventeenth century were imprecise, not only because of conflicts in land grants, but also because Long Island towns had refused to submit their patents, Dutch land briefs, and Indian deeds to the governor for confirmation.[5] These efforts to deny jurisdiction of the Duke of York over the Long Island settlements made it impossible to determine just where the bounds of those towns actually were. For this reason the jurisdiction of the Courts of Constable and Overseers was constantly open to challenge upon the basis of some disputed town boundary.

The Court of Sessions, according to the Duke's Laws, was to be a tribunal of general jurisdiction throughout Long Island and Westchester. To this court were assigned civil cases where the amount in dispute did not exceed £20, all cases concerning title to real property, and those causes appealed from the Courts of Constable and Overseers. The Courts of Sessions, in addition, were empowered, at least in theory, to try all criminal matters, including those punishable by death. In practice, however, nearly all prosecutions for felonies were instituted before the Court of Assizes.[6] Further inroads into the general jurisdiction of the Courts of Sessions were made possible by provisions in the Duke's Laws which conferred concurrent jurisdiction upon the Court of Assizes in civil cases where the amount in litigation exceeded £20.[7] Because of this situation, any party wishing to pay the higher costs in the Court of Assizes could avoid the jurisdiction of his local Court of Sessions. To the extent that the substantive law applied in the Court of Assizes might differ from the local law applied in the Court of Sessions, the opportunity to select a more favorable court presented an unfair advantage to the plaintiff.

Not surprisingly, there are numerous instances where the Court of Assizes transferred cases originally commenced before it, to the Courts of Sessions for trial.[8] The short term during which the Court of Assizes met, coupled with the inconvenience of assembling juries from distant counties in New York City, made such transfers desirable. However, had the Courts of Sessions been permitted a general jurisdiction in their various ridings, the Court of Assizes could have functioned more efficiently as a tribunal of appellate jurisdiction.

From the foregoing description, it may be seen that, intentionally or otherwise, the jurisdiction of the Courts of Sessions was left in an amorphous state. In cases where the amount in litigation was less than £20, the jurisdiction was clearly vested in the Sessions Court; in cases where the cause involved more than £20, and in all criminal cases, the Sessions Court exercised whatever authority the Court of Assizes was willing to permit. Litigants selected their court without any clear-cut guide lines concerning whether the case would be heard by the court in which it was commenced or transferred to some other court. Added to this uncertainty was the possibility of selecting a court that would apply the legal system most favorable to a party's position.

The dynamic force behind the judiciary in proprietary New York was the General Court of Assizes, the highest court in the Province. Composed of the governor, his Council, and all of the justices of the peace of the Province, this court met annually in October, usually in New York City, the capital of the Province. Because of its composition, the Court of Assizes exercised both legislative and judicial authority, much like the English House of Lords.[9] While we need not be concerned with the legislative authority of the court in this essay, it is important to realize that the plenary power of the Court of Assizes resulted in procedures quite different from those in the inferior courts. Particularly noteworthy in this regard was the rule that should the Court of Assizes be confronted with a criminal case where the offense had not been prohibited by the Duke's Laws, the court itself was empowered to try the offense after deciding whether it was a punishable trangression. Professor Julius Goebel has noted the large number of crimes that were not enumerated in the Duke's Laws, including manslaughter and rape. In these and other like offenses, the Court of Assizes apparently fixed the penalty after convicting the accused.[10]

In its capacity as the highest court in New York, the Court of Assizes possessed the power to resolve conflicts of jurisdiction between the various lower courts. For example, in 1667 a judgment of a Westchester town court was vacated, presumably for lack of jurisdiction, and the case was referred to the local Court of Sessions for the North Riding.[11] In its supervisory capacity, the Assizes Court was frequently plagued by the petitions of unsuccessful litigants who demanded that the local judges be censured or removed because of decisions adverse to the petitioners. To put a stop to this practice, the Court of Assizes in 1681 declared its support for the judges and thereafter enforced a policy that relief from adverse judgments could be had only by way of appeal.

Appellate procedure before the Court of Assizes was formal in nature, and was begun by a petition filed by the applicant. This petition was the basis upon which the appellant argued his case before the court. Prior to filing such a petition the appellant was required to post a bond to secure the costs of the appeal and to file a notice of appeal with the clerk of the Court of Assizes. Failure to post the bond or to file the notice of appeal was adequate ground for a non-suit.[12] An interesting departure from this procedure occurred in 1682 when the clerk of the Assizes Court was instructed to prepare the case for a group of Indians who were claiming an injustice at the hands of their local Court of Sessions.[13] Such an extraordinary step gives evidence of the importance the New York governors attached to amicable Indian relations.

According to the Duke's Laws, the Assizes Court could hear new evidence only in those cases where a material witness was not heard by the court of original jurisdiction. This rule was amended in 1666 to confer upon the court the power to hear appeals on the facts, as well as the law, whenever "... the Court shall see Cause."[14] After this change, review by the Court of Assizes of facts on appeal was virtually unlimited and its control over inferior courts vastly increased. Usually the Court of Assizes remitted cases to a Court of Sessions for retrial. However, in those causes bearing upon public policy, such as the titles to township lands and Indian affairs, a new hearing of the evidence normally occurred before the Court of Assizes.[15] In at least one of these cases, the Court of Assizes overruled the verdict of a seven-man jury rendered in the lower court.[16]

With the establishment of the office of justice of the peace in the Province of New York, English common law practices began to intrude on the local level. On the provincial level, the impact of English common law was made evident in the Court of Assizes. The preference for trying felonies before the Court of Assizes closely paralleled the tradition in England where felony prosecutions pending before the Courts of Quarter Sessions of the Peace would be held for the arrival of the justices on the assize instead of having such causes tried by the local justices of the peace, who in Quarter Sessions, possessed the requisite jurisdiction.[17] Before the Court of Assizes, there was a conscious attempt to duplicate the English writ system, and the minutes of that Court's proceedings contained references to the English forms of action.[18] Apparently the authorities were attempting to introduce English modes of practice through the provisions of the Duke's Laws and the activity of the Court of Assizes. Yet the numerous departures from the English common law norm emphasize the strong resistance to English legal institutions that still prevailed in seventeenth-century New York.

If the judicial system established by the Duke's Laws had been the sole basis of legal development in proprietary New York, it is possible that the conflicting jurisdictions referred to above may have been resolved, and the Province might have started down the path toward a gradual reception of English common law. That such was not the case was due to the continued existence of the Dutch courts, left relatively unchanged by the conquest in 1664, and to the creation of a system of private manorial courts. Both these courts functioned outside the court system established by the Duke's Laws.

Dutch civil law survived in the province of New York primarily because the population of the colony was predominantly Dutch and any inroads into Dutch institutions might prove particularly dangerous. Estimates for the years 1672 and 1673 indicate that approximately three-fifths of the people in the Province were Dutch and one-fifth were composed of disaffected Englishmen on Long Island, who, because of their Puritan inclination, desired to become a part of the corporate colony of Connecticut. While the Englishmen were more vocal in proclaiming their rights, the Dutch remained secure in their preponderance of numbers. Despite the occasional protests from Long Island, the Puritan towns gradually lost their independence as the Duke's Laws began to take effect. The Dutch, on the other hand, became taciturn under English rule and succeeded in resisting English legal institutions for several decades. Accepting the superficial changes made in their traditional Court of Burgomaster, Schepens and Schout, which was renamed the Mayor's Court of the City of New York, they continued to operate the court according to Dutch rules.[19]

One of the more bizarre results of the English attempt to alter the Dutch court, was the compromise reached in regard to jury trials during the proprietary period. In complying with the English insistence upon jury trials, the Dutch were ostensibly more conscientious than required by the Duke's Laws. The Mayor's Court of New York always utilized a twelve-man jury, while in those areas where the Duke's Laws were applied, a seven-man jury was usually employed.[20] Having thus complied with the conqueror's whim, the Mayor's Court proceeded to use a trial jury in a suit for separation from bed and board. This may well have been the only time that a jury was used in an English matrimonial case. In this suit for separation, as in a criminal case that followed, the court rendered its decision, and then as if an afterthought, requested the jury to ratify the verdict already given by the court.[21] In still another case, the trial jury was asked to rule on whether a party should be non-suited for failing to produce a document before the court.[22] Whether these unorthodox practices were the result of Dutch intransigence, or whether they resulted from a complete ignorance of the proper function of a trial jury is difficult to assess. However, the English towns of New Netherland had been permitted to use trial juries under the Dutch government, and this past familiarity with jury trials indicates that the Mayor's Court was employing the trial jury as a protective device by which it could shield itself from a charge by the governor that the court was exceeding its powers. After the Mayor's Court was called before the Court of Assizes in 1681 to answer a charge of treason concerning its alleged denial of a jury trial, the Court's attitude toward the "formality" of jury trial seems to have been substantially altered.[23]

Although the Mayor's Court of New York reluctantly accepted the English system of jury trials, it nevertheless continued to exercise its traditional probate jurisdiction under Dutch law. Furthermore, the Mayor's Court possessed a criminal jurisdiction equivalent to, or perhaps even greater than, the penal authority of the Courts of Sessions. One of the lasting vestiges Dutch law left upon the New York legal system was its extensive use of arbitration in the settlement of law suits.[24]

While the first English commission to the Mayor's Court confined its territorial jurisdiction to Manhattan Island, the court had traditionally exerted its authority beyond those limits. From the cases heard by the court, it would appear to have been the rule that the court would entertain any cause arising in adjacent territory provided that there was no court functioning in that area. Consequently, a contract of sale executed in New Jersey in 1668 was the subject of litigation in the Mayor's Court, as were other cases involving "bronx-Land" and the town of Fordham.[25] While in each instance the presence of the parties gave jurisdiction to the Mayor's Court, there can be little doubt that the doctrine of *forum non conveniens* played a small role in early Manhattan jurisprudence.

The Mayor's Court under the English also continued to exercise its maritime jurisdiction. Before the appointment of a judge of admiralty in 1683, the court frequently received a commission from the governor to sit as a court of admiralty in a particular cause.[26] There were, however, a number of instances in which the Mayor's Court of its own volition heard suits concerning seamen's wages and maritime contracts.[27] It is almost impossible to ascertain those cases tried solely upon the basis of a special commission and those cases which determined solely upon the existence of certain inherent powers of the court. We can only conclude from the evidence that the Mayor's Court exercised independent admiralty jurisdiction, subject to the prohibition of the governor in certain cases.[28]

Of all the courts in the judicial system of proprietary New York, the Mayor's Court of New York City was most clearly the one that took a hybrid form. Retaining a large part of its jurisdiction from the Dutch period, it gained new powers by grant of the English governors, or by various provisions of the laws enunciated by the governor and Council. Neither entirely statutory nor entirely customary in its source of authority, the Mayor's Court derived its power from both sources. For this reason it is nearly impossible to determine the limits of the Mayor's Court jurisdiction during the proprietary period. However, once the majority of the population was no longer Dutch and the English authorities could move with greater assurance against the independence of the Mayor's Court, its unique characteristics began to disappear. It became, in fact, a court of common pleas for New York City.

Contrary to the policy of *laissez-faire* evidenced by the English concerning the Dutch court system in New York City, the governors of the Province of New York took positive steps with regard to the establishment of private manorial courts. Although these courts in themselves were merely appendages to the manorial land grants, they served to further complicate and confuse the already complex system of courts within the Province.

As historians have long noted, the New York manors were created to serve two principal functions: defense and social control. Along the shores of Long Island and the outlying settlements in the Hudson River valley, the manorial grants were made in strategically located areas to guarantee the loyalty of leading citizens in the event of Dutch revolt or Indian attack. In the case of the manorial grants on Long Island, a class of large landowners with aristocratic privileges was formed to curb the extreme republican tendencies of the Puritan townspeople. To this extent the manorial lords of New York served a useful function in making possible a stronger political control of the Province by English governors.[29]

By far the most extensive grant of privileges made by the Duke of York was that to Thomas Mayhew, who, at the age of eighty, was made governor for life of Martha's Vineyard. Simultaneously Mayhew was made lord of Tisbury Manor, but his jurisdiction as governor extended far beyond the boundaries of this manor. As governor, he presided over the annual general court for Martha's Vineyard and Nantucket, which exercised civil jurisdiction without appeal in all cases below £50. This court also served in a legislative capacity, and its laws were binding upon the people under its control, subject only to confirmation by the governor in New York City. In the exercise of criminal jurisdiction, all transgressions other than those punishable by forfeiture of life or limb, or banishment, could be heard before Mayhew's general court.[30] The authority granted to Mayhew was subject only to judicial review by the New York Court of Assizes, and to confirmation of legislative acts as noted above. For most purposes, Martha's Vineyard continued to be substantially independent of New York until it, along with Nantucket, was re-annexed to the Bay Colony by the Massachusetts charter of 1691.

The extent to which private jurisdictions, such as that of Mayhew and the manorial lords, were used to avoid the authority of provincial courts is difficult to determine. We know that at least one manor lord was quite jealous of his prerogatives. John Archer, lord of Fordham Manor, refused to accept service of process from the Mayor's Court of New York, and erected a manorial court to rule the town of Fordham. According to a petition to the Mayor's Court, he fined an opponent in a lawsuit pending in the Mayor's Court the sum of £20 when he found that unfortunate man in the town of Fordham and hence subject to the jurisdiction of his manorial court.[31] Another manor lord, John Pell of Pelham Manor, was also challenged for avoiding the power of the provincial courts by utilizing his own jurisdictional privileges.[32] In the long run, however, the impact of these private jurisdictions upon the development of New York law was probably very slight. What is of importance, is the fact that these manorial grants weakened the power of the provincial courts. They made equal justice under the law unavailable when one's adversary was a manor lord and undermined the power and prestige of the courts held under the authority of the governor. In this way, manorial grants originally made to secure military and political objectives, worked against the governor's efforts to establish a sound judiciary in the Province.

As a result of the inroads of private jurisdictions and the persistence of Puritan "Bible Codes" and Dutch civil law institutions, the Province of New York during the proprietary period presented an intricate patchwork pattern of local law. While the government gave clear indications of its desire to impress an English pattern upon the court system, the implementation of the Duke's Laws resulted in a jumble of jurisdictions between the town courts, the Court of Sessions, and the Court of Assizes. The situation was only compounded by the continued existence of the indigenous legal systems which continued to function to a greater or lesser degree after the English conquest.

When in 1683 the English population of New York had reached a point where a General Assembly could safely be called, the people of the Province began to pay more attention to the court system. The result was a bill to revise the judiciary passed in 1683. Characteristically the jurisdiction of the local town courts was again reduced, and the Courts of Sessions were placed under the immediate supervision of Courts of Oyer and Terminer. Appeals from the Courts of Oyer and Terminer could be prosecuted to the High Court of Chancery at New York, consisting of the governor and Council, or to the Privy Council in England.[33] Once this new system of courts was in operation the old Court of Assizes was abolished.[34]

The court system erected under the Judiciary Act of 1683 enjoyed but a short tenure and was superseded in rapid succession by the courts of the Dominion of New England and the military tribunals of Leisler's revolt. Practice under the 1683 Act was so brief that it could not have been of much assistance to the lawyers who became engaged in setting up the Supreme Court of Judicature in 1691. Nevertheless, the example of the 1683 Judiciary Act, coupled with the declining influence of the Long Island town courts and the New York City Mayor's Court, provided a rare opportunity to completely revise the system of law in the Province of New York. With the establishment of the Supreme

Court of Judicature, the day of redemption for English common law in the Province of New York was at hand.

Mere alteration of a court system does not of itself indicate a change in the substantive law of a region. Indeed, it is possible that some remnants of the old indigenous legal systems formed a part of the New York law during the opening decades of the eighteenth century. However, with the confusing state of jurisdiction in the seventeenth century it is most likely that the substantive law was in an equally disheveled state by 1691. The era was one of drastic change in the political life of the mother country, and the trend was toward greater simplification and efficiency in government. New York lawyers having long suffered from the diversity of laws in the Province, no doubt welcomed an opportunity to eliminate from New York law all of the precedents based upon local law and were glad to substitute instead a legal system deriving its precedents and procedures from English common law.

This supposition is supported by the tradition among eighteenth-century New York lawyers, that the law of the Province prior to 1691 was to be considered identical with the common law of England.[35] For the eighteenth-century attorney, this rule meant that he could substitute the readily available materials of English common law for the seventeenth-century colonial precedents which were available only in manuscript. In addition, had such a rule been applied in 1691, it would have saved New York lawyers of that day from the frustrating experience of attempting to ascertain any consistent pattern in the precedents of the proprietary province. Either by agreement in 1691, or by the established practice of the bar in the following decades, the complex system of local law that prevailed in proprietary New York was relegated to the limbo of "pre-history," and the years from 1664 to 1685 became, in fact, the "dark age" of New York's legal history.

If the foregoing be true — that in 1691 a revolutionary change in New York law resulted in the elimination of precedents created during the proprietary period — the lawyer may well question the value of spending time in the study of proprietary law. Since the rules developed before 1691 have no binding effect upon future courts, they possess what many might consider to be merely an antiquarian interest. Yet a careful study of various aspects of New York law in the seventeenth century promises to yield large dividends to those who have the tenacity to pursue the subject. In addition to having the opportunity to study the legal development of the Province during its most inventive period, the legal historian approaching proprietary New York finds a clash of legal systems that serves as an antecedent for similar events that occurred later in American legal history. What happened in proprietary New York is, I submit, not substantially different from the adjustments that had to be made in later years when English common law came into contact with different legal systems. Examples of such conflicts may be found in the development of legal institutions in the states of Louisiana, Missouri, Texas and California. A study of New York in the proprietary period provides a fascinating introduction to the study of clashing legal systems; such an entree into this subject of laws in conflict, has too long been neglected and deserves closer attention in the years ahead.

FOOTNOTES

1. Dutch practice in the New Amsterdam Court of Burgomaster, Schepens and Schout, established in 1653, closely paralleled the laws of the Netherlands and particularly the customs of the city of Amsterdam, Richard B. Morris, ed., *Select Cases of the Mayor's Court of New York City, 1674-1784*, in *American Legal Records*, II (Washington: 1935), at 42; Berthold Fernow, ed., *Records of New Amsterdam from 1653 to 1674 Anno Domini*, 7 vols. (New York, 1897), IV, 122. For notarial practice see Edmund B. O'Callaghan, trans., Register of Solomon Lachaire, Notary Public of New Amsterdam 1661-1663, City Clerk, New York City, and Edmund B. O'Callaghan, trans., Register of Walewyn van der Veen, Notary Public of New Amsterdam, 1662-1664, City Clerk, New York City. It is notable that the Dutch permitted English settlers within their province to use a trial jury, see *Minutes of the Town Court of Newtown 1656-1690*, in Historical Records Survey, *Transcripts of Early Town Records of New York* (New York: 1940), 27. Appeal from New Netherland courts was to to the Director-General and Council, see Fernow, ed., *Records of New Amsterdam*, IV, 251.
2. George L. Haskins and Samuel E. Ewing, "The Spread of Massachusetts Law in the Seventeenth Century," *University of Pennsylvania Law Review*, CVI (1958), 414-417.
3. The Long Island settlers wished complete independence or political attachment to Connecticut; both Richard Nicolls and his successor, Francis Lovelace, resorted to every art of diplomacy to gain their support. It was to no avail, for the Puritans persisted in resistance to the the Governor's authority. The numerous retreats by the governors in the face of Long Island intransigence are striking examples of what groups exercised political power in the Province. Edmund B. O'Callaghan, ed., *Documents Relating to the Colonial History of the State of New York*, 15 vols. (Albany: 1856-1883), III, 157, 158; XIV, 542, 545, 551, 620, 681. Victor Hugo Paltsits, ed., *Minutes of the Executive Council of the Province of New York . . . 1668-1673*, 2 vols. (Albany: 1910), I, 80, 81; Josephine C. Frost, ed., *Records of the Town of Jamaica, Long Island, New York 1656-1751*, I (Brooklyn: 1915), 29, 47, 48. See also Julius Goebel, Jr., "Some Legal and Political Aspects of the Manors in New York," Order of Colonial Lords of Manors in America, *Publications*, No. 19 (1928), 4.

   For brief period of Dutch resistance, and the use of gifts and offices to palliate them see Fernow, ed., *Records of New Amsterdam*, V, 145; VI, 198; Paltsits, ed., *Minutes of the Executive Council*, I, 329-330.
4. The preamble to the Duke's Laws cites its New England heritage, *The Colonial Laws of New York from the Year 1664 to the Revolution*, I (Albany: 1894), 7. For parallel texts and a narrative account of the enactment of the Duke's Laws see Morton Pennypacker, *The Duke's Laws: Their Antecedents, Implications and Importance*, in Paul M. Hamlin and Richard B. Morris, eds., *Anglo-American Legal History*

Series, 1st ser., No. 9, 30-31. The results of requiring the governor to have a veto over the selection of town officials are discussed in Richard M. Bayle, *Historical and Descriptive Sketches of Suffolk County* (Port Jefferson, N.Y.: 1874), 34, 35, and Henry J. Scudder, "The Formation of the Civil Government of Suffolk County," in *Bicentennial: A History of Suffolk County* (Babylon, N.Y.: 1885), 24. In at least one case local resentment resulted in the beating of a constable, see O'Callaghan, *Documents . . . Colonial History*, XIV, 582. For jurisdiction, personnel and supervision of Court of Constable and Overseers, see applicable provisions of the Duke's Laws, at *Colonial Laws New York*, I, 7, 44, 48, 55, 63, 88, 90, 91; criminal jurisdiction see *ibid.*, I, 63; power of justice of peace to preside over town courts, see *ibid.*, I, 31.

5. An example of a contested town boundary is that of Jamaica, which was challenged by Newtown, Hempstead, and Flushing, see Frost, ed., *Town Records of Jamaica*, I, 33, 86, 190. The Southold-Southampton line was one of many settled by the Court of Assizes, O'Callaghan, ed., *Documents . . . Colonial History*, XIV, 599.
6. For jurisdiction of Sessions Courts see *Colonial Laws of New York*, I, 7, 23, 25, 27, 31, 75. The allocation of criminal jurisdiction is discussed at length by Julius Goebel, Jr. and T. Raymond Naughton, at *Law Enforcement in Colonial New York: A Study in Criminal Procedure 1664-1776* (New York: 1944), 61.
7. See cases at Paltsits, ed., *Minutes Executive Council*, I, 132-133 (Jamaica), 115 (Gravesend), Fernow, ed., *Records New Amsterdam*, VI, 151 (Mayor's Court, N.Y.C.).
8. Paltsits, ed., *Minutes Executive Council*, I, 131, 132, Fernow, ed., *Records New Amsterdam*, VI, 175.
9. *Colonial Laws New York*, I, 44.
10. *Ibid.* See also Goebel and Naughton, *Law Enforcement*, 61.
11. Orville C. Ackerly, Calendar of the Proceedings of the Court of Assizes 1665-1672 (in the New York State Library), Manuscript Division, New York Public Library, New York City, 20. When the Court of Assizes was not in session the conflicts were resolved by the governor and Council, Goebel and Naughton, *Law Enforcement*, 299.
12. *Colonial Laws New York*, I, 12, 75, 76; Fernow, ed.,*Records New Amsterdam*, V, 151; Mayor's Court Minutes 1677-1682, Division of Records, New York County Clerk, Hall of Records, New York City, 24. See *Osborne* v. *Tuder*, at Proceedings of the General Court of Assizes Held in the City of New York, October 6, 1680 to October 6, 1682, New York Historical Society *Collections*, XLV (New York: 1913), 20. But if tender to the clerk should be shown, appellant could renew at the next term, *Martinoe v. Latten*, *ibid.*, 20, 23.
13. *Tackapowsha v. Town of Hempstead*, *ibid.*, 32
14. *Colonial Laws New York*, I, 11, 90.
15. Paltsits, ed., *Minutes Executive Council*, I, 42, 326.
16. O'Callaghan, ed., *Documents . . . Colonial History*, XIV, 572; *Tacka-*

powsha v. *Town of Hempstead*, Proceedings General Court Assizes, New York Historical Society *Collections*, XLV, 32, 33.

17. Bertram Osborne, *Justices of the Peace 1361-1848* (Shaftesbury, Eng.: 1960), 83; Michael Dalton, *The Country Justice: Containing the Practice Duty and Power of the Justices of the Peace* (London: 1746), 83, 84. Appellate procedure under the Duke's Laws seems to have followed English precedents, see Dalton *ibid.*, 63, 66; Charles A. Beard, *The Office of the Justice of the Peace in England: Its Origin and Development* (New York: 1904), 77, 78, 153; Osborne, *ibid.*, 35, 51.
18. For example the court minutes contain references to an " . . . action of trover and Conversion", *Archer* v. *Orchard*, an " . . . action of assault and battery", *Coursen* v. *Orchards*, and the notation that the defendant craved a nonsuit and the court adjudged that the plaintiff did not have a cause of action and granted the request, *Osborne* v. *Tuder*, all at Proceedings General Court Assizes, 19, 20.
19. The 1672 and 1673 population figures have been graphically presented in Herbert A. Johnson, *The Law Merchant and Negotiable Instruments in Colonial New York 1664-1730* (Chicago: 1963), 48. The figure for Suffolk County is from *History of Suffolk County New York* (New York: 1882), 62, for the year 1673. Under their own Dutch governors, the Dutch were not slow in asserting their rights, see Fernow., ed., *Records of New Amsterdam*, V, 60.
20. *Ibid.*, V, 267; *Colonial Laws New York*, I, 42, 91 (Sessions Courts used twelve man juries only when trying capital crimes.)
21. Fernow, ed., *Records of New Amsterdam*, V, 282; VI, 16.
22. *Ibid.*, VI, 75, 78.
23. Use of jury in English towns under Dutch, see *Newtown Court Minutes*, 27. Procedure against Mayor's Court recorded in case of *Tuder* v.*Rumbouts, et al.*, Proceedings . . . General Court of Assizes, New York Historical Society *Collections*, XLV, 13, 22.
24. Probate jurisdiction, see Morris, ed., *Select Cases Mayor's Court*, 46; Mayor's Court Minutes, 1675-77, 208 for appointment of curators in accordance with Dutch practice. For penal jurisdiction see Goebel and Naughton, *Law Enforcement*, 66, 67; that this practice was a continuation of the Dutch practice, cf. Fernow, ed., *Records of New Amsterdam*, V, 93, 96 with *ibid.*, VI, 11, 35, but also see *ibid.*, V, 287, 288, where one accused of assault and battery was held for the Court of Assizes. On use of arbitration see Morris, *ibid.*, 44, for a 1670 arbitration see Fernow, ed., *Records New Amsterdam*, VI, 271.
25. Fernow, ed., *Records New Amsterdam*, V, 249, 326, VI, 7, 213, 234-235, 325 [bronx-Land and Harlem], see also *ibid.*, VI, 120 [Bergen in "New Garsie"], and Mayor's Court Minutes, 1675-77, 253-254.
26. Paul M. Hamlin and Charles E. Baker, eds., *Supreme Court of Judicature of the Province of New York 1691-1704*, I (New York: 1959), 25-27; see also Fernow, ed., *Records New Amsterdam*, VI, 304, 341, and Mayor's Court Minutes, 1675-77, 76.
27. *Ibid.*, VI, 185-188; 305-341.

28. O'Callaghan, ed., *Documents . . . Colonial History*, III, 264, XIV, 617-619, 625; Fernow, *ibid.*, VI, 117; Paltsits, ed., *Minutes Executive Council*, I, 76.
29. Goebel, "Some Legal and Political Aspects of . . . Manors", Order of Colonial Lords of Manors in America, *Publications*, No. 19, 11, 12, 15. See also John Henry Livingston, "The Minor Manors of New York," Order of Colonial Lords of Manors in America, *Publications*, No. 12 (1923), 14, and Howland Pell, "The Pell Manor," Order of Colonial Lords of Manors in America, *Publications*, No. 5 (1917), 5.
30. *Colonial Laws New York*, I, 1; Paltsits, ed., *Minutes Executive Council*, I, 361, 367, 375; John M. Wightman, "The Mayhew Manor of Tisbury," Order of Colonial Lords of Manors in America, *Publications*, No. 10 (1921), 29.
31. Harry C. W. Melick, *The Manor of Fordham and its Founder* (New York: 1950), 80, 81, 84, 89; see also Fernow, ed., *Records New Amsterdam*, VI, 325, 326. See petition of Johannes Vervelen, Mayor's Court Minutes 1675-77, 75 — this is probably the paper noted in Goebel, "Some Legal and Political Aspects of . . . Manors," at p. 19.
32. Goebel, "Some Legal and Political Aspects of . . . Manors," 14.
33. *Colonial Laws New York*, I, 125; Hamlin and Baker, eds., *Supreme Court of Judicature*, I, 14, 15; Julius Goebel, Jr., *Cases and Materials on the Development of Legal Institutions* (Brattleboro, Vt.: 1946), 525.
34. *Colonial Laws New York*, I, 172.
35. The rule was enunciated by William Smith and Daniel Horsmanden shortly before the Revolution, Hamlin and Baker, eds., *Supreme Court of Judicature*, I, 378-379. For the disruptive effect of the year 1691 see Fred S. Hall, "Common Law Marriage in New York State," *Columbia Law Review*, XXX (1930), 2-3, and Johnson, *The Law Merchant*, 35.

The Prerogative Court of New York, 1686-1776

The appearance of a bishop's mitre as the principal device on the seal of the Prerogative Court of the Province of New York is one of the strangest paradoxes in colonial legal history. Opposition to the appointment of an Anglican bishop resident in North America was widespread throughout British North America, and an episcopate was not to become a reality in New York until well after the American Revolution had run its course. Yet New York colonials were willing to accept not only a mitred court seal, but also a probate tribunal modelled after the English ecclesiastical courts. While the colony did not trace its origins to dissenting emigres driven from England by the persecutions of Anglican bishops, it did have deeply rooted Calvinist traditions in the Dutch Reformed churches of the southern counties and Albany, and in the Congregational strongholds in Long Island and Westchester County. Clearly the decision to institute a Prerogative Court in 1686 was not due to an extraordinary amount of affection on the part of the colonists for the institutions appendant to the hierarchy of the Anglican church.[1]

With the exception of the Prerogative Court of New Jersey, New York's sister province, and possibly the probate courts of Maryland and South Carolina, the New York Prerogative Court was unique in colonial America. As a recent writer on probate courts has demonstrated, the typical colonial court system assigned probate and administration matters to local courts charged with this specialized jurisdiction. At times these probate courts were subject to review by local courts of general civil jurisdiction, but just as frequently they enjoyed a dignity equal to that of the common law courts. All matters concerning decedent estates were handled in these probate courts, while the New York Prerogative Court shared its jurisdiction with the common law courts and the Court of

1. See generally, A. L. Cross, *The Anglican Episcopate and The American Colonies* (1902), and C. Bridenbaugh, *Mitre and Sceptre: Transatlantic Faiths, Ideas, Personalities, and Politics, 1689-1775* (1962).

Chancery.[2] For most colonies, the single probate court meant a simplification of the jurisdictional labyrinth which delayed the administration of decedent estates in the multitudes of interested courts in the mother country, and at the same time eliminated the need for a court which by its name and practice memorialized in America those unpopular English ecclesiastical institutions which had done their part in expelling dissenters from England.

Concentration upon the New York Prerogative Court provides a legal historian with two opportunities. In a general sense, he is enabled to examine the American colonial Prerogative Court in relation to its English prototype, a comparative approach which highlights the adaptations which American conditions and customs made in the Old World institution. The Prerogative Court, in this sense, was an outstanding example of what happened when an English institution was transferred to the English colonies of North America. In a more narrow sense, the legal historian may find in the history of the New York Prerogative Court a substantial amount of information concerning the substantive and adjective law of colonial New York, as well as a firm foundation upon which to base a future study of the gradual evolution of the Surrogates' Courts of New York from their colonial antecedents.

The Structure of New York's Probate System

When the English conquered Dutch New Netherlands they did not alter the existing legal systems in the province. Rather than risk the enmity of the residents, consisting of Dutchmen and disaffected Puritans, the proprietary government permitted the indigenous courts to continue to function. Among the powers exercised by local courts was that of admitting wills to probate and granting administration over intestate estates. This jurisdiction was confirmed by the Duke's Laws of 1665, and only slightly abridged in 1670 when the Court of Assizes passed an ordinance requiring all wills and grants of administration to be recorded in the provincial secretary's office in New York City.[3]

2. R. H. Limbaugh, "The Sources and Development of Probate Law," 1957 *Wash. U.L.Q.* 419, 427-435; a good brief summary statement can be found at J. Goebel, Jr., 1 *History of the Supreme Court of the United States: Antecedents and Beginnings to 1801* 8, fn. 14; on Maryland see E. McQueen, "The Commissary of Colonial Maryland" 25 *Md. Hist. Mag.* 190. Massachusetts conducted probate business through local courts of probate in the various counties, subject to review by the governor and council, 1 Wroth & Zobel, *Legal Papers of John Adams* xliv (1965). In North Carolina local precinct courts exercised probate jurisdiction, 2 Parker, *North Carolina Higher-Court Records, 1670-1696* lxiii (1968).

3. 1 *Colonial Laws of New York* 9, 10 (1894) (hereinafter cited as

This system of local probate continued to dominate the law of New York until the accession of James II resulted in New York becoming a royal province. At that point the powers of granting probate and administration were vested in the royal governor, and all subsequent authority in those matters was derived from, and appended to, that of the governor.[4] Although a vestigial form of local probate and administration continued to apply to small estates even after the introduction of the Prerogative Court in 1686, it is entirely proper to draw a sharp line of distinction between local probate before and after 1686.[5] As we shall see, the local tribunals that acted in the later years were mere agents of the governor, and were delegated only those powers that were essential to assist him in the work of his Prerogative Court.

Probate of wills and grants of administration in England were, for the most part, powers vested in the bishop of the diocese in which a decedent had made his residence. Such authority was known as "Ordinary" power, and in the province of New York this jurisdiction was granted to each royal governor by virtue of his instructions from the crown.[6] Although general ecclesiastical jurisdiction over the spiritual life of New York was granted to the archbishop of Canterbury in 1686 and transferred to the bishop of London in 1690, the right to probate wills and grant letters of administration over intestate estates were among those powers specifically excepted from this general authority. Overall supervision of decedent estates in colonial New York was therefore firmly established in the hands of the governors of the royal province.[7]

Col. Laws of N.Y.); see also H. Johnson, *The Advent of Common Law in Colonial New York, Law and Authority in Colonial America* 74-91 (Billias, ed., 1965).

4. The royal instructions are conveniently analyzed at 2 L. Labaree, *Royal Instructions to British Colonial Governors* 489-490 (1935); a specific instruction prohibiting deputizing ordinary powers to anyone not exercising gubernatorial powers appears at *Id.*, 491 (instruction issued in 1733). See also 8 E. O'Callaghan, *Documents Relative to the Colonial History of New York* 372 (1853-1887) and 4 *Id.*, 288, 5 *Id.*, 849 (hereinafter cited O'Callaghan, *Documents*.

5. For a fuller discussion of probate practice and jurisdiction before 1686 see F. Setaro, "The Surrogate's Court of New York: Its Historical Antecedents," 2 *New York Law Forum* 283-290, and G. Wingate, "The Surrogate's Court of the State of New York, Its Early History and Present Equitable Jurisdiction," 2 *Brooklyn L. Rev.* 165-167.

6. See authorities at note 4, *supra*.

7. Naturally the separation of probate business from other ecclesiastical jurisdiction created the need for some adjustment in procedure. An example is the English diocesan court's recourse to excommunication, a sanction not found in New York practice.

While the succession of the lieutenant governor or, in his absence, the president of the council, to the powers of the governor was usually sufficient basis for the acting governor to assume the powers as ordinary, a problem arose in 1697 when the governor found it necessary to travel to the frontier regions of the province. Since he remained within its territory, New York ordinary jurisdiction could not be considered vested in his substitute as it would have in the case of his absence. This difficulty was solved by the appointment of councillor Stephen Van Cortlandt, a justice of the Supreme Court of Judicature, to be a "delegate for the proving of wills and granting administrations." This power was more extensive than that conferred upon the surrogates, who merely took proofs, but did not seal the letters issued under the Prerogative Seal that were necessary to appoint an executor or an administrator. In effect this was equivalent to the appointment of a commissary in an English diocese, and was a rare practice in the province of New York. The 1733 instruction prohibiting such a delegation of authority, issued to the governor of the Leeward Islands, indicates that the practice did not have the approval of the home government.[8]

While many of the early governors insisted upon personally administering the necessary oaths in probate matters, it soon became common to leave the routine affairs to the so-called "Prerogative Office",[9] at times called the "Prerogative Court." Whatever its designation in the judicial system of New York, it is clear that this tribunal was a branch of the provincial secretary's office, which from the very first days of English rule had played a recording role in regard to decedent estates. With the passage of time after 1686 the functions of the secretary in this field became so closely identified with the secretaryship itself that, as we shall see, the British Privy Council upheld the claim of the secretary that he or his deputy held office as register of the Prerogative Court of

---

8. Van Cortlandt appointment at 25 *N.Y. Hist. Soc'y Colls.* 272; for prohibition against deputizing ordinary powers see 2 Labaree, *Royal Instructions* 491.

9. A summary of the English rules concerning proof of wills is at 2 H. Swinburne, *A Brief Treatise of Testaments and Last Wills* 59 (cor. ed., 1640) (hereinafter cited as Swinburne, *Brief Treatise*). Proofs before the New York governors acting *in personam* are at New York County Wills, Old Series, f. 204 (John Hendrick De Bruyn, 1709), Historical Documents Collection, Queens College Library; *Id.*, at f. 206 (William Van Niuwenhinson, 1707); *Id.*, at f. 212 (Peter Manet, 1712); *Id.*, at f. 661 (Cornelia Norwood, 1724), and *Id.*, at f. 671 (Lowrens Wessels, 1724). (Hereinafter this collection will be cited NY Co. Wills (O.S.), HDC/QC, f. —)

New York and principal surrogate of the province, even against the wishes of the incumbent governor.

With the geographical dispersal of settlements after 1686, it became the practice to appoint delegates or "surrogates" to take depositions of witnesses to wills and to administer oaths to executors and administrators who were unable to travel to New York City. These surrogates were also charged with other miscellaneous matters, such as caring for infants' shares in intestate estates. From the recitations of authority endorsed upon the wills transmitted to the Prerogative Court, it is impossible to determine whether these appointments were limited to one particular estate or if they were general delegations of authority.

The records of the Prerogative Court do not contain a commission delegating authority to local surrogates, and the fact that the authorizing instrument was termed a *dedimus potestatem* does not help in determining the tenure of the office.[10] However, the recurrence of the same officer's name on the endorsements submitted within a given county would indicate that the authority was a continuing grant rather than a single act by the governor.

While no list of these appointments has survived, extant documents, supplemented by the abstracted names printed by Pelletreau, provide a fairly complete list of the individuals appointed. From this roster, printed as Appendix A, it is apparent that men of varying degrees of distinction were appointed to perform "surrogate's" duties. In the counties the appointees were frequently justices of the county courts, local members of the bar, or members of prominent colonial families. Several of these county surrogates served for periods extending over two, and in one instance, three decades. While the roster is not complete enough to provide a basis for studying nepotism in the office of surrogate, it does suggest that some county surrogateships were held within single families through several generations. The Hoffmans in Dutchess county, the Smiths in Suffolk County, and John DePeyster's succession to the Albany county post held by his father-in-law Myndert Schuyler, are suggestive of such a pattern. Finally, we should note that in the case of Suffolk county in 1730, two surrogates were appointed, one for the "west end" and one for the "east end" of that county.[11] Overlapping dates for surrogates

10. The term *dedimus potestatem* is a general one denoting a delegation of authority from a court, empowering an official to take testimony on behalf of the court. In New York records it appears at 25 *N.Y. Hist. Soc'y Colls.* 275 (Constant Sylvester, 1696) and 26 *Id.* 214 (Richard Gorish, 1719).

11. See estates of John Bayley and Ananias Conkling, both committed to administration in 1730, at 27 *N.Y. Hist. Soc'y Colls.* 9.

appointed for Westchester and Dutchess counties suggest that a similar territorial division of labor may have been utilized in those counties.

At the middle of the eighteenth century it also became the practice to appoint surrogates for the city of New York.[12] Since remoteness from the Prerogative Office could not serve as justification for these appointments, it is reasonable to conclude that they were made to reduce the work load of the principal surrogate, and were a product of motives other than those attendant upon the appointment of the county surrogates.

It should be noted that English ecclesiastical practice provided for one surrogate to act upon behalf of the ordinary, principally in regard to testamentary matters. He was domiciled at the cathedral seat of his ordinary, unlike the commissary who administered probate affairs at some remote region of the diocese. The canons of the church required that the surrogate be a cleric in orders who held either a bachelor of law (i.e., civil law) or a master of arts degree. This level of education and training was not required of the delegates appointed to be "surrogates" by the governors of New York, and it is fairly obvious that the English "surrogate" served a far different function from the multitude of men appointed to assist in the work of the New York Prerogative Court.[13] Clearly the appointment of New York surrogates was to facilitate the submission of papers to the Prerogative Court from the outlying counties of the province, and to expedite the work of the secretary's office in the last years of British rule.

Superior to these county surrogates in jurisdiction and function, was the deputy secretary of the province who, as already noted, also served as register of the Prerogative Court. Dr. John Bridges, an English trained civil lawyer, occupied the post of

---

12. See appendix A, for a list of names. Significantly two of the New York City surrogates were Daniel Horsmanden and James Delancey, both of whom were justices of the Supreme Court of Judicature when appointed to the surrogate's position. Lambert Moore, already holding the lucrative post of naval officer for the province of New York, was also appointed a New York City surrogate.

13. 2 Swinburne, *Brief Treatise* 62; W. Nelson, *Lex Testamentaria* 436, 438 (2nd ed., 1724), 3 R. Burn, *Ecclesiastical Law* 538 (4th ed., 1781); C. Ritchie, *The Ecclesiastical Courts of York* 65 (1956). New York surrogates apparently were authorized to take proof from close relatives, as did Samuel Clowes from his father in 1757, see NY Co. Wills (N.S.), HDC/QC, f. 1058 (will of Joseph Latham). The usual practice of utilizing one surrogate per diocese did not apply in the Prerogative Court of Canterbury, where the pressure of business compelled the appointment for six or more surrogates to handle the business in London.

register briefly in 1702, and it was he who first used the title "surrogate" to describe his authority as a delegate of the governor.[14] Again a full list of incumbents is unavailable but a reasonably full roster can be obtained from the original wills. It is attached as part of Appendix A, and consists of the names of men who served as deputy secretary of the province. In those instances where a secretary acted *in personam* rather than by deputy, that fact is noted. The single extant delegation of authority to the principal surrogate is that issued by Governor Benjamin Fletcher on October 21, 1692 empowering Secretary Matthew Clarkson or David Jamison, his deputy, to administer the oath of probate of wills and testaments, to take the oaths of executors and administrators, and to administer the oath of executors and administrators swearing to the truth and accuracy of their accounts and inventories.[15]

The deputy secretary, or principal surrogate as we shall refer to him, functioned throughout the territorial limits of the province of New York. This office of principal surrogate, coupled with the registry of the Prerogative Court, gave rise to a constitutional struggle of considerable importance during the last years of British rule. Through the earlier decades of the eighteenth century, the monetary significance of the offices of register and principal surrogate of the Prerogative Court had been slight. The fees of the secretary (and hence of his deputy) arose from the function as register. That officer was required to record in the libers of the Prerogative Office every will admitted to probate, as well as inventories, accounts and other related documents; the revenues were proportional to the number and size of estates administered in the province of New York. The fees had been fixed by an ordinance passed in 1693 at the request of the General Assembly.[16]

---

14. NY Co. Wills (O.S.), HDC/QC, f. 256 (Peter Bilson, 1702); and inventory of the estate of Jeudah Samuel, sworn to before Bridges on December 2, 1702, at New York County Surrogate's Court Inventories, Historical Documents Collection, Queens College (hereafter NYCo Inventories, HDC/QC). Bridges subsequently became chief justice of the Supreme Court of Judicature, and had a distinguished, albeit short-lived, career on the bench, see 3 P. Hamlin & C. Baker, *Supreme Court of Judicature of the Province of New York, 1691-1704*, 27-29 (1959). On the relationship between the local surrogates and the deputy secretary, see C. Daly, *The Nature, Extent, and History of the Jurisdiction of the Surrogate's Courts of the State of New York* 13-17 (1863).

15. The commission is at 25 *N.Y. Hist. Soc'y Colls.* 206.

16. The fee table of 1693 was in the form of an ordinance but passed at the request of the Assembly. It provided for a 10 shilling fee to the Governor for each letters testamentary or letters of administration. The

A subsequent attempt by the General Assembly to insure by statute that the fees remain fixed began a struggle over the constitutional position of the Assembly and Council that occupied the better part of the years from 1710 to 1712 and met with failure when the statute was disallowed. Nonetheless, the Council eventually permitted the 1693 fee ordinance to remain in force, and it did so until the American Revolution.[17]

Thus, as the eighteenth century wore on, the fees in individual cases remained constant, and the value of the office might have eroded through inflation had there not been a rapid expansion of population and accumulated wealth. As it was, the aggregate of fees grew substantially, and in the wake of the quarrels between the New York General Assembly and the governors over the issue

---

secretary's fees were 3 shillings for recording a will, inventory or account under 24 lines, and 9 pence for each additional line. For issuing letters on estates of less than £100, the secretary received 6 shillings. His fee for issuing a certificate of the probate of a will was 4 shillings; a quietus of administration brought a fee of 6 shillings. For copying a record the secretary received a 3 shilling fee for the first sheet of 24 lines, and an additional fee of 6 pence for each additional page. When a will was proved in the common pleas courts, the fee was 3 shillings, with an additional 1 shilling 6 pence fee for transmitting a certificate of proof to the secretary's office. See "A Catalogue of Fees Established by the Governor and Council at the Humble Request of the Assembly," *The Laws & Acts of the General Assembly for Their Majesties Province of New York,* Appendix 1, 3 (1694, Grolier Club Ed., 1894).

17. Essentially the struggle was over the constitutional right of the Assembly to pass a fee bill, the Queen indicating that all fees should be regulated by ordinance. When disallowance of the 1709 statute became known, a committee of the Council, led by Roger Mompesson and May Bickley, was appointed to draw up a table of fees, which after debate was passed and made effective November 11, 1710. 1 *Journal of the Legislative Council* 298, 299-301, 305 (1861). George Clarke, acting governor in the absence of Robert Hunter, advised the Board of Trade that the fees so fixed were far too low, but that he had acquiesced in the ordinance since the fees were better than none at all. Assembly opposition blocked the effectiveness of the fee ordinance, and the Council agreed to table it. Again the governor, Robert Hunter, conferred with the Board of Trade, which advised that there was no objection to permitting the 1693 fee table from being continued in effect, by statute or otherwise, see 5 O'Callaghan, *Documents* 238, 298, 334. Thus it was the 1693 fee table that governed probate practice in colonial New York, and not the 1709 statute or the 1710 ordinance, cf. 1 Hamlin & Baker, *Supreme Court of Judicature of the Province of New York 1691-1704* 271, 276 (1959). The fees before 1693 are detailed at 1 *Col. Laws of* N.Y. 34, 89; the text of the disallowed 1709 statute is at 1 *Id.* 639. On fees in English ecclesiastical courts see Ritchie, *Ecclesiastical Courts of New York* 52 (1956).

of revenue collection that reached a critical point in 1764-66, the office of principal surrogate and register became too substantial a piece of patronage to be ignored. Not surprisingly its value was apparent both to the incumbent and to newly appointed governors. George Clarke, veteran secretary of the Province of New York, had been partaking of a moiety of the Prerogative Office registry and surrogate's fees for many years, and administered the office through his deputy, Goldsbrow Banyer. Clarke's family had held these, and countless other judicial and administrative offices besides, for nearly seventy years when in 1772 the governor, William Tryon, filed his complaint of multiple office holding.[18] Actually Tryon's next past predecessor, Sir Henry Moore, also had sought to obtain the register's office in 1766 as a means of compensating his private secretary. Sir Henry had ousted Clarke's deputy, and taken custody of the seal of the Prerogative Court. A motion for reinstatement, brought by Clarke later in the same year, was dismissed by the Privy Council; however a year later a royal patent was issued to Clarke that in future years was to guarantee his right to the register's office and the attendant surrogateship.[19]

With the death of Sir Henry Moore on September 11, 1769, the controversy over the register's office became moot. Both Lieutenant Governor Cadwallader Colden, and Lord Dunmore, the new governor, permitted Clarke to exercise his office, and restored custody of the Prerogative Court seal to Banyer as Clarke's deputy. This was changed by the transfer of Dunmore to Virginia and the arrival of General William Tryon in the spring of 1771. Tryon immediately installed his private secretary, Edward Fanning, in office and Clarke lodged his second and more successful petition with the Privy Council on December 26, 1771. On March 21, 1772 the Privy Council sent a copy to Governor Tryon with the request that he frame an answer. When Tryon's reply reached Whitehall, it was apparent that he categorically denied that any secretary's commission issued since 1664 had authorized that official to "intermeddle" in the business of the Prerogative Court. On the contrary, he argued, law and express provisions in the governor's instructions and the 1692 act of the New York General Assembly granted probate of wills and the grant of administration to the governor or such persons as he might delegate. Some additional papers were submitted

18. Governor Tryon's impassioned plea to the Board of Trade is at 8 O'Callaghan, *Documents* 326 (Dec. 1, 1772).

19. The earlier controversy between Moore and the Clarke family can be traced at 31 *N.Y. Hist. Soc'y Colls.* 6 (Banyer ousted), 7 O'Callaghan, *Documents* 830, 927, 5 *Acts of the Privy Council, Colonial Series* 47 (1912) and 6 *Id.*, 440, and 12 *Journal of the Commissioners for Trade and Plantations* 321, 322 (1936).

with Tryon's reply when it was filed on December 1, 1772, and on February 21, 1774 the entire matter was ordered referred to the Board of Trade. By its report of March 21, 1774 the Board of Trade asserted that probate business was legally part of the functions of the provincial secretary and that the usage that had grown up in this regard had been confirmed by letters patent issued to the secretary in 1770. The act of 1692 had not severed the registry from the secretary's office as Tryon contended, but rather that statute, by requiring submission of proofs to the secretary's office, was further evidence of the secretary's constitutional authority to issue probates. On the basis of this report by the Board of Trade, the Privy Council ordered George Clarke reinstated in the offices of register of the Prerogative Court and principal surrogate.[20]

Vindication of Clarke's claim by the Privy Council served to provide constitutional sanction for an institutional arrangement that had persisted in substantially the same form since 1686. Through the passage of time and gubernatorial acquiescence, it had become a part of the judicial establishment of New York. For all intents and purposes, the Prerogative Court had been, and continued to be, the focal point of probate business in the province; and the most important provincial official in this field was the register and principal surrogate of the Prerogative Court.

In addition to the numerous group of surrogates in the counties, and their constitutionally protected superior, the principal surrogate of the Prerogative Court, other colonial officials played a minor, but not insignificant role in the conduct of probate business. In 1690 wills had been proved before courts of sessions, continuing the practice instituted by the Duke's Laws of 1665. A will was also proved in 1690 before the Leislerian court of oyer and terminer.[21]

20. For correspondence with Board of Trade detailing the events after Moore's death, see 8 O'Callaghan, *Documents,* 187, 188-189, 283-284, 321-327. The order reinstating George Clarke is at 8 *Id.,* 417 (Apr. 13, 1774). Proceedings before the Board of Trade are at 13 *Journal of the Commissioners of Trade and Plantations* 112, 218, 389, 391 (1937); action by the Privy Council is synopsized at 5 *Acts of the Privy Council, Colonial Series* 47-49, and 6 *Id.,* 507, 527-529, 555.

21. Local probate before 1686 can be seen in probate before courts of sessions, at NY Co. Wills (O.S.) HDC/QC, f. 77 (Barnabas Horton, Sessions of East Riding of Yorkshire, 1670) NY Co. Wills (O.S), HDC/QC, f. 19 (Samuel Drake, Sessions, Westchester Co., 1670), NY Co. Wills (O.S.), HDC/QC, f. 62 (Thomas Huston, Sessions, Queens Co., 1670). Probate before Mayor's Court of New York is illustrated in NY Co. Wills (O.S.), HDC/QC, f. 18 (Judith Stuyvesant, 1686). Probate before court of sessions in 1690, see 25 *N.Y. Hist. Soc'y Colls.* 157-158 (William Cox, New York City). Probate before Oyer and Terminer, 25 *Id.* 156, 157 (Thomas Wandell, Queens Co.).

However the act of 1692 regularized matters and provided for the taking of witnesses' proofs and the oaths of fiduciaries before certain local common law courts, provided that the counties involved were sufficiently remote from the provincial capital at New York City. The courts of common pleas in those counties might conduct such business on behalf of the Prerogative Court in New York City, and transmit their proceedings under seal to the Prerogative Office. In the vacation of the county courts of common pleas, any judge of that court, in conjunction with two justices of the peace of the county, might convene a "special meeting" to take proofs or administer oaths. While proof before surrogates was a far simpler procedure, the local courts continued to enjoy a fairly constant flow of probate business under the terms of the 1692 statute.[22]

These local courts in the "remote" counties also had jurisdiction to admit wills to probate and grant letters of administration if the assets in the estate did not exceed £50. In transacting this business the courts were subject to review by the governor or his delegate at New York City, provided an appeal was brought within three months after the grant of probate or issuance of letters of administration. Since no central record was kept of wills proven, or letters issued, in regard to small estates, few records concerning this practice survive. However we do know that the Westchester County Court of Sessions in 1694 prepared a form for the grant of administration in which it referred to itself as the "Prerogative Court for the County of Westchester." From this we may assume that the local courts patterned their practice and activities after that of the Prerogative Court held under the governor's authority in New York City.[23]

---

22. The 1692 act is at 1 *Col. Laws of N.Y.* 300-304; it designated the counties of New York, Orange, Richmond, Westchester and Kings as those areas where local probate would not be permitted; all other counties were "remote." The act of 1750, 3 *Col. Laws of N.Y.* 780, designated Orange County as "remote," permitting local probate in that county; the act of 1772 made the same provision for the new counties of Tryon, Charlotte, Cumberland and Gloucester, 5 *Id.*, 414. For wills proven before common pleas courts see NY Co. Wills (O.S.), HDC/QC, ff. 217, 545, 548, and NY Co. Wills (N.S.) HDC/QC, f. 1257, see also 25 *N.Y. Hist. Soc'y Colls.* 376, 26 *Id.*, 116-117, 129-130, 172-178, 183, 230-231, 315; 28 *Id.* 57-58, 431, 29 *Id.*, 22, 337-338, 32 *Id.*, 59. For wills proven before a judge and two justices see NY Co. Wills (O.S.), ff. 218, 259, and 26 *N.Y. Hist. Soc'y Colls.* 96-97, 147, 170-171, 28 *Id.*, 303-304, 425, 29 *Id.*, 34.

23. See 1 *Col. Laws of N.Y.* 302-303, for statutory sanction to the practice of local probate of small estates, and providing for an appeal to governor or his delegate in the Prerogative Office. The letter of administration from Westchester County is at Minutes of the Court of Sessions

Despite the large number of officials involved in the business of the Prerogative Court of New York, we must not lose sight of the fact that the governors, acting through the secretary in the Prerogative Office, had retained ultimate authority to grant probate (letters testamentary) and to issue letters of administration over intestate estates.[24] Only in the case of small estates under £50 in value might probate be granted or letters issued by another tribunal; and even then the Prerogative Court retained authority to regulate such practice through appellate review. Under normal conditions an estate could not be administered without the commission from the governor under the seal of the Prerogative Court. Proofs might be taken elsewhere, and oaths might be sworn before officials designated by statute or delegated by the governor, but the final step remained firmly in the hands of the Prerogative Court.

Depending ultimately upon the authority derived from the governor's instructions, the system of surrogates, local courts and Prerogative Office was flexible enough to accommodate the needs of the residents of the most distant outposts of the province. Convenience in submitting proof and taking affidavits was the result of a generous delegation of authority. At the same time the long tenure of the secretary and his deputies in the bureaucratic functions of the Prerogative Court insured regularity and a strong sense of continuity. Although the offices in the Prerogative Court undoubtedly were sinecures, the very fact that they remained untouched by the fluctuations of provincial or imperial politics gave added status to the Prerogative Court and precedent value to the administrative decisions of its veteran clerks and surrogates.

The Substantive Law of Inheritance

Unfortunately our knowledge about the intestacy laws of

(1657-1696) Westchester County, 2 Fox, *Westchester County Historical Society Publications* 122 (1924).

24. It is perhaps wise to note that "probate" in colonial New York was not synonymous with "proof of a will," as it is in contemporary practice. Rather "probate" was the confirmation by a court of competent jurisdiction, attesting to the validity of the will and appointing a fiduciary to administer the estate, see Nelson, *Lex Testamentaria* 462 (2nd ed. 1724), and 2 J. Woerner, *A Treatise on the American Law of Administration* 715 (3rd ed. rev., 1923). New York usage seems to have followed contemporary English terminology in the eighteenth century. In New York colonial records I have found no indication that the probate of a will was evidenced by the preparation of a decree; rather the submission of written proofs was endorsed on the reverse and the issuance of letters testamentary, or letters of administration with the will annexed, was the only evidence of probate.

New York from 1664 to 1754 is quite vague and imprecise, although we can be sure that at some time during that period early Dutch and Puritan influences must have been purged from New York jurisprudence or reduced to the status of local custom. One piece of early information is that, shortly after the first English conquest of New York in 1664, an ordinance was promulgated establishing a system for the distribution of the personal estates of persons dying intestate. After the payment of funeral expenses and debts, the residuum of personalty would be divided between the widow, who received a one-third share, and the children, who received two-thirds of the estate between them in equal shares, except that the eldest son was to be entitled to a double portion. The widow or a child might apply to the next Court of Sessions held after the date of death, but if another relative or a creditor wished to apply for letters of administration, he was required to wait until the third Court of Sessions to be held after the date of death.[25] We cannot, however, be certain for how long or to what degree this ordinance was given effect.

In 1670 the English law of intestate succession to personalty was changed by Parliamentary statute. Thereafter the widow took one-third of the estate after debts and funeral expenses, and the other two-thirds were to be divided between the children equally. If a widow but no child survived, the personalty remaining in the estate was divided one-half to the widow, and one-half to the next of kin in equal degree, or to their representatives. No representation was to be permitted among collaterals more distant than brother's or sister's children. This English rule of intestate succession was not formally adopted by New York legislative act until March 9, 1774. However, an examination of the administration bonds filed by administrators of intestate estates indicates that about 1754 the bonds began to include references to the 1670 English statute, and at that time the administrators were required to abide by its provisions in their actions concerning the estate.[26] While it is possible

25. Act of April 2, 1664, 1 *Col. Laws of* N.Y. 9, 10

26. 22 and 23 Car. 2, c. 10 (1670), made perpetual by 1 Jac. 2, c. 17 (1686), and act of March 9, 1774, 5 *Col. Laws of* N.Y. 614 *et seq.* Early New York bonds do not mention the 1670 English statute; bonds drawn in 1754 occasionally omit the mention of the English statute; those drawn after 1754 always mention the 1670 statute. Administration Papers, Court of Appeals, Box Brown-Byvanck, f. 3-131 (estate of Richard Burtt, 1687); *id.* Box Ha, f. 3-412 (estate of William Hay, 1712); *id.* Box a, f. 3-17 (estate of East Apthorpe, 1718); *id.* Box L, f. 3-567 (estate of Hoseah Cooper, 1754); *id.* Box Ha, f. 3-392 (estate of David Halsey, 1754); *id.* Box B, f. 3-23 (estate of Daniel Baker, 1754); *id.* Box Ca-Coe, f. 3-160 (estate of Theophilus Clark, 1755); *id.* Box a, f. 3-18 (estate of

that the English rule had been adopted by custom at an even earlier date, it can safely be said that the 1774 New York legislation was merely a recognition of a reception which had occurred at least two decades previously.

Fortunately we know much more about New York's law of testate distribution. First, it appears that New York followed rigid English rules of priority concerning payment of debts, legacies and other charges upon the estate. Under those rules, funeral expenses constituted a primary claim on the decedent's estate, subject to the limitation that if the estate were insufficient to pay all obligations, it should not be burdened with excessive charges for the funeral banquet. Next, the fiduciary was required to pay his expenditures in proving the will of the deceased. Following this, debts were to be paid in an order of priority ranging from those payable upon judgments and recognizances down to simple open book accounts and oral promises to pay. Finally, if there were any surplus, specific and general legacies were to be satisfied.[27]

Second, we know a good deal about New York's law of testamentary capacity and about the formalities required for execution of a will within the province. At English law all persons twenty-one years of age and of sound mind could execute valid devises of real property. Testaments of personal property could be effectively executed by a young man of fourteen or a girl of twelve. The English law concerning capacity to devise land was enacted into law in New York in 1684; while no similar action was taken in regard to testamentary dispositions of personalty, it seems safe to assume that the English law, setting the age of fourteen for men and twelve

---

Jonathan Archer, 1758); *id.* Box Brown-Byvanck, f. 3-119 (estate of Abraham Buckhaut, 1758); *id.* Box Taffe-Townshend, f. 3-907 (estate of James Terry, 1758); *id.* Box Heard-Hits, f. 3-438 (estate of Coe Hinman, 1758); *id.* Box A, f. 3-15 (estate of Ziprah Anderson, 1765); *id.* Box A, f. 3-14 (estate of Mahershalalkashbaz Anderson, 1768); *id.* Box Be-Blue, f. 3-65 (estate of Samuel Betts, 1773); *id.* Box A, f. 3-8 (estate of Benjamin Allen, 1774), all at HDC/QC.

27. T. Wentworth, *The Office and Duties of Executors* 32, 116-117, 129-135 (1728); H. Swinburne, *A Treatise of Testaments and Last Wills* 369 (1728); for the interrelation between these rules and the New York practice, see discussion at note 26, *supra.* This, and the surviving examples of New York colonial accounts, leads to a strong presumption that these priorities were also applicable in New York, see estate of William Holleyken (1703), NY Co. Will Liber IV (1702-1708), 60-65; estate of Peter J. Marius (1706), *id.* at 133-136; estate of Huybert Aartse (1710), Albany Inventories, Ser. 2, f. 1; estate of Germanicus Andrew (1718), *id.* f. 7; all at HDC/QC. There seems to be some evidence in the Marius estate, a particularly large and well-to-do estate, that legacies and debts were being paid simultaneously.

for women, was accepted as a customary usage in New York.[28] Excepted from this broad class of persons possessing testamentary capacity under English and New York law were lunatics, idiots and persons suffering from senility or the debilitative effect of chronic alcoholism.[29] Last, but not least, both New York and English law excluded most married women from the right to execute valid wills of realty or personalty.

In regard to a married woman's testamentary capacity, New York appears to have moved slowly away from the fairly liberal rules of Roman Dutch law and toward the limitations of English common and ecclesiastical law. As Professor Goebel has pointed out, the earlier Dutch practices permitting a separation of property during coverture without the intervention of trustees gradually were superseded by the use of trustees. By the time that the Prerogative Court was established in 1686 the process was well under way, but the drift toward English law had not been completed.[30]

A fairly common form of testamentary disposition in the Dutch period was a will executed jointly by the husband and wife, providing for the transfer of their assets to the surviving spouse. Obviously the husband's consent could be inferred from the disposition as well as from the fact that he signed the will simultaneously with his wife. Yet it is important to note that under English law a wife could not devise realty, even to her husband and with his consent. Examples of joint wills exist in the late seventeenth-century New York records, and from their contents give some evidence of realty being the subject of the testamentary dispositions.[31]

In addition to the occasional use of joint wills, the pre-nuptial agreement appears to have retained much of its original vigor in eighteenth-century New York. Well into that century married women executed wills devising realty and bequeathing personalty according to powers conferred upon them by pre-nuptial accords. Mary Horsmanden, wife of the chief justice of the province, executed

---

28. J. Godolphin, *Orphan's Legacy* 23 (4th ed., 1701); 1 *Col. Laws of N.Y.* 145 (1684). There is some question whether the statutes enacted by the 1683-84 session of the New York general assembly survived beyond 1691, see generally Beers v. Hotchkiss, 256 N.Y. 41 (1931). For further evidence of English rules see 2 Swinburne, *Brief Treatise* 61-62, and R. Fowler, *Decedent Estate Law of the State of New York* 78 (1911).

29. Swinburne, *A Treatise of Testaments;* Nelson, *Lex Testamentaria,* 173-174.

30. J. Goebel, *Development of Legal Institutions* 538-546 (7th ed. rev., 1946).

31. See the will of Jan Joosten Van Rollegon and Tryntie Jans Van Bartenburgh, husband and wife, probated February 10, 1694, 25 *N.Y. Hist. Soc'y Colls.*, 278-279.

a will in 1763 upon the basis of a pre-nuptial contract, and significantly, the abstract of her will does not mention trustees joining in her testamentary act, nor does it indicate that her husband, Daniel Horsmanden, signed the will as evidence of his consent. Such an independent act seems also to apply to the will of Dorothy Tarpy in 1712, which confirmed a pre-nuptial land grant to her husband by devising the same land to him in her will.

However, by the middle of the eighteenth century it is safe to say that married womens' rights to execute wills and testaments were based upon rules quite similar to those applied in England. For example, trustees were usually part of the pre-nuptial arrangements made to secure property for the benefit of women about to marry. The will of Elizabeth Sands, proved in 1760, is thus typical of the prevailing English practice that undoubtedly gained general acceptance in New York. Executed with the consent of her husband and signed by him and her trustee, the will includes bequests of personalty and devises of real property.[32] Obviously such trustee arrangements, and even the simpler matrimonial property adjustments of the earlier years, were necessary only in the case of relatively affluent brides; most New York women who died during coverture left no wills.

A great deal of English law concerning the formalities of executing wills was adopted in New York, but adoption was not an automatic process, nor is the record entirely without ambiguities. It seems most proper to observe at this point that English rules concerning the execution of wills were only selectively adopted into the law of the province of New York, and that any broad generalizations based upon the law of England when New York was settled (1664), or when its first assembly met (1683) are not at all helpful. We turn first to the formalities required for devises of realty and then to those required for bequests of personalty.

Under the English statute of wills, real property held in fee simple might be devised by a last will and testament in writing. Significantly, no formalities of execution, other than a written evidence of the devise, were required. Writers on English law during the years after the enactment of the statute of wills are quite specific in stating that any form of writing would be sufficient to

32. For the Horsmanden will see 30 *N.Y. Hist. Soc'y Colls.*, 283-284; a similar will is that of Anna Thompson, proved in 1750, and abstracted Dorothy Tarpy's will is at 26 *N.Y. Hist. Soc'y Colls.*, 101-102. An English will of a feme covert which refers to a pre-nuptial agreement, but not trustees, is that of Jane Trahern (1760), Prob. 11/854, ff. 128, PRO, London. The Sands will is abstracted at 29 *N.Y. Hist. Soc'y Colls.* 357-358, and discussed at length at Goebel, *Development of Legal Institutions* 544-545.

satisfy the requirements of the statute. There is even evidence that an oral, or nuncupative will might be a valid devise of realty provided it was reduced to writing by someone, not necessarily the testator, before the testator's decease. This rather simple requirement was altered by the enactment of the statute of frauds by Parliament in 1677. This required, among other things, that thereafter all wills devising real property, in addition to being in writing, had to be witnessed by three or more credible witnesses.[33]

There has always been serious doubt whether the English statute of frauds of 1677 had been adopted as part of the law of the province of New York.[34] One piece of evidence concerning the adoption of the English statute of frauds is a 1705 decision of the New York Court of Chancery, embodied in a decree overruling a plea in bar to the complainant's bill. The defendant's plea was based solely upon the provision of the 1677 English statute, which required that all agreements to be performed in one year or more should be evidenced by a memorandum in writing. The transcript of the decree makes it clear that both complainant and defendant agreed that the contract was not to be performed within one year; since that crucial fact was undisputed, the Chancery Court's decision rested solely upon the question whether the English statute applied in New York, and the court answered that question in the negative.[35]

The evidence in the original wills remaining on file in New York, supplemented by a more exhaustive study of the abstracts of those wills, confirms the premise that substantial portions of the 1677 English statute of frauds did not apply in New York, and specifically, that the section requiring three witnesses to wills

33. The Act of Wills, Wards and Primer Seisins, 32 Hen. 8, c. 1, sec. 2 (1540). Technically the statute does not refer to fee simple estates, but rather permits the devise of lands held in socage tenure of lords other than the king, and provides for limited alienability by devise for lands held by military tenure or directly of the king. For New York purposes at least, it is safe to overlook these subtleties of the 1540 statute. See also Godolphin, *Orphan's Legacy* 11, 12-14. The English statute of frauds is 29 Car. 2, c. 3 (1677).

34. In *Beers v. Hotchkiss*, 256 N.Y. 41 (1931), the New York Court of Appeals held that a land distribution by allotment in Suffolk County, was sufficient as an *inter vivos* conveyance of title, even though the deed requirements of the 1677 English statute of frauds had not been met. The court held that no convincing evidence of the adoption by custom of the English statute had been submitted, but that, on the contrary, allotment of lands by entry in town records had been a matter of local custom.

35. *Benson v. Rose*, 2 Orders in Chancery 9-10, Historical Documents Collection, Queens College Library, Flushing, New York, but *cf.* 29 Car. 2, c. 3, sec. 4(5).

of real property did not become part of the law of the province. A small but nevertheless significant number of wills of real property, ranging in date from 1687 to 1776, were admitted to probate with but two subscribing witnesses. Of these the will of Leonard Lewis of Dutchess county, probated in 1759, is most valuable for our purposes. One of the subscribing witnesses to Lewis' will was Bartholomew Crannel, a practicing attorney who served as surrogate for Dutchess county at the time the will was executed.[36] Certainly a man so well acquainted with probate matters would not have permitted a will to be executed with an insufficient number of witnesses. To further show the inapplicability of the 1677 English statute of frauds provisions concerning witnesses, we must note that two early wills of real property were admitted to probate with but one witness, and one will, that of Richard Cornell, was admitted to probate in 1694 even though it had no witnesses whatsoever.[37] These two-, one-, and no-witness wills are of course, exceptions to the rule, for most New York colonial wills devising realty bore the signatures of at least three and perhaps more witnesses. However,

36. Two witness wills of realty appear at 25 *N.Y. Hist. Soc'y Colls.* 144-145 (John Holt, 1684), *id.* 151 (Matthew Taylor, 1688), *id.* 156-157 (Thomas Wandell, 1690), *id.* 157-158 (William Cox, 1690), *id.* 179-80 (David Schuyler, 1691), *id.* 245 (Susannah Brasier, 1694), *id.* 263-264 (Peter Silvester, 1696), *id.* 357 (Abraham Lutine, 1702), *id.* 422 (Jacob Teunis DeKay, 1706), *id.* at 454 (Marten Peterse Wyckoff, 1708), 26 *N.Y. Hist. Soc'y Colls.*, 70 (Olphert Suerts, 1711), *id.* 79-80 (John Hunt, 1711), *id.* 112 (Jan Lequere, 1713), *id.* 136-137 (John Roe, 1714), *id.* 139 (Johannes Hardenbrook, 1714), *id.* 141-142 (Lawrence Van Alen, 1714), 27 *N.Y. Hist. Soc'y Colls.* 24-25 (John Kearle, 1731), 26 *N.Y. Hist. Soc'y Colls.* 239 (Teunis Egbertse, 1721), *id.* 352 (John Hicks, 1730), *id.* 163-164 (Richbell Mott, 1734), 27 *N.Y. Hist. Soc'y Colls.* 255-257 (Benjamin Scudder, 1739), *id.* 332 (Benjamin D'Harriette, 1741), *id.* 407 (Rem Remsen, 1743), 28 *N.Y. Hist. Soc'y Colls.* 71 (Caleb Carman, 1746), *id.* 115-116 (James Ferris, 1747), *id.* 257 (Timothy Tredwell, 1748), *id.* 362 (John Brundage, 1751), 29 *N.Y. Hist. Soc'y Colls.* 72 (Jacob King, 1755), *id.* 40 (Cornelius Van Duyn, 1754), *id.* 182-183 (Joseph Kniffen, 1757), *id.* 226 (Jacob Duryee, 1758), 30 *N.Y. Hist. Soc'y Colls.* 107 (Monmouth Hart, 1761), *id.* 365-366 (Christophel German, 1765), 31 *N.Y. Hist. Soc'y Colls.* 77-78 (John Kennan, 1767), 32 *N.Y. Hist. Soc'y Colls.* 131 (John Cornell, 1773) *id.* 139 (John Snedeker, 1773), *id.* 265-266 (Constant Booth, 1774), *id.* 364 (Daniel Knapp, 1774), *id.* 180-181 (Jacobus Ryder, 1774), *id.* at 349-350 (Johannes Yates, 1776). The will of Leonard Lewis, witnessed by Bartholomew Crannel, is at 29 *N.Y. Hist. Soc'y Colls,* 331, and devises land in both Ulster and Orange Counties.

37. One witness wills are at 25 *N.Y. Hist. Soc'y Colls.* 258-259 (Mary Grigg, 1695) and 27 *N.Y. Hist. Soc'y Colls.* 99 (John Smith, 1733). Richard Cornell's will with no witnesses, as at 25 *N.Y. Hist. Soc'y Colls.* 240-242 (1694).

the number of exceptions to the three witness rule, and the case of Lewis's will, seem to indicate that the English statute of 1677 was not considered binding in New York as far as formalities of executing wills was concerned.

Thus, any will in writing would be sufficient to devise New York realty.[38] Indeed, even a will drawn at the direction of the testator and declared by him to be his voluntary testamentary act in the presence of the requisite number of witnesses, could be proved and held valid under the law of both England and New York, even though the testator had not signed the document. Papers on file concerning the will of Dennis Power, proved in October 1759, show the nature of the proofs that the New York Prerogative Court required in such cases.[39]

---

38. But see the Act of May 13, 1691, 1 *Col. Laws of* N.Y. 247, providing that ". . . All wills in writing, *attested by three or more Credible Witnesses shall* be of the same force to Convey Lands as other Conveyances being proved and Registered in the proper office in each County within [blank] days after the Testator's death." (emphasis added). It should also be noted that the will of Maurice Sullivan, submitted to the Prerogative Office in 1755, was signed by but one subscribing witness and bears the annotation "proved"; however it does not appear that letters testamentary issued on this will, perhaps because of a lack of at least one more witness, see NY Co. Wills (N.S.) f. 931. It is also important to note that the act of March 19, 1774, 5 *Col. Laws of* N.Y. 619, purportedly "Adopted" the 1677 statute of frauds as part of the customary law of the province of New York and raised it to statutory dignity.

The English rules concerning real property wills may be found at 2 Swinburne, *Brief Treatise* 30-33, H. Conset, *The Practice of Spiritual or Ecclesiastical Courts* (3rd rev. ed., 1708), 373-374; G. Gilbert, *Law of Devises, Revocations and Last Wills* 91-93 (1761), W. Cockburne, *The Clerk's Assistant in the Practice of Ecclesiastical Courts* 130 (4th ed., 1792).

Although it was sufficiently unusual to cause notation by the Prerogative Office clerks, a young man of seventeen could be a competent witness to a will, see the 1774 probate of the will of John Cockle at NY Co. Wills (N.S.), f. 2629. In some instances a testator and the witnesses signed each page of the original will, see NY Co. Wills (O.S.), f. 233, and for signatures by mark of the testator, see *id.* ff. 2, 4, 8, and 13.

39. An affidavit by the draftsman, John Burnett, recounted that he had read the will aloud to the testator in the presence of Lewis Pintard, and that the testator assured them both that it was his last will and testament and accurately represented his wishes. Then Burnett, a tidy scrivener, returned to his office to draw up a fair copy, and a short time afterward, handed it to Pintard who was to gather two witnesses and call at the dying man's home. This Pintard did, but left with the witnesses when told that the would-be testator was asleep. At one o'clock in the morning, not having received word of the ill man's awakening,

New York formalities concerning personal property wills were more in line with the existing English practice. The written English testament of personalty was in sufficient form if it was executed before two witnesses.[40] A similar rule seems to have applied in New York, and most mariner's wills and wills of persons of modest means were generally witnessed by two persons. In most large estates where there was a likelihood of English or out-of-province American realty passing under the will, three or more witnesses would be employed.

The most common form of will in Dutch New Netherlands had been a notarial will, declared in the presence of a duly appointed notary public, who, after the testator's death, could testify to its due execution and provide a copy from his notarial register. This practice survived despite English occupation of New York, and seems to have been tolerated well into the last decade of the seventeenth century.[41] I have not found a notarial will admitted to probate after 1700, and although there might be a few, it seems safe to conclude that the Dutch form of testamentary disposition ended with the turn of the century. Since all testators who executed notarial wills bore Dutch surnames it is plausible that the English permitted the Dutch practice to continue in respect for the surrender rights afforded to the Dutch inhabitants in 1664. However with

---

Pintard decided to try again. This time the testator was awake when Pintard and his entourage of witnesses arrived, but had grown so weak that he was unable to sign the will; he died shortly thereafter. On the basis of the affidavits of Burnett and Pintard, submitted with the fair copy of the will and the depositions of the two witnesses, the document was admitted to probate and letters testamentary were issued. NY Co. Wills (N.S.), HDC/QC, f. 1243; see also will of Thomas Terry (1672), NY Co. Wills (O.S.), HDC/QC f. 26. The Dennis Power wills and supporting documents are at NY Co. Wills (N.S.), f. 1259, HDC/QC.

40. 2 Swinburne, *Brief Treatise* 30-33; Cockburne, *Clerk's Assistant* 130; Godolphin, *Orphan's Legacy* 65.

41. Examples of notarial wills in the English period after 1686 are at New York County Surrogate's Court, Liber II, 209-211 (Georgia Rutgers, 1691); *id.* 237-240 (Stofel and Heltje Jans, 1691). NY Co. Wills (O.S.), f. 1 (Dirck Johnson Dyer, 1683) and *id.* f. 15 (Gulian Ver Planck, 1684), provide examples of the notarial form used before 1686. One possibility of a notarial will executed in the eighteenth century is that of Cornelius Jansen, admitted to probate in 1706, after being executed before a "clerk," Jan Tiebout, who had been admitted before the Mayor's Court of Harlem, see 25 *N.Y. Hist. Soc'y Colls.* 418-419; however, there were three witnesses to this will. The notarial registers of Solomon Lachair and Walewyn van der Veen, in the New York City Clerk's Office, Municipal Building, New York City, are the best source for a number of notarial wills prepared and executed under the Dutch government.

the passing of the old generation and the submersion of Dutch law and courts that followed the jurisdictional reforms of 1691, the use of the notarial wills declined rapidly and eventually disappeared entirely from the law of New York. But while the notarial will retained its vitality, it constituted an exception to the English statute of frauds, for, following Dutch practice, the notarial will was a valid devise of both realty and personalty.

Holographic testaments of personalty, that is, those in the testator's handwriting but not witnessed, were admissible under English ecclesiastical law if found among the testator's papers after his death, or under such other circumstances as to preclude the likelihood of fraud. If offered with proof that the handwriting compared favorably with that known to be the testator's, the holograph might be admitted to probate.[42] An unusual holograph that illustrates the value of admitting informal documents to probate is a 1775 letter written by the testator, John Backhouse, to his brother, William. Dated on the eve of John's departure for South Carolina, the letter asked the brother, in the event of John's death, to turn all of his assets over to John Barrow of Lancaster ". . . to be divided amongst my suffering creditors in England." Admitted to probate by the New York Prerogative Court, the letter made possible a prompt settlement of the testator's affairs in accordance with his wishes.[43]

The uncertainty concerning the adoption of the 1677 English statute of frauds in New York makes it difficult to determine whether a holographic will might contain valid devises of New York realty. As we have noted previously, at least one holograph, the 1694 will of Richard Cornell, included devises of realty.[44] However, it is the only instrument of this nature to be uncovered, and the lack of similar cases in the later colonial period would seem

42. For the English rule see Cockburne, *Clerk's Assistant* 139; Swinburne, *A Treatise of Testaments* 300, 301; and Gilbert, *Law of Devises* 85; for forms used in proof, see *The Clerk's Instructor in Ecclesiastical Courts* 507-509 (1740); and for the rules see *id.* 47, 48. Proof in the Prerogative Court of Canterbury by two booksellers familiar with a local rector's handwriting, see will of William Purbeck, 1740, Prob 11/700/21, PRO, London. For New York practice see Fowler, *Decedent Estates Law* 48, 51. The King will probate papers are at NY Co. Wills (N.S.), f. 1674; the Wraxall will is at *id.* f. 1274. For other holographs and circumstances justifying their admission to probate, see 25 *N.Y. Hist. Soc'y Coll.* 305 (John Stout, 1699), 28 *N.Y. Hist. Soc'y Colls.* 348-349 (Paul Michaux, 1751), 29 *N.Y. Hist. Soc'y Colls.* 239-241 (Abraham Lodge, 1758) and 31 *N.Y. Hist. Soc'y Colls.* 107-109 (Witham Marsh, 1767).

43. NY Co. Wills (N.S.), f. 2716.

44. See discussion at n. 37, *supra*.

to indicate that the practice of the bar, if not the custom of the province, was against the use of holographs to devise real property. To this extent at least, we may assume that there was a selective adoption of the 1677 statute of frauds in that witnesses were required for the validity of real property devises. Perhaps the principle of the English statute of frauds—that witnesses being present prevented fraudulent or coerced devises—was considered valid and adopted into New York law, even though the rigid requirement of three witnesses was adjudged inapplicable to New York conditions.

Nuncupative, or oral wills, were also used on an infrequent basis in the province of New York. At English law an oral will of personalty might be declared by the testator in the presence of two witnesses, who would then swear to its contents after his death. In 1677 the English statute of frauds increased the number of required witnesses to three in the case of personal estates that exceeded £30 in value. Additionally, the English statute added the requirements that the testator make an affirmative declaration that his statements were to be taken as his last will and testament, and that the declaration be made in the course of the testator's last illness while he was in his dwelling house or prevented from reaching his home by virtue of a sudden onslaught of a fatal illness. The English statute further required that nuncupative wills be proved within six months after the date of their declaration, unless they had been reduced to writing by the witnesses no more than six days after the date of declaration. Specifically exempted from the provisions of the 1677 statute were wills of soldiers and mariners.[45]

If the wills of New York military men and seamen are disregarded, it seems clear that certain portions of the 1677 English statute of frauds applied to nuncupative wills executed in New York during the colonial period. An examination of nuncupative wills admitted to probate during the period from 1702 to 1772 indicates that the witnesses did, as a general rule, swear that the will was declared to them by the testator to be his will, that it was so declared in his dwelling house, and in several cases it is apparent that they reduced the oral will to writing within six days after its declaration. A memorandum in the papers of attorney John Tabor Kempe, discussing points of law involved in the probate litigation

---

45. R. Richardson, *The Law of Testaments and Last Wills* 23 (2nd ed., 1769); *Clerk's Instructor in Ecclesiastical Courts* 504; Godolphin, *Orphan's Legacy* 65; Act for the Prevention of Frauds, 29 Car. 2, c. 3, secs. 19-21, 23, 24; Wentworth, *Office of Executors* 7; Gilbert, *Law of Devises* 85.

of *New v. Sharpe* (1773), gives further evidence that it was the practice to reduce nuncupative wills to writing within six days and that the £30 limitation of the 1677 English statute of frauds also applied in New York. Significantly, the three-witness rule of this clause of the English statute of frauds was not adhered to in New York; thus the practice of the Prerogative Court was to ignore the three-witness requirement for nuncupative wills, just as it ignored the three-witness requirement devises of realty. As a result, most New York nuncupative wills have two, rather than three witnesses.[46]

Similarly, the New York court ignored the requirement of a 1660 English statute requiring that a testamentary appointment of a guardian be made by a will executed in the presence of two or more witnesses, when in a 1720 case it gave effect to an oral deathbed nomination. The court acted, however, with the consent of the minor for whom the guardian was appointed;[47] perhaps that consent was vital since, in the absence of a will, a boy of fifteen and a girl of fourteen might nominate their own guardian in New York, and appointments of guardians for children nine years of age or older were always made with the infants present in court.[48]

---

46. On New York practice see Fowler, *Decedent Estate Law* 84-85. Two early New York nuncupative wills are at NY Co. Wills (O.S.), HDC, Queens College, f. 28 (Samuel Moore, 1676) and f. 32 (Robert Ashman, 1683). More recent nuncupative wills of inhabitants not in military or maritime service, are at 25 *N.Y. Hist. Soc'y Colls.* 338 (George Dod, 1702); 29 *N.Y. Hist. Soc'y Colls.* 92-93 (Richard Shaw, 1755); 30 *N.Y. Hist. Soc'y Colls.* 64-65 (Richard Kirby, 1761); and 32 *N.Y. Hist. Soc'y Colls.* 82 (Silas Horton, 1772); of these only the last was executed before three witnesses. Wills of mariners or soldiers are at 25 *N.Y. Hist. Soc'y Colls.* 193 (Charles Lambert, 1691), 26 *N.Y. Hist. Soc'y Colls.* 327-328 (Peter Walker, 1725), 26 *N.Y. Hist. Soc'y Colls.* 46-47 (Paul Fountaine, 1710), *id.* 277 (Elias Hughes, 1723); 28 *N.Y. Hist. Soc'y Colls.* 52 (John Ward, 1745); 28 *N.Y. Hist. Soc'y Colls.* 342 (Charles Greenfield, 1751); 29 *N.Y. Hist. Soc'y Colls.* 208-209 ("Captain Harbord," 1757). The rules on reducing a nuncupative will to writing are at *Clerk's Instructor in Ecclesiastical Courts* 54, 1 Woerner, *A Treatise of the American Law of Administration* 115, Wentworth, *Office of Executors* 6; for papers in *New v. Sharpe* see Lawsuits, Unsorted P-U, John Tabor Kempe Papers, New York Historical Society, New York City.

47. Administration Papers, Court of Appeals, Box Be-Blue, f. 68 (estate of James Bord, 1720), HDC/QC.

48. Cockburne, *Clerk's Assistant* 145; Wentworth, *Office of Executors* 321-322; 12 Car. 2, c. 24, sec. 8, 9 (1660). Guardian appointments by New York courts are at 25 *N.Y. Hist. Soc'y Colls.* 365 (Robert Puddington, 18 years old, 1703); *id.* 439 (Catherine and Mary Donaldson, 13 and 12 years old, 1706); NY Co. Wills (O.S.), f. 253 (Jacob Smith, over 12,

We should note in passing that in regard to estates that were bequeathed by nuncupative wills and were less than the £30 limitation, the formalities of the 1677 statute of frauds were not required in England. From an examination of the records of the New York Prerogative Court it is not possible to determine whether this exception applied in New York. The strong likelihood is that few residents of the province had estates valued at less than £30 in New York currency, and that if they did, its descent was probably by intestate succession. Previously we noted the fact that the local courts in the "remote" counties had, under the 1692 New York statute, the right to admit to probate wills of persons whose estate did not exceed £50. Consequently a study of probate practice at the county level is necessary before any definite conclusions can be drawn concerning nuncupative wills and small estates in New York.

It thus appears that the Prerogative Court gradually and selectively received into New York law the English statute of 1670 concerning intestacy, the English statute of frauds of 1677, and the English statute concerning guardianship of infants passed in 1660. In the case of the first two statutes there is strong evidence that the statutes were known and understood by the New York bar. It is equally clear that only portions of those statutes were received into New York colonial law, and that the reception was by custom rather than by legislative action. Only at the end of the colonial period did the New York General Assembly pass a series of statutes which brought the statutory law of the province into line with the customary reception of these English statutes. Of particular interest is the fact that New York law was fairly consistent in refusing to adopt English rules concerning witnesses required to validate legal acts. Possibly the sparcity of population in New York may explain this reluctance. On the other hand, the close relationships among colonial New Yorkers, a product of intermarriage and frequent social contact, might very easily have rendered unnecessary the more formal protections against fraud required in the more heterogeneous and impersonal society of eighteenth century Eng-

1696), HDC/QC; 4 Orders in Chancery 322 (Hannah Montgomery, 9 years old, 1740); 5 *id.* 1-3 (Joseph Haynes, for George Baker and Sarah Baker, both under 5 years of age, 1748); *id.* 12-13 (Lawrence Hardman, 15 years old, 1749); *id.* 13 (Elizabeth Smith, 14 years old, 1750); *id.* 18-19 (John George Cooke, 13 years old, 1751); all at HDC/QC. See also Albany Inventories, Ser. 2, f. 8 (Richard Ashfield, over 15 years of age, 1703, appointed under seal of Prerogative Court), HDC/QC. Godolphin, *Orphan's Legacy* indicates that an infant executor over seventeen could not assent to the payment of legacies, but he might sell goods of the estate, and execute a valid release for true and real satisfaction.

land. This is an area of study which has only been briefly discussed, but which promises to yield rich rewards to legal historians willing to pursue the evidence concerning the gradual reception of English statutes into colonial New York law.

Procedure

The procedure of New York's Prerogative Court, like the substantive law that it applied, was modeled upon English law, although there was again some variation. In England two procedures were available for the proof of formal wills. The first and simplest was proof in "common form," an *ex parte* proceeding whereby the nominated executor swore that he knew the circumstances of the will's execution, and that he would undertake the administration when the document was admitted to probate.[49] Proof in common form was predicated upon the presumption that a will, undoubtedly in the testator's hand and subscribed by him, was in fact his last will and testament. It was available only when there was no controversy concerning the validity of the will. If there was a controversy, proof in form of law would be required.[50] This, the second method for proving formal testaments, required that the widow or next-of-kin be cited to appear before the court, and that, in their presence the witnesses would be examined concerning the circumstances under which the purported will was executed.[51] Proof in form of law carried greater weight than proof in common form, the English rule being that proof in form of law could be challenged only within thirty years of probate, but that proof in common form could be controverted at any time.[52] It should be understood that proof and probate of a will was not properly *res judicata* in law, but only evidence of the facts proved in the

---

49. Wentworth, *Office of Executors*, 48; 2 Woerner, *A Treatise on the American Law of Administration*, 712, 714; Godolphin, *Orphan's Legacy* 62, 65; Nelson, *Lex Testamentaria* 463; 2 Swinburne, *Brief Treatise*, 69-70; A. Redfield, *The Law and Practice of Surrogate's Courts in the State of New York* 2, 3 (5th ed., 1894).

50. For presumption of validity, see Wentworth, *Office of Executors*, 4, 5; presumption of death, see H. Swinburne, *A Treatise of Testaments and Last Wills*, 362 (1677); Godolphin, *Orphan's Legacy*, 61.

51. Godolphin, *id.* 62; Cockburne, *Clerk's Assistant* 133.

52. A certain degree of presumptive validity attached to a common form proof that went unchallenged for ten years, see Swinburne, *A Treatise of Testaments* 362. The principle seems to have been that proof in common form could be challenged at any time, but that a will admitted to probate after solemn form proof could not be challenged more than thirty years after probate, see Godolphin, *Orphan's Legacy* 62; Swinburne, *A Treatise of Testaments* 362; Nelson, *Lex Testamentaria* 463.

course of taking depositions. For this reason English common law courts were not bound by the probates of the ecclesiastical courts.[53]

Both methods of proving wills were used in New York, and by the end of the colonial period the clerks in the Prerogative Office were well versed in the distinction between them. The will of Peter Rezeau, proved in 1725, indicates that common form proof was in use by that date, and perhaps even earlier.[54] Common form proof was resorted to most frequently when a will executed outside New York before non-residents of the province was to be proved in New York.

Proof in form of law, or "solemn form" proof, was undoubtedly the most general method for proving wills in colonial New York. English custom required that two witnesses to the execution be examined before probate in solemn form would issue. New York practice seems to have followed this general pattern. While the form of witness's oaths varied somewhat, particularly in the seventeenth century, the substance remained remarkably constant. Under normal circumstances the witnesses were expected to affirm the solemn ceremony of execution and testify concerning testamentary capacity and soundness of mind. Typical of most is the oath endorsed on the will of Josiah Hunt (1732), where the witnesses swore that they saw testator sign, seal, and declare the instrument to be his last will and testament, that he was then of a disposing mind, and of sound mind and body, and that they signed the will in the presence of the testator as subscribing witnesses and witnessed the signature of each other.[55]

---

53. Richardson, *Law of Testaments* 336-339.

54. NY Co. Wills (N.S.), f. 2374 (Goslin), HDC/QC; *id.* f. 2421 (Van Veghte), and NY Co. Wills (O.S.), f. 679 (Rezeau), HDC/QC; see also 28 *N.Y. Hist. Soc'y Colls.* 181-182 (William Wily, 1748).

Since wills proved in a sister province were usually not available to be exhibited in New York, common form proof was usually adequate when coupled with an exemplified copy of the will and letters admitted the executor to the administration of the estate, N.Y. Co. Surrogate's Court Liber II (1682-1692), 296; 25 *N.Y. Hist. Soc'y Colls.* 391-392 (William Corbin, Mass. probate, confirmed in N.Y. in 1704); *id.* 390-391 (Jacob Mayle, Jamaica probate, confirmed in N.Y. 1704); 26 *id.* 11 (Fitzjohn Winthrop, Conn. probate, confirmed in N.Y. 1708); *id.* 20 (Andrew Duany, Penna. probate, confirmed in N.Y., 1709); 28 *id.* 43-431 (Francis Ferrari, St. Eustatius probate, confirmed in N.Y. 1753). On occasion proof in form of law might be required, see NY Co. Wills (N.S.) f. 2168 (Mary and William Walton, N.J. probate, confirmed in N.Y. 1768), HDC/QC.

55. The Hunt materials are at NY Co. Wills (O.S.), f, 84, HDC/QC; an earlier form of oath, appended to the will of Adam Mott (1691), states that the witnesses saw the testator sign, seal and execute the in-

The fact that a man was sworn as a subscribing witness did not disqualify him from assuming the duties of an executor or an administrator cum testamento annexo. The absence of New York wills witnessed by legatees or devisees would indicate that a beneficiary under the provisions of the will was not considered a competent witness. Prior to 1752 a will so witnessed would have been invalid under English law, and the statutory relief provided after that date saved the validity of the will by the expedient of cancelling the devise or bequest. There is no evidence that the 1752 English statute was adopted in New York through usage; of course a careful draftsman would have avoided the difficulty which, even with the more liberal post-1752 English rule, was most prejudicial to interested witnesses.[56]

The requirement of two witnesses was a flexible rule permitting proof of a witness' handwriting or other testimony to compensate for the absence of witnesses. A New York will executed in 1742 was proved in 1769 by the affidavit of testator's sister that the signature was that of the testator, supplemented by proof of the death of two of the subscribing witnesses and the "unsound mind" of the third witness. Similarly the testimony of a non-subscribing

---

strument as his will, that he published it as his will, and that at the time they knew him to be in his perfect senses and to be of sound memory, *id.* f. 48; a more abrupt affidavit from 1675 attests only to ". . . the reality and verity of the above will . . .", while the witnesses to a 1687 will swore that they ". . . saw her sign, seal, and declare the Will, of which the within is a true copy." Will of John Elton (1675), *id.* f. 11; will of Grizzel Sylvester (1687), *id.* f. 83. By way of contrast the deposition of a subscribing witness taken in an English ecclesiastical court was very precise concerning the execution of the will, its preparation, the behavior of the testator and the behavior of others present at the time of execution, and also contained positive allegations concerning the absence of fraud or undue influence. See *Clerk's Instructor in Ecclesiastical Courts* 91-95. For wills witnessed by Jews, see NY Co. Wills (N.S.), f. 1620, HDC/QC, and 29 *N.Y. Hist. Soc'y Colls.* 96 (Philip Isaacs, 1755). For a general discussion of Jewish wills and estates see L. Hershkowitz, *Wills of Early New York Jews (1704-1799)* (1967). On Quakers see the Act of May 18, 1691, 1 *Col. Laws of N.Y.* 257; 26 *N.Y. Hist. Soc'y Colls.* 382 (Robert Eddas, 1727); English practice was similar, see *Clerk's Instructor in Ecclesiastical Courts* 58, 228, 229.

56. See will of Sampson Simpson (1774), NY Co. Wills (N.S.), f. 1694, HDC/QC, for administrator *cum testamento annexo* testifying as a witness. The legatee-witness situation is discussed at Wentworth, *Office of Executors*, 5-8; Swinburne, *A Treatise of Testaments* 295-296. The will of Anne Chambers, executed in 1767 and naming John Jay as a legatee, was not witnessed by Jay, even though he would have normally done so as one of the drafting attorney's clerks, 32 *N.Y. Hist. Soc'y Colls.* 168-170. The English statute is 25 Geo. 2, c. 6 (1752).

witness to a will executed in 1740 was sufficient to support probate requested in 1768. Even an oath verifying the authenticity of the signatures of the two witnesses to a will might be adequate.[57]

As we have noted above, proof in common form was available only when there was no controversy in regard to the validity of a will; when a will was contested, solemn form proof was needed. Although no substantial amount of documentation has survived concerning New York probate contests, it is nevertheless possible to outline with some accuracy the procedures which were followed in determining such cases.

As in English practice a caveat was filed by the party wishing to contest the validity of the will. When the proponent appeared in the Prerogative Court to file his proofs and obtain letters testamentary, he was confronted with the caveat and compelled to prepare and file a formal petition for probate if he wished to proceed further. On the basis of such a petition the Prerogative Court issued its citation in the form of an order to show cause, requiring the caveator to appear on a certain date, and to give his reasons why letters testamentary should not issue.[58]

On the return date the caveator appeared and filed his written answer to the petition, which began with the ritual objections to the vagueness and inaccuracy of the petition; such formal objections formed part of most of the pleadings filed in the New York Court of Chancery in the colonial period. In addition, the answer specifically admitted or denied the allegations in the petition, and might also plead affirmative objections to the granting of probate.[59] After this interchange of the petition and answer, it was possible for the parties to continue pleading by way of filing replications and rejoinders. But none of these documents survive, and if they ever did exist, it is quite possible that they, like similar pleadings

---

57. Swinburne, *A Treatise of Testaments* 293; Cockburn, *Clerk's Assistant* 135-1371, 31 *N.Y. Hist. Soc'y Colls.* 269-270 (John Frans Walter, 1760); *id.* at 181 (Frederick Williamse, 1768); 28 *N.Y. Hist. Soc'y Colls.* 328 (John Burroughs, 1751). See also proof of handwriting of only one of the three deceased subscribing witnesses, 30 *N.Y. Hist. Soc'y Colls.* 182-183 (Dirck Dyckman, 1762). If the original will were lost after proofs were taken before a county surrogate, it might be confirmed upon the filing of the surrogate's affidavit explaining the loss, 29 *N.Y. Hist. Soc'y Colls.* 420-421 (Benjamin Van Steenbergen, 1760).

58. William Livingston, Cost Book II, Supreme Court of New York (1759-1772), pp. 371-372, Manuscript Room, New York Public Library, New York City. For petition of proponent after discovering a caveat, see the will of Thomas Bishop (1760), Administration Papers, Court of Appeals, Box Be-Blue, f. 3-70, HDC/QC.

59. The answer is in the Thomas Bishop will file, *op. cit. supra*, 58.

in the New York Court of Chancery, were merely formal reaffirmations of the truth and accuracy of the respective petition and answer.

After all pleadings had been served and filed with the Prerogative Court, the cause stood ready for the preparation of proofs. Depending upon the difficulty of the issues raised by the pleadings, and perhaps upon the convenience and efficiency of the proctors retained by the parties, the delay between pleading and the commencement of the deducing of proofs could range from a few days to as much as six months.[60]

Absent any minutes covering the proceedings of the New York Prerogative Court, we have no way of telling the extent to which the court policed the interchange of pleadings or what type of orders, if any, may have been necessary for the purpose of expediting the progress of the case at this stage. However it is clear that interrogatories and cross-interrogatories were prepared by the proctors for each party, and that these were filed with the register (also the principal surrogate) of the Prerogative Court. Then the witnesses were summoned, occasionally by brief citations, similar only in bare essence to those used in England, to appear before the register, who put them under oath and took their testimony on the basis of the questions submitted by the proctors. We do not know whether proctors for all parties were present at the examinations by the register, but it is most likely that the examinations and depositions were not generally available to all counsel for all the parties until the taking of proofs was finished and "publication" had passed. This was in keeping with the practice of the English Court of Chancery, and was in use in the New York Chancery Court.[61]

"Publication" would pass in both English and New York chancery practice when the parties required no further examinations before the case would be set down for decree. New York chancery court practice fixed the time for publication to pass by an order of the court, entered upon the motion of the parties. The one example of New York Prerogative Court publication practices to come to light is a stipulation by the proctors agreeing that publication should pass as of the date of signing the stipulation. The document is endorsed "so ordered" and signed by the principal surrogate, suggest-

60. *Ibidem.* The Bishop pleadings were exchanged May 26, 1760; a citation to examine subscribing witnesses issued June 3, and interrogatories were drawn and filed with the register between June 11 and 18, *ibidem.* The delay in the Stillwell case was over six months, Livingston Cost Book II, 371-372, New York Public Library.

61. A set of interrogatories, cross-interrogatories and depositions is in the Bishop file, *op. cit. supra,* n. 58. English chancery practice is discussed at W. J. Jones, *The Elizabethan Court of Chancery* 238-239 (1967).

ing that an order of the court was required for the validity of the stipulation, and that the normal practice would be by motion to the governor. The latter procedure would of course be required if one of the proctors would not consent to publication.[62]

The matter was set down for hearing once publication was passed. While no records of argument survive, we do know something about the rather informal manner in which a motion was set for hearing by the governor. On the morning the two parties wished to argue their case, their proctors called upon the governor who then fixed the time and place of the hearing. In the single example of this procedure which is extant, the proctors were given two hours to appear to argue their motion.[63]

The relatively simple procedure followed before the New York Prerogative Court was significantly different from English church court practice. This is evidenced by the informal matter of noticing motions before the governor as ordinary, and it also appears in the brevity of pleadings and the brief citations; both pleadings and citations usually retained only the essence of procedural forms used in the English ecclesiastical courts. In addition, no decree admitting a will to probate has been found, and no reference to such decrees are contained in the court's records. This strongly suggests the possibility that such decrees were not prepared, but that the letters testamentary served as a substitute for the formal decree.

Two of the contested probate proceedings survive in the form of documents which provide information concerning the nature of the objections to the wills offered for probate. In the case of Samuel Stillwell it was alleged that he had destroyed his will by attempting to burn it, and that he had thereby revoked its provisions. The will had been rescued from the flames and sewn together by his sister, and the issue raised was Stillwell's mental state at the time of attempted revocation. The Prerogative Court held the revocation ineffective and admitted the will to probate. In the will contest concerning Thomas Bishop's estate, a daughter by a previous marriage

62. Jones, *Elizabethan Court of Chancery* 248-250; 1 Orders in Chancery 23 (*Smith v. Smith*, 1701); *id.* 24 (*Lawrence v. Woolsey*, 1701); 4 *id.* 45 (*Rapeltje v. Hansen*, 1723). The stipulation and order on consent is in the will file of Thomas Bishop, *op. cit. supra*, n. 58, p. —.

63. Motion practice can be found in the will contest of *Biggs v. Smith* (1759). William Wickhaam, Supreme Court Register A, verso pp. 4, 5, Columbia University Law Library, New York City; see discussion at 1 Goebel, *The Law Practice of Alexander Hamilton* 23, 24 (1967). The motion is of further interest in that it was a request for a continuance by the contestant, coupled with the proponent's request for an order of the court authorizing him to harvest and sell wheat partially owned by the estate.

claimed lack of testamentary capacity and undue influence upon the testator by his second wife. After testimony concerning the estrangement between the testator and his daughter, as well as proof concerning execution of the will, the court admitted it to probate.[64]

Once proofs of a will were on file with the Prerogative Court, the nominated executor or the administrator cum testamento annexo (c.t.a.) appointed by the court took his oath before the deputy secretary or one of the subordinate surrogates. These qualification procedures were nearly identical to those followed in the Prerogative Court of Canterbury, even including the frequent use of Latin to record the fact that the oath had been administered to the New York fiduciary. There was a short period in New York history when the governors personally administered oaths to executors and administrators, but this was limited to the first thirty years of the New York court's existence. Thereafter the routine procedure was to delegate such duties to the deputy secretary (principal surrogate and register) or to a surrogate.[65]

English law required no words of art to constitute an executor, as long as duties of executorship were imposed upon the individual mentioned in the will. The New York rule was similar, for as we have noted in the case of the 1775 probate of the "will" of John Backhouse, a mere letter requesting the testator's brother to settle accounts with creditors, was sufficient as a holographic will, and competent to authorize the brother's appointment as executor.[66]

Executors might be appointed in England from among a fairly large class of individuals, the testator's discretion being limited by the legal exclusion of traitors, felons, excommunicants,

64. The Stillwell case is described in the cost book entries of William Livingston, *op. cit. supra*, n. 58, p. —; and in an answer in chancery filed after the American Revolution in a related case, Decrees before 1800, S-79, HDC/QC.

65. New York original wills bear endorsements showing qualification before the deputy secretary. See the will of John Stryker (1759), NY Co. Wills (N.S.), f. 1257. Qualification before New York governor at NY Co. Wills (O.S.), ff. 217, 218 (1708-10), HDC/QC.

Qualification in the Prerogative Court of Canterbury can be traced in the registry books. See the will of Henry Chatfield (1691/2), Prob 10/1226; will of Abraham Clarke (1691/2), Prob 10/1226; will of John Cooke, Prob 10/1226; will of Elizabeth Childers (1724/5), Prob 10/1655; will of Thomas Pinfold (1739/40), Prob 10/1890 and Prob 11/700, all in PRO, London. See also *Clerk's Instructor in Ecclesiastical Courts*, 129.

In the Prerogative Court of Canterbury the proofs and oaths of the executors or administrators are recorded in Latin until 1740. New York registrars and surrogates used English at an earlier date, but inevitably took the oaths "*Coram me.*"

66. See discussion at n. 43, *supra*.

outlawed persons, libellers, sodomites, recusants, apostates and usurers. An infant might be designated executor, but letters could not issue to him or her until he or she reached the age of 17. A feme covert was not barred from administration by canon law, but the common law concerning coverture gave rise to the principal in English ecclesiastical courts that a feme covert might not accept executorship without her husband's consent. Her husband, on the other hand, might accept the fiduciary duty and exercise it upon her behalf.[67] New York Prerogative Court documents do not provide any indication whether these various rules applied in New York. Certainly most of the spiritual offenses which served as bars to appointment in England would be unknown in New York; on the other hand there are so few appointments of femes covert to administer decedent's estates that we can surmise that English law in this connection did generally apply in the province of New York.

When it became impossible to assemble all of the executors before one officer, it was the New York practice that those who were present might qualify by taking their oaths, while those absent would be permitted to do so at a later time, either before the same official or some other delegate of the governor. This closely followed the system utilized in the Prerogative Court of Canterbury, and there it came to be known as "double probate."[68] Again it is necessary to recall that "probate" in the côlonial and English context was not proof of a will, but rather the qualification of the executor of a valid will and the issuance of letters testamentary to him.

---

67. Godolphin, *Orphan's Legacy* 75, 82, 85, 102, 109, 110; Nelson, *Lex Testamentaria* 329-330; Wentworth, *Office of Executors* 202-203, 205. In 1757 a N.Y. feme covert renounced administration with the consent of her husband; in 1770 a feme covert accepted administration, her husband not consenting but serving as surety on her bond. Administration Papers, Court of Appeals, Box Ba-Be, f. 3-51 HDC/QC (estate of Catherine Bedford, 1757; *id.* Box Mc-Met, f. 2-614 (estate of Thomas Marsh, 1770).

68. A New York example of separate qualification is in the proceeding concerning the will of former Supreme Court of Judicature justice John Chambers (1764), where one executor was sworn before the deputy secretary and nine days later the second executor qualified by taking his oath before a surrogate, NY Co. Wills (N.S.), f. 1742, HDC/QC.

The procedures in the Prerogative Court of Canterbury are shown in regard to the will of Henry Hawley (1724), Prob 11/599, f. 208; will of Daniel Lawrence (1724), Prob 11/600 and Prob 12/95; will of Jane Pym (1739/40), Prob 11/700, ff. 19, 20. "Double probate" is a term used in the index to the registry books of the Prerogative Court of Canterbury, see entry on the estate of Daniel Lawrence (June 1725), second probate), at Prob 12/95. All of the foregoing at PRO, London. See also Godolphin, *Orphan's Legacy* 79.

Hence "double probate" was the subsequent qualification of an additional executor, and not the second proof of the will. Although the term "double probate" does not seem to have been used in New York, it is clear that the English rules concerning it were closely followed.

Should an executor decide to renounce the administration of the will, both New York and English law required that this be done in writing. No specific formality was necessary, but English practice required that a renunciation be an act recorded in the ecclesiastical court. Consequently the writing had to be executed in the presence of a judge (i.e., ordinary, commissary or surrogate) of the court.[69] New York seems to have varied from this requirement. Although renunciations in New York were in writing and filed with the Prerogative Court, they varied in form from those taken before the deputy secretary or surrogates to those sworn to before one or more witnesses. Occasionally New York renunciations were executed in the presence of notaries public, and a renunciation in the form of an indenture also appears to have been acceptable to the New York Prerogative Court.

It is not possible to determine whether the elaborate English rules concerning acts which would prevent an executor's renunciation, applied in New York. But it does appear that the English rule which permitted a renouncing executor to later qualify during the lifetime of his co-executor was applicable in the province of New York, and that use of an indenture as a form of renunciation was needed to contractually prevent a renouncing executor from later changing his mind.[70]

Absence or death of the nominated executor would permit a New York colonial surrogate, like his English counterpart, to administer the oath of a fiduciary to an administrator c.t.a. In New York the most frequent c.t.a. appointments occurred in the

---

69. *Clark's Instructor in Ecclesiastical Courts* 192; Wentworth *Office of Executors* 33-41, 326.

70. New York renunciations are at NY Co. Wills (O.S.), f. 705 (Clement Elsworth, 1726—two witnesses to renunciation); NY Co. Wills (N.S.), f. 253 (Charles Cornelius, 1744—two witnesses to renunciation); NY Co. Wills (O.S.), f. 706 (Peter DeRiemer, 1726—one witness to renunciation); NY Co. Wills (N.5), f. 74 (Thomas Dickerson, 1738/9—renunciation signed but not witnessed); *id.* f. 1077 (Samuel Boyd, 1757—two witnesses and in indenture form); *id.* f. 404 (James Ferris, 1747—renunciation sworn to before Queens county surrogate); all in HDC/QC.

While English practice permitted a renouncing executor to qualify and administer during the lifetime of his co-executor who had qualified, his right to qualify terminated upon the death of the last appointed executor. See Godolphin, *Orphan's Legacy* 88, 141-142.

case of British soldiers who died while stationed in the province. Since their nominated executors usually were non-residents, officers from deceased soldiers' regiments were usually appointed administrators c.t.a.[71] Normally appointments as administrator c.t.a. would follow the general rules applicable in cases of intestacy. As we shall later see, these favored the appointment of next of kin to administer the estate. However, in appointing an administrator c.t.a., an English ecclesiastical court might exclude next of kin if the decedent's will contained a residuary legacy and the legatee was willing to serve as administrator c.t.a. There is some slight evidence that this preference for a residuary legatee also applied in New York colonial law.[72]

There is also evidence that New York applied English principles and procedures in the appointments of administrators de bonis non cum testamento annexo (d.b.n.c.t.a.), and administrator de bonis non (d.b.n.). The evidence consists of the use of the terms de bonis non (d.b.n.) and cum testamento annexo (c.t.a.) in the records of the New York Prerogative Court, from which we may presume that the English ecclesiastical court practice concerning these successor fiduciaries was followed, in a general way, in colonial New York.[73]

---

71. English practice at Conset, *Practice of Spiritual Courts* 14; 2 Swinburne, *Brief Treatise of Testaments* 28; for New York procedures see the estate of Thomas Johnston (1771). NY Co. Wills (O.S.), f. 66; will of John River (1767), NY Co. Wills (N.S.), f. 2040; and will of James Alburtis (1771), NY Co. Wills (N.S.), f. 2351, all at HDC/QC.

Where the nominated executor was absent, administration c.t.a. might be granted in New York and England. See will of Thomas Jackson (1769), NY Co. Wills (N.S.) f. 2218; will of John Dumaresque (1723), 26 *N.Y. Hist. Soc'y Colls.* 266, 267. In the Prerogative Court of Canterbury a citation was issued to a nominated executor, a resident of Calcutta, whose nonappearance permitted administration c.t.a. to be granted. Will of John Penning (1740), Prob 11/700, f. 20, PRO, London.

72. Godolphin, *Orphan's Legacy* 83, enunciates the rule on the residuary legatee and administration c.t.a. For appointment of next-of-kin to administer c.t.a., see will of Anna Medford (1687), 25 *N.Y. Hist. Soc'y Colls.* 140-141; grant to a creditor who "purchased" the rights of children, see will of Hope Carpenter (1713), 26 *id.* at 132, 133.

73. An executor's executor succeeded to the administration if the deceased executor was the sole surviving executor, and if the deceased executor had been admitted to the administration. If the deceased executor had not been admitted, but was the residuary legatee, then letters of administration c.t.a. might issue to his executor. Godolphin, *Orphan's Legacy* 87, 230; see also Cockburne, *Clerk's Assistant* 147; T. Atkinson, *Handbook of the Law of Wills* 577, 582 (2d ed., 1953); 1 Woerner, *Treatise on the American Law of Administration* 605 (3d rev. ed., 1923). New

In New York colonial practice the issuance of letters of administration or letters testamentary was reserved to the governor, and the appropriate letters issued out of the Prerogative Office, signed by the secretary or deputy secretary on behalf of the governor, and sealed with the seal of the Prerogative Court. Under English practice, buttressed by statutory enactment in 1670, a final step was required of a fiduciary before letters would issue—that he give bond to secure the performance of his duties in accordance with law and the orders of the court. Penal bonds, conditioned upon faithful performance of the fiduciary, were utilized in New York as early as 1666, and continued to be required until the end of the colonial period.[74] The deputy secretary of the province, acting as principal surrogate, fixed the penal amount of the fiduciary's bond, and notified the local surrogate of the amount to be taken in security.[75]

Upon his appointment and qualification before the Prerogative Court, the New York fiduciary entered upon the administration of the estate entrusted to his care, and normally there was no further need for the Prerogative Court to assist him in his duties or to regulate his administration. By virtue of his appointment by the Prerogative Court the executor had unquestioned standing to sue on behalf of the estate in the New York courts of common law and

---

York references to c.t.a. administrations are at n. 72, *supra*. The term d.b.n. occurs at William Livingston, Supreme Court of Judicature Cost Book II, 360 (1767), and at 29 *N.Y. Hist. Soc'y Colls*. 77 (will of Johannes Beekman, 1755).

74. Wentworth, *Office of Executors* 381, notes that pursuant to "23 Car.2" (presumably 22 & 23 Car. 2, c. 10 (1670)), an ordinary or judge of an ecclesiastical court might take bond with two or more sureties, from administrators in accordance with the form of the statute. As we shall see later, 22 & 23 Car. 2, c. 10 was not considered applicable in New York until about 1754. New York bonding practices thus evolved from the traditional ecclesiastical court procedures, which were recognized and approved by the English statute of 1670.

See NY Co. Wills (O.S.), f. 57 (estate of Edward Jessup, 1666); NY Co. Wills (N.S.), f. 2351 (estate of James Alburtis, 1771); Administration Papers, Court of Appeals, Box A, f. 3-17 (estate of East Apthorpe, 1718); *id.* Box Heart-Hitz, f. 3-418 (estate of Gilbert Heathcote, 1730); *id.* Box Ca-Coe, f. 3-160 (estate of Theophilus Clark, 1755); *id.* Box A, f. 3-4 (estate of Jonathan Adams, 1757); *id.* Box A, f. 3-15 (estate of Ziprah Anderson, 1765); *id.* Box Be-Blue, f. 3-65 (will of Samuel Betts, 1773); *id.* Box B, f. 3-24 (estate of Remember Baker, 1776); all at HAD/QC.

75. Administration Papers, Court of Appeals, Box B, f. 3-24 (estate of Remember Baker, 1776); *id.* Box A, f. 3-5 (estate of William Adams, 1761); *id.* Box A, f. 3-8 (estate of Benjamin Allen, 1774); all at HDC/QC.

equity and to undertake all other tasks necessary to full administration of the estate.

Procedure in cases of intestacy was parallel to that in cases seeking probate of wills. Upon the appearance of a person claiming administration of an intestate's estate, the surrogate would require renunciations from individuals having a prior right, or in the alternative, request that citation issue against such persons. If the petitioner's right to administration was unquestioned, or went uncontested, the surrogate administered the oath to the administrator, accepted the filing of the administrator's bond, and then granted a certificate "admitting" the individual to administer the assets. The certificate and bond were then transmitted to the Prerogative Office, which, in due course, issued the formal letter of administration.[76]

Absent careful genealogical investigation into the family condition of each individual to whom letters of administration were granted, it is not possible to provide an accurate picture of the rules of law which governed grants of administration in colonial New York. Clearly the 1664 statute expressed a preference for widows and children, and this preference continued throughout the colonial period. Later proceedings in the Prerogative Court indicate that a widow's right to administer was considered superior to that of her child or children, and that among surviving sons, the eldest son had a prior right to administer. Creditors might be admitted to administration only upon the renunciation of the widow, children and next-of-kin, or, in the alternative, if those individuals having prior right and being cited did not appear before the Prerogative Court to request letters of administration.[77]

---

76. The appointment of administrators can be traced in the estate of Thomas Gray (1701), Administration Papers, Court of Appeals, Box G, f. 3-371; estate of John Bennet (1729), *id.* Box Be-Blue, f. 3-56; estate of John Hearsen (1740), *id.* Box Heart-Hitz, f. 3-417; estate of William McBride (1753), *id.* Box McMet, f. 3-594; estate of Anneltie Acker (1757), *id.* Box A, f. 3-2; estate of Johannes Hitz (1759), *id.* Box Heard-Hitz, f. 3-440; estate of Lewis Leonard (1760), *id.* Box L, f. 3-565; estate of John Lowere (1770), *id.* Box L, f. 3-589; estate of John Haunes (1775), *id.* Box Ha, f. 3-384; all in HDC/QC.

Formalities might be expedited for prominent fiduciaries. For example when in 1730 Margaret Heathcote, widow of the late Councillor Caleb Heathcote, wished to administer her son's estate, the governor instructed the deputy secretary, Isaac Bobin, to make out two letters of administration and to "wait upon" the lady to take her oath as administratrix. Administration Papers, Court of Appeals, Box Heard-Hitz, f. 3-418, HDC/QC.

77. Surrogate's certificates admitting administrators occasionally provide justifications for their by-passing individuals having a prior right to administer. For example see a petition of a creditor for admin-

In determining entitlement to letters of administration, the Prerogative Court and county surrogates may well have taken into account renunciations by widows and children which specifically requested the appointment of a given individual. In nearly every instance where a renunciation is so limited, the individual so nominated was appointed to administer.[78] Of course the ultimate recourse in this matter would be to the discretion of the governor as ordinary, who presumably might elect to disregard the terms of the renunciation.

New York Prerogative Court procedure thus conformed in the main to English practice. The most substantial deviations were in the direction of greater simplicity, notably in pleading and in the issuance of citations and in the absence of formal decrees admitting wills to probate. But simplicity in practice is rarely a goal in and of itself. Rather it is usually a reflection of underlying conditions which make the more complicated procedures inappropriate or unattainable.

In the case of the New York Prerogative Court there was a total isolation from the clerical influences which pervaded the English church courts, impelling them to cling to Latin records well after other courts abandoned it for everyday English. New York lawyers, with the only possible exception being Dr. John Bridges, received no training in Doctors Commons and hence there was no basis for the development of the expertise and rather esoteric knowledge deemed necessary for a general ecclesiastical practice in the mother country. New York attorneys, practicing in a bar undifferentiated by degree of barrister and solicitor, and concerned with general practice in both law and equity, gained their

---

istration of the estate of Lewis Leonard (1760), setting forth their interest and specifically referring to a lack of next-of-kin or other creditors willing to undertake administration, Administration Papers, Court of Appeals, Box L, f. 3-565, HDC/QC. An admission certificate mentioning the fact that the administrator appointed was the eldest son, is in the estate of Oliver Beasly (1746), at *id.* Box Be-Blue, f. 3-63. A certificate stating that deceased left no friend or relation that could be located, is in estate of John Heartsen (1740), *id.* at Box Heard-Hitz, f. 3-417. A "particular friend and countryman" of deceased admitted after showing that there were no relatives or creditors in America, estate of Johannes Hitz, *id.* at f. 3-440. For English rules on intestacy and grants of administration see Nelson, *Lex Testamentaria* 22, 23; Conset, *Practice of Spiritual Courts* 14, 15.

78. An example is in the case of the estate of James Mosher (1747), where the widow renounced in favor of Ebenezer Holly, who was qualified as administrator, Administration Papers, Court of Appeals, Box Mitchell-Myford, f. 3-654, and 28 *N.Y. Hist. Soc'y Colls.* 484.

knowledge of ecclesiastical law from English text books, which they purchased and used extensively. These works included John Godolphin's *Orphan's Legacy*, a remarkably well-written and forthright treatise, as well as William Nelson's *Lex Testamentaria* and Henry Swinburne's two-volume *Brief Treatise of Testaments and Last Wills*. Other titles used in New York included Thomas Wentworth's *Office and Duties of Executors* and Henry Swinburne's shorter work, *A Treatise of Last Wills and Testaments*.[79] In a very real sense these are New York ecclesiastical law treatises as well as sources of English law upon the subjects they treat. However, since it is not possible to measure the impact these books had upon New York law and practice, they have been used in this paper only as evidence of English law.

While it is helpful to note the ecclesiastical treatises known to have been in New York colonial law libraries, it is equally valuable to note the lack of treatises on aspects of ecclesiastical law other than testamentary matters, and most significantly, the lack of practice manuals based upon English church court practice. It is a truism to suggest that lawyers buy those textbooks which are most helpful to them in their practice; consequently, we may safely conclude that general matters of clerical discipline, church administration and even probate practice in the English church courts were not of any great concern to members of New York's colonial bar. New York lawyers were vitally interested in the substantive law of the English ecclesiastical courts in probate and intestacy matters, and these were the areas in which they felt a need to supplement their education through study of English treatises. They were interested in English procedure, on the other hand, only to the extent that they wished to conform to its general principles, while ignoring its burdensome details.

The Emergence of Unique American Rules

At the same time that increasing reference to English substantive law and to English probate manuals was bringing the law of New York's Prerogative Court into increasing conformity with English law, special conditions that were unique either to New York in particular or characteristic of the American colonies in general were causing New York's probate law to diverge in several significant ways from its English model. It is to these special conditions and to the resulting divergency that we must now turn.

---

79. For law library lists see P. M. Hamlin, *Legal Education in Colonial New York* 173-195 (1939), and Johnson, John Jay; Colonial Lawyer" (unpub. Ph.D. diss., Columbia University, 1965), p. 191, 274. For a discussion of law libraries in eighteenth-century Philadelphia see Edwin Wolf 2d's discussion in American Lawyer's Library," 61 *Law Lib. J.* 440-450.

One way in which the Prerogative Court of New York differed from its counterpart at Canterbury was in its jurisdictional subordination to the Canterbury court through the operation of the principle of *bona notabilia.* This series of rules and customs, far too complex to be examined in detail in this paper, determined which church court had the right to issue letters of administration or grant probate over a decedent's estate. English canon law required that this authority be exercised by the court of the ordinary within whose jurisdiction the decedent resided at the time of his death. However, if goods of a certain value (which varied from diocese to diocese) were located in the diocese of any other ordinary, probate or administration had to be granted by the next highest ecclesiastical court, that of the archbishop of Canterbury or the archbishop of York. In the event there were *bona notabilia*, or goods of the requisite value, in both the province of York and the province of Canterbury, there was no alternative to a dual probate or a dual grant of administration. Since few New York decedents left goods in England, the situation rarely presented itself, but a 1764 endorsement to the documents concerning the estate of a London merchant, Thomas Cryer, makes it clear that the Prerogative Court of New York knew the rules of *bona notabilia.* In Cryer's estate, the certificate of probate before the Prerogative Court of Canterbury was accepted in New York as basis for issuing ancillary letters as requested by the Canterbury appointed executor. Obviously the ordinary of New York was considered subordinate to the jurisdiction of the province of Canterbury and no second proof of the will was necessary.[80]

This subordination of the province of New York to the ecclesiastical jurisdiction of the Prerogative Court of the archdiocese of Canterbury is further shown by an interchange of letters between one of New York's early governors, Lord Cornbury and the Board of Trade. In 1706 Cornbury had issued letters of administration over the estate of the Reverend Mr. Edmund Mott, then chaplain to Her Majesty's military forces in New York, and one of the original applicants for a portion of a land grant in the Minisink patent. Several months after granting letters of administration over the minister's estate, Lord Cornbury discovered that Mott had left goods and outstanding debts in England. As a result, administration had

80. Nelson, *Lex Testamentaria* 115-119; Conset, *Practice of Spiritual Courts* 304; 2 Swinburne, *Brief Treatise* 60; ancillary administration of the estate of Thomas Cryer is at NY Co. Wills (N.S.) HDC/QC, f. 1747. The conclusion is supported by the N.Y. Chancery Court's overruling the plea "no executor" entered in N.Y. by an executor appointed by the Prerogative Court of Canterbury. See *Heming v. Cross*, 3 Orders in Chancery 10-11 (1711), HDC/QC.

issued out of the Prerogative Court of Canterbury. Blustering that the invalidation of the New York fiduciary's appointment by the arrival of the Canterbury letters was in derogation of powers granted to the governor by his royal instructions, Cornbury lost no time in demanding an explanation from the Lords of Trade. While their reply has not survived, it is obvious that they patiently explained to the Queen's distant relative the intricacies of the doctrine of *bona notabilia*.

The situation facing Cornbury must have arisen before, and the Lords of Trade applied to attorney general Edward Northey, asking him to address himself to the general problem of a decedent dying in the colonies leaving goods or debts in England. Northey held that whenever a man died intestate in the colonies, leaving personal estate or debts in England, the right of granting administration vested in the archbishop of Canterbury. Consequently the letters issued by a governor in exercise of his ordinary powers, would be void upon the receipt of a duly authenticated copy of the English administrator's appointment. However the colonial administrator would be given credit for the just debts of the decedent that had been paid by him, provided that he had paid them in order of priority and that all English debts of equal dignity were also settled. In effect Northey's opinion precluded all future administrators appointed by colonial governors from settling any debts other than those payable to the Crown or those due on final judgments of the courts, unless they could be certain that there were no goods or debts in England. This, Northey admitted, was inconvenient, but the same rule applied to the payment of debts by administrators appointed by ordinaries junior in jurisdiction to either of the archbishops in England. To further buttress his opinion, Northey cited Pennsylvania enactments that had attempted to provide for the payment of Pennsylvania debts out of Pennsylvania assets; those laws he noted, had been disallowed by the Privy Council as being prejudicial to the interests of the kingdom of England.[81]

Wills admitted to probate before the Prerogative Court of the archbishop of Canterbury were thus admitted to probate in New York upon the presentation of a duly exemplified copy of the will and the letters issued out of the English court. Technically a second probate was not essential since under the doctrine of *bona notabilia*, the English court had the exclusive right to issue letters where there was property in New York as well as in the province of Canterbury.

81. The interchange can be found at 4 O'Callaghan, *Documents* 1182, 5 *id.* 2-3; 1 *Journal of the Commissioners for Trade and Plantations* 299, 340 (1920); and *Calendar of State Papers, Colonial Series, America and West Indies*, 1706-1708, 327, 415 (1916).

Even in those cases where no goods were present in England to confer such jurisdiction, English merchants could nevertheless protect their financial interests through a special statutory proceeding instituted by act of Parliament in 1732. The statute provided that affidavits executed before certain English magistrates, pertaining to obligations owed by colonial subjects, were to be received as testimony in open court throughout the colonial empire. This 1732 statute "for the more easy Recovery of Debts in His Majesty's Plantations and Colonies in America" provided a useful method for probate when the subscribing witnesses were in England, but the assets in their entirety were in America.[82] Such a circumstance existed in the estate of Laurance Reade, and the three witnesses were sworn before Frederick Bull, Lord Mayor of London, concerning the execution of Reade's will.[83] When submitted to the Prerogative Court, they were by law entitled to the same evidentiary weight that depositions taken in New York would be accorded. Hence the court was bound to accept them as oaths of subscribing witnesses and grant probate as a consequence of the statute.

English doctrine was further modified in New York by the absence in America of any intercolonial court to assume probate jurisdiction over estates having assets in more than one colony. In England, as we have seen, the normal rule when an estate had assets in more than one diocese was for an archdiocesan court to assume jurisdiction; dual probate was required only if the estate had assets in both of England's archdioceses. In America, on the other hand, dual probate apparently was required whenever a decedent had assets in more than one colony; the New York cases indicate, for example, that New Jersey fiduciaries did not have standing in New York courts to administer their estates and similarly that New York wills were probated a second time in a sister province if administration in the sister province was required.[84]

82. 5 Geo. 2, c. 7 (1732). While the act refers to actions or suits in any court of law or equity, it does not specifically refer to probate proceedings, *id.* sec. 1.

83. NY Co. Wills (N.S.), f. 2685, HDC/QC.

84. Canterbury fiduciary's standing in New York law was established by the 1711 Chancery case, *Hemings v. Cross*, discussed at n. 80, *supra*, p. —; for concensus of opinion among colonial New York lawyers on the incapacity of a New Jersey executor in New York, see Minutes of the Moot, December 7, 1770 and January 4, 1771, Collection of John Jay DeBois, on deposit at Columbia University Libraries. As an outgrowth of the relative ease with which a New York fiduciary might leave the province, a 1771 act of the New York General Assembly authorized actions and suits against New York executors and administrators who, after qualification, left New York, 5 *Col. Laws of N.Y.* 201.

A third difference between English and New York practice concerned the jurisdiction of common law courts in cases in which an executor or an administrator c.t.a. "suppressed" a legacy. English law permitted legatees to commence a proceeding against such a fiduciary either in an appropriate ecclesiastical court or in the High Court of Chancery. Both these forms of relief were also available in New York, but in 1743 an act of the New York General Assembly made an additional action in the common law courts available for this purpose. The New York act, describing the "previous method" of suits in the Prerogative or Chancery Court as tedious and expensive, permitted actions of debt, detinue or account to be instituted once a legacy was past due. If the amount involved exceeded £20, the action might be brought in the Supreme Court of Judicature; otherwise, it was to be commenced in the inferior courts of the province. Before commencing his action under the 1743 statute, a legatee was required to make a demand for payment upon the executor, and to offer a bond with two sureties to secure his promise to refund the legacy, should unforeseen obligations to creditors arise after the legacy had been distributed. If no time for the payment of legacies were specified in the will, the statute required that the legatee wait one year after the executor qualified before commencing his action.

Should the defendant executor plead *plene administravit*, or lack of assets, the statute authorized the court to refer the matter to auditors who would hear evidence and report their findings to the court. If a sufficiency of assets was reported, the plaintiff would be awarded the legacy plus the costs of bringing the action. On the other hand, if the assets were sufficient to cover the debts of the deceased, but not to pay all of the legacies, the statute provided that the legacies would abate proportionately and the plaintiff would receive his appropriate share. Although the 1743 statute was directed primarily at actions to collect legacies, it is important to note that it specifically included within its scope actions against administrators c.t.a. for the same purpose, and also actions against administrators of intestate estates who were guilty of unduly delaying distribution of shares to the proper distributees.[85]

The enactment of the 1743 law did not eliminate the pro-

85. English rules are at 2 Swinburne, *Brief Treatise of Testaments* 25; Cockburne, *Clerk's Assistant* 147; Conset, *Practice of Spiritual Courts* 309; see also 3 *Col. Laws of* N.Y. 308 *et seq.* (act of December 17, 1743). Conset, *Practice of Spiritual Courts*, 309, indicates that administration of an intestate's estate would be vacated upon the discovery of a valid will and the commencement of a proceeding in a "cause of legacy." If the proceedings on a legacy in the New York Perogative Court were used in this manner, no evidence seems to have survived.

ceeding for the payment of a legacy in the Prerogative Court. Not only was the proceeding in the Prerogative Court still in use at the end of the colonial period, but it does not seem that actions brought under the terms of the statute were particularly numerous. The first action of this class to be brought in the New York City Mayor's Court arose in 1745, and the first to be found in the minutes of the Supreme Court of Judicature did not occur until 1752.[86]

In addition to the foregoing proceedings for the collection of a legacy, a New York legatee had the further possibility of bringing a bill in chancery to demand similar relief. Because of the relatively higher counsel's fees and long delays in the New York Chancery Court, litigants after 1744 would probably have favored the common law actions. One proceeding in chancery to recover a charitable legacy, however, was brought by the attorney general in 1708. Upon the finding of sufficient assets the Court decreed that the legacies be paid.[87]

In the event that neither a fiduciary nor a beneficiary appeared to compel administration of an estate, it was possible for the Prerogative Court to take charge of the estate and appoint "sequestrators" who would administer the assets on behalf of the crown. The English rule pertinent to these procedures was that four months from date of death was ample time for the nominated executor or next-of-kin to take steps to secure appointment to administer the assets; while the New York cases are too few to deter-

---

86. Daly, *The Nature, Extent and History of the Jurisdiction of the Surrogate's Courts* 18-19. John Jay, in the course of his seven years' practice, commenced three proceedings in a cause of legacy in the Prerogative Court. John Jay Ledger 1774, Manuscript and History Division, New York State Library, Albany, New York; Johnson, "John Jay; Colonial Lawyer" (unpub. Ph.D. diss., Columbia University, 1965), pp. 191, 274.

The Mayor's Court proceeding, *Van Evert v. Roll's Estate*, was one in which the executor pleaded *plene administravit*, and the court entered an order awarding the legatee any assets *in futuro*. Minutes of the Mayor's Court of the City of New York, August 24, 1742-February 7, 1749, p. 233, New York County Clerk's Office, Hall of Records, New York City. The case in the Supreme Court of Judicature, *Yates v. Hubbard's Estate*, involved the same plea; three auditors were appointed and they reported sufficient assets. Upon this report the Court adjudged the legacy due and payable to the plaintiff and awarded him five percent interest on the amount due, calculated from the date upon which the legacy should have been paid. Minutes of the Supreme Court of Judicature, October 16, 1750-April 21, 1756, pp. 106, 121, New York County Clerk's Office, Hall of Records, New York City.

87. *Queen v. Cullen*, 2 Orders in Chancery 144-148 (1708), HDC/QC.

mine the applicability of this limitation, it seems plausible that such a procedure in England would gain acceptance with the New York Prerogative Court.[88]

If, on the other hand, administration of an estate had commenced but an accounting had not been rendered within the one-year period required under New York law,[89] any interested party would again have a remedy in the Prerogative Court, although not under the 1743 statute in a common law court. The remedy was by way of a petition requesting the court to cite the fiduciary to render his account. Not infrequently, citations to file inventories, if returnable one year after appointment, would also require that an accounting be rendered upon the return date.[90]

---

88. Godolphin, *Orphan's Legacy* 61; Wentworth, *Office of Executors* 327; Swinburne, *A Treatise of Testaments* 319-320; a New York case where proof was compelled is at 27 *N.Y. Hist. Soc'y Colls.* 145-146 (Abraham Depeyster, 1734); an appointment of sequestrators in New York, 25 *id.* 334; and 26 *id.* 17-18 (Ouzel Van Swieten, 1702-1708). Citations to appear and prove will or undertake administration, are at Administration Papers, Court of Appeals, Box G, f. 3-347 (will of Peter Garrine, 1757); *id.* Box Ba-Be, f. 3-40 (will of Barnet Barryt, 1763); and *id.* Box Be-Blue, f. 3-60 (will of Matthew Benson, 1765); all at HDC/QC.

89. Bonds of New York administrators required the submission of an accounting under the oath of the administrator within one year from his or her appointment. A similar rule undoubtedly applied to the accounts of executors, as it did to the accounts of administrators c.t.a. See NY Co. Wills (O.S.), f. 57 (estate of Edward Jessup, 1666), NY Co. Wills (N.S.), f. 2351 (estate of James Alburtis, 1771); Administration Papers, Court of Appeals, Box A, f. 3-17 (estate of East Apthorpe, 1718); *id.* Box Heart-Hitz, f. 3-418 (estate of Gilbert Heathcote, 1730); *id.* Box Ca-Coe, f. 3-160 (estate of Theophilus Clark, 1755); *id.* Box A, f. 3-4 (estate of Jonathan Adams, 1757); *id.* Box A, f. 3-15 (estate of Ziprah Anderson, 1765); *id.* Box Be-Blue, f. 3-65 (will of Samuel Betts, 1773); *id.* Box B, f. 3-24 (estate of Remember Baker, 1776), all at HDC/QC.

English ecclesiastical practice left the time to file an account within the discretion of the ordinary, but one year was the usual date set for the completion of this requirement. Wentworth, *Office of Executors* 221, 582; 2 Swinburne, *Brief Treatise of Testaments* 87, 88; Swinburne, *A Treatise of Testaments* 363-364, 377.

90. A New York citation to compel the filing of an accounting may be found at Administration Papers, Court of Appeals, Box L, f. 3-564 (estate of Samuel Levi, 1762). New York practice seems to have deferred the distribution of legacies until after the account had been judicially allowed. See the bond filed in the case of the will of Stephen Stevenson (1713), *id.* Box Stevens-Sylvester, f. 3-876, HDC/QC. For the English rules concerning this practice, see Wentworth, *Office of Executors* 221; Cockburne, *Clerk's Assistant* 138; Conset, *Practice in Spiritual Courts*, 290, 291.

As an alternative to a citation to account in the Prerogative Court a New York legatee might file a bill in chancery with the Chancery Court. This was in accordance with English practice, which by the eighteenth century relied quite heavily upon the High Court of Chancery to police the accounts of executors and administrators. At least three cases of bills for an equitable accounting were brought in New York during the colonial period. In all of these suits the executors were ordered to submit their accounts and record books to a master in chancery, who took evidence and submitted a report, upon which the Chancery Court entered its decree.[91]

A final major difference between English and New York practice developed in regard to the use of a formal inventory of an estate, made before and approved by two interested parties, usually creditors, legatees or next of kin, to fix its value. In England, an executor or an administrator could always resort to a formal inventory on his own account and could also be compelled to prepare one upon the motion of any interested party.[92] But, if the fiduciary did not file an inventory and no interested party applied for redress, no inventory of a decedent's assets would be taken. In such a case, the fiduciary assumed the risk that the assets were sufficient to cover the decedent's outstanding obligations; if they were not, the fiduciary might, under certain circumstances, be personally liable for the deficiency. During the eighteenth century an increasing number of English executors and administrators were willing to assume this liability, for the number of inventories filed in the Prerogative Court of Canterbury declined sharply from 1718 to 1782.[93]

New York and English rules concerning the preparation and filing of inventories are discussed at n. 92-96, *infra*.

91. For English developments see Atkinson, "Brief History of English Testamentary Jurisdiction," 8 *Mo. L. Rev.* 118. The New York cases are *Teller v. Bayard*, 2 Orders in Chancery 11, 35, 53-54, 75-76 (1706); *Brett v. Rombouts*, 2 *id.* at 39, 41-43 (1706), HDC/QC; and *Pemberton v. Buvelet* (1773) Law Suits P-U; John Tabor Kempe Papers, New York Historical Society, New York City.

92. Godolphin, *Orphan's Legacy* 151-153; Cockburne, *Clerk's Assistant* 132-133; Swinburne, *Brief Treatise of Testaments* 57; Wentworth, *Office of Executors* 50-52; Conset, *Practice of Spiritual Courts* 303; Nelson, *Lex Testamentaria* 353-354. Swinburne, *Brief Treatise of Testaments* 55, indicates that the time for filing an inventory was a matter lying within the discretion of the ordinary. However, Godolphin, *Orphan's Legacy* 150, an early eighteenth century text, is quite clear that the thirty-day rule stated herein was generally applicable, the only exception being that made in the case of widely dispersed assets.

93. Godolphin, *Orphan's Legacy*, *id.* 151. The declining number of

From the earliest days of English occupation of New York, executors and administrators were required to file inventories under penalty of being held liable for judgment against their personal estate regardless of the assets in decedent's estate. The bonding requirements of the Prerogative Court specified that inventories were to be filed six months from the date of appointment. During the early years of the Prerogative Court's existence, a defaulting executor or administrator might be ordered to file his inventory before a local court of sessions, a justice of the peace or a mayor's court.[94] The more general, and preferred practice in later years, was based upon a citation, also called a mandate, issued by the Prerogative Court. Issuing upon the written petition of an interested party, it ordered the fiduciary to appear before the court and to submit his inventory. The return date in the surviving citations varies from three days to a month after the date of issuance. When inventories were demanded over a year from the date of appointment, the citation also required that the respondent appear and render his account, to be sworn to before the court. The citation was served by the sheriff of the county in which the respondent resided, and was duly served by being read to the respondent. If difficulty in service was apprehended, the citation might contain a clause permitting service by fastening a copy of the citation to the door of the respondent's dwelling place, or, if he be continuously absent, then to the door of the parish church where the respondent resided. This latter provision for service at the parish church is not unlike service of an English ecclesiastical court's citation by posting on the door of the Royal Exchange.[95]

Canterbury inventories is noted in the search list entitled "Prerogative Court of Canterbury, List of Inventories, 1702, 1718-1782, 8/66B," in PRO, London.

94. Act of April 2, 1664, 1 *Col. Laws N.Y.* 10, *supra;* early inventories are at NY Co. Will Libers I (1677-1685), 10 (estate of Thomas Rudge, 1690); *id.* II (1682-1692), 52 (estate of John Evans, 1700); *id.* 302 (estate of Anthony Wright, 1680). Later inventories are at NY Co. Wills (O.S.), f. 425 (estate of Henry Filkin, 1736); Albany Inventories, Series 2, f. 1 (estate of Huybert Aartse, 1710); *id.* 3 (estate of Joseph Allison, 1755); *id.* 11 (estate of Micah Baker, 1723); *id.* 20 (estate of Charles Beatty, 1727); *id.* 182 (estate of Joseph Miller, 1728); *id.*, 192 (estate of William Nottingham, 1731); *id.* 207 (estate of John Pinhorne, 1763); and *id.* 21d (estate of John Reeve, 1713). All at HDC/QC.

95. For citations against fiduciaries to compel filing inventories, see Administration Papers, Court of Appeals, Box Mitchell-Myford, f. 3-661 (estate of Henry Myer, Jr., 1746); *id.* at Box L, f. 3-253 (will of Samuel Lawrence, 1761); *id.* at Box Be-Blue, f. 3-54 (will of William Beekman, 1770); *id.* Box Taffe-Townshend, f. 3-921 (will of Christopher Tobias, 1772); *id.* Box G, f. 3-349 (will of Daniel Gautier, 1775), all at HDC/QC.

New York inventories vary in the amount of care taken to enumerate the decedent's assets, but the formalities of inventorying are quite uniform. Two witnesses were always present, and not infrequently an appraiser was appointed by a "warrant" of the governor, to evaluate the assets. The executor or administrator then swore to the truth and accuracy of the inventory; if he were a Quaker he would be permitted to declare its correctness "under penalty of perjury." Oaths and affirmations concerning inventories might be taken before the governor in person, before the principal surrogate, one of the county surrogates, or even before a local justice of the peace.[96]

The continued use of inventories in eighteenth century New York, while the practice was on the decline in the province of Canterbury, is a striking divergence between the two forms of practice. Some basis for the difference may be assigned to the persistence of Dutch practice, which followed many of the canon law rules and presumptions concerning inventories. On the other hand, it is much more likely that the relative inactivity of the New York Chancery Court at various times during the colonial period may have put beneficiaries on their guard since bills in chancery against defaulting fiduciaries were expensive and at times, unattainable, proceedings.

Conclusion

With due consideration to all the distinctions, differences and variations, the New York Prerogative Court was indeed a very close copy of its English prototypes. Its redeeming virtue was the simplicity of its procedures and the lack of preoccupation on the part of its bar and judges with the sterile formalism which ultimately led to the downfall of the English church courts in 1857. The Prerogative Court of colonial New York performed its functions with a suitable respect for traditional English practice and substantive law. But at the same time it adapted its jurisprudence

---

Substituted service of citations appear at *id.* Box L, f. 3-547 (estate of Caleb Lawrence, 1723); and *id.* Box Mitchell-Myford, f. 3-661 (estate of Henry Myer, Jr., 1746). For English decrees to be served by posting on door of the Royal Exchange, see *Clerk's Instructor in Ecclesiastical Courts*, 62-64, 66-67.

96. For the New York method of executing inventories, see Albany Inventories cited at ft. nt. 92, *supra;* a Quaker's affirmation is at 29 *N.Y. Hist. Soc'y Colls.* 312 (estate of Margaret Duncan, 1703). Appraisal in accordance with gubernatorial "Warrant," is shown in the estate of John Coessaert, 1700, N.Y. Co. Will Liber II (1682-1692), 177; another appraisal, not mentioning a warrant, occurs at *id.* 149 (estate of William Teller, 1701).

and procedures to the demands of colonial conditions and the undifferentiated nature of the New York bar.

Although we may find vestiges of Prerogative Court practice in the organization, jurisdiction and practice of the present day Surrogate's Courts of the State of New York, it seems quite clear that the courts which have conducted probate business under the sovereignty of the independent State of New York are quite distinguishable from their colonial predecessor. The mere continuance of the title of "surrogate" is a totally misleading happenstance, for the current "Surrogates" are in effect, principal surrogates and ordinaries for their separate counties. New York has returned to the local probate system of the early years of English settlement; it has surrogates without ordinaries; it permits common law appellate review of ecclesiastical decisions; and it uses juries to determine will contests on oral testimony. New York's colonial lawyers would be appalled!

APPENDIX

Principal Surrogates

Matthew Clarkson (Secretary)	1691-98
David Jamieson	1691-98
Daniel Honan	1702
John Bridges	1702-03
Samuel Shelton Broughton	1704
Henry Wileman	1711-21
Isaac Bobin	1722-29
George Clarke (Secretary)	1727-35
Frederick Morris	1730-36
John Robinson	1740
George Joseph Moore	1741-45
John Catherwood (Secretary)	1745-46
Goldsbrow Banyer	1744-66 1769-70
John French	1766-67
Philip Livingston	1768
Edmund Fanning	1771
Samuel Bayard	1774

Albany County

James Cruger	1711
Johannes Cuyler	1711
Johannes Cruger	1713
Robert Livingston	1719
Killian Van Rensselaer	1726
Myndert Schuyler	1731-54
John De Peyster	1756-75
Jacobus C. Ten Eyck	1760
William Hanna	1766-70
Peter Lansingh	1769-73
Stephen Delancey	1770-75

Cumberland County

Thomas Chandler	1771
Brean Bush	1775

Dutchess County

Barent Van Kleek	1726
Jacob Ter Boss	1736
Bartholomew Crannell	1747-73
Theodorus Van Wyck	1750
Martin Hoffman	1750
Anthony Hoffman	1764-75

Kings County

Henry Filken	1706
Richard Stillwell	1735-44
Andrew Larned	1748

New York City

Daniel Horsmanden	1745, 1747, 1758
Pierre Depeyster	1751
James Delancey	1753
John Godby	1754-58
Lambert Moore	1755
Edward Smith	1763-65
Francis Filken	1763
Francis Child	1768-69
John Bowles	1769-71
John Gromly	1773
Carey Ludlow	1774-75

Orange County

Henry Ludlow	1739-43
William Finn	1755-56
John Gale	1759-71

Queens County

Thomas Wenham	1704-09
John Jackson	1711-19
John Johnson	1720
Thomas Chatfield	1726
John Messenger	1736-38
Adam Lawrence	1741-48
Samuel Clowes	1749-60
Samuel Smith	1760

Queens County (Continued)

Thomas Braine	1760-69
Henry Dawson	1769-74
John J. Troup	1774-75

Richmond County

Walter Dongan	1732-48
Benjamin Seaman	1760-75

Suffolk County

Giles Sylvester	1706-07
Joseph Fordham	1709
Jonathan Smith	1710
Henry Smith	1712
Benjamin Youngs	1719
Daniel Young	1719
William Booth	1719
Brinley Sylvester	1724-51
Henry Smith	1738-66
Elijah Hutchinson	1754
Maltby Gelston	1754-72
William Throop	1755-56
Samuel Langdon	1757-68
Richard Miller	1767-68
William Smith	1767-75
Jared Landon	1768-72
Nathaniel Woodhull	1770-75
David Gelston	1775

Tryon County

Bryan Lafferty	1774

Ulster County

William Nottingham	1714
Jacob Rutsen	1724
Edward Whitaker	1727-45
John Crooke	1746-59
Jan Eltinge	1760-61
Jacobus Bruyn	1761-70
Patrus Edmundus Elmendorph	1762-65
George Clinton	1767-76
Joseph Gasherie	1767-75
John Bruyn	1772

Westchester County

Caleb Heathcote	1712-20
Gilbert Willett	1727-31
Israel Honeywell	1742-53
Samuel Purdy	1742-51
John Bartow	1754-67
Caleb Fowler	1761-75
David Dayton	1766-75
Timothy Wetmore	1770-75

Some Nice Sharp Quillets of the Customs Law: The *New York* Affair, 1763-1767

With
DAVID SYRETT

STATUTES, like men and women, grow palsied when they age; few retain the same capabilities in their centennial year that they possessed in youth. By 1763 the old Acts of Trade and Navigation, tailored to meet the vastly different imperial conditions of the previous century, had become ineffective controls upon commercial activity and contained inadequate procedures for enforcement and administration. Predicated upon the acts of the Restoration Parliaments in 1660 and 1663, they had been slightly supplemented by the 1696 legislation under William III, but for the most part the British Empire entered the second half of the eighteenth century with its mercantile system a ramshackle and archaic product of seventeenth-century law makers. The lawyers of the North American colonies were well aware of the disheveled state of the British Acts of Trade, and lost no opportunity to make new breaches in the system of enforcement. In this they were aided by ambiguities that existed in the terms of the statutes themselves, and the anachronisms that evolved through applying old law to new situations.

Even before Parliamentary revisions were made in the administration of colonial customs by the Sugar Act of 1764, British courts had begun to grapple with the problem of how the antiquated rules of enforcement could be reinterpreted in the light of changing colonial conditions. One such attempt at judicial reformation and tightening of pre-existing practices is to be found in the *New York* affair, a series of related cases that originated in the province of New York. The conclusion of this complex and costly litigation, which was far from a clear definition of the law, indicated the limitations upon judicial power and discretion in meeting the challenge.

On Friday, December 2, 1763, the merchant ship *New York,* bound for New York City from Port au Prince, was met at a considerable distance from the American coast by two New York harbor pilots, William Fandeau and John Driskill. They were accompanied by Thomas Kerks, who carried a letter for Alexander Claxon, master of the *New York*. At the same time Kerks delivered the letter, the pilots informed Claxon that H. M. S. *Hawke* was off Sandy Hook and would doubtless intercept and search the *New York* for illegal cargo. Consequently they offered to carry any such goods ashore in the pilot boat. Claxon refused this offer, and after taking the letter and presumably reading its contents, he ordered the pilots to guide the *New York* to Amboy Roads to await further orders.[1] James Miller, one of the sailors on the *New York*, overheard this conversation, and subsequently reported it under oath. Miller also testified that he distinctly heard Claxon tell the pilots that he did not intend to run any illegal goods into New York City or to break bulk while there.[2]

Subsequent to these alleged conversations, the *New York*, on course for Amboy Roads, proceeded toward the entrance to Lower New York Bay. As she passed Sandy Hook, or shortly before, she was intercepted by H. M. S. *Hawke* and searched for illegal goods. When it was discovered that the *New York* carried European goods that had not been cleared through an English port as required by the 1663 Navigation Act, the ship was arrested and carried to New York City by a boarding party from the *Hawke*.[3]

When Captain John Brown arrived in New York City aboard the *Hawke*, he consulted with the attorney general of the province, John Tabor Kempe, before taking legal action against the *New York*. When Kempe advised him to prosecute, Brown in turn asked Lambert Moore, the New York collector of customs, to assume responsibility for bringing the *qui tam* action. This was the statutory procedure by which the vessel, her equipment, and cargo could be declared forfeited, and the proceeds from their sale divided among the ship making the seizure,

[1] Deposition of William Fandeau, Feb. 21, 1764; deposition of James Miller, Mar. 2, 1764; deposition of Cornelius Berrian, Mar. 17, 1764, File Papers, Vice-admiralty Court, Province of New York, Box "Customs Cases M-Z," Record Group 21, National Archives.

[2] Deposition of James Miller, Mar. 2, 1764, *ibid.*

[3] 15 Car. 2d. c. 7, sec. 6. This act is commonly called the Staple Act. For report of seizure see Dec. 2, 1763, Admiralty Group, Class 51, Piece 437, Public Record Office. Hereafter cited as Adm. 51/437.

the governor, and the Crown. After considering his own interests, Moore replied that he could not bring action unless he had express instructions from the American Board of Customs or the surveyor general of customs at Boston. On the other hand, if Brown would withdraw his boarding party from the *New York* and thereby forfeit his claim to a portion of the seized property, Moore would immediately order the ship libelled and proceed with his own *qui tam* action.

Unwilling to forego the monetary advantages that might accrue to himself and his crew, Brown decided to write to John Temple, the surveyor general of customs for the Northern District of America. In due course Temple's instructions concerning the case arrived from his Boston office; they merely affirmed Moore's position, and cautioned all New York customs officers that they should assist Brown "as far as they are Able without becoming principals."[4] In this circumstance Brown, relying upon the advice of the attorney general, but without any support from the American customs service, took it upon himself to institute a *qui tam* action against the *New York* in the Vice-admiralty Court for the province of New York. For himself, the king, and the governor, Brown filed a libel in the Vice-admiralty Court on December 19, alleging that he had been deputed "an officer of the Customs to seize etc. prohibited and unaccustomed goods." Acting in pursuance of this authority he had seized the *New York* on December 2, 1763, along with her tackle, furniture, ammunition, and apparel, plus thirty casks of wine and twenty boxes of soap, the cargo seized being products of European origin imported into America contrary to the Staple Act. As to the other goods on the *New York*, including molasses, rum, candles, sugar, ship staves, and umbrellas, no libel was filed and it is clear that the proceeding against those goods was not contemplated.[5]

The proceeding against the *New York* was based upon the court's possession of the goods and the vessel, or what in the law is known as *in rem* jurisdiction. Once property was before the court, the interests of all individuals who had notice of the action would be determined by the decree. Consequently it was an integral part of the procedure that a series of proclamations be made in open court before the judge

[4] Adm. 1/482, 334-335, 341-342, 344; Adm. 1/1494, May 16, 1764.

[5] Dec. 19, 1763, Minutes of the Vice-admiralty Court of the Province of New York, III, 288, Record Group 21, National Archives; Libel, Dec. 19, 1763, File Papers, Vice-adm. Ct., N. Y., Customs, R. G. 21, National Archives.

could proceed to hear the case. In theory at least, this permitted all interested parties to have notice and to retain counsel to protect their property rights. In the *New York* case the first proclamation was made on the same date the libel was filed on behalf of Brown. Three days later the second proclamation was made and entered in the minutes of the court. Just prior to the third, and last, proclamation, John Morin Scott appeared for the claimants and obtained leave of the court to perfect their claim. Then the last proclamation was read, and any further claims were thereby precluded.[6]

On behalf of his clients Scott filed a most unusual claim. He commenced by admitting the fact that the wine and soap *were* products of Europe, and also that they did not originate in any of the English ports designated in the Staple Act of 1663. However, Scott claimed that the seizure of the *New York* took place upon the high seas, that is, outside Lower New York Bay, and he denied that there had been an *importation* into New York or any other British plantation in North America, for the ship was allegedly enroute to the Isle of Man. On this basis the claimants prayed that the libel be dismissed, and that the costs of the litigation be assessed against Brown, the libellant.[7] Five days after this paper was filed, Scott obtained an order from Vice-admiralty Judge Richard Morris requiring the attorney general to file Captain Brown's reply within two days. Although Scott had benefitted from a delay of five days in which to file his answer, the attorney general was permitted only two days in which to file his reply. Nevertheless he did so with the assistance of Whitehead Hicks, who then appeared for the first time as advocate for the libellant. The replication of Brown, and the rejoinder of the claimants, merely reasserted the accuracy of their respective libel and answer.[8]

Simultaneous with the filing of libellant's (Brown's) replication, a bond for costs in the sum of £50, New York currency, was executed before Judge Richard Morris and filed in court on behalf of Brown. This

[6] Dec. 19, 22, 28, 1763, Vice-adm. Min., N. Y., III, 288-290, R. G. 21, National Archives. Scott (1730-1784) was one of the leading members of the New York Bar, a member of the so-called Presbyterian triumvirate, and quite active in opposition to British imperial policies.

[7] Answer and Claim, Jan. 2, 1764, File Papers, Vice-adm. Ct., N. Y., Customs, R. G. 21, National Archives.

[8] Jan. 7, 1764, Vice-adm. Min., N. Y., III, 292, R. G. 21, National Archives; Jan. 11, 1764, File Papers, Vice-adm. Ct., N. Y., Customs, R. G. 21, National Archives.

bond obligated Archibald Kennedy, collector of customs at New York, to secure the costs, if any, to be assessed against Brown.[9] The parties then began to examine the witnesses and file documents deemed essential to their case.[10] From the interrogations and answers thereto, it is apparent that the attorneys for both parties were interested in three questions: Did the seizure take place within New York harbor? Was the *New York* at the time of her seizure on her way to land goods of European origin in New York or New Jersey? Had there been an importation into New York or New Jersey, despite the fact that no actual landing had taken place in either province?

According to Brown's interrogatories Claxon, master of the *New York,* stated that his entire cargo was consigned to Cornelius Skinner of Amboy.[11] Further, the ship's manifest, prepared at Port au Prince, showed that the destination of the entire cargo was New York City. A seaman from the *New York* asserted that he had signed on for a round trip voyage to Port au Prince and immediate return to New York. Finally, a mariner not connected with either H.M.S. *Hawke* or the *New York* testified that he understood the *New York* was to make a voyage to Port au Prince and then return directly to New York; he had never heard the Isle of Man mentioned until the *New York* was seized.[12]

The claimant's witnesses confirmed the defense, asserting that the *New York* was to wait for orders and instructions at Amboy Roads before proceeding to the Isle of Man. For example, there was some hearsay evidence that the *New York* was at anchor in Amboy Roads when she was seized. Well before she arrived off Sandy Hook her charterer, Thomas White, had contracted with the owners, Walter and Samuel Franklin, for a voyage to the Isle of Man. Further, Claxon stated that while on the high seas, twenty-four hours before being arrested by H.M.S. *Hawke,* he had received orders to proceed to the Isle of Man, and was enroute to Amboy Roads for further instructions before sailing for Europe. In addition, immediately upon seizure, the

[9] Jan. 11, 1764, File Papers, Vice-adm. Ct., N. Y., Customs, R. G. 21, National Archives.

[10] See notices, cross-notices, interrogatories, and cross-interrogatories, Feb. 16, 20, 21, 24, 25, 1764; Exhibit A, Feb. 25, 1764, *ibid.*

[11] Deposition of John Shapcote, a seaman on H.M.S. *Hawke,* Feb. 25, 1764, *ibid.*

[12] Exhibit B, filed Feb. 25, 1764; deposition of James Miller, Mar. 1, 2, 1764; deposition of Alexander Ker, Mar. 24, 1764, *ibid.*

officers of the *New York* had reported her to the customs officials as outward bound for the Isle of Man.[13]

As briefly outlined above, the evidence was at some points contradictory, and certainly not helpful in resolving the questions of law arising from the pleadings. The intention on the part of the owners of the *New York* to import European goods into New York or New Jersey, if proven, would have been strong circumstantial evidence that they were stopped while in the course of effecting this illegal goal. On the other hand, it was the *importation* that was prohibited by statute, and not the attempt to import or a conspiracy to import. The precise timing of the instructions to proceed to the Isle of Man could also be important circumstantial evidence. If orders to that effect were issued prior to the seizure, it was far less likely that they would have been self-serving. Still, it might be standard procedure for smugglers to issue such orders *pro forma* to all of their inbound vessels. If seized while in the possession of such instructions, they could interpose just such a defense as was being utilized in the case of the *New York*. Once access to the harbor was gained, the goods could be easily landed clandestinely. Finally, the location of the *New York* at the time of her seizure, and the question as to whether she was at anchor or in motion, had to be resolved. All of these factual questions required decision, but even more significant was the main issue of law in the case: had there been an *importation* of such a nature that it would fall within the proscription of the statute?

With these issues delineated, the attorneys for the claimants brought the case on for trial by a motion addressed to the court.[14] Prior to the hearing the attorney general moved that the deposition of Thomas White, an owner of certain goods legally on the *New York* at the time of seizure, be suppressed because of White's interest in the outcome of the suit. The motion was denied, the court being of the opinion that White's interest in the outcome of the litigation was so remote that it was not sufficient ground to suppress his testimony but could only be used to minimize his credibility. Upon Judge Morris's decision concerning this

[13] Deposition of George Coitmore, Feb. 29, 1764; deposition of Richard Mercer, Mar. 13, 1764; deposition of Peter Bard, Mar. 17, 19, 1764; deposition of James Emmot, Notary Public, Mar. 30, 1764, *ibid.* It should be noted that the log of H.M.S. *Hawke* gives the impression that the *New York* was in motion when intercepted, for it reads "Stoped the New York." Dec. 2, 1763, Adm. 51/437.

[14] May 4, 1764, Vice-adm. Min., N. Y., III, 300, R. G. 21, National Archives.

motion, the pleadings were read in open court, and Kempe then proceeded to argue the case for Brown. When this argument was complete, Scott successfully moved for a delay of eight days during which he might prepare his answer to the argument.[15]

On May 18, 1764, Scott argued on behalf of the claimants. Pointing to the assertions of witnesses that Claxon had reported the entire cargo for shipment to the Isle of Man and that he had refused to land the *New York* or to place the illegal goods on the pilot boat, Scott presented a persuasive view of the claimant's case. He then called to the judge's attention the fact that the judge himself had had a conversation with Walter Franklin, one of the *New York*'s owners, several weeks before her arrival in New York and that in the course of that conversation Franklin mentioned his intention to ship goods then on the *New York* to the Isle of Man.[16] To this argument the attorney general replied on May 26, and then moved for a decree condemning the *New York* and the illegal goods. The court took the matter into consideration, but refused to enter a decree immediately. On May 30, upon the motion of Scott, the decree was delivered in favor of the claimants.[17]

Hitherto Judge Morris had declined to consider his conversation with Walter Franklin to be part of the evidence in the case, citing the fact that any testimony he might give would of necessity be unsupported by an oath, for he could not swear himself to tell the truth. Consequently the decree of May 30, ostensibly without resort to this evidence, directed that the ship and goods were not subject to forfeiture under the statute, and required the informant, Captain John Brown, to pay the claimants their costs in the suit.[18] A notice of appeal to the High Court of Admiralty dated May 31, 1764, was immediately filed and signed by John Tabor Kempe and Whitehead Hicks, proctor and advocate for the libellant.[19] The arguments of counsel before the Vice-admiralty Court, particularly those in regard to the definition of the term "import," had raised issues calling for determination before the appellate court in London. In

[15] May 11, 1764, *ibid.*

[16] Argument for Claimants, File Papers, Vice-adm. Ct., N. Y., Customs, R. G. 21, National Archives.

[17] Vice-adm. Min., N. Y., III, 301, 302, R. G. 21, National Archives.

[18] This preliminary decision was made on Apr. 2, 1764, Charles M. Hough, ed., *Reports of Cases in the Vice Admiralty of the Province of New York . . .* (New Haven, 1925), 217-218.

[19] File Papers, Vice-adm. Ct., N. Y., Customs, R. G. 21, National Archives.

addition, although Judge Richard Morris had maintained a fair degree of objectivity in this case, could he have avoided being influenced by his prior knowledge of the matter? Further, Morris was a native born New Yorker whose family had held the Vice-admiralty judgeship for two generations; in a case such as this, where the law was closely disputed, and the facts far from clear, would he not be likely to decide in favor of colonial interests and sacrifice the unpopular and abstract interests of the Crown?

Moreover, even prior to the acquittal of the *New York,* Captain Brown had been subjected to "a most Public Insult" when he was arrested in a coffee house on April 27th at the suit of Walter and Samuel Franklin, owners of the *New York,* and of Thomas White, owner of part of the cargo. Brown pleaded with the lieutenant governor and the customs officers at New York for assistance, but these officials declared that they did not have funds "for Defraying the Expences of a Law Suit." After this refusal, two merchants came forward with an offer of bail for Brown; however, the plaintiffs granted him a parole on the condition that he not leave New York until the affair was settled in the High Court of Admiralty.[20] Yet Brown did not long enjoy his liberty, for on November 20, 1764, he was rearrested when the plaintiffs decided that his word was not sufficient security and that he must post a bond. In a report to the Admiralty Captain Archibald Kennedy, senior navy officer at New York, stated on November 15 that Brown had received orders to proceed to sea with H.M.S. *Hawke* "to cruise between Sandy Hook and great Egg Harbour, for the more effectual prevention of smuggling" and that Brown had been rearrested to "prevent His Majesty's service from being executed."[21] After being arrested for a second time, Brown again requested that the Crown officers at New York provide him with bail. Despite what he had written to the Admiralty indicating his view of the reasons for Brown's second arrest, Kennedy agreed with the customs officers in refusing to post bail, "not chusing to make a precedent of it"; in this they were joined by Lieutenant Governor Cadwallader Colden. Consequently Brown languished in jail until orders were received from England in March of 1765 directing that his bail be posted.[22]

In view of the widespread official support for Brown's enforcement

[20] Adm. 1/482, 398; May 16, 1764, Adm. 1/1494.
[21] Nov. 20, 1764, Adm. 1/2012; Adm. 1/482, 420.
[22] Nov. 29, 1764, Adm. 1/1494.

activities, this delay is astonishing. No less an authority than Colden himself had declared that the use of warships to enforce customs regulations had resulted in a "great decrease" in illicit trade.[23] Captain Archibald Kennedy, in regard to Brown's case, requested that the Admiralty take "some more effectual measures for protecting the Sea Officers in cases of seizure, otherwise it will be impossible for any Officer to execute his duty in this place, where the minds of the People are so much inflamed against them that I believe on the most trivial occasion they would give the most unreasonable damages against the Crown or the Officers of the Crown."[24] From jail Brown wrote to the Admiralty that he had been told by Attorney General Kempe "if the Cause [in the High Court of Admiralty] is even given in my favour [I] shant be able to recover any Damages for my Confinement, and if such are not prevented by Bail we shall be liable to be put in Gaol for every seizure and that with Impunity for they Glory in such things here."[25]

Dispatches describing the jailing of Brown for seizing the *New York* reached the Admiralty at the beginning of 1765. Philip Stephens, a secretary to the Admiralty, unofficially sent all the relevant papers to Charles Jenkinson, a secretary to the Treasury, who after a "Perusal" of the documents suggested on January 15, 1765, that the matter be placed before the Treasury. On January 17 the Admiralty followed Jenkinson's suggestion.[26] After studying the seizure of the *New York* and the resulting "ill treatment" of Brown, the Treasury directed on January 25 that the commissioners of customs "take every proper and legal method to support Captain Browne in the execution of his Duty."[27]

Jenkinson, however, had unofficially informed the customs board of the case and it had already issued a series of rebukes and directives to the customs officers in America. On January 19 John Temple, surveyor general for the Northern District of America, was directed to order his subordinates at New York to provide bail for Brown,

> and as we apprehend there may be many attempts of the like kind to deter the Officers of the Navy from Acting in their Duty as Officers of the

[23] Treasury Group, Class 29, Piece 36, 84, Public Record Office. Hereafter cited as T. 29/36.
[24] Nov. 20, 1764, Adm. 1/2012.
[25] Nov. 29, 1764, Adm. 1/1494.
[26] Jan. 15, 1765, *ibid.*; Jan. 17, 1765, Adm. 3/72.
[27] T. 29/36, 124.

Revenue, We direct you to give Orders to the several Collectors and Comptrollers within your District, that they give immediate Notice to you when any Officer of the Navy is arrested on account of acting in his Duty as an Officer of the Revenue, acquainting you with the whole circumstances thereof, and if it shall appear to you, that the Officer has not subjected himself to such Arrest by any unjustifiable Conduct, but barely by the proper exertion of himself in the execution of his Duty as an Officer of the Revenue. We hereby impower you . . . to give Orders to the Collector and Comptroller of the Port where such Officer has been arrested, to enter Bail for him, and in all Cases, where the interest of the Revenue is so essentially concerned, you must exert yourself in support of the Officers who will otherwise be deterred from doing their Duty; and you must repeat our Directions to the officers of the several Ports within your District, that they Aid and assist the Officers of the Navy, acting in their Duty as Officers of the Revenue, to the utmost of their Power.[28]

At the same time the customs board informed the customs officers at New York that their excuses for permitting Brown to be jailed were "frivolous." The board also wrote to Brown informing him that orders had been issued to procure bail for him.[29]

Although the customs board's directives procured the release of Captain Brown from jail, they could not liberate him from the legal trap in which the seizure of the *New York* had ensnared him. In late March of 1765 he emerged from the New York City jail,[30] freed on bail only to face trial of one of the civil lawsuits instituted against him earlier. This was the action by Thomas White, owner of part of the *New York*'s cargo, who claimed damages amounting to £8,000 New York currency.[31] Brown's attorney, John Tabor Kempe, duly entered a plea of "not guilty" and noticed the matter for trial on October 18, 1765. Prior to the opening of the trial Kempe strongly urged Brown to gather his witnesses. Particularly he observed, "I think your Officers are good Witnesses for you. They ought to be present at trial."[32] Whether Brown complied is

[28] Board of Customs to John Temple, Jan. 19, 1765, T. 1/441.

[29] Jan. 19, 1765, Adm. 1/4286; Board of Customs to Collector and Comptroller at New York, Jan. 19, 1765; Board of Customs to John Brown, Jan. 19, 1765, T. 1/441.

[30] For dockets showing issuance of *capias ad respondendum* (civil arrest) writs, see Pleadings 1754-1837, M 203, W 159, New York County Clerk's Office, Records Division, Hall of Records, New York City. Defendant's notice of bail is filed *ibid.*, W 159, and is dated Mar. 26, 1765.

[31] The complaint, or narrative, is filed *ibid.*, W 159. It is endorsed to show service upon John Tabor Kempe on June 3, 1765.

[32] Defendant's plea is filed with the complaint *ibid.* The notice of trial was served

impossible to ascertain, for the case was not reached on the trial calendar before the Stamp Act crisis caused suspension of civil litigation. Not until a year later did the Supreme Court of Judicature again hear and try civil lawsuits.

During the intervening year, Brown and Kempe exchanged harsh words over a debt of £120 which the navy officer owed his lawyer. This altercation most likely destroyed the harmonious relationship which should exist between client and attorney before a trial. It was only after he had received assurances that Brown would remain stationed at New York for three more years that Kempe withdrew his threat to commence suit on the obligation and agreed to continue to represent Brown.[33]

Whatever his personal feelings may have been, the attorney general did his best to protect Brown's interests in the case of *White* v. *Brown*. As might be anticipated, the debate over the meaning of the word "import" played as significant a part in this case as it did in the litigation before the Vice-admiralty Court. Kempe's adversary, John Morin Scott, contended that an importation is a laying of the cargo upon land, citing English precedents in support of this position; Kempe disagreed, pointing to the fact that the commonly accepted meaning, as well as the meaning of Parliament in enacting the Staple Act of 1663 was that an importation was merely bringing a cargo into the territory or territorial waters of some political subdivision, and that it carried with it no implication of landing or breaking of bulk.[34] This delicate question of statutory construction formed a major part of the legal arguments on behalf of both Brown and White.

Not content to rest his case solely upon statutory construction, Kempe proceeded to argue that Brown should not be liable for trespass, since he had not acted with malice, and that under English law a customs officer had a right to seize goods and bring them into court so that property rights could be adjudicated. Finally, he asserted that Brown had never proceeded against the goods of White, or against the vessel

on Oct. 8, 1765, and the date noted for trial was Friday, Oct. 18, 1765. Letter of John Tabor Kempe to John Brown, Oct. 9, 1765, *ibid.*

[33] Kempe to Brown, July 24, 1766, *ibid.*

[34] John Morin Scott, Notes for Summing Up, *ibid.*, citing *A Case of Custom*, 12 Coke Rep., 77 Eng. Rep. Full Reprint 1299 (1583), and 4 Geo. 3d. c. 15, sec. 46 (1764). Whitehead Hicks, Brief for Defendant in *White* v. *Brown*, *ibid.*, W 742, citing among other precedents, *Sauk* v. *Roberts*, 1 Salk. 14, 91 Eng. Rep. Full Reprint 14, 15 (1708).

New York, but only against the cargo of the two Franklins which he had ample reason to believe was illegally imported. In his argument Kempe was only partially correct. The libel clearly indicates that the proceeding was instituted against the ship *New York*, her guns, tackle, and furniture, as well as against certain cargo of the vessel. On the other hand it is fairly clear that no legally imported cargo carried on the *New York*'s manifest was listed in the libel. Unfortunately Kempe made another mistake by referring to the newly enacted British statute which provided that Crown officers could not be subjected to civil suit if their seizures under the revenue laws were made with probable cause for the attachment.[85] On this point he was in error, for the act was not in effect at the time Brown seized the *New York*, and hence had no place in the law of the case. This mistake the attorney general discovered when, on November 1, 1766, the court refused to issue the certificate of cause referred to in the statute. The court was of the opinion that *White* v. *Brown* did not come within the purview of the statute.[86]

Kempe, while paying careful attention to the law of the case, also took steps to secure as impartial a jury as could be obtained in New York in 1766. This required obtaining a "struck jury," a relatively simple procedure that permitted trial counsel the right to eliminate twenty-four potential jurors from a panel of forty-eight returned by the sheriff. From the twenty-four remaining the sheriff selected the twelve man trial jury by lot.[87]

Before the trial began Kempe subpoenaed those witnesses for White whom he wished to examine, notified Brown of the impending trial, and requested that he bring to the proceedings all of the officers of H.M.S. *Hawke* who could give evidence in his favor.[88] Yet when the

[85] Hicks, Brief for Defendant, *ibid.*, citing 4 Geo. 3d. c. 15, sec. 46, effective Sept. 29, 1764.

[86] See Scott, Notes for Summing Up, *ibid.*, W 159, referring to statute, and Nov. 1, 1766, Minutes of the Supreme Court of Judicature, July 31, 1764-Aug. 2, 1766, 29, 30, New York County Clerk's Office, Records Division, Hall of Records.

[87] Aug. 2, 1766, Minutes, Sup. Ct. Jud., July 31, 1764-Aug. 2, 1766, 444. The jurors marked off belonged to prominent mercantile families, including a DePeyster, a Bayard, a Beekman, a Van Horne, and a Cuyler. Defendant's List of Jurors Struck, Oct. 20, 1766, Pleadings 1754-1837, W 159. The jury sitting on the case included Nicholas Low, a prominent merchant of the city. Oct. 29, 1766, Minutes, Sup. Ct. Jud., Oct. 21, 1766-Jan. 21, 1769, 23.

[88] Subpoena directed to plaintiff's witnesses, dated Oct. 21, 1766, returnable Oct. 27, 1766, Parchments 197 D-8, New York County Clerk's Office, Records Division, Hall of Records.

trial began neither Brown nor any other commissioned officer of H.M.S. *Hawke* appeared. Only Dr. Andrew Lawson, a warrant officer who served as surgeon of H.M.S. *Hawke,* was present to testify for Brown. The circumstances surrounding this dearth of witnesses for Brown and the absence of Brown himself are obscure. We do know that throughout the trial Brown and H.M.S. *Hawke* were in the Delaware River hunting smugglers and did not return to New York until November 5, 1766. Brown wrote Captain Archibald Kennedy on November 20, explaining that the failure to appear had "been instigated thro' the different orders I received from time to time." But Kennedy, in a report to the Admiralty, disagreed with this version. He stated that Brown should have made "application" to his superiors for permission to proceed with H.M.S. *Hawke* to New York in order to attend the trial. "I imagine," Kennedy concluded, "if he had made such application to Capt. [John] Corner . . . he wou'd have given him an order for that purpose, but I know of no such application having been made."[39]

Although Brown and Kennedy might debate responsibility for the failure of the captain of the *Hawke* to appear at the trial, neither officer would deny that his absence made a strong defense impossible. Scott examined no less than thirteen witnesses, including the Vice-admiralty judge Richard Morris; Kempe had to content himself with the examination of Dr. Andrew Lawson of H.M.S. *Hawke* and the custodians of the official records pertaining to the seizure of the *New York*. The case went to the jury, who after an hour's deliberation returned with a verdict of over £4,000 for the plaintiff White.[40] Two weeks later, Kempe expressed his outrage and humiliation in a letter to Brown: "I cannot sufficiently express the Chagrin I then felt and still feel in being obliged to try a Cause of so much Importance under such Circumstances, deserted by my Client and without Witnesses." Reminding Brown that the case had been heard "by a special Jury which I got struck for that Purpose that you might have as fair a Trial as possible," Kempe went on to explain that he had been too busy to examine all of Brown's witnesses the previous July and that he generally believed it best to have all witnesses testify in open court whenever possible.[41] Furthermore, Kempe continued that he

39 Sept. 11-Nov. 5, 1766, Adm. L/H76, National Maritime Museum, Greenwich; Aug. 29, 1766, Adm. 1/1609; Nov. 20, Dec. 3, 1766, Adm. 1/2012.

40 Oct. 29, 1766, Minutes, Sup. Ct. Jud., Oct. 21, 1766-Jan. 21, 1769, 23.

41 Kempe to Brown, Nov. 19, 1766, Pleadings 1754-1837, W 159. Kempe was quite justified in explaining that he was too busy in July of 1766 to examine witnesses

had no intention of proceeding further in *White* v. *Brown* and would take no steps in the newly instituted case of *Franklin* v. *Brown,* unless Captain Brown promptly settled his outstanding debts to Kempe for court costs and counsel's fees.[42]

Upon his failure to pay the £4,000 judgment against him, Brown again faced imprisonment. His attorneys, Kempe and Whitehead Hicks, advised him that, in the light of the decision of the Privy Council in *Forsey* v. *Cunningham,* there could be no appeal from the verdict of a common law jury.[43] They had also suggested that Brown might sell the cargo seized from the *New York* to obtain funds with which to pay the judgment debt.[44] Apparently this suggestion was predicated upon the fact that, pending the appeal to the High Court of Admiralty, Brown retained possession of the goods. While in possession of the goods Brown had been sued for their wrongful seizure and conversion to his own use. This action in the Supreme Court of Judicature in effect determined that Brown had taken the goods and that £4,000 was the value of the seized property. White's judgment thus was equivalent to a forced sale to Brown for the amount of the judgment. It would therefore follow that Brown might sell the goods in his possession to obtain funds with which to settle the £4,000 judgment outstanding against him. Actually, such a sale by Brown would involve the risk of not realizing the full amount of the judgment, for the purchasers at auction would not be bound by the Supreme Court jury's assessment of damages. This was the chance Brown took at the end of November when the goods were sold.[45] However, Brown did not pay the sum realized to White; for on December

on behalf of Brown, because it was during this month that the leaders of the tenant riots in Westchester and Dutchess counties were being tried by Court of Oyer and Terminer, with Kempe as principal prosecuting attorney.

[42] *Ibid.*

[43] Kempe and Hicks to Andrew Elliott and Lambert Moore, Apr. 6, 1767, *ibid.* The reference is to a decision of the Privy Council, overruling the opinion of Lieutenant Governor Cadwallader Colden, and affirming the position of the New York Supreme Court. Based upon this decision, it was firmly established that once a common law jury verdict had been entered in the New York Supreme Court, only formal errors in the proceeding were legal cause for reversal on appeal by writ of error. The Governor in Council could not reverse upon the facts, or reduce the amount of the jury verdict.

[44] Nov. 27, 1766, Case and Opinion for Captain Brown, by Attorney General and Mr. Hicks, *ibid.*

[45] Judgment at Parchments 108 H-4; Dec. 3, 1766, Adm. 1/2012; *New York Gazette or Weekly Post-Boy,* Nov. 27, 1766.

5, a judgment was entered against Brown in the New York Supreme Court. Three days later Brown set sail for England in H.M.S. *Hawke,* arriving at the Downs on January 25, 1767. When he died at London on March 19, 1767, the New York judgment was still outstanding.[46]

After Brown's departure for England a *capias ad satisfaciendum,* or warrant of arrest, was issued against Brown by the New York Supreme Court. The collector and the comptroller of customs at New York, Andrew Elliott and Lambert Moore, "by the Express Orders of the . . . Commissioners of Customs," posted bail for Brown on the same day.[47] On February 18, John Morin Scott filed Thomas White's declaration in the New York Supreme Court claiming that Elliott and Moore, as pledges and manucaptors for themselves and Captain John Brown, owed White the amount of the judgment, namely £4,168 6*s* 0*d* New York currency. The declaration asserted that numerous demands made upon Moore and Elliott were unavailing and that the judgment remained unsatisfied. Kempe and Hicks decided that their best course was to demur to the complaint in the hope that instructions would arrive from London before the plaintiff's attorneys could obtain a hearing before the court in regard to the demurrer. Scott moved for argument on the demurrer on April 21, 1767, and after some additional argument on April 25, the demurrer was overruled and judgment was entered for the plaintiffs on April 28. The judgment roll, which is unfortunately missing from its place, is indexed as being filed on April 30, 1767. No executions appear to have been issued on this judgment, and as far as we can tell, no instructions were ever received from London. It is most likely that Moore and Elliott paid the judgment rather than to go to jail and that thereafter they attempted to recoup their losses from the Treasury or customs board. There is no record to show whether or not they succeeded.[48]

In the meantime the admiralty case appeal had moved forward on the calendar of the High Court of Admiralty in London. On June 7, 1765, the case of *Brown* v. *Kenyon* first appears on a petition filed on

[46] Jan. 25, 1767, Adm. 1/1494; Dec. 8, 1766, Adm. L/H76; *Gentleman's Magazine* (1767), 144.

[47] On motion of Scott, the sheriff was directed to return execution by arrest of Brown, Jan. 20, 22, 1767, Minutes, Sup. Ct. Jud., Oct. 21, 1766-Jan. 21, 1769, 82, 86. Recognizance of bail, dated Jan. 22, 1767, Parchments 9 K-10.

[48] Declaration at Pleadings, 1754-1837, W 253; Kempe and Hicks to Elliott and Moore, Apr. 6, 1767, *ibid.,* W 159; Minutes, Sup. Ct. Jud., Oct. 21, 1766-Jan. 21, 1769, 111, 144, 160. The judgment roll should be filed at Parchments 180 E-10, but is missing.

behalf of Brown by Thomas Tyndall. Roger Altham appeared on July 3 and at his request was granted permission to represent the appellee. At the same time Tyndall, proctor for Brown, was assigned to libel by the first day of the next term.[49] On January 21, 1766, Tyndall's libel was tendered, filed, and received by the court, and Altham was ordered to file a reply on behalf of the appellee by the next sitting of the court. Subsequently Altham requested and received three continuances.[50]

The proceedings finally resumed on April 15 when Altham presented the court with a "Negative Issue," or a general denial of the appellant's case. As a consequence of this joinder of issue on the facts as well as the law, the court proceeded to a rehearing of the case based upon the documentary record before it, and Tyndall, Brown's proctor, was "assigned to prove [his libel] by the last Session" of Easter term. However there was a delay until Trinity term when the court on May 27 directed that Tyndall produce proofs and make his plea by the third session of the term. After a continuance until June 24, Tyndall filed his papers, and then with the consent of Altham the court postponed the assignation until the next term. Again the proceedings were delayed, this time by the death of Brown's proctor, Tyndall, who was replaced by George Gostling, Jr.[51]

On February 17, 1767, the trial resumed, and the proctors for both parties presented arguments and proofs to the court. Counsel for the appellees argued that the *New York* had been seized on the high seas while enroute to the Isle of Man and that no importation in fact or in law had taken place. Precedents were cited to show that the word importation implied breaking bulk and physically placing goods on the shore. However the appellees' case was greatly weakened by the failure to produce in court a number of crucial documents such as the charter party of the *New York* which called for the voyage to the Isle of Man. Counsel for Brown, the appellant, argued that the *New York* had been arrested within the jurisdiction of the province of New York while attempting to smuggle illegal goods into the province. Statutes of Parliament were cited to show that an importation could be effected without

[49] June 7, July 3, 1765, High Court of Admiralty Group, Class 5, Piece 139, Public Record Office. Hereafter cited as H.C.A. 5/139. Nov. 6, 1765, H.C.A. 5/140.

[50] Jan. 21, 28, Feb. 5, 24, 1766, H.C.A. 5/140.

[51] Apr. 15, May 10, 27, 1766, *ibid.*; June 11, 24, Nov. 4, 22, Dec. 9, 1766, Jan. 1, 1767, H.C.A. 5/141.

actually breaking bulk and physically placing goods on land. Brown's counsel, citing the lack of documentary evidence, dismissed the argument that the *New York*'s destination was the Isle of Man as nothing more than an attempt to cover up the fact that the ship was engaged in a smuggling voyage. The pleading ended on February 24, when "Gostling prayed the Appeal to be pronounced for and that the Decree of the Judge below may be reversed with Costs, and that the said Ship New York with all her Guns Tackle Furniture Ammunition and Apperel and the thirty Casks of wine and twenty boxes of soap the goods seized may be pronounced and declared to be forfeited as being on a Trade contrary to the Statutes in that Case made and provided and be condemned accordingly." Then "Altham prayed the Judge to affirm the Decree of the Judge below and to admit the Cause and to condemn Gostling's Client . . . [Brown] in Costs."[52]

Immediately upon the termination of the arguments of counsel, the High Court of Admiralty promulgated its decision. Reversing the New York Vice-admiralty Court's decree, Judge Sir Thomas Salisbury wrote a decision that is remarkable for its ambiguity. Noting the general lack of documentary evidence to support the claimant's position, he observed: "I think this is a trade which it is highly incumbent upon Great Britain to regulate and place upon a better footing than it stands at present. The seizure is sufficiently justified by the European goods on board, which I decree to be confiscated pursuant to the statute, and condemn the appellate [appellee] in costs as well o[n] the first instance as this; but I restore the ship."[53] The contemporary editor, Sir William Burrell, was perplexed and added to his report of the case the query: "Does the statute leave any discretionary power in the judge to restore the ship? Do not prohibited goods create an absolute forfeiture of the vessel whereon they are laden?"[54]

Central to the confusion is the fact that Salisbury did not specify *which* statute formed the basis of his condemnation of the illegal cargo while he restored the vessel to her owners. Clearly it could not be the 1663 Staple Act, for under its terms the condemnation of illegal goods resulted in the forfeiture of the vessel within which they were "imported."

[52] Feb. 17, 24, 1767, H.C.A. 5/141; Reginald G. Marsden, ed., *Reports of Cases Determined by the High Court of Admiralty . . . 1758-1774. By Sir William Burrell* . . . (London, 1885), 30-46.

[53] Marsden, ed., *Reports*, 46.

[54] *Ibid.*

Further, at no point in his brief decision did the judge resolve the legal issue of importation that had figured so prominently in the arguments before him, as well as in the courts below. Apparently the issue of importation was not sufficiently proved to form a part of his decision. Hence there was only one basis upon which to decide the suit—the "hovering statute"[55] that provided for the forfeiture of goods found on vessels standing off the coast without adequate explanation. The rule to be applied in forfeitures under this statute was that all vessels over fifty tons burden were not subject to forfeiture, but that any illegal goods they carried could be condemned.

This statute, originally enacted in regard to the British Isles in 1718, had been extended to the colonies by Parliamentary act in 1762. It had been in effect for only six months when the *New York* was seized, but Attorney General Kempe had wisely included it in the libel. There it remained unnoticed by counsel for either of the parties until the case was debated before the High Court of Admiralty. Then it was noted in argument, and brought to the attention of Salisbury, who took the easiest course available to him in the disposition of the appeal.[56] He had been urged to construe strictly the penal statutes providing for forfeiture, and the question of "importation" under the Staple Act was one which, *strictissimi juris,* would have been resolved in favor of the claimants. While the evidence did not rise to the level required to prove "importation," it did present a good case for the application of the "hovering statute." Consistent with the terms of this statute, Salisbury condemned the cargo but acquitted the vessel, since she was over fifty tons burden.

By this construction the law had been interpreted to limit the scope of the Acts of Trade and to reduce the penalty for most instances of hovering to a mere seizure of the illegal goods. Smugglers were in effect given the assurance that they might hover in vessels of over fifty tons and endanger only their illegal cargoes. Since the High Court of Admiralty refused to reverse on the basis of the broad interpretation of the term "import" that had been urged by Brown's counsel below, it was fairly certain that only an actual landing or breaking of bulk would constitute an offense under the Staple Act of 1663. The only apprehension of a large vessel carrying illegal goods that would result in

[55] 5 Geo. I, c. 11, sec. 8 (1718), and 3 Geo. III, c. 22, sec. 9 (1762).

[56] Marsden, ed., *Reports,* 39, 43, 44.

forfeiture of the vessel as well as the illegal goods was, therefore, a seizure while the vessel was in the process of landing illegal goods or breaking bulk. The function of the Royal Navy in searching and clearing all "hovering vessels" off the American coast thus became a critical, albeit impossible, task of customs enforcement. The High Court of Admiralty decision in the *New York* case meant that the likelihood of any smuggling vessel being forfeited was substantially reduced.

As if to add insult to injury, the costs assessed against the owners of the *New York* were never paid. Taxation of costs dragged on through term after term of the High Court of Admiralty, and ultimately the matter was forgotten in the outbreak of the American Revolution.[57] In retrospect it can be said that only the American merchants engaged in smuggling gained benefit from the *New York* case. Captain John Brown, the libellant, was long dead when the High Court of Admiralty partially reversed the decision below and awarded him part of the libelled goods; his bondsmen in New York appear to have been left some £4,000 poorer by virtue of their part in the litigation; the Royal Navy and customs officers faced an even more difficult task of enforcement because of the High Court of Admiralty's decree.

Uncertainties concerning the scope of the term "import," coupled with strict construction of penal statutes had tipped the scales against a judicial decision that would have facilitated revenue collection. Although the judge saw the need to put enforcement "upon a better footing," he could not find a legal basis to decree forfeiture of the offending vessel, and the property rights of her owners and charterers prevailed. The court recognized the need for more vigorous revenue collection but, in the absence of more comprehensive statutory sanctions, could go no further than it did in the *New York* situation.

Clearly it was the duty of Parliament to provide a basis upon which a more efficient customs enforcement program could be instituted, and the courts were unable to take the lead in evolving these new rules of law. Bound by rules of statutory construction, judges on both sides of the Atlantic were sorely hampered by what they could do, and in the case of American Vice-admiralty judges sharply restricted in what they were inclined to do, to assist Crown officers charged with enforcement. Had the Acts of Trade been revised periodically, there would have been

57 H.C.A. 6/1-7, *passim*.

no need for a radical departure in enforcement techniques during the last half of the eighteenth century. Altered conditions in America and the decreasing enforcement capabilities of the customs service and Royal Navy could have been taken into account in 1710 as well as in 1764. In all likelihood there would have been less resistance to the change in the earlier years of the century, and the Acts of Trade would have been held in higher respect because their frequent revision would have caused them to coincide with the realities of the day.

Undoubtedly cases such as that of Captain Brown brought the situation to the attention of Parliament, for in 1764 and the years to follow statutory alteration and revision did take place. Reaction then was vocal and widespread in America; yet in the light of the *New York* case it is fairly obvious that no matter how unpopular the new statutes might be in the colonies, it would have been impossible to tighten revenue enforcement in the empire by any other means. Little solace could George III draw from the realization that the "radical" step he took in 1764 could have been accomplished gradually by his predecessors, Anne and the first two Georges. A queen and two kings checkmated the commercial system of the British Empire and left Farmer George a rapidly adeeming legacy on the North American continent.

John Jay: Lawyer in a Time of Transition, 1764-1775

Unlike many of his associates in the leadership of the American Revolution, John Jay was already well established in law practice when the war broke out. Born into a financially secure and prominent mercantile family, he had been trained at King's College and in the law offices of Benjamin Kissam, a well known New York City attorney. Although young in years and experience, Jay had built up a large and remunerative practice before he began his public career in 1774.[1] For this reason his life at the bar is a valuable point of departure for studying the legal profession in the last decade of the colonial period and for considering the role of the lawyer in colonial society and in the coming of the American Revolution.

I. Legal Education

Few periods in colonial New York were less auspicious for entering the legal profession than the years 1762 and 1763. In 1756 the attorneys of New York had agreed to restrict bar admissions by refusing to accept clerks for the next fourteen years.[2] Aspiring lawyers were thus to be deprived of the substantial benefits of training in a law office within the province. With that path to the profession seemingly blocked when John Jay decided upon a law career in 1762, his family was forced to look elsewhere for his legal education. Peter Jay, John's father, consulted with relatives in England.[3] He concluded that legal train-

[1] At the end of the American Revolution, Jay was minister to Spain and a member of the American commission appointed to negotiate a peace treaty. Before he returned to the United States, Jay intended to resume his law practice. Appointments as Secretary for Foreign Affairs and subsequently as first Chief Justice of the United States, however, prevented his returning to private life.

[2] Agreement of the Bar of New York City, *dated* Oct. 1756, in P. Hamlin, Legal Education in Colonial New York 160-61 (1939) [hereinafter cited as Hamlin].

[3] The relatives were Sir James Jay, John's brother who was then in London, and David Peloquin, of Bristol, a cousin of Peter Jay and his commercial correspondent.

ing in the mother country would be an extremely expensive proposition. Mindful of the heady social atmosphere of the Inns of Court and their lack of pretension to serious legal education, Peter Jay wrote to David Peloquin, his Bristol cousin and commercial correspondent: "[T]hough I have hitherto no Reason to doubt of his behaving Well, as he is a youth remarkably sedate, and is well disposed, but nevertheless it's prudent to gard, as much as possible, against the danger of bad Company he would be exposed to in London . . . ."[4] Peloquin, on the other hand, felt that because he lacked the proper contacts with members of the local bar, he probably would not be able to obtain a suitable clerkship placement for John in Bristol.[5]

Quite fortunately for the Jay family, and for John in particular, an unanticipated change in the policy of the New York bar resulted in the revocation of the 1756 agreement.[6] Within eleven days of the repeal of the suspension of clerkships, Peter Jay entered into preliminary arrangements with Benjamin Kissam, a New York City lawyer with an extensive practice, whom Peter Jay described as a "Gentleman eminent in the Profession."[7]

Despite the alacrity with which the anxious father and son accepted the apprenticeship terms, the choice of John Jay's master proved to be wise. As a well-known and extremely busy attorney, Kissam at least equaled any other practitioner in the city of New York in the advantages he could provide a clerk studying the law. Little information concerning the man, however, has been preserved. We know that Kissam was about thirty-four years of age when Jay began his clerkship. Although Kissam was a member of a family prominent in Queens County legal circles, he centered his practice in New York City, where the highest courts of the province held their sessions.[8] During the clerkship, Benjamin Kissam and John Jay developed a rare

---

[4] Letter from P. Jay to D. Peloquin, Apr. 14, 1763, in 3 Peter Jay Letterbook (Columbia University Libraries, Special Collections). *See* F. MONAGHAN, JOHN JAY: DEFENDER OF LIBERTY AGAINST KINGS AND PEOPLES 29 (1935).

[5] Letter from D. Peloquin to P. Jay, July 26, 1763 (private collection of John Jay (a descendant), Williamstown, Mass.).

[6] Agreement of the Bar of New York City, *concluded* Jan. 5, 1764, in HAMLIN, *supra* note 2, at 163-64.

[7] Letter from P. Jay to D. Peloquin, May 15, 1764, in 3 P. Jay Letterbook, *supra* note 4.

[8] E. KISSAM, THE KISSAM FAMILY IN AMERICA FROM 1644 TO 1825, at 20-21 (1892). A number of attorneys practicing before the Queens County Court of Common Pleas were named Kissam. Daniel Kissam (1726-1782) and Daniel Kissam (1739-1812) were judges of that court.

form of camaraderie,[9] which must have rendered more bearable the grueling and tedious writing tasks assigned to all law clerks in the colonial period.

Jay entered his apprenticeship with a full appreciation of the difficult years that would intervene before his admission to the bar. When he had first announced his desire to enter the profession, his father had admonished him: "[A]s its [*sic*] your inclination to be of that Profession, I hope you'll closely attend to it with a firm resolution that no difficulties in prosecuting that Study shall discourage you from applying very close to it, and if possible, from taking delight in it."[10]

Twenty years before, young William Livingston had published two anonymous essays attacking the drudgery of his life as a law clerk and the inattention of the attorneys who accepted law clerks without training them in the law. The attendant publicity may have helped draw the bar into a reconsideration of its duties to the young men committed to its charge.[11] Arduous copying duties were lightened by a growing reliance upon the use of printed litigation forms and papers prepared by scriveners.[12] Nevertheless there still remained lengthy pleas in chancery, bulky briefs of counsel, wills and non-routine deeds and contracts, all of which required preparation in the handwriting of law clerks. John Jay and probably other senior law clerks were also expected to manage the business affairs of the law office by keeping accurate registers of costs and disbursements, preparing bills for services rendered, and drafting routine correspondence.[13] The colonial law clerk performed all of the duties which today are assigned to a legal stenographer, as well as the functions of a managing clerk and a legal researcher.

---

[9] Specific incidents are recounted in H. Johnson, John Jay: Colonial Lawyer 70-71, June 1, 1965 (unpublished doctoral dissertation in Columbia University Library) [hereinafter cited as Colonial Lawyer].

[10] Letter from P. Jay to John Jay, Aug. 23, 1763, in 1 THE CORRESPONDENCE AND PUBLIC PAPERS OF JOHN JAY 1763-1781, at 1 (H. Johnston ed. 1890) [hereinafter cited as CORRESPONDENCE].

[11] T. SEDGWICK, JR., A MEMOIR OF THE LIFE OF WILLIAM LIVINGSTON 48, 52, 56-57 (1832). When the shields of anonymity slipped, however, the outburst resulted in the transfer of Livingston's indenture to another attorney.

[12] HAMLIN, *supra* note 2, at 41-43. An example of a pleading prepared by a scrivener can be seen in the case of Dugdale v. Carr (1775) (Mayor's Court Papers, Benjamin Salzer Collection, Columbia University Libraries, Special Collections). While the formal nature of Supreme Court litigation appears to have lent itself to printed forms, the niceties of practice seem to have dictated that papers be handwritten.

[13] *See* note 29 *infra* & accompanying text.

While reliance upon the clerks as scriveners decreased in the twenty years between Livingston's and Jay's clerkships, the time that a busy attorney could devote to the clerks' legal education probably did not increase significantly. In the course of their studies or work for their masters, clerks were confronted with a vast array of inadequately indexed sources which, only after a large expenditure of time and effort, might yield an answer to their questions. Peter Van Schaack, a close friend of Jay's, commented on his own clerkship:

> For my part, how many hours have I hunted, how many books turned up for what three minutes of explanation from any tolerable lawyer would have made evident to me! It is vain to put a law book into the hands of a lad without explaining difficulties to him as he goes along.[14]

Van Schaack found that not more than one or two attorneys in the entire province did tolerable justice to their obligations to educate their clerks.

Jay's clerkship is most fully documented in the large number of litigation papers that were prepared in Jay's handwriting and were then filed by Kissam in the Supreme Court of Judicature. Lacking Jay's signature, the papers have survived the ravages of time and the petty thievery of autograph collectors. Sixteen of the seventeen judgment rolls filed by Kissam in the Supreme Court from June, 1764, to November, 1765, are in John Jay's hand, and the other judgment roll is in the hand of Kissam's senior clerk, Lindley Murray, the future grammarian. Jay's hand also appears on the endorsements to writs and on two writs of inquisition; from this we may conclude that his duties as junior clerk included carrying these papers to the judge or the sheriff, and thence to the Supreme Court clerk for filing.[15]

---

[14] Letter from P. Van Schaack to Henry Van Schaack, Jan. 2, 1769, in H. VAN SCHAACK, THE LIFE OF PETER VAN SCHAACK, LL.D. 9 (1842). Van Schaack later established a law school at Kinderhook, N.Y., a step toward the separation of legal education from active practice and clerkship training. HAMLIN, *supra* note 2, at 24 n.3; *see* text accompanying note 130 *infra*. Members of the bar were not unmindful of their clerks' need for guidance. One of the William Smiths, for example, drew up a list of books to be included in a law student's course of study. *Id.* 61-62, 197-200; Klein, *Rise of the New York Bar: The Legal Career of William Livingston*, 15 WM. & MARY Q. 357 (3d ser. 1958). Klein claims that Hamlin is incorrect in identifying William Smith, Jr., as the author, and that the list was drawn up in 1747 by William Smith, Sr.

[15] For a detailed listing of the judgment rolls and other documents prepared by Jay, see Colonial Lawyer, *supra* note 9, at 28-29, 72-73. Judgment rolls were written on

The documentary evidence indicates that Kissam's practice involved primarily commercial matters. Only one tort claim for assault and battery was handled in the first twenty months of Jay's clerkship. One interesting manuscript, drawn up in Jay's neat hand on March 5, 1765, deals with the construction to be placed upon a will and codicil.[16] Participation in the research and drafting of such a legal opinion was apparently one of the rare opportunities that John Jay had to improve his analytic skills. In a day before New York cases were regularly reported and before current English decisions received wide circulation, a lawyer's opinion was probably the closest a colonial law clerk could come to a "recent decision on the law."

The absence of reported opinions of New York courts in the colonial period and a substantial lack of law reporting from the other provinces of British North America are matters well known to students of legal history but surprising to those not familiar with colonial practice and jurisprudence. Throughout the colonies the acts of the assemblies were printed and periodically revised to eliminate repealed matter and to provide an easy guide to the statutory law of the province. Yet in New York no efforts were made during the colonial period to reduce the case law of the province to a written or printed form.[17] English law

---

parchment measuring about six inches in width; the membranes were stitched together, and when completed the document was rolled tightly for filing in a small square slot.

[16] The will and codicil, executed on the same day by Elizabeth Hamilton, left the rights of beneficiary Abraham DePeyster in confusion. The will left two-sevenths of the testatrix's residuary estate to DePeyster. The codicil indicated DePeyster was entitled to a certain entailed estate and no more, provided that upon evaluation the entailed estate equaled two-sevenths of the residuary estate. The testatrix subsequently broke the entail. At her death the question arose whether she intended, in the absence of the entail, to give DePeyster nothing or two-sevenths of the residue of the estate. Kissam's opinion was that the will and codicil were to be read as one document. The provision that DePeyster take only from the entailed estate merely modified and did not supersede the bequest of the residuary estate. When the entail was broken the limitation became meaningless and thus could be eliminated. The bequest of the two-sevenths of the estate was left standing. Miscellaneous Manuscripts, Elizabeth Hamilton (New-York Historical Society, New York City).

[17] The first regularly reported New York cases date from 1794. J. WALLACE, THE REPORTERS 343 (3d rev. ed. 1855). The colonial laws of New York were published in compilations in 1694, 1718, 1752, and 1773. Session laws were also published. 1 N.Y. COLONIAL LAWS v-vi (1894).

The only colonies with reports of pre-Revolutionary cases were Pennsylvania, Maryland, and Virginia. J. WALLACE, *supra*, at 339-52. Some colonies had abridgments of the statute law. *See* J. BISSET, ABRIDGMENT AND COLLECTION OF THE ACTS OF ASSEMBLY OF THE PROVINCE OF MARYLAND, AT PRESENT IN FORCE (1759); J. MERCER, AN EXACT ABRIDGEMENT OF ALL THE PUBLIC ACTS OF ASSEMBLY, OF VIRGINIA, IN FORCE AND

reports were used by New York lawyers on a fairly extensive scale, if the law libraries listed by Paul Hamlin are at all characteristic.[18] English precedents were undoubtedly a rich source of law and custom in New York. In addition, English statutes, readily available in the province, had often been received into New York provincial law through usage and custom. We may speculate that what case law there might have been prior to the Revolution was concerned principally with identifying those English precedents that had been accepted in New York courts as binding upon the province. Unfortunately no extant documentation reports the opinions of the New York courts or their rulings on the law, and for that reason it is impossible to say how far they departed from the simple acceptance or rejection of English precedents.

The oral tradition of the bar preserved the major decisions in the memory of the select group that had been trained in New York clerkships. Reliance upon memory seems remarkable to lawyers of a later generation, trained to research the written precedents of courts and to present arguments based upon analysis of authorities. Yet apparently both judges and lawyers in early American courts were inclined to rely upon their mutual recollections of unreported cases.[19]

Even law clerks, in preparing their student notes, often failed to reduce legal opinions to written form. A clerk would customarily copy into a "commonplace book" the necessary forms of practice, such precedents as might prove useful, and such legislative acts as bore directly upon the conduct of a law practice.[20] Jay's commonplace book, begun during his first

---

USE, WITH PRECEDENTS IN LAW AND CONVEYANCING (1737). Of course the acts passed at any given legislative session were printed immediately after the end of the session. In contrast, Thomas Jefferson's collection of Virginia colonial cases was not published until 1829; Josiah Quincy's collection of Massachusetts Superior Court cases from 1761 to 1772 was not published until 1865, and Thomas Harris's and John M'Henry's collection of Maryland law cases from 1658 to 1799 was not published until 1809. Historians actually know more about colonial case law today than could have been widely known in colonial America.

[18] HAMLIN, *supra* note 2, at 171-96.

[19] *See* the colloquy between court and counsel in Kirman Holmes & Co. v. Duncan (1788), in 1 THE PAPERS OF JOHN MARSHALL 250-51 (H. Johnson ed. 1974).

[20] John Jay, Commonplace Book (New York State Library, Albany) may be compared with the more extensive commonplace books of James Alexander (New-York Historical Society, New York City) and of Joseph Murray and John Chambers (Columbia University Law Library).

twenty months as a clerk, is surprisingly brief, containing outlines for only those procedures rarely used in everyday practice.[21]

Even with this extensive oral tradition, it is remarkable that no movement developed for the reporting of Supreme Court of Judicature opinions in the years immediately preceding the American Revolution. The lack of interest in perpetuating the reasoning of the courts in written records may perhaps be attributed to two factors. First, the traditional method ensured that lawyers from the mother country or sister provinces could not easily invade the monopoly of the local provincial bar. Second, the small size of the Supreme Court bar and the manner in which matters of law were adjudicated created no necessity for written opinions. While the number of admitted lawyers increased sharply prior to the Revolution, at no time did the group exceed fifty. All practiced in the City of New York and were in regular attendance at the Supreme Court and the occasional sessions of the High Court of Chancery. When the Supreme Court was sitting, Saturday of each week was designated motion day, permitting the bar to dispose of trial business during the week and to attend the motion day to hear and present arguments.[22] With all of the lawyers and most of their clerks in the courtroom when motions were decided, including the important decisions on cases stated and cases reserved, very little reason remained for reduction of the decisions and opinions to written form to serve those lawyers.

In accordance with his apprenticeship agreement, Jay had permission to attend sessions of court when his office duties permitted.[23] Very likely he took advantage of this opportunity to attend the famous trial of *Forsey v. Cunningham* in 1764, a matter

---

[21] Jay singled out for particular attention the proceedings to recover possession under the act against forcible entry and detainer, not unlike summary proceedings available against a holdover tenant today; proceedings under the attachment act, which permitted prejudgment seizure of an absconding debtor's property; and proceedings on the act for preventing trespasses, a procedure somewhat in the nature of an injunction used to delay lumbering until title to realty could be ascertained. John Jay, *supra* note 20.

[22] *See* Minutes of the Supreme Court of Judicature, April 21, 1772-Jan. 21, 1776; Minutes of the Supreme Court of Judicature, April 18, 1769-May 2, 1772; Minutes of the Supreme Court of Judicature, Oct. 21, 1766-Jan. 21, 1769 (New York County Clerk's Office, Hall of Records, New York City). [The three volumes are collectively cited hereinafter as Judicature Minutes.]

[23] Although the agreement does not survive, this provision is mentioned in a letter from P. Jay to D. Peloquin, May 15, 1764, in 3 Peter Jay Letterbook, *supra* note 4.

that rallied the full weight of the New York bench and bar behind the Supreme Court of Judicature and its refusal to allow an irregular mode of appeal from the verdict of a common law jury.[24] Lieutenant Governor Cadwallader Colden, temporarily in charge of the province of New York, insisted that the governor's instructions[25] permitted civil law appeals from the Supreme Court of Judicature as well as review through writs of error. A higher court could, in Colden's view, reverse on the facts the verdict of a jury. Chief Justice Daniel Horsmanden and all the justices of his court, with the unanimous support of the bar and the royal attorney general, opposed this measure, which they deemed an unconstitutional alteration of the form of government of the province of New York. Eventually this stand by the New York legal profession was upheld.

During Jay's clerkship the bar was caught up in another attempted exercise of imperial power—the implementation of the Stamp Act within the province. That Act required that all legal instruments and litigation papers filed with the courts be submitted on stamped paper. The New York bar, however, was not forced to decide whether to defy the imperial authorities directly by conducting business without stamps. With the stamped paper unavailable because of a tactical move by royal authorities, the courts were pressured into closing down for civil matters to avoid such a confrontation. Shutting down the courts demonstrated the profession's willingness to abet a protest against Parliament's taxes when British authority was not directly and unlawfully challenged. Because of this passive resistance,

---

[24] J. Smith, Appeals to the Privy Council from the American Plantations 390-416 (1950). *See also* E. Alexander, A Revolutionary Conservative: James Duane of New York 26-27 (1938); A. Keys, Cadwallader Colden: A Representative Eighteenth Century Official 300-02 (1906); T. Sedgwick, *supra* note 11, at 121-25; Johnson, *George Harison's Protest: New Light on Forsey versus Cunningham*, 50 N.Y. History 61 (1969). Klein, *Prelude to the Revolution in New York: Jury Trials and Judicial Tenure*, 17 Wm. & Mary Q. 439 (3d ser. 1960).

[25] The governor's commission and instructions were drawn up by officials of the British Board of Trade and forwarded to the Privy Council for issuance in the monarch's name. Although a specific formula evolved for these documents, some changes were made over the centuries of colonial rule. Because the commission and instructions formed the basic constitutional documents of the royal colonies, these changes could, and did, have constitutional significance. The commission was promulgated upon its bearer's arrival in the colony; the instructions were made public in a selective fashion, either by virtue of an instruction that certain portions of the document be made public, or by the governor's exercise of his discretion to publicize a given instruction. *See* 1 Royal Instructions to British Colonial Governors 1670-1776 vii-x, 16-17, 45-46 (L. Labaree ed. 1935).

only criminal cases, which were exempt from the tax, were tried between November, 1765, and May, 1766, when news of the repeal was received.[26]

The reaction of the New York bar to the Stamp Act and its earlier unified resistance to the lieutenant governor's position on appeals from the Supreme Court contrast markedly with the profession's sharp division into patriot and loyalist parties on the eve of the American Revolution. The role of the bar in these events of the 1760's indicates that both patriot and loyalist New York attorneys were opposed to the constitutional alterations being made in the name of King George III. Their differences arose from their selection of the means of opposition. Patriots decided to leave an empire that increasingly threatened the liberties they claimed as Englishmen and loyal subjects of the Crown; loyalists preferred to work within the framework of English law and constitutionalism to voice their opposition to the imperial administration.

The cessation of court business during the Stamp Act crisis forced Jay and his fellow clerks to take a vacation, a relief from the drudgery of office copying and an illustration for them of the depth of opposition to the Crown. Jay retired to his family home at Rye to read in the classics and to continue his legal studies on a more leisurely schedule. On April 25, 1766, Benjamin Kissam notified him to be ready to come to town to help reap a "Luxuriant Harvest of Law" as soon as the news of the repeal was received.[27] A month was to pass before notice of royal approval of the repealing bill reached the city, reopening the New York courts to litigation. With the clerkship of Lindley Murray, Jay's senior colleague, nearing its end, Jay's return to his writing desk in May, 1766, brought the promise of new responsibilities. He continued to prepare judgment rolls, thirteen in number from May, 1766, to October, 1768, when he was admitted to the bar, but Kissam had frequent recourse to scriveners and other clerks to keep up with the stenographic tasks. Twenty-one judgment rolls are in hands other than that of

---

[26] C. Becker, The History of Political Parties in the Province of New York, 1760-1766, at 40 & nn. 68-69 (reprint 1968); E. Morgan & H. Morgan, The Stamp Act Crisis: Prologue to Revolution 174-75 (1953); Morris, *Legalism versus Revolutionary Doctrine in New England*, 4 New Eng. Q. 195, 206 (1931).

[27] Letter from B. Kissam to John Jay, in 1 Correspondence, *supra* note 10, at 3; F. Monaghan, *supra* note 4, at 36.

John Jay, although his endorsements remain on most of them.[28] Jay's added responsibilities included the management of Kissam's appearance dockets and the maintenance of the disbursement and fee registers of the office.[29]

The routine and urgency of office duties, coupled with time taken to study Kissam's law books, would not seem to have permitted much freedom for other activities. Yet John Jay took an active part in the Debating Club, a group organized by the young men of New York City to debate issues of ethics, natural law, and political theory. While a substantial portion of the membership was either law clerks or recently admitted members of the bar,[30] the purposes of the Debating Club were as much social and intellectual as they were professional. In January, 1768, the Club debated the question, "Whether in an Absolute Monarchy it is better that the Crown should be elective than hereditary?" Jay argued that elective monarchy was preferable. If the son of a king was entitled to rule, Jay said, his father's interest would secure him the election. If, on the other hand, the election was contested between members of the nobility, the elective process would guarantee a contest between men of the greatest merit, for the nobility have an equal interest with the people in the government of the state. Finally, if a man was elected King in a constitutional way from among candidates of equal merit, the people would submit. To quote from the written argument of Jay and his associate, "People won't risque by Rebellion their Lives & Property to get rid of a good King."[31]

The consideration of morality, law, and politics extended beyond the formal meetings of the Debating Club. Studying law in a crowded colonial seaport city, the young clerks were made aware of the functions of law as a system of police and social control. While they learned to value law as the cement of society, they also began to question the need for the harsh penalties that

---

[28] Colonial Lawyer, *supra* note 9, at 72-73.

[29] Bill to Florus Bancker, *et al.*, Trustees of James Duthrie, in IX Miscellaneous Manuscripts 22 (New-York Historical Society, New York City). Kissam's registers do not survive, but this bill for legal services in Jay's hand supports the theory that office management was part of a senior clerk's duties.

[30] The Debating Society membership included Lindley Murray, as well as Egbert Benson and Peter Van Schaack, fellow students with Jay at King's College and clerks with other New York lawyers. F. MONAGHAN, *supra* note 4, at 39.

[31] Manuscripts of the Debating Society (BV Sec (Moot), New-York Historical Society, New York City). In contrast, the signers of the Declaration of Independence mutually pledged "our Lives, our Fortunes and our sacred Honor."

were then part of the criminal law. John Jay's close friend, Robert R. Livingston, Jr., prepared a piece for publication decrying the sorry circumstances of a young woman whose death sentence had been delayed so that she might give birth to an illegitimate child, who would then be orphaned by her execution.[32] But for the most part Jay's circle probably agreed with Peter Van Schaack that the "Altar of Justice requires such Sacrifices—to preserve human Society Individuals must bleed . . . ."[33] This generation of lawyers, however, would do much to alter the most sanguinary portions of the criminal law inherited from the mother country.

In the summer of 1766 John Jay witnessed a forceful demonstration of the role of the lawyer in society: His mentor, Kissam, defended William Prendergast and his associates in the Dutchess County rent riots against charges of high treason.[34] Tenant resistance to the New York system of land tenure and to suspect claims of the Dutchess County landholders intensified when the courts were closed in response to the Stamp Act. When the courts reopened in the spring of 1766, the sudden and widespread collection and ejectment effort stirred additional resentment. By summer, resistance to payment resulted in a violent outbreak against lawful authority in Dutchess County and elsewhere. The May riot on the Livingston Manor compelled the royal governor to send the Twenty-Eighth Regiment of regular troops up the Hudson River to put down the rebellion against the civil authorities. Several militiamen, supporting the regular troops, were killed in the affray with the tenants, and Sir Henry Moore, the governor, appointed a special Court of Oyer and Terminer to try the rebel leaders, including Prendergast.[35] This

---

[32] Manuscript, Nov. 3, 1768, [Box 1] Livingston Papers, (New-York Historical Society, New York City).

[33] Letter from P. Van Schaack to Peter Silvester, Jr., Aug. 1, 1768 (Van Schaack Papers, Columbia University Libraries, Special Collections).

[34] *See* I. MARK, AGRARIAN CONFLICTS IN COLONIAL NEW YORK 135-148 (1940); Mark & Handlin, *Land Cases in Colonial New York, 1765-1767, The King v. William Prendergast*, 19 N.Y.U.L.Q. REV. 164 (1942).

[35] The court that tried the Dutchess County rioters was one of Oyer and Terminer, and not merely a special sitting of the Supreme Court of Judicature. *See* letter from Gov. Moore to the Lords of Trade, Aug. 12, 1766, in 7 DOCUMENTS RELATIVE TO THE COLONIAL HISTORY OF THE STATE OF NEW YORK 849 (E. O'Callaghan ed. 1856) [hereinafter cited as DOC. REL. COL. HIST. N.Y.]; letter from Gov. Moore to Sec. Conway, July 14, 1766, in 7 DOC. REL. COL. HIST. N.Y. 845. William Smith, Jr., then a private attorney, recounted his own reluctant acceptance of a seat on the special court. HISTORICAL MEMOIRS FROM 16 MARCH 1763 TO 9 JULY 1776 OF WILLIAM SMITH 33-34 (W. Sabine ed. 1956) [hereinafter cited as WILLIAM SMITH].

court, armed with commissions to try high crimes and misdemeanors, was separate from the Supreme Court of Judicature, which did not exercise criminal jurisdiction in these matters. Composed of specially commissioned justices, it was heavily balanced in favor of the landlord interests, and a number of the future leaders of the American Revolution in New York served on this tribunal.[36] William Prendergast challenged the members of the court: If opposition to government was rebellion, then no member of the court was qualified to sit in his case.[37]

To that Court of Oyer and Terminer rode Benjamin Kissam, entrusting his cases before the Supreme Court and his court appearances to John Woods. He had taken upon himself the awesome burden and unpopular task of defending Prendergast. To Jay, his clerk, he wrote, "[W]hat their fate will be, God only knows; it is terrible to think that so many lives should be at stake upon the principles of a constructive murder: for I suppose that the immediate agency of but a very few of the party can be proved."[38] The reference to constructive murder indicates that Kissam was engaged in the defense of Prendergast's followers, which began on August 14, 1766.[39] It is not known whether Kissam took part in the cross-examination of the Crown witnesses. He did advance a strong argument that Prendergast and his associates had been asserting their private rights rather than staging a public demonstration to redress a public grievance or to alter the law. Under English law, riots over private grievances would not subject the participants to the penalties for high treason.[40] Kissam's abilities could not prevail against the contrary

---

[36] William Smith's account indicates that the court had a large bench, including both him and his father, a Supreme Court justice. WILLIAM SMITH, *supra* note 35, at 33-34. Mark and Handlin state that the Court of Oyer and Terminer consisted of Chief Justice Daniel Horsmanden, John Watts, William Walton, Oliver DeLancey, Joseph Reade, William Smith, Whitehead Hicks, and John Morin Scott. Mark & Handlin, *supra* note 34, at 167 n.3.

[37] The remark, no doubt based on hearsay evidence, is recounted in Captain John Montresor's journal. THE MONTRESOR JOURNALS 384 (New-York Historical Society Publication Fund No. 14, 1881).

[38] Letter from B. Kissam to John Jay, Aug. 25, 1766, in 1 W. JAY, THE LIFE OF JOHN JAY 19, 21 (1833) [hereinafter cited as LIFE].

[39] Notes on July 1766 Assizes, Dutchess County (New-York Historical Society, New York City).

[40] The citations used by Kissam are reproduced in Mark & Handlin, *supra* note 34, at 194. The works are Kelyng's Reports 75 [Messenger's Case], 84 Eng. Rep. 1087 (Exch. Ch. 1680); Popham's Reports 122 [Case of Bradshaw & Burton], 79 Eng. Rep. 1227 (K.B. 1597); SIR MICHAEL FOSTER'S REPORT AND DISCOURSES 211 (1762); 1 W. HAWKINS, A TREATISE OF THE PLEAS OF THE CROWN 34, 37 (1724-26). For a discussion

contentions of the Crown attorneys, nor could he successfully refute the large number of witnesses obtained by the Crown, in a number of cases through promises of immunity from prosecution.[41] The case ended with Prendergast's conviction and sentence to be hanged, castrated, disemboweled, beheaded, and quartered.[42] Fortunately for him, the execution was suspended by the governor and he was subsequently pardoned by the Crown.[43]

John Jay's attitudes toward the Prendergast case are not known, but Kissam's letter to him concerning the trials conveyed a compassion and humanity that must have impressed his clerk. The letter reveals a warm-hearted man, shocked by the violence of the agrarian revolt, but nevertheless reluctant to permit a wholesale execution of the participants to satiate the thirst for revenge that permeated the propertied classes.

While training in legal draftsmanship and litigation formed the backbone of John Jay's legal education, clerkship had been for him a time of maturation and growing sensitivity to the social and political consequences of the law in colonial New York.

II. Admission to the Bar and Commencement of Practice

Events during Jay's clerkship undermined the assumptions of the agreement he had made with Benjamin Kissam in January, 1764. Under its terms Jay was to serve a five-year term as a clerk before he would be certified for examination by his mentor.[44] A 1767 rule of the Supreme Court of Judicature required that college graduates, a class into which Jay fell, were to serve only three years.[45] On the other hand, the suspension of Jay's clerkship during the Stamp Act crisis deprived Kissam of his clerk's services. Kissam and Jay probably considered these variables and agreed that Jay would apply for admission to the bar about six months earlier than originally planned. Their parting appears to have been cordial, for thereafter Kissam was most

---

of the law of treason in the colonies, see Hurst, *Treason in the United States* (pts. 1-3), 58 Harv. L. Rev. 226, 395, 806 (1944-1945).

[41] Appearance Bond, Aug. 1, 1766, Miscellaneous Manuscripts, Dutchess County (New-York Historical Society, New York City).

[42] Mark, *supra* note 34, at 147.

[43] S. Lynd, Anti-Federalism in Dutchess County, New York 50-51 (1962).

[44] The five-year term was required by the Agreement of the Bar of New York City, *concluded* Jan. 5, 1764, in Hamlin, *supra* note 2, at 163.

[45] Hamlin, *supra* note 2, at 39.

helpful in securing employment for his former clerk, and in some instances, referring cases to him.

In the fall of 1768 Benjamin Kissam recommended Jay for admission to the bar. Although the 1764 agreement concerning admission required that the candidate's name be endorsed for examination, it is unclear whether such examinations were in fact conducted. Where the attorneys in New York City were personally aware of the abilities of the applicant, the examination may have been eliminated entirely.[46] We do not have any record of Jay's being examined, but on October 26, 1768, Governor Sir Henry Moore, "being well assured of the Ability and Learning of John Jay, Gentleman,"[47] appointed him an attorney-at-law and authorized him to appear in all of the provincial courts of record in accordance with the laws of New York and England.[48] Now a fully qualified attorney, Jay stood at the threshold of his career in the law, a profession he believed was to be his life's work.

Jay's prospects for success may have fallen considerably during his clerkship. When Jay entered Kissam's office the Supreme Court of Judicature bar was a relatively small group of thirty-six attorneys, averaging thirty-eight years of age, and closely related by blood or marriage to the large landowners and prosperous merchants of the province.[49] Their numbers had been purposely restricted by the 1756 bar agreement eliminating New York clerkships.[50] John Jay would have gained ready acceptance into this group by virtue of his social position,[51] and he also would

---

[46] For a discussion of admissions procedures, see *id.* 38, 50; Letter from P. Van Schaack to Peter Silvester, Aug. 1, 1768 (Van Schaack Papers, Columbia University Libraries, Special Collections).

[47] Jay's license to practice law, signed by Governor Moore, is in the Columbia University Libraries, Special Collections.

[48] Five days later Jay appeared in the Supreme Court of Judicature and produced his license. The presiding justice then administered the prescribed oaths and declaration, and the newly admitted attorney signed the roll of attorneys. Minutes of the Supreme Court of Judicature, Oct. 21, 1766-Jan. 21, 1769, at 567 (New York County Clerk's Office, Hall of Records, New York City); Roll of Attorneys, Oct. 26, 1754-June 3, 1847, Ledger J, Parchment Roll 1 (New York County Clerk's Office, Hall of Records, New York City).

[49] For a listing of Supreme Court attorneys, with age, education, and family relationships, see Colonial Lawyer, *supra* note 9, at 253.

[50] *See* notes 2-6 *supra* & accompanying text.

[51] John Jay was related to the leading landowning and mercantile families of New York. Through his paternal grandmother he was related to the Bayards, his mother was a member of the Van Cortlandt family, and his first cousins included DePeysters, DeLanceys, and Stuyvesants. *See generally* L. WELLS, THE JAY FAMILY OF LAROCHELLE AND NEW YORK (1938).

have prospered as older members of the Supreme Court bar retired from practice or were appointed to the Supreme Court. While Jay was a clerk, however, this monopoly of the law began to crumble, first with the liberalized clerkship rule of 1764[52] and subsequently with the 1767 reduction of college graduates' clerkships to three years.[53] In 1767 the number of admissions rose to three a year from one a year for the preceding period of two years. Although only Jay and Livingston were admitted in 1768, six attorneys were admitted in 1769, and twelve in 1770.[54] The net result was that from 1765 to 1770, twenty-five lawyers were added to the original, small group of seasoned practitioners.

The neophytes, whose preparation and abilities varied greatly, were all in competition for the limited legal business that was likely to fall to new practitioners. As the number of attorneys practicing before the Supreme Court of Judicature increased, the economic life of New York settled into a lethargy caused by new British commercial restrictions,[55] the Townshend Acts, and a decreasing money supply.[56] Not surprisingly, of the twenty-five men admitted to practice from 1765 to 1770, only eleven continued in active practice before the Supreme Court.[57] That Jay remained within this active group evidences not only his abilities and tenacity, but also his capacity to attract clients and secure business on referral from other attorneys.

Jay's first step toward survival was the formation of a partnership, a form of practice almost unheard of in colonial New York, with his college classmate and close friend, Robert R. Livingston, Jr. Even with the combined clientele of the Jay and Livingston families, the partnership seems to have made a precarious start.[58] In January, 1769, business was so modest that Jay was able to conduct it alone while Livingston traveled to his ancestral home at Clermont.[59] The April, 1769 motion calendar

---

[52] *See* note 6 *supra* & accompanying text.

[53] *See* note 45 *supra* & accompanying text.

[54] Minutes of the Supreme Court of Judicature, Oct. 21, 1766-Jan. 21, 1769, at 28, 29, 50, 247, 567, 606-07; Minutes of the Supreme Court of Judicature, April 18, 1769-May 2, 1772, at 15, 107, 113, 186, 188, 194, 243, 288, 319 (New York County Clerk's Office, Hall of Records, New York City).

[55] Klein, *supra* note 14, at 354.

[56] 5 C. Becker, *supra* note 26, at 26, 53-94.

[57] *See* Judicature Minutes, *supra* note 22.

[58] *Contra*, 1 Life, *supra* note 38, at 21.

[59] Letter from John Jay to R.R. Livingston, Jr., Jan., 1769, [Box 1] Livingston Papers (New-York Historical Society, New York City).

lists only four Jay-Livingston cases. Of these, at least two originated among Jay's relatives.[60] Had the partners begun practice without family backing and pooling their respective cases, both would have been quickly forced out of business. The partnership arrangement continued until October, 1771, when Jay's cases were ruled off in the joint law register that he and Livingston maintained for their Supreme Court of Judicature matters.[61] In 1771, Jay paid as much in clerk's fees for his individual cases as the Jay-Livingston firm had paid to the same clerk during the entire three years of its existence.[62]

During the partnership period matters other than law practice apparently occupied most of Jay's time. He rapidly replaced his elder brother, Augustus Jay, as the New York City representative of Jay family interests.[63] During the summer and fall of 1769 he was actively involved as clerk to the New York-New Jersey Boundary Commission, a royal body appointed by the Privy Council to fix the northern boundary of New Jersey. As clerk, Jay was expected to keep a thorough account of all of the proceedings, recording the activities of the commissioners in a minute book and preserving the written interrogatories of witnesses for future consideration.[64] Because the Commission followed civil law procedure and appeals were permitted from it to the Privy Council, Jay's clerkship experience with litigation papers for the Vice-Admiralty Court, which followed similar procedures, proved most valuable.[65] Jay's work with the Commission gave him a solid grounding in the operations of a mixed com-

---

[60] Minutes of the Supreme Court of Judicature, April 18, 1769-May 2, 1772, at 53 (New York County Clerk's Office, Hall of Records, New York City).

[61] The dissolution of the partnership began in January, 1771, when Jay and Livingston appeared in court separately as well as in pursuit of partnership matters. Their partnership register was closed in October, 1771. Law Register of John Jay and Robert R. Livingston, Jr. (BV Sec. New-York Historical Society, New York City); Minutes of the Supreme Court of Judicature, April 18, 1769-May 2, 1772, at 336, 384-85, (New York County Clerk's Office, Hall of Records, New York City).

[62] Entries for John Jay and Jay & Livingston in Account Book of George Clark, Clerk of the Supreme Court (New-York Historical Society, New York City).

[63] *See* John Jay's advertisements to rent family property, in N.Y. Gazette and Weekly Post Boy, Feb. 8, 1768; N.Y. Mercury, Jan. 19, 1767; *id.* Jan. 25, 1768. *See also* letter from Frederick Jay to John Jay, June 5, 1769 (Columbia University Libraries, Special Collections).

[64] A complete set of minutes, interrogatories and other Boundary Commission papers is in [Box 7] Jay Papers (New-York Historical Society, New York City). For a discussion of the commission and its proceedings, see Colonial Lawyer, *supra* note 9, at 100-17.

[65] *See* Johnson, *Civil Procedure in John Jay's New York*, 11 AM. J. LEGAL HIST. 69, 79 (1967).

mission. Colonial, and particularly Jay's, familiarity with this British imperial institution laid the basis for use of the device not only for the settlement of interstate boundary disputes under the Articles of Confederation, but also for adjustment of complex issues in international disputes.[66]

Benjamin Kissam, one of the agents selected by the New York General Assembly to argue the province's case, may have prompted Jay's appointment as clerk to the Boundary Commission. Certainly Kissam's referrals of law cases to Jay in the years following 1769 evidence his continuing encouragement of the young attorney. While Jay was trying some cases in the up-river counties, Kissam wrote him:

> If it was not for you, or some other such apostolic lawyer, my clients would be left in the lurch this court [*sic*], as I am afraid I cannot attend myself. But, sir, you have now a call to go forth into my vineyard; and this you must do, too, upon an evangelical principle—that the master may receive the fruits of it. . . .
>
> . . . I wish you good success with my consignments, and hope they'll come to a good market. If they don't I am sure it will not be the *factor's* fault; and if my clients' *wares* are bad, let them bear the loss.[67]

Despite Kissam's levity, he clearly took a considerable risk in trusting the trial of cases on circuit to his former clerk. The circuit ridings of the Supreme Court of Judicature resulted in the returns of jury verdicts to the court clerk, ready for the formal imposition of judgment by the court en banc; consequently, it was quite easy to do irreparable damage to the case during the trial on circuit. No greater compliment could be given to Jay's abilities than this vote of confidence by his former master.

III. Success at the Bar

From 1771 to 1775 John Jay established a successful and remunerative practice,[68] and by the eve of the Revolution he was

---

[66] J. Smith, *supra* note 24, at 462-63. For a discussion of Jay's association with the mixed commission, see Lillich, *The Jay Treaty Commissions*, 37 St. John's L. Rev. 260 (1963).

[67] Letter from B. Kissam to John Jay, Nov. 6, 1769, in 1 Life, *supra* note 38, at 21, 22.

[68] For a discussion of the mechanics of colonial law practice, see Johnson, *supra* note 65.

among the better known attorneys in the province of New York. Although family connections and referrals from Kissam played a part in his success, only hard work and determination elevated him above the level of his contemporaries. Jay's first step as an independent practitioner was to restrict the geographical area of his practice. He left the Dutchess County causes with his former partner, Livingston,[69] concentrating his country practice in the Common Pleas Court of Westchester County.[70] At the November, 1770, term of the Supreme Court of Judicature he opened eighteen cases in his individual name, and at the following term in New York City he added an additional eighteen cases to his independent trial docket.[71] The increased case load soon took its toll on Jay's health. From the fall of 1770 until the summer of 1771 he was under the care of three doctors for a swelling of muscles in his neck and a lingering fever.[72] The illness conquered, he returned to the task of increasing his store of pending cases. By late 1773, he had reached the apparent peak of his caseload, with 136 cases pending in the Supreme Court of Judicature and 118 pending in the Westchester County Court of Common Pleas.[73] Subsequent to this rapid expansion, Jay seems to have been content to open relatively fewer cases in the years 1773 and 1774. The loss of registers and court minutes limits the statistics available on his practice for the years from 1774 to 1776, but it seems likely that after late 1773 the time consumed by longstanding litigation curtailed the number of new cases he could open.

The pending cases in Jay's office included nearly every phase of civil litigation. Of those with identifiable subject matter, fifty-one were actions of debt on writings obligatory, twenty-five

---

[69] D-F Minutes of the Dutchess County Court of Common Pleas, 1766-1775 (Dutchess County Clerk's Office, Poughkeepsie, N.Y.).

[70] Minutes of the Westchester County Court of Common Pleas, 1723-1773; Minutes of the Westchester County Court of Common Pleas, 1774-1793 (Westchester County Clerk's Office, White Plains, N.Y.).

[71] Statistics on case openings in the Supreme Court are based on returns of *capias ad respondendum* writs reflected in the Minutes of the Supreme Court of Judicature, April 18, 1769-May 2, 1772, (New York County Clerk's Office, Hall of Records, New York City); Minutes of the Westchester County Court of Common Pleas, 1723-1773 (Westchester County Clerk's Office, White Plains, N.Y.). A writ book, also known as a praecipe book, provides the data for the Mayor's Court of New York City.

[72] Letter from John Jay to Samuel Kissam, Aug. 27, 1771, in Monaghan, *Samuel Kissam and John Jay*, 25 COLUM. U.Q. 127, 130-31 (1933).

[73] For a graphic representation of Jay's case openings and pending caseload in various courts, see Colonial Lawyer, *supra* note 9, at 256-64.

were actions in trespass for assault and battery, eleven were actions in ejectment, and nine were proceedings in certiorari.[74] Jay's practice involved him in minor litigation[75] as well as in the most significant cases of the period.

In January, 1773, Jay became defense counsel for Nathaniel Underhill in *King v. Underhill*, a case instituted by Attorney General John Tabor Kempe to compel the Supreme Court to render a strict interpretation of the suffrage requirements in Westchester borough elections.[76] Although the case was litigated by several well-known attorneys, and enjoyed considerable prominence at the time, its precise details appear to have been lost. Jay's principal service to Underhill, whose election as mayor of the borough was being challenged, was to secure two continuances until July, 1773. By then, the Crown Attorney seems to have lost interest in the case, and no further effort was made to try it. Underhill remained in office until well after the State of New York had declared its independence. In 1773 and 1774 Jay also represented the officials of the town and borough of Westchester in a mandamus action to order them to admit Gilial Honeywell and Isaac Legget to the offices of aldermen.[77] Jay used

---

[74] Law Register of John Jay (New York State Library, Albany). Certiorari in colonial New York practice was used by the Supreme Court of Judicature as a form of review of the administrative decisions of inferior courts of common pleas and general sessions. In all cases examined the certiorari was issued to the justices of the inferior court as a collegiate group; the normal form of appeal in common law matters was by writ of error.

[75] In the assault and battery action of *Budd v. Tompkins*, Jay defended three Westchester men charged with beating a schoolmaster who had sued them for his salary. Jay promptly moved for and obtained a change of venue from New York County, where his clients were imprisoned, to Westchester County, where they were better known. His affidavit in support of the motion alleged that all of the material witnesses were in Westchester. The convenience in taking testimony, of course, was secondary to the advantage of having a jury empaneled in Westchester to try the case. There was conflicting evidence concerning the original obligation upon which the schoolmaster had brought his action and concerning the defendants' claim that he had stolen corn from them. The jury, swayed by Jay's argument and influenced no doubt by sympathy for their neighbors, held for Jay's clients. Law Register of John Jay, *supra* note 74, at 22; [A-B] Lawsuits, John Tabor Kempe Papers (New-York Historical Society, New York); Minutes of the Supreme Court of Judicature, Apr. 18, 1769-May 2, 1772, at 306 (New York County Clerk's Office, Hall of Records, New York City). For a full discussion of the case, see Colonial Lawyer, *supra* note 9, at 148-51.

[76] H. Dawson, Westchester County, New York During the American Revolution 4 (1886); G. Pellew, John Jay 18-19 (1890); 1 J. Sparks, The Life of Gouverneur Morris 20 (1832); Law Register of John Jay, *supra* note 74, at 176; [S-U] Lawsuits, John Tabor Kempe Papers (New-York Historical Society, New York City).

[77] Minutes of the Supreme Court of Judicature, Apr. 21, 1772-Jan. 21, 1776, at 101, 131, 153 (New York County Clerk's Office, Hall of Records, New York City).

procedural motions to exclude the pair from office for the period from July, 1773, to April, 1774, but he was unable to prevent the Crown from eventually directing their installation. These two cases involving royal officials' meddling with local elections may have enhanced Jay's recognition and popularity throughout the province.

Jay was also involved in one of the most important cases of the day in the provincial High Court of Chancery, *Bloomer v. Hinchman*, a struggle by proxy between the vestry and the governor for control of a parish. When the first rector of the parish[78] received a call to another church, the vestry installed a Presbyterian divine in his place. The governor, however, intervened. Without vestry concurrence, the governor, who had the ecclesiastical power of nomination of clergymen by virtue of his commission, appointed as rector the Reverend Mr. Joshua Bloomer, an Anglican. The vestry countered by withholding Mr. Bloomer's salary. Caught between the two contending forces, Mr. Bloomer was forced by necessity to commence a suit against the vestrymen to collect his arrears in salary.[79] When Jay entered the case on Bloomer's behalf is unknown, but by December, 1771, Jay had come to the conclusion that he was being ignored by John Tabor Kempe, another attorney retained by Bloomer. Affronted at not being consulted at an important stage of the litigation, Jay dressed Kempe down in indelicate terms, drawing a sharp rebuke from Jay's senior counsel. Jay righteously continued to demand an explanation, which Kempe steadfastly refused to give.[80] The interchange indicates that Jay, whose social position was apparently superior to Kempe's, was willing to risk the enmity of the older man to protect his reputation at the bar. No further record of Jay's participation exists, although the biographer of his co-counsel, James Duane, gives Jay credit for participation in later phases of the case.[81] As might have been

---

[78] Established and incorporated in the spring of 1761, the parish, now known as Grace Church in Jamaica, had the Reverend Mr. Samuel Seabury as its first rector. A Thomas Hinchman, probably a relative of the defendant in this chancery case, was among the first vestrymen. Vestry Minutes and Register, 1764-1862, at 2 (Grace Church Parish Hall, Jamaica, N.Y.). Mr. Seabury was called to a Westchester County church. E. ALEXANDER, *supra* note 24, at 22.

[79] E. ALEXANDER, *supra* note 24, at 22; H. ONDERDONK, JR., ANTIQUITIES OF THE PARISH CHURCH, JAMAICA 68 (1880); 4 Minutes of the High Court of Chancery 46, 64, 69 and BM-1425-B (New York County Clerk's Office, Hall of Records, New York City).

[80] The interchange of letters is in [Box 2] Sedgwick Papers (Massachusetts Historical Society, Boston).

[81] E. ALEXANDER, *supra* note 24, at 22. Jay's connection with the litigation was prob-

anticipated, the governor, sitting in his capacity as chancellor, upheld his constitutional right to appoint rectors of the established church in the province of New York. The vestry's appeal to the Privy Council was interrupted by the outbreak of the American Revolution.

Although modest in relation to his practice in the Supreme Court of Judicature, Jay's practice in the Court of Chancery was quite respectable by 1772. Since fees in Chancery were slightly higher than those in Supreme Court practice, the added effort and care required to prepare a Chancery case were well compensated.[82] Had his practice continued beyond the Revolution, it is quite likely that Jay would have achieved a distinguished position as a counselor in the Chancery Court; his meticulous work habits[83] in drafting pleadings would have made him a most valuable adviser.

While practice in Chancery required exhaustive attention to detail, matters before the Prerogative Court of the province tended, for the most part, to be mere formalities. Acting as ordinary[84] for the province of New York, the governor bore the responsibility of admitting wills to probate and granting letters of administration for intestate estates. The primary activity of

---

ably as a counselor in the chancery, responsible for arguing the case and helping to draw the pleadings and interrogatories.

[82] *Compare* Chancery fees *with* Supreme Court fees, in William Livingston, Cost Book in the Supreme Court of Judicature, 1759-1772, at 438-39, 485 (New York Public Library). For a discussion of the constitutional struggle between the New York Council and the Assembly concerning the right to set Chancery and Admiralty Court fees, see 1 P. HAMLIN & C. BAKER, SUPREME COURT OF JUDICATURE OF THE PROVINCE OF NEW YORK 1691-1704, at 269-71 (New-York Historical Society Collections No. 78, 1945). In 1710 the conflict was resolved in favor of fees established by ordinance rather than by act of the Assembly. In Prerogative Court, the fees remained those established by a 1693 statute that had been ratified by a subsequent ordinance and royal approval. Johnson, *The Prerogative Court of New York*, 1686-1776, 17 AM. J. LEGAL HIST. 95, 101-02 (1973).

[83] Later when he was Chief Justice of the United States, Jay wrote to explain to his son how a letter should be answered. "[W]hen you answer a Letter, it is always advisable to read it over carefully and attentively, and to mark accurately *what part* it may be proper or necessary to answer, and what not." Letter from John Jay to Peter Augustus Jay, Dec. 4, 1790 (collection of John Jay DuBois, Rye, N.Y.). While he was a college student Jay kept a writing desk near his bed to make changes in compositions that occurred to him during the night. 1 LIFE, *supra* note 38, at 13.

[84] In ecclesiastical court practice the ordinary was the official in charge of a diocese or archdiocese and thus was empowered to act in probate matters. His jurisdiction could be limited by specific grant of a "peculiar" authority to another official. The ordinary in England was most commonly a bishop. *See generally* W. NELSON, LEX TESTAMENTARIA (1724). Although the bishop of London had general ecclesiastical supervision of New York, the authority to grant probate and letters testamentary in the province was vested in the royal governors. Johnson, *supra* note 82, at 97.

the Prerogative Court was the recording of wills, letters testamentary, and letters of administration. The court also had the power to compel an executor to file an inventory at the suit of legatees, a jurisdiction rarely exercised because it was shared with the High Court of Chancery and the Supreme Court of Judicature. The three cases noted in Jay's law register concerning the Prerogative Court involve such applications to the court for relief.[85]

Supplemented by an extensive backlog of cases in the Westchester County Court of Common Pleas and the Mayor's Court of the City of New York, John Jay's pending cases in the central courts at New York City promised him a comfortable living for several years to come. On the eve of the Revolution the loyalist Supreme Court Justice, Thomas Jones, noted that Jay was a gentleman of eminence in the law who had a sufficiency of ambition, a proper share of pride, and a reverence for the British constitution in church as well as state.[86] Another loyalist claimed that Jay's practice yielded him about £1,000 per annum, no mean sum when it is compared to the £1,287 per annum attributed to the veteran lawyer William Livingston or the £ 1,400 attributed to James Duane.[87]

IV. Continuing Legal Education

The extreme pressures of an active practice, coupled with the increasing competition for cases, could easily have robbed the colonial New York bar of its energy and interest in self-improvement. Yet men who had learned their law as clerks, squeezing self-education in amidst an avalanche of paper and heavy responsibilities, were able to cope with day-to-day practice and still find time to enhance their understanding of the law through reading and discussion. John Jay was quite representative of the group of colonial lawyers that made the decade before the American Revolution one of the golden ages of legal learning in the province. They did this through book purchases and participation in a legal discussion group called the Moot.

---

[85] Law Register of John Jay, *supra* note 74. For the procedures available to compel the filing of an inventory, see Johnson, *supra* note 82, at 138-39.

[86] 1 T. Jones, History of New York During the Revolutionary War 35 (E. DeLancey ed. 1879).

[87] Klein, *supra* note 14, at 355. Thomas Barclay claimed before the Commissioners on Loyalist Claims that Jay offered him a partnership and that Jay's business amounted to more than £1000 per year. Hamlin, *supra* note 2, at 94.

In the mid-1700's, the law of the province of New York was derived from the common and statutory law of England, as modified by the acts of the New York General Assembly and as either received or rejected by the usages of the courts in New York.[88] Since the opinions of New York courts were not available in printed reports, it is not surprising that the bulk of the volumes in John Jay's law library was printed in England and pertained to English common law. These materials were cited before the courts of the province, formed the basis for discussion at the Moot, and were the fundamental law for all practical purposes. Jay had been fortunate to inherit a good working library from his godfather and uncle, former Supreme Court Justice John Chambers, who died in 1764.[89] This legacy included all the volumes of the reports of Sir Edward Coke, Sir George Croke's *Reports*, the two then-published volumes of Peere Williams's *Reports*, and reports of Keilwey and Kelyng. Among the Chambers treatises in Jay's library were Matthew Hale's *History of the Pleas of the Crown*, Giles Jacobs' *Lex Mercatoria*, and William Nelson's *Lex Testamentaria*. Not content to rely upon this good basic collection, Jay conducted a program of purchases from 1770 through 1774. Jay first had substantial earnings from practice in 1771, and he seems to have spent part of his income from that year on the expansion of his library. Thereafter he apparently limited purchases to newly published case reports. For example, in 1773 he purchased William Salkeld's *Reports*, the new edition of which had been published in London earlier in the same year. In 1772, Jay purchased the third volume of Peere Williams's *Reports*, which had been published in 1768.

Jay's membership in the Moot also greatly advanced his legal education. From 1770 to 1774, this select group of lawyers met to debate points of law. At the same time they agreed to refrain from arguing the political issues that sharply divided them and soon destroyed not only the Moot, but royal government in New York and the society they knew. Jay's name is listed as a charter member of the Moot. From 1771 to 1772 he served as secretary of the organization.[90] The group's debates illustrate the complex

[88] For a discussion of the process of reception and modification, see 1 P. HAMLIN & C. BAKER, *supra* note 82, at 378-412.

[89] The discussion of Jay's library is based upon a physical examination of the extant library (Columbia University Law Library, Treasure Room). For a complete catalog, see Colonial Lawyer, *supra* note 9, at 264-72.

[90] Minutes of the Moot (private collection of Dr. John Jay DuBois, Rye, N.Y.)

problems of colonial practice that were relatively unknown in England. For example, the Moot debated whether a New Jersey decedent's estate, represented by a New Jersey executor, might be sued in New York for the decedent's obligation when the executor happened into New York. The members of the Moot considered the English rule that an executor may be sued even before a will is admitted to probate by the ecclesiastical court. Despite that rule and its implication that an executor is amenable to suit outside the jurisdiction granting representative capacity, they held that a New Jersey executor could be sued in his representative capacity only in New Jersey. New York and New Jersey, they recognized, had a special jural relationship quite unlike that between English counties or dioceses. The interprovincial problem was unique, and English precedent offered no solution.

Another Moot discussion of interprovincial legal relationships demonstrates that conflict of laws was among the legal issues foremost in the minds of colonial practitioners. The debate involved the effect of a New Jersey insolvency proceeding upon the rights of creditors residing in the province of New York. The hypothetical situation posed was that a New Jersey debtor, having obtained relief in New Jersey, then moved to New York, where he was sued by his New York creditors, some of whom had contracted with him in New Jersey. Could the New York creditors sue the New Jersey expatriate in spite of his release under the laws of the province of New Jersey? The Moot opined that as to debts actually contracted in New Jersey, there could be no recovery. Creditors who had appeared in the New Jersey insolvency proceeding would also be precluded from asserting their rights against the New Jersey insolvent. From the Moot's discussion we may assume that the situs of the making of the contract determined the law controling insolvency proceedings against the debtor. An appearance in the New Jersey insolvency proceeding by a creditor who had made his contract in New York, however, would constitute submission to the jurisdiction of the New Jersey court and a consent to the debtor's discharge under New Jersey law. New York creditors who had taken the precaution of contracting in New York, and who had

[hereinafter cited as DuBois Minutes]; Minutes of the Moot (BV Sec (Moot), New-York Historical Society) [hereinafter cited as Society Minutes]. For a more detailed treatment of the debates, see Colonial Lawyer, *supra* note 9, at 177-85.

not waived their rights by an appearance in the New Jersey insolvency proceeding, retained their privilege to institute collection actions in New York.

The Moot also struggled with difficult problems of New York law that continue to puzzle legal historians.[91] One debate that ended without a resolution concerned the 1677 English Statute of Frauds[92] and its applicability to the province. The statute, which antedated the creation of a New York General Assembly, did not expressly apply to His Majesty's dominions. Thus, identification of the parts of the statute that did apply depended on the arcane process of statutory reception—a combination of legal mythology, pragmatism, and mechanics. Resolution of questions of reception required fine constitutional reasoning as well as precise knowledge of the unwritten usages of the colonial practice. Evidence apparently unknown to the Moot, for instance, indicates that New York courts had, by usage, selectively adopted certain portions of the 1677 English Statute of Frauds.[93]

Although the debating functions of the Moot were of primary importance, the organization also served more public and regulative purposes. Its membership made it the outstanding professional organization in colonial New York, and it took strong positions against attorneys' advancing expenses on behalf of their litigating clients.[94] This stand coincided with the rules against champerty that Jay and others were already following. The limitation tended to remove the lawyer from the more commercial aspects of practice and to elevate him to a position similar to that of the English barrister. The Moot also evidenced concern for the bar's public relations. When court cryer Richard Wenman found himself in financial distress because attorneys

---

[91] *See, e.g.*, Beers v. Hotchkiss, 256 N.Y. 41, 175 N.E. 506, (1931) (Cardozo, C.J., on the Statute of Frauds).

[92] 29 Car. 2, c. 3. *See generally* Costigan, *The Date and Authorship of the Statute of Frauds*, 26 Harv. L. Rev. 329 (1913).

[93] New York had accepted that some witnesses, but not necessarily three, were required to validate a will of real property. Also accepted in New York were the English statute's requirements for nuncupative wills of personalty. Johnson, *supra* note 82, at 115-17. In 1774 the Assembly declared that the statute had been received by usage and then proceeded to amend it. Act of March 19, 1774, ch. 1678, 5 N.Y. Colonial Laws 689. An earlier attempt to enact an omnibus reception of those English statutes passed after the establishment of the provincial legislature was disallowed as an affront to royal rights. Act of Dec. 24, 1767, ch. 1327, 4 N.Y. Colonial Laws 953, *disallowed*, Order of Dec. 9, 1770, § 168, 5 Acts of the Privy Council of England (Colonial Series) 284.

[94] Society Minutes, *supra* note 90, at 17-18.

had failed to pay his fees, the Moot voted him an advance of 40 shillings per member to relieve his necessitous condition.[95]

The members of the Moot recognized a collective responsibility to the courts and cooperated in making their expertise available to the judges. Chief Justice Daniel Horsmanden sought their advice concerning the procedures to be used in examining the attorneys' fees after judgment and later asked them for proposals on the regulation of juries taken from the courtroom to view lands for purposes of valuation. The Moot carefully discussed both questions and certified its answers to the Chief Justice.[96]

It was proposed that a committee from the Moot attend the sittings of the Supreme Court on the first Friday of each quarterly term en banc and prepare for Moot members a list of the questions of law that would be argued during the term.[97] No record of the appointment of such a committee and no evidence of such cooperative action survive. Presumably this list would have permitted members to attend the arguments on issues in which they were interested. Unfortunately, the step from this activity to recording and publication of arguments and decisions was never taken by the Moot or by anyone else in colonial New York. The American Revolution intervened, breaking up the fellowship of the Moot and ending its activities.

V. The Quest for a Judgeship

The scholarly discussions of the Moot and the opinions rendered in New York City courts contrasted sharply with the earthy ad hoc decisions occasionally handed down by the laymen who served in the outlying county courts of justice. Attorneys practicing solely in those courts served relatively short apprenticeships and were badly versed in the English common law. These circumstances led John Jay and his former partner, Robert R. Livingston, Jr., to suggest that legally trained men be appointed to ride circuit among the various courts as advisers to the common pleas judges. When the proposal was originally submitted to the Council by Governor William Tryon in November, 1772, little objection arose. The matter was tabled, however, and attorney William Smith left the Council meeting

---

[95] DuBois Minutes, *supra* note 90.

[96] Society Minutes, *supra* note 90, at 18-19.

[97] *Id.* 15.

correctly convinced that delay was tantamount to the defeat of the proposal. The prominent political leader Oliver DeLancey realized that political capital could be made of the rural resentment that would greet the proposal. At the next meeting of the Council he characterized the plan as a repudiation of the work of the county magistrates. Again the matter was tabled. According to William Smith, DeLancey partisans sent letters to the counties to arouse local opposition to the proposal. The Livingston political faction rallied against the DeLanceys, but even the suggestion by Jay and Livingston that the advisers serve without compensation failed to obtain a favorable vote in the Council. In the end, Chief Justice Horsmanden agreed with the DeLancey councilors that the arrangement would raise public clamor and was therefore inexpedient.[98]

The proposal next emerged in 1774 in correspondence between Jay and John Vardill, a known loyalist who turned out to be an English spy. Vardill, apparently with the approval of his English superiors, had offered Jay a royal post. Writing in reply, Jay noted his lack of influence with Governor Tryon and suggested that Vardill might better serve Jay by pushing the idea of circuit-riding advisers. In 1784 Vardill used this letter as evidence of his own efforts on behalf of the Crown in proceedings before the Commissioners on Loyalist Claims. There is no evidence that the promise of influence swayed Jay's loyalties or led him to break his pledge to keep secret the deliberations of the First Continental Congress.[99]

Jay obviously desired a post on the bench. He was married in April, 1774, and was completing his sixth year in practice. He no doubt wished to move on to the ease, perquisites, and emoluments of the colonial Bench. Indeed, with marriage, he had already limited his cases outside New York City. But Jay's political position in the colony did not support his desires. The DeLancey faction, opponents of the Livingstons with whom Jay was linked by former partnership and marriage,[100] had already frustrated the proposal for court advisers. Nor did Jay have sufficient influence with Tryon, who in 1773 had found Robert

---

[98] WILLIAM SMITH, *supra* note 35, at 51, 129-30, 132-33.

[99] Letters from John Jay to J. Vardill, May 23, 1774, and Sept. 24, 1774 (AO 13/105/283, 321, Public Record Office, London). *See* F. MONAGHAN, *supra* note 4, at 53-54.

[100] Jay's wife was the former Sarah Livingston, daughter of William Livingston. *See generally* 2 T. JONES, *supra* note 86, at 474-75.

R. Livingston, Jr., the post of recorder for the City of New York.[101] Even with Vardill's solicitude, Jay was not to find a judicial post within the British Empire.

VI. Law and Society in Eighteenth-Century New York

The outbreak of the American Revolution in the province of New York obscures the fundamental changes that had already begun in the law and legal profession of the province.

At first glance, it is true, the New York bar had not changed since the late 1600's.[102] Admission to the profession continued to be based upon the traditional system of clerkship. Despite the infusion of new practitioners after 1765, the organized Supreme Court bar remained a relatively small and homogeneous group.[103] The monopolistic tendencies of the colonial advocates surfaced in the 1756 agreement to prohibit clerkships, and even the liberalizations of 1764 and 1767 maintained high barriers to entry into the profession.[104] Retaining financial and familial connections with the mercantile and landholding interests, the bar at times staunchly defended the status quo.[105] Initial success at the bar was dependent to a considerable degree on family referrals and the continued interest and patronage of one's mentor.[106] Access to an administrative office, such as Boundary Commission Clerk[107] or assistant to county judges,[108] was governed as much by personal contacts as by ability. In short, the Supreme Court bar in 1771, as in 1691, was a relatively small group of professionals closely tied to the powerful landholding and merchant families and dependent upon personal and official favor for advancement.

Yet the old relationships between the bar and society had begun to change. Reliance upon centralized gubernatorial pa-

---

[101] Minutes of the Court of General Sessions, May 21, 1772-Nov., 1790, at 65, 89 (New York Criminal Court Building, New York City). *See also* The Burghers of New Amsterdam and the Freemen of New York, 1675-1866, at 557 (New-York Historical Society Publication Fund No. 18, 1885).

[102] The Supreme Court of Judicature opened its first term on Oct. 6, 1691. For a description of its early bar, see 1 P. Hamlin & C. Baker, *supra* note 82, at 99-110.

[103] *See* text accompanying note 54 *supra*.

[104] *See* text accompanying notes 2-6, 45 *supra*.

[105] *See* text accompanying notes 34-43 *supra*.

[106] *See* text accompanying notes 57-62, 67 *supra*.

[107] *See* text accompanying notes 64-66 *supra*.

[108] *See* text accompanying notes 98-101 *supra*.

tronage may have begun to decrease in the years after 1760, with the mercantile community emerging as a more diffuse source of income and power. In order to supplement the modest rewards of practice, the bar traditionally had looked to appointments as surrogates to the Prerogative Court or as clerks in the High Court of Chancery.[109] We may surmise, however, that the increase in outside sources of income decreased the dependence on gubernatorial favor. Otherwise it would be strange that an established lawyer of Kissam's reputation would have undertaken the defense of William Prendergast,[110] stranger yet that Jay opposed the governor and attorney-general in the *Underwood* case.[111] And it would also be odd that Jay devoted so little effort to obtaining a judicial position.[112] Indeed, the unusually large number of debt collection cases in the practices of Jay and Kissam demonstrates that the mercantile community was a major source of litigation fees. Jay's comments on patronage posts, made in 1800, come as no surprise:

> Such offices give their Possessors no additional consideration, but on the contrary tend to diminish Confidence in their Professional Merit and Qualifications. The Emoluments of them are not worth the Time they consume, and cannot compensate for the Neglect of professional Studies and Pursuits. An Eminent Counsellor will attract more Respect, and command more influence, as well as money, than almost any office can confer or produce.[113]

Such a sentiment, ringing with pride in the profession and its independence, would have been out of place coming from a colonial lawyer of 1735.

Armed with this new-found independence, but still possess-

---

[109] Surrogate appointments, and a struggle over the principal surrogate's office, are discussed in Johnson, *supra* note 82, at 99-100, 102-04, 143-44. In the absence of a careful study of chancery procedure in New York, it is impossible to evaluate the patronage value of an appointment as a clerk in the chancery. The minutes of the court and file papers on deposit at the Historical Documents Collection, Queens College, Flushing, N.Y., indicate that all chancery papers were filed with a clerk, usually one of the leading Supreme Court attorneys, who was then entitled to fees for making copies of the originals.

[110] *See* text accompanying notes 34-43 *supra*.

[111] *See* text accompanying notes 76-77 *supra*.

[112] *See* text accompanying notes 98-101 *supra*.

[113] Letter from John Jay to Peter Augustus Jay, Dec. 18, 1800 (Columbia University Libraries, Special Collections).

ing its traditional connections with the sources of economic power in New York, the bar was not lacking in political power on the eve of the War for Independence.

In many ways the American Revolution was a lawyer's rebellion, for the critical issues concerned imperial constitutional law and the prerogatives of the Crown in the North American colonies. Lawyers were essential to the shaping of the peculiar constitutional rhetoric of the political pamphleteering, and a number of the popular issues were based upon technicalities of the law. The public agitation over appeal by writ of error, rather than by civil law appeal methods, was a problem of procedural law with constitutional overtones. Even when one considers the deft change of emphasis in characterizing *Forsey v. Cunningham* as an attack upon the institution of common law juries,[114] it is hard to imagine today how such matters flamed the coals of revolution. The electoral franchise, as defended by Jay in the *Underhill* case,[115] would seem to have been far better grist for the revolutionary's mill, and yet it went unheralded in the pre-Revolutionary history of New York. The Stamp Act, a simple revenue measure, was attacked not as a tax, but rather as an unconstitutional form of taxation by Parliament.[116] Again, the issue was one that in other times would probably have caused concern only among constitutional lawyers. Legal issues were the sparks that ignited the revolution.

Some New York lawyers may have contributed more than issues to the kindling of Revolution. A few, purportedly following the path of passive resistance, may have actually directed the Stamp Act mobs.[117] The Sons of Liberty placarded one John Cogshill Knap,[118] who was a threat to the legal community, suggesting that the profession did indeed help to select the targets of radical wrath. Knap, an English barrister, had been refused

---

[114] *See* text accompanying notes 23-25 *supra*.

[115] *See* text accompanying notes 76-77 *supra*.

[116] *See* text accompanying note 26 *supra*.

[117] E. MORGAN & H. MORGAN, *supra* note 26, at 184-85.

> The Lawyers levelled at, by the people, to be at the bottom of this disloyal Insurection and seconded by many people of property of the place and its neighbourhood.
>
> /Nov./7th the lawyers deemed by the people here to be Hornets and Firebrands of the Constitution. The Planners and Incendiaries of the present Rupture.

THE MONTRESOR JOURNALS, *supra* note 37, at 339. Captain John Montresor, a British Army engineer, held the "rabble" in utter contempt.

[118] THE MONTRESOR JOURNALS, *supra* note 37, at 342.

admission to the bar by the Supreme Court of Judicature but still attempted to practice law in the colony.[119] Although he had been harrassed prior to the effective date of the Stamp Act, afterwards the Sons of Liberty suggested that he be hunted "as with hounds."[120]

Nevertheless, the New York bar retained a strong element of conservatism, based upon its close affiliations with the landholding and merchant elite of the province. Many of its members viewed the rioting of tenants in the up-river counties with alarm.[121] The Court of Oyer and Terminer that condemned William Prendergast was composed of many of the lawyers who played a role in the resistance to royal power in New York City, not only in the courtroom but also, perhaps, in the direction of the New York City mob.[122] The Dutchess County trials resulted in the return of an anti-lawyer vote in the 1768 General Assembly elections.[123]

Like the general population of New York, the lawyers were sharply divided in their allegiances when the Revolution came. Approximately one-half of the men who were in practice with John Jay chose to become leaders in the struggle for independence; the remainder were loyal to the Crown.[124] Jay's affiliation with the patriot party does not seem to have come from pecuniary motives,[125] personal friendships,[126] or private resentments.[127] Rather, he was convinced by the justice of the patriot cause, and chose to sacrifice his lucrative practice in order to attend the meetings of the Continental Congress as a New York delegate and later to serve in prominent roles in the struggle for independence.

---

[119] The activities of Knap and the public attacks in the press may be followed in New York Gazette and Weekly Post Boy, June 14, July 5, 12, 26, Aug. 2, Sept. 13, 1764, Mar. 7, Apr. 25, 1765.

[120] The Montresor Journals, *supra* note 37, at 342.

[121] *See* notes 34-42 *supra* & accompanying text.

[122] John Morin Scott, a member of the court, apparently called for repeal or revolution during the Stamp Act crisis. *See* C. Becker, *supra* note 26, at 59-60.

[123] *Id.* 59-60; S. Lynd, *supra* note 43, at 51-53; I. Mark, *supra* note 34, at 158-59.

[124] Colonial Lawyer, *supra* note 9, at 233-34.

[125] Jay's clientele seems to have been equally divided between loyalists and patriots. *Id.* 234. This mix of clients suggests that the New York bar had not suffered the polarization that took place in Massachusetts. *See* Morris, *supra* note 26, at 205-15.

[126] Benjamin Kissam, Jay's friend and mentor, was among the loyalists. Colonial Lawyer, *supra* note 9, at 233-34.

[127] The frustration of Jay's quest for a judicial post, *see* text accompanying notes 98-101 *supra*, does not correlate with his emergence as a patriot.

Even more profound than the legal profession's impact upon the events leading to the American Revolution was the change in the study and analysis of law, as demonstrated by John Jay's brief legal career. Trained in the traditional clerkship method, Jay had the additional experience of working with the Debating Club and discussing theoretical, philosophical, political, and ethical issues. Furthermore, he associated with young men who were sensitive to the cruelties of the criminal law of the day, and later in life he was to show compassion toward condemned criminals and men and women bound in perpetual servitude. Bred in a generation of lawyers who found their precedents in English statutes and casebooks, Jay amassed a respectable library of those sources and a professional ability directed toward their prompt citation. Yet he also purchased books less useful to New York law and practice—titles on natural law and jurisprudence[128]—which opened his mind and the minds of his fellows to legal subjects beyond the pronouncements of the courts and parliaments at Westminster.

Most symptomatic of the subtle change in the New York legal profession was the rise of the Moot in 1770 and its survival for four years despite the sharp political controversies that threatened to divide its membership.[129] In a city teeming with social diversions, congeniality alone could not have preserved the Moot's popularity among the leading lawyers; rather, the challenging intellectual task of debating and resolving the troublesome legal problems of the day drew the attention and enthusiasm of Jay and his friends. As successful practitioners, they had the time to devote to discussion of law in the abstract, divorced from the hurried pressures of practice. The Moot may have been another product of the prosperity of the New York bar, but it is significant that the members of that bar, far from spending their time in nonprofessional pursuits, chose to devote themselves to matters of legal interest.

Had the Moot continued, it might have begun to publish opinions of the Supreme Court of Judicature and records of its own debates, stimulating more complex and current legal analysis. And the Moot may have had a direct impact on legal education. A member, Peter Van Schaack, established law

---

[128] *See* text accompanying notes 89-90 *supra*.

[129] *See* notes 90-97 *supra* & accompanying text.

classes at Kinderhook, New York, after the Revolution.[130] Van Schaack's school and the Litchfield Law School of Tapping Reeve[131] may well be considered the precursors of the academic law schools established in mid-nineteenth century America. The Moot may have been the connecting link between clerkship and pure academic training, the intermediary institution that recognized the need to sharpen the practitioner's legal arts through *both* analysis and observation. When the method of the Moot was applied to student as well as practitioner, the nature of training and the quality of the bar itself were totally altered.

The broadening views of law and jurisprudence would not have any discernible impact upon legal history until well after the American Revolution, but they undoubtedly had a significant influence upon the men of Jay's generation who were summoned to shape the public and private law of New York State and the United States. Similarly, the compassion felt by Jay and his friends toward the suffering of men in society would only gradually result in amelioration of the penal laws. Jay and his contemporaries were products of an age in transition—legal professionals who were fortunate to have been trained by more than the clerkship method alone, but nevertheless men who would never fully appreciate the dynamic and evolutionary qualities of jurisprudence. They built new states and a new nation, but the next generation—that of John Marshall, James Kent and Joseph Story—had to develop the legal framework of their creations.

---

[130] *See* H. VAN SCHAACK, *supra* note 14.
[131] HAMLIN, *supra* note 2, at 24 n.3.

Civil Procedure in John Jay's New York

IN HIS SEVEN YEARS OF LAW PRACTICE prior to the American Revolution, John Jay was retained in a large number of cases pending in the Supreme Court of Judicature, the Mayor's Court of the City of New York, and the Common Pleas courts of Dutchess and Westchester counties. In addition, he was engaged as counsel in several cases before the Court of Chancery, and as a law clerk had drawn pleadings for Benjamin Kissam in regard to Vice Admiralty proceedings. From a study of Jay's early career, one may gain considerable insight into the procedure before these various courts, and this article is the result of drawing generalizations concerning procedure from the court records pertaining to Jay's practice.

Like most lawyers of his day, Jay did not prepare a practice manual for his own use. Trained by a four-year clerkship, he had already been well indoctrinated in the mysteries of practice when he was admitted to the Bar. The technical phrases of pleading, the preparation and service of process, motion practice and calendar practice, were all second nature to a young lawyer who had prepared all of the litigation papers his master required. What is stated below is therefore not what Jay wrote he should do, but what he and his adversaries actually did in the conduct of litigation.

* * *

The Supreme Court of Judicature, created in 1691, possessed all of the powers vested in the English courts of King's Bench, Common Pleas and Exchequer.[1] Since procedures in the English prototype were not uniform, the Supreme Court of Judicature had a variety of alternatives from which to choose its practice rules. Consequently the colonials could adapt to their peculiar situation those English procedures that were most useful, and reject those practices at Westminster that were either inappropriate or cumbersome.

Although the Supreme Court possessed broad civil and crimi-

---

[1] Paul M. Hamlin and Charles E. Baker, eds., *Supreme Court of Judicature of the Province of New York 1691-1704* (New York: 1959), I, 68.

nal jurisdiction, an act of 1728 limited civil litigation before the Court to causes in which the amount in controversy exceeded £20.[2] Shortly after John Jay's admission to practice in October of 1768, the New York General Assembly raised the minimum amount to £50, and provided that a party beginning suit in the Supreme Court and recovering less than that amount, would be assessed to pay the defendant's costs.[3] These prohibitions and penalties against instituting certain cases in the Supreme Court also applied to the transfer of actions by means of habeas corpus or certiorari from the lower courts over which the Supreme Court of Judicature exercised appellate jurisdiction.

Preliminary process was necessary to bring an individual within the jurisdiction of the Supreme Court, thereby conferring upon the Court the power to render judgment against him. In the case of a resident of New York county, or a defendant found within the territorial limits of that county, the plaintiff's attorney drew up a Bill of New York, and issued the document to the sheriff for service. When the potential defendant resided in any other county, the attorney for the plaintiff drew up a *capias ad respondendum* and forwarded this writ to the sheriff of the defendant's county.[4] In either case the sheriff had to return the defendant in his custody at the next term of the Court, at which time the necessary *pro-forma* rule would be made to retain the defendant in the Court's custody until the matter had been determined. Usually the defendant endorsed his appearance on the writ, and the plaintiff moved that his appearance be entered; this procedure conferred jurisdiction upon the Court through the consent of the defendant. Should defendant refuse to so endorse his appearance, or if he were a stranger likely to leave the Province, he would be arrested and held in custody until bail was posted or judgment was rendered. In this situation the sheriff, upon returning the writ or bill, would be ordered by the Court to have the defendant in Court at the next term or the sheriff would be amerced forty shillings for contempt. Once the defendant was brought before the Court, he would be committed to prison to await the decision of his case. These preliminary steps, and the so-called "common rules"

---

[2] *Colonial Laws of New York from the Year 1664 to the Revolution* (5 vols., Albany: 1894), II, 462, 464 (September 20, 1728), hereafter cited as *N. Y. Colonial Laws.*

[3] *Ibid.*, IV, 1088 et. seq. (May 20, 1769).

[4] Law Register of John Jay, New York State Library, Albany, N. Y., p. 180 (hereafter Law Reg. Jay), where a bill of New York was used, with p. 147, where a capias was utilized. The matter is fully discussed in Julius Goebel, ed., *The Law Practice of Alexander Hamilton* (1 vol. to date, New York: 1964), I, 63, nt. 2.

mentioned above, involved a minimum of work for the attorney, and it is likely the lawyer did not have to appear in Court to request that the "common rule" be entered.[5]

Because of the routine nature of "common rule" entries, the clerk's minutes in the Westchester and Dutchess Common Pleas courts were limited to listing the common rules in the minutes immediately after the last entry for each term. Subsequently in New York State practice "common rule books" came into use for this purpose.

Doubtless some abuses arose through the commencement of vexatious actions, and the foregoing rules of preliminary process were to some degree ameliorated by several acts of the New York Assembly. For example the defendant in a replevin action was guaranteed interim possession of the property to which the action pertained.[6] A plaintiff bringing action in trespass, assault, false imprisonment or ejectment was deterred from acting precipitately by the rule that the defendant's costs would be assessed against the plaintiff should the defendant be held not guilty.[7] Furthermore, special bail in Supreme Court matters could be obtained by the defendant and his bondsmen appearing before local officials in the county of his residence, rather than travelling to New York to appear before a justice of the Supreme Court, as had been required previously.[8]

In instances where the plaintiff failed to post a bond as security for costs, or to file his declaration within twenty days after entry of the common rule, the defendant might move to "non-pross" him.[9] This remedy was also available if the plaintiff delayed in taking steps to bring the case to an early trial. The motion to "non-pross"

---

[5] The usual common rule required the defendant to plead in 20 days after receipt of the rule with the declaration of the plaintiff, Minutes of the Supreme Court of Judicature, New York County Clerk's Office, Hall of Records, N. Y. C. October 21, 1766-January 21, 1769, p. 624 (*Beekman v. Noxon*). If the defendant were in custody of the sheriff, upon the sheriff's certificate that he had received the papers on behalf of a defendant, the plaintiff might move for judgment for lack of a plea, Min. S. Ct. Jud., July 25, 1775-April 28, 1781, p. 94 (*Jay v. Lawrence*). In early New York State practice a personal appearance by the attorney was not required for the entry of a common rule, Goebel, *ibid.*, I, 57.

[6] *N. Y. Colonial Laws*, V, 76, 77 January 27, 1770). Replevin is an action to recover possession of certain personal property which plaintiff claims defendant unlawfully detains from him.

[7] *Ibid.*, V, 287, 288 (February 26, 1772).

[8] *Ibid.*, II, 464, 465 (September 20, 1728).

[9] Law Reg. Jay, p. 170 (*Ross v. Costigan*).

a plaintiff was usually made twice, and judgment was entered after the plaintiff failed to heed the first order of the Court.[10]

Once jurisdiction over the person of the defendant had been secured, the parties then proceeded to make whatever pre-trial motions they deemed necessary. Demurrers on formal grounds were discouraged, and an attorney asserting a formal defect in his adversary's pleading had to specify the formal defect; it was statutory policy that a large number of such flaws would not defeat judgment upon the merits, and that demurrers based upon formal grounds would ordinarily be denied.[11] In addition to demurring to the declaration or answer, or instead of demurring, a party might move for a change of venue so that the trial would be held in a county other than the one in which the defendant was served with process. This motion for change of venue was utilized very effectively by John Jay in his defense of a group of men accused of attacking and falsely imprisoning a Westchester schoolmaster. A bill of New York had been served upon the Westchester men while they were in New York City, and they were scheduled to stand trial before a New York county jury. After the change of venue was granted, Jay pleaded his clients "Not Guilty", and the Westchester county jury returned a similar verdict. Had the trial been held in the more sophisticated environs of New York county, and away from the area of the defendants' homes, a contrary verdict would have been much more likely.[12] It is significant that Jay's motion was made upon the ground of greater convenience for witnesses rather than the less plausible assertion of prejudice in New York county against his clients or their anti-intellectual activities. However either ground could have been advanced as the basis for the motion.

With preliminaries completed, the case was ready for trial either before the Supreme Court *en banc* at New York, or in cases arising outside the county of New York, before a circuit sitting of the Supreme Court at a county courthouse in the appropriate county. Circuits were held in Richmond county during the last week in May, in Orange, Dutchess, Ulster and Albany, in that order in June. The September circuit was constantly rearranged during the period of Jay's practice. In 1769 it was held first in

---

[10] Min. S. Ct. Jud., April 18, 1769-May 2, 1772, pp. 164, 268 *(Axtell v. Remsen)*; see also *N. Y. Colonial Laws*, V, 207, 208 (February 16, 1771).

[11] *Ibid.*, V, 537 (March 8, 1773).

[12] Venue motion papers, consisting of notice and affidavit, were served three days before the return date; see Law Register, Jay and Livingston, New York Historical Society, N. Y. C., p. 22 (hereafter Law Reg. Jay & L.).

Kings county, then in Suffolk, Queens and Westchester. With 1770 and 1771 the order was changed to Kings, Queens, Suffolk and Westchester. In 1772 the sequence was again altered to Westchester, Queens, Kings, and Suffolk, and this routine was retained in 1773, only to be changed in 1774 to Westchester, Queens, Suffolk and Kings.[13] Since Jay's practice was limited to appearances in the first circuit named, and in Westchester county, the confused pattern of sittings in Long Island would not have greatly inconvenienced him.

The circuit sittings of the Supreme Court were held before one Justice of the Court, and two or more judges of the county Court of Common Pleas.[14] The issue roll, prepared by the plaintiff's attorney, was delivered to the Clerk of the Circuit Court; during John Jay's period of practice, this office was held by Richard Morris who in addition served as the unsalaried Judge of the Court of Vice-Admiralty. Should the plaintiff's attorney neglect to file the issue roll, the defendant could move to compel the plaintiff to do so upon pain of suffering a non-suit.[15] Once the issue roll, containing the declaration and answer, was on file with the Clerk of the Circuit, the case could be noticed for trial in the usual manner.

Cases were placed on the calendar for trial by means of a notice for trial. After May 1, 1771 the moving party was required to give fourteen days' notice of trial if the other party resided more than forty miles from the place the trial would take place. When the other party resided at a lesser distance, eight days' notice would be sufficient; however, the customary procedure before the Bar was to give approximately three weeks' notice of trial, and the notice could be countermanded upon the opposing party's motion within six days of trial.[16]

---

[13] Min. S. Ct. Jud., April 18, 1769-May 2, 1772, pp. 17, 18, 62, 189, 235, 352, 359, 396, 522; *ibid.*, April 21, 1772-January 17, 1776, pp. 27, 92, 110, 152, 162, 191; *ibid.*, July 25, 1775-April 28, 781, p. 84.

[14] This procedure continued well into the nineteenth century, the courts so held in each county being termed "Circuit Courts and Special Terms of the Supreme Court."

[15] *N. Y. Colonial Laws*, V, 207, 208. The importance of having an attorney available at New York City for service would seem readily apparent. However it was not until the Supreme Court order of October 13, 1772 that attorneys who did not maintain city offices were required to file with the court clerk a designation of an agent who would receive process on their behalf. If no agent was designated, the clerk was authorized to accept process in the name of a non-resident attorney. The rule became effective Apr. 1, 1773, Min. S. Ct. Jud., April 21, 1772-January 17, 1776, p. 61.

[16] *N. Y. Colonial Laws*, V, 207, 208 (February 16, 1771). Cf. Hamilton's Practice Manual, Goebel, ed., *Law Practice Hamilton*, I, 59, with Law Reg. Jay, p. 137, showing a 25-day notice of trial in 1773.

Since 1699 the assembling and selection of a jury had been regulated by acts of the General Assembly. The attorney bringing his case to issue was therefore required to comply with the statutory procedures, which were subject to suspension only when a foreign jury had to be selected.[17] After the case had been noted for trial, the attorney who had noticed the matter obtained a writ of venire which directed the sheriff of the county to assemble qualified jurors to serve in the case. All male inhabitants between the ages of 21 and 70 listed in the county assessment lists, and possessing a freehold in land of the value of £60 or more, were eligible to serve on juries.[18] In the event a freeholder summoned had served within the previous year, the Court would excuse him from service.[19] The normal procedure was that the jurors, not less than forty-eight nor more than seventy-two in number, would be returned by the sheriff at least six days before the first day of the term at which they were to serve. Attorneys for the litigants would receive at least five days' notice of the jurors returned.[20] Should either party desire a special jury, he might request the sheriff to bring before a Justice of the Court, a list of jurors, and upon three days' notice to his adversary, move to strike a jury. This process permitted the attorneys to select from the sheriff's list a panel of twenty-four, the jurors so selected being certified to the Clerk of the Court as having been specially selected to serve in the particular case.[21]

Precisely what occurred at a jury trial in the Supreme Court of Judicature is left to the reader's conjecture, for no written transcript of those hearings was made.[22] The minute books of the Court reflect only the names of witnesses and upon whose behalf they

---

[17] Act of May 16, 1699, *N. Y. Colonial Laws*, I, 387-388, renewed and amended November 11, 1726, *ibid.*, II, 345; act regulating practice in Jay's time was that of December 6, 1726, *ibid.*, II, 185-192, made perpetual on November 27, 1741, *ibid.*, III, 599. Foreign juries were used in causes involving the law merchant.

[18] *N. Y. Colonial Laws*, II, 185-187 (December 6, 1726).

[19] *Ibid.*, II, 187.

[20] *Ibid.*, II, 188, 189. The names would be picked for each petty jury at random from a box, and counsel would be extended the opportunity to challenge any juror so selected to try the case.

[21] Law Reg. Jay, p. 137. Cf. Goebel, ed., *Law Practice Hamilton*, I, 61. The three-day notice would seem subject to waiver by the parties, *Leadbetter v. Harison*, Min. S. Ct. Jud., April 18, 1769-May 2, 1772, pp. 349-350.

[22] From Chief Justice Horsmanden's comments concerning jury trials in *Report of an Action of Assault and Battery . . . Between Thomas Forsey and Waddel Cunningham*, p. 12, it is clear that no written transcript of trial proceedings was taken.

were called to testify. In Jay's case of *Leadbetter v. Harison,* Jay called ten witnesses for the plaintiff who was suing his former business partner for slander. In opposition, Jay's college classmate, Richard Harison, called three witnesses to testify for the defendant, and then took the stand himself in support of his kinsman's case.[23] One may surmise that the trial was conducted by direct, cross and re-direct examination of the witnesses, and the testimony adduced should have entertained the throngs who customarily assembled in colonial court rooms. From contemporary proceedings in the Court of Chancery, we know that the two litigants in the Supreme Court action had been involved in a lengthy and bitter dispute over their respective shares in a brewery business, and that Jay's client had been subjected to considerable embarrassment and ridicule by the principal partner, George Harison.[24] Unfortunately the testimony in the slander case did not inspire any of the onlookers to reduce it to writing; and since the judgment roll is not in existence, the harsh words exchanged between the partners are no longer available to us.

A month after Jay's admission to practice in 1768 there was enacted a statutory method for resolving issues of fact without trial by jury in the Supreme Court; this involved a reference of the matter to three referees when the controversy would require the examination of lengthy accounts.[25] The referees were authorized to make a decision upon the case, and their report in favor of the plaintiff would be confirmed as a judgment upon motion to the Court. If their determination was in favor of the defendant, judgment of non-pross would be entered and the action dismissed. One case where Jay represented the successful plaintiff was handled in this manner, and consumed a total of two days in hearings.[26] After decision was given for Jay's client, judgment was entered upon the filing of the referee's report and motion to the Court.

When trial was had before the Supreme Court *en banc* at New York City the judgment roll prepared by the successful party was

---

23 Min. S. Ct. Jud., April 18, 1769-May 2, 1772, pp. 358-359.

24 Chancery Minutes, IV, 21, 137, New York County Clerk, Record Division, Hall of Records, N. Y. C.; bill in chancery at Decrees Before 1800, Chancery Room, Court of Appeals Hall, Albany, N. Y., L-76.

25 *N. Y. Colonial Laws,* IV, 1040-1042 (December 31, 1768). Actually the use of arbitration in New York courts was common in the seventeenth century and persisted throughout the colonial period; this statute merely regularized procedures in the Supreme Court of Judicature.

26 *Halstead v. Lyons,* Law Reg. Jay, p. 65; the referee's report is filed under "Attachment vs. Vessels 1752-1835", N. Y. Co. Clerk's office, Hall of Records, N. Y. C.

presented to the Chief Justice for signature, and then filed with the Clerk of the Court. Thereafter execution could issue on the judgment. However when trial was had at a circuit sitting of the Court, the issue roll, duly endorsed by the Clerk of the Circuit with the jury verdict, was approved by the Court at its next sitting *en banc,* and then filed with the Clerk of the Court, thereby reducing the matter to judgment.[27] Appeals by writ of error were possible, initially to the Governor and Council; final appeals to the King in Privy Council were available in certain cases.

After judgment had been entered and docketed, two forms of execution were available to the judgment creditor. Execution by *fieri facias* directed that the judgment debtor's goods be seized in satisfaction of the judgment; should the sheriff return that he had seized the property of the defendant and it remained in his hands for lack of buyers, a *venditione exponas* would issue on the motion of the plaintiff, instructing that the goods be sold at public auction.[28] Far more likely to succeed was the second form of execution by *capias ad satisfaciendum,* requiring that the defendant be arrested and held in confinement until the judgment was satisfied.[29] In transmitting either writ to the sheriff, the attorney for the plaintiff was required to endorse on the reverse the amount of the debt with interest and costs. Should the case involve a penal bill obligatory, the attorney issuing the execution was charged with endorsing only the amount of the debt, without regard to the penalty in the bond.[30]

In the county Courts of Common Pleas and the Mayor's Courts of Albany, New York and Westchester Borough, the foregoing outline of procedure seems to have been followed. However, the Common Pleas courts were to some degree hampered by the absence of province-wide jurisdiction. The Westchester Common Pleas court, for example, issued an order that all parties defendant appearing without attorneys would be subject to service by posting notices in the Common Room of the county courthouse. Service of

---

[27] See Jay's case of *Downing v. Oakley,* Parchment 1 K-2, N. Y. Co. Clerk, Hall of Records, N. Y. C. For regulation of recording of judgments see *N. Y. Colonial Laws,* V, 636-638 (1774).

[28] *Smith v. Hickman,* Law Reg. Jay & L., p. 15.

[29] *White v. Abeel,* Law Reg. Jay, p. 205. Even in colonial times the harsh results of this type of execution were ameliorated; see *N. Y. Colonial Laws,* III, 753-756 (Act of October 4, 1732).

[30] *N. Y. Colonial Laws,* II, 676 (October 29, 1730). The unjust situation that existed before 1730 is described in my study, *The Law Merchant and Negotiable Instruments in Colonial New York 1664-1730* (Chicago: 1963), p. 32-33.

papers upon the official in charge of the room was to be considered due and sufficient service of the papers.[31]

Appeals from the lower courts by writ of error were not uncommon and John Jay had his share of this type of practice. Once the writ of error was returned to the Supreme Court with the record attached, the appellant filed his assignment of errors and the appellee joined issue with a rejoinder. The matter was then set down for a hearing in the Supreme Court by means of a motion made in the term preceding the term in which the hearing was to take place. The Supreme Court, after argument of the points of law at the hearing, entered its order either reversing the court below or confirming its judgment.[32] The procedures in regard to a writ of certiorari, directed to justices of the peace and Courts of General Sessions, were approximately the same as those outlined for writs of error.[33]

Although appeal by writ of error was the usual mode of relief from adverse judgments in the Court of Common Pleas, in the outlying counties where Jay did not practice, motions in arrest of judgment were popular. For example, in the Tryon County Court of Common Pleas, I have found two cases in which executions on judgment were stayed and motions in arrest of judgment entertained. In one of those cases, judgment was actually arrested.[34] The obvious advantage of this procedure over the writ of error was that the delay and inconvenience incident to appellate review at New York City were thereby eliminated.

Quite distinct from the procedures followed in the common law courts were the steps necessary to prosecute a suit in the New York Court of Chancery. This tribunal exercised broad equitable jurisdiction, being concerned in the appointment of guardians for infants and incompetents, the foreclosure of equities of redemption in real property, the prevention of breaches of trust and confidence, and the granting of injunctive relief. Unfortunately the Governors, who occupied the office of Chancellor by virtue of their guberna-

---

31 Minutes of the Court of Common Pleas, Westchester County Clerk's office, White Plains, N. Y., I, under date November 8, 1771.

32 See *Bemus v. Fellows*, Law Reg. Jay, p. 138; *Hunt v. Leggett*, *ibid.*, p. 155. The practice was regulated by the act of December 23, 1765, *N. Y. Colonial Laws*, IV, 801, 802. If appellee failed to appear he was compelled to do so by a *scire facias ad audendum errores*, see *Vrooman v. Zeele*, *ibid.*, p. 143.

33 *Ibid.*, pp. 128, 197.

34 Tryon County Common Pleas Minutes, Division of History, Montgomery County Clerk's Office, Fonda, New York, under date December 14, 1774 *(Whitmore v. Shew)*, and September 14, 1774 *(Hough v. Whitmore)*. In the first case judgment was ordered arrested.

torial commissions, were usually laymen, and the Chancery Court was hampered by its presiding officer being inexpert in law and limited in the amount of time he could devote to proceedings before the Court. With the appointment of a Master of the Rolls in 1773 the proceedings became more formal and hearings were held at more frequent intervals.

Chancery proceedings were commenced by filing a bill in chancery with one of the clerks in chancery.[35] The bill in chancery was drawn upon a large piece of parchment that was approximately three feet square. After being signed by the solicitor and counsel for the complainant, the bill was ready for filing. This was done before an official termed a clerk in chancery. Precisely how one was appointed to this office is difficult to determine. It is obvious, however, that the leading attorneys of the Province of New York functioned as clerks in chancery; among their number are included James Duane and John McKesson. The clerk in chancery was not counsel or solicitor for either party to the suit, but all papers in the suit were filed with the same clerk, who would provide certified copies at a fixed fee per folio page. One is compelled to conclude that the clerk in chancery was a member of the Bar who made his office available as a repository for papers in chancery litigation. When the Chancellor called a term of court, the various clerks were alerted to attend the session, at which time they were to make available the bills, answers, interrogatories, and other papers deposited with them. In this way the Chancery Court could sit wherever the Chancellor happened to be, and the clerk in chancery provided all of the papers deemed necessary for the Chancellor's consideration of the cause. Also, the presence of an independent lawyer serving as clerk in chancery would make available to the Governor a disinterested expert to whom he could turn for advice.

Testimony in chancery matters was usually taken by means of interrogatories of witnesses. Questions and answers would be reduced to writing, sworn to before the clerk in chancery, and then filed for future use in the case. In this manner testimony could be obtained at the convenience of the parties, and the affidavits and documents could be preserved until some later date when the case would be presented to the Chancellor for decision and decree.[36] As opposing parties were always given the opportunity to cross-examine the witnesses, the eliciting of evidence by this method was rea-

---

[35] This discussion is based upon my examination of papers filed in the Chancery Room, Court of Appeals Hall, Albany, N. Y. and the N. Y. Co. Clerk's Office, Hall of Records, N. Y. C.

[36] *Jager v. Van Benthuysen,* Chancery Decrees Before 1800, V-33, Chancery Room, Court of Appeals Hall, Albany, N. Y.

sonably satisfactory, although the Chancellor did not have the opportunity to observe the deportment of the various witnesses and evaluate their credibility for himself. Once the Chancellor had reached a decision and signed his decree, a party wishing to appeal to the King in Council began this appellate procedure by filing a notice of appeal.[37]

Jay did not try a case in the Court of Vice-Admiralty during the period of his practice. This was not unusual for the number of causes heard in Vice-Admiralty in peace time was extremely small. However, as a law clerk Jay did prepare the litigation papers for two Vice-Admiralty cases tried by his master, Benjamin Kissam.[38] These papers reflect that proceedings in Vice-Admiralty were substantially similar to those outlined above for the Court of Chancery. However the post of Judge of Admiralty was occupied by an appointee of the Crown, traditionally from the Morris family of New York. As a result the Court met regularly at monthly intervals to hear any causes that might be brought to issue before it. Since the Judge was unsalaried, it became the custom to sweeten his personality and lighten the spirit of the proceedings by the parties to the case providing some rum or wine for the use of the Court, and the clerk taking the minutes was careful to record the "refreshment" provided in the minutes of the Court. Once a decree was reached after the hearing, a party wishing to appeal could do so. Appeals would lie to the Court of Admiralty in England in all cases except those involving British treaties, in which case appeals would lie to the King in Privy Council. In either case the appeal was commenced by filing of a notice of appeal.

Civil practice in New York in the last decade of the colonial period was fairly close to the English pattern, both in common law and equity courts. Attorneys of John Jay's generation were, of necessity, men of learning in the common law of England and the less certain but more pertinent law of the Province of New York. To properly plead a case and bring the matter to issue in any of the above courts required a thorough knowledge of procedure,

---

37 Decree and Notice of Appeal in *Bloomer v. Hinchman*, at BM-1425-B, N. Y. Co. Clerk, Hall of Records, N. Y. C.

38 The cases are *Sinclair v. The Nancy*, with file papers at Vice Admiralty Court, Province of New York, File Papers, Salvage Papers A-Z, National Archives, Washington, D. C., with decree at Charles M. Hough, *Reports of Cases in the Vice Admiralty Court of the Province of New York . . .* (New Haven: 1925), pp. 225-227, and *Apthorpe v. The Prince of Wales*, file papers at Vice Admiralty Court, Province of New York, File Papers Customs Cases, M-Z, National Archives, Washington, D. C., with decree at Hough, *Reports*, pp. 219-222.

which then, as now, was drawn from a variety of court rules and statutes. What is surprising is the degree to which this pre-Revolutionary procedure was perpetuated in the early national period of American history. Until the enactment of the procedural codes in 1848, New York courts continued to follow the colonial pattern, and John Jay would have been just as familiar with litigation procedures in 1825 as he had been fifty years before when he left practice to begin his career of public service.

George Harison's Protest: New Light on *Forsey* versus *Cunningham*

A waterfront sword fight between two New York merchants in 1763 led to a constitutional conflict affecting the right of trial by jury. A document recently acquired by the New-York Historical Society gives new information on the case and also provides the only known description of legal procedure in a New York colonial court.

FEW LEGAL CASES of constitutional significance arose in colonial New York, and it is for this reason that the litigation in *Forsey* v. *Cunningham* is of paramount importance to the student of early New York legal history.[1] Involving the right of a party to appeal to the Governor and Council from what was allegedly an excessive verdict by a common law jury, *Forsey* v. *Cunningham* eventually became the focal point of a political struggle between the acting executive, Lieutenant Governor Cadwallader Colden, and the entire Bench, Bar and Royal Council of the Province. Each new development was

[1] See Alice M. Keyes, *Cadwallader Colden* (New York: Columbia University Press, 1908), pp. 300-309; Edward P. Alexander, *A Revolutionary Conservative, James Duane of New York* (New York: Columbia University Press, 1938), pp. 26-27; George Dangerfield, *Chancellor Robert R. Livingston of New York, 1746-1813* (New York: Harcourt, Brace & Co., 1960); Milton M. Klein, "Prelude to Revolution in New York: Jury Trials and Judicial Tenure," *William and Mary Quarterly*, 3rd ser., XVII (1960) 439-462 [hereafter, Klein, "Prelude," *Wm&MQ, XVII*.]; Joseph H. Smith, *Appeals to the Privy Council from the American Plantations* (New York: Columbia University Press, 1950), pp. 392-416 [hereafter, Smith, *Appeals*]. A primary source is *The Report of a Case of, Assault, Battery and Wounding Tried in the Supreme Court of Judicature for the Province of New York between Thomas Forsey, Plaintiff, and Waddel Cunningham Defendant* (New York: John Holt, 1764), Evans Nos. 9660 and 10190, [hereafter, *Report*].

brought to the attention of the public through newspaper articles or printed pamphlets; simultaneously each contestant sought the approval and support of both the Board of Trade and Privy Council in London. Thus it was that from a felonious assault two law cases developed, and the second of these led to the presentation of a constitutional issue that far transcended the interests of the actual parties and the petty infighting between colonial politicians.

As is so frequently the case, a technical question of legal procedure vitally affected not only the substantive rights of the parties, but also the constitutional structure of the judicial system of the Province of New York. The issue in *Forsey* v. *Cunningham* involved the right of a party deeming himself aggrieved by the verdict of a common law jury to appeal from that verdict. Common law appeals in New York since the creation of the Supreme Court of Judicature in 1691 had been entirely by writ of error. This system required the party to set forth specifically what his exceptions were to the various papers filed in the case or the orders entered by the Court. It was necessary to present for review the filed paper or a transcript of the order of which the appealing party complained. Since no record was kept of testimony, there could be no appeal on the basis of facts, and hence the jury's verdict, which is essentially a finding of facts, could not be altered through the means of an appeal by a writ of error. This was the invariable practice until the case of *Forsey* v. *Cunningham* in 1764. Established by the custom and usage of the Bar and the ancient practice of the Court, ratified by successive gubernatorial instructions, this tradition was firmly embodied in the fundamental law of the Province. For all intents and purposes it was an old usage which had been elevated to constitutional status in the law of New York. Yet it is important to note at the outset that the issue in *Forsey* v. *Cunningham* was not whether the Governor and Council could hear appeals. This was a tradition dating back to the first days of English occupation of New York; rather the issue in this case was *how* an appeal could be taken in conformance with the constitution of the Province of New York.

Crucial to the constitutional issue in the case was an alteration in the gubernatorial instructions issued to Sir Danvers Osborne in 1753. At that time the clerks in the Board of

Cadwallader Colden, by an unknown artist. [*Courtesy of* New-York Historical Society, *New York City.*]

Trade forwarded to the Privy Council an instruction that was slightly different from the previous one governing appeals to the New York Governor and Council. The earlier phraseology had been to permit "appeals by writ of error," whereas the 1753 instruction deleted the last four words. Quite possibly the change was a clerical error, but once committed it was perpetuated in all subsequent instructions. A 1754 case, *Obriant* v. *Bryant,* had construed another part of the altered instruction,[2] but as far as the law of New York was concerned, the issue presented in *Forsey* v. *Cunningham* was a novel one.

The case found its bloody inception in a violent waterfront argument between Thomas Forsey and Waddell Cunningham on the 29th of July 1763. Both were merchants of means, but when tempers flared swords were drawn and in the resultant combat Cunningham stabbed Forsey through the lungs. A criminal prosecution was instituted and Cunningham was fined £50 because of the assault, but Forsey's recovery precluded any homicide case being brought against Cunningham. Before news of Forsey's recovery had arrived at Whitehall, the Earl of Halifax as Secretary of State had informed Lieutenant Governor Colden that should Cunningham be convicted of manslaughter or murder, execution should be stayed.[3] Historians have yet to delineate the complex web of political and personal loyalties that were responsible for this interest in Cunningham's fate. Suffice it to say that the imperial authorities were to follow the development of this case with more than their usual detached concern.

Even before the criminal prosecution for assault and battery had gone to judgment against Cunningham, Forsey instructed his attorneys, John Morin Scott and William Smith, Jr., to commence a civil action for damages against the assailant. The declaration alleged that Forsey had been incapacitated for eighty-two days and that his injuries amounted to some £5,000.[4] Defendant Cunningham appeared and denied all of the material allegations and the matter was set down for trial on October 25, 1764.[5] It is the events of this and the five days following that are illuminated by a document recently acquired by the New-York Historical Society—the "Protest" of George Harison, a New York notary public.

[2] Dorothy R. Dillon, *The New York Triumvirate* (New York: Columbia University Press, 1949), pp. 66, 68.

[3] *Report,* p. 1; Grand jury presentment, July 30, 1763, Miscellaneous Manuscripts, Waddel Cunningham, New-York Historical Society; Smith, *Appeals,* p. 390; Klein, "Prelude," *Wm&MQ,* XVII, 454; "The Letters and Papers of, Cadwallader Colden, Vol. VI," New-York Historical Society *Collections,* LV, 236 [Sept. 5, 1763], [hereafter, "Colden Papers, VI," NYHS Collections, LV].

[4] Declaration at PL 1754-1837,F 402, New York County Clerk's Office, Hall of Records, New York City. As to postponements and subsequent proceedings see the judgment roll at Parchments 21 A-8, New York County Clerk's Office, Hall of Records, New York City [this repository will hereafter be cited, NY Co.Clk., HR, NYC].

[5] Judgment roll, *ibid.,* and Minutes of the Supreme Court of Judicature, July 31, 1764-Aug. 2, 1766, p. 56 [Oct. 17, 1764], NY Co.Clk, HR, NYC.

Attestation page of George Harison's Protest. [*Courtesy of* New-York Historical Society, *New York City.*]

According to the "Protest", Harison had been asked to attend the trial by Robert Ross Waddell, who had been appointed attorney-in-fact to represent Cunningham who was in England at the time the case was tried. Waddell wished Harison and two other notaries public to listen to the trial and to take down the proceedings in such a way that a record of the case would be available. Harison did so, assisted by James Emott and attorney-at-law Benjamin Kissam. When the evidence was submitted to the jury the Court adjourned for the day, and before it reconvened the following morning Waddell had discovered that the verdict was against Cunningham. At this point Waddell attempted to persuade various members of the Bar to appeal the case to the Governor and Council, but since no attorney would undertake the appeal upon the facts, Harison agreed to do so. No notary public had appeared in Court as an attorney since the last days of Dutch rule in

New York, and the justices of the Supreme Court properly refused to recognize him as a practitioner at its bar. After the denial of Harison's "motion" for an appeal, he and Waddell prepared a more formal request for permission to enter the appeal before the Supreme Court. This consisted of an appeal bond, a copy of the Governor's instructions concerning appeals, and a formal written request that an appeal be entered. On October 26th this document was filed with the Court, which again vehemently refused to recognize Harison's right to appear in Court nor to permit such a mode of appeal.

On October 30th, possibly with the "Protest" in hand, George Harison and Robert Ross Waddell called on Lieutenant Governor Cadwallader Colden. Apparently John Tabor Kempe, the Attorney General, was present and advised them and Colden that an appeal by writ of error was the only procedure available to them. Harison, having read of the ecclesiastical court's writ of inhibition, questioned Kempe concerning it, but the Attorney General assured him that this relief was available only in courts operating under civil law procedures. Colden informed all present that he intended to do right in the matter, and then stated to Harison and Waddell that they should call again the next day. In the intervening period, Kempe submitted a detailed memorandum of law unequivocally denying any right of appeal in New York common law courts other than by writ of error.[6]

True to his word, Colden the following day issued a "writ" prepared in a form roughly similar to that of a subpoena, addressed to the Chief Justice and Justice of the Supreme Court of Judicature, directing that all proceedings in *Forsey* v. *Cunningham* be stayed. Three days later Colden issued another "writ," directing all of the Supreme Court judges to appear before the Governor and Council. They were to bring with them ". . . all and every . . . Proceedings, . . ." in the case. In defiance of the first "writ," Chief Justice Horsmanden signed the judgment roll after the "writ" was served upon him.[7] However the clerks of the Court refused to file the judgment roll and no writ directing execution by seizure of defendant's

[6] Harison to Colden, Oct. 30, 1764, "Colden Papers, VII", NYHS *Collections,* LV, 387, 388.

[7] A judgment roll is an engrossed parchment record of the pleadings and disposition of the case, prepared by the successful litigant, signed by the presiding justice and entered (filed) by the Clerk of the Court.

property was issued.[8] The date set for the appearance of the justices of the Supreme Court before the Council was November 14th, and in the intervening two weeks neither Colden nor the lawyers of New York remained idle.

Attorney William Smith, Jr., having withdrawn from the employ of Cunningham, became most active in the opposition to Lieutenant Governor Colden and the attempt to apply a new form of appellate review in the Provincial courts. In this Smith was undoubtedly aided by having the ear of the absent Governor, Robert Monckton. Their relationship dated to the time of Monckton's arrival in New York when Smith had assisted the new Governor in collecting one-half of the Governor's salary from the Lieutenant Governor. Since Monckton's Lieutenant Governor at the time was none other than Cadwallader Colden, Smith's intercession with Monckton in regard to appeals was not likely to be without influence. To Monckton the younger Smith wrote on November 5th, 1764:

> The Term Appeal is borrowed from the Civilians, and I suppose those who introduced it [*into the Governor's instructions*] intended to give it a Civil Law Operation, and render the Administration of Justice amongst us controulable by the King, as that of the Pretor in the Roman provinces on the Appeal to Caesar. . . . What Construction the Government will adopt is a Matter of anxious Expectation—I have for many years been fearful of the day in which the Experiment will be made—A late Verdict will now bring it on.[9]

Colden, too much a veteran of New York political intrigues to be caught without an explanation on hand in London, hastened to set forth his views in a letter to the Lords of Trade. Pleading for support he pointed to the array of judges and lawyers who acted in concert against him.[10]

While the appearance of the Supreme Court justices was postponed to the 19th of November, Colden again sought the advice of his Attorney General. Kempe's reply shows that Colden had taken to the lawbooks himself in search of a pos-

[8] The judgment roll was signed on the 31st of October 1764, but Scott, plaintiff's attorney, was not permitted to file it until Jan. 11, 1765, Parchment 21 A-8,N.Y.Co.Clk.,HR,NYC. William Smith, defendant's former attorney, erroneously states that Scott was refused property execution by the Clerk, see *Memoirs,* I,24, but such execution could not be requested before the judgment was filed and entered by the Clerk.

[9] Smith, *Memoirs,* I, 26.

[10] Edmund B. O'Callaghan, ed., *Documents Relative to the Colonial History of the State of New York* (15 vols., Albany: Weed, Parsons & Co., 1856-1861) VII, 676-677 [Nov. 7, 1764]. This set is hereafter cited *Doc. Rel. Col. Hist. NY.*

sibility of entertaining an appeal from a common law jury's verdict. These he set forth at length, and to each point Kempe made a detailed reply. After admitting that writs of error were not used in the practice before the House of Lords in Ireland nor in the Courts of Stannaries in Devon and Cornwall, Kempe patiently explained to Colden that these were courts of civil law origin, and hence their precedents were not applicable. He assured Colden that he had searched every book in his office, and every volume in the more extensive library of William Smith, Jr., but that he could find no basis for the Lieutenant Governor's "writs."[11]

Matters stood in much the same condition when Colden met with the Council on November 19 to hear the reasons offered by Chief Justice Horsmanden for disobeying the "writs" issued by the Lieutenant Governor. The Chief Justice began by calling the Council's attention to the unexceptionable circumstances of the trial. A jury had been selected in accordance with Cunningham's request for a "struck" jury. This was a procedure which permitted both parties the right to select a panel of twenty-four from which the twelve trial jurors ultimately would be chosen; thus, the danger of being surprised by the nature of the jurors was minimized. No evidence offered by either party was rejected by the Court. Plaintiff was represented by three attorneys at trial, but defendant had secured the services of four.

Aside from the fair nature of the trial, continued Horsmanden, there was very good reason to limit appeals on the facts from common law jury verdicts. *Forsey* v. *Cunningham* required twelve hours of testimony in open Court, none of which had been officially reduced to writing. If this and every similar case were to be so conducted that an official transcript was available, the time consumed would be greatly magnified, and the time of the Governor and Council would be sorely taxed in hearing appeals from these judgments. Finally Horsmanden demanded the Council consider ". . . whether a Single Word in the Royal Instruction will Warrant your Assuming this great and important power." The issuance of Colden's "writs" was ". . . an unwarrantable abuse of the King's name, and his Judges." "Old Horsey" had never before spoken with such great authority as the representative of the lawyers of

[11] "Colden Papers," VI, NYHS, *Collections*, LV, 378.

the Province; his stand against Colden endeared him to every member of the Bench and Bar, as well as to the populace who anxiously followed the proceedings in the press.[12]

On December 12th, Justices William Smith and Robert R. Livingston lent their support and erudition to the stand of Horsmanden, and one can imagine the impact upon the Councillors and Colden. Smith bluntly told the Council that the powers of the Supreme Court were limited by the justices' commissions; those commissions conferred only the authority vested in the English judges of the courts of Common Pleas, Kings Bench and Exchequer. Since no appeals from jury verdicts were known in these common law courts at Westminster, they as justices of the Supreme Court of Judicature were incompetent to permit such an appeal in New York.[13] Livingston shrewdly pointed out that even if Colden had issued a writ of error, it would have been ineffective in this case, for judgment would have to have been filed and entered before the writ could be issued and returned. In short even if the form of Colden's writ be conceded for purposes of argument, there was no final judgment until the judgment roll was entered and filed. Colden had acted prematurely and Horsmanden was quite within his powers in ignoring both of Colden's "writs." Informing the Council that they were unable to judge the merits of the verdict because they could not be advised of the jury's grounds for finding the verdict, Livingston concluded, ". . . the Monarchs of the illustrious House of Hanover, could never be justly charged with taking a single Step towards infringing the Liberties of their People."[14]

Justice Thomas Jones followed the lead of Horsmanden and Livingston in his formal reply to the Council delivered on December 26. Colden's reply to the allegations of the judges was presented on January 9. It consisted primarily of arguments drawn from treatises and ignored the pertinent questions of practice at Westminster and the customary procedure in the Province of New York. In effect Colden's argument was that the King was the fountainhead of justice, and that the King's representative in the Province should function as the guarantor of the liberties of all the King's people. The Council

[12] *Ibid.*, pp. 378-385.
[13] *Report*, p. 16.
[14] Ibid., pp. 21-26. At the same meeting Justice Jones' response was postponed until December 26th, *ibid.*, p. 15.

heard Livingston's forceful rebuttal on the same date and then voted not to entertain any appeal in *Forsey* v. *Cunningham* except by writ of error.

Colden's brief before the Council left little room for doubt that he felt that a flexible system of appeals was necessary to obtain justice. Furthermore he believed that the limited New York appellate practice unduly restricted opportunities to appeal to the King in Privy Council. His distrust for lawyers in general and for the New York Bar in particular is clearly shown in his paper. He began, perhaps unfortunately, with a cynical apology, observing,

> The Law has not been my Study, . . . If I cannot deliver my conception without a multiplicity of perplexual Argument & Verbose harangs, you will have just reason to think, that my Conceptions of the matter are not clear: for a Multiplicity of Words generally arises either from a perplexed imagination, or from a view to perplex others, . . .

In other words, as far as Colden was concerned, the elaborate citations to precedent on the part of the Supreme Court justices were merely to confuse the Councillors. However in the body of his argument, as Livingston sagely pointed out in rebuttal, Colden woefully confused procedures in the English common law courts with the entirely distinct and different practice which applied in English courts governed by the civil law. The distinction was basic to the fundamental law of New York, just as it was the clearest delineation made by the lawyers of England. The Englishman of station who did not understand the difference was a dolt indeed, and Colden trespassed on the patience of his Council by attempting to blur the distinction they all knew quite well.[15]

The one strong point in Colden's brief was also its greatest weakness. He had argued that if no appeal were to be permitted except by writ of error, then the Supreme Court of Judicature would be virtually independent as to any review on points of fact. This, Colden contended, would subject the people of New York to the tyranny of the judges. What he failed to consider, but what the lawyers and judges used effec-

[15] Common law procedure applied in English courts of King's Bench, Common Pleas and Exchequer, as it did in their New York counterpart, the Supreme Court of Judicature. On the other hand English and Provincial courts of admiralty and chancery proceeded by civil law standards which included among other things "apostella", or written, testimony.

tively against him, was the fact that the lack of control was not over *Justices of the Supreme Court,* but rather over *juries* selected from among the freeholders of the Province of New York. Judges and lawyers might at times be unpopular with the people, but common law juries were so deeply enshrined in tradition as a fundamental right of English subjects that a trespass upon their independence was bound to raise strong opposition.[16]

Actually the Lieutenant Governor's most telling and subtle argument was never aired before the Council nor in the public announcements concerning the controversy; he revealed this unpopular position only to the Earl of Halifax, the Secretary of State. The New York courts, he held, were creatures of the Royal Prerogative, and not subject to protection under the common law. While it was true that the common law was a part of the law of the province of New York, the courts were not common law courts and their procedures were therefore subject to alteration by royal command. According to Colden, this was readily apparent to one who considered that the New York Supreme Court of Judicature combined the powers of the Westminster courts of King's Bench, Common Pleas and Exchequer. Such a court would not be created by royal command in England, but its authority had never been questioned in New York. The very procedures for appealing common law verdicts for which Colden contended, he was quick to point out, were used in New England. However he neglected to note that this was applied in appeals from the inferior common law courts to the highest common law court in the colony, as well as from the highest common law court to the Governor and Council. As we have noted, these arguments were made in secret to the Secretary of State; Colden wisely left such unpopular statements out of his arguments before the Council.[17]

The Council gave its opinion on January 11th, 1765, and as was to be expected, the Councillors with Colden dissenting, upheld the justices of the Supreme Court. They rejected out of hand Colden's citations to appellate methods in Ireland and the Channel Islands. The acts of 1696 clearly established

16 "Colden Papers, VII", NYHS *Collections,* LVI, 1-12.

17 "The Colden Letterbooks, Vol. I, 1760-1765", New-York Historical Society *Collections,* IX, 429, 430; L. Kinvin Wroth and Hiller B. Zobel, eds., *The Legal Papers of John Adams* (3 vols., Cambridge, Mass.: Harvard University Press, 1965), I, xli-xlii.

the law of New York as that of England in 1664, and this included the practice of the English common law courts at Westminster. Finally, the right of jury was one, the Council pointed out, which the English enjoy over all nations, and it should be maintained with the utmost firmness as the birthright of every British subject.[18]

As we have already noted, the judgment roll was filed on the day the Council rendered its decision, and an execution for the seizure of Cunningham's property was issued a week later. A writ ordering his arrest was then obtained and returned with the endorsement that he was not to be found within the Province of New York. The plaintiff's attorneys undoubtedly knew of Cunningham's continued residence in London, but execution by this *capias ad satisfaciendum* was a necessary step toward commencing an action to collect the amount of the judgment from his bondsmen in New York City.[19] This action was begun shortly thereafter against William Kelly; unfortunately the records concerning it are missing, but it is likely that Kelly paid the amount of the judgment after the Council refused Cunningham's request that execution be stayed pending an appeal of its decision to the Privy Council.[20]

With legal maneuvering in New York City at a standstill, both Colden and his numerous opposition turned their efforts toward influencing the Board of Trade and Privy Council. Colden's letter of December 13th, 1764 was a diatribe against the conspiracy of lawyers and judges arrayed against him. Concerning Chief Justice Horsmanden, he noted that he was sorely tempted to suspend him from his office, but decided to await the Privy Council's advice before taking such drastic action. Even more telling in regard to the agitated state of Colden's mind is his reference to the fact that Horsmanden, as senior member of the Council would ". . . succeed to the Administration of the Government . . ." in the event of Colden's death. It was Horsmanden, and it could be no other, who had released copies of Colden's writs to the press and had written such an inflammatory preface to them.[21]

[18] *Report,* pp. 32-56 [Jan. 11, 1765].
[19] Note 11, above. Parchment 21 A-8, the judgment roll was filed on Jan. 11, 1765. Writ of *fieri facias* issued Jan. 18, 1765, Parchment 186 K-3, with arrest attempts endorsed thereon [sic.], all at N.Y.Co.Clk.,HR,NYC.
[20] *Doc. Rel. Col. Hist. NY,* VII, 679-683, 695-699.
[21] *Ibid.*

A month later the entire Council came within the condemnation of Colden, as he wrote to London to accuse them of delaying proceedings for eight weeks so that Horsmanden could perfect his "harang." As far as Colden was concerned Attorney General Kempe was totally unreliable, for here in the midst of the hottest legal controversy in years, he had been of no use to the acting Governor. Lamented Colden, ". . . what can a Man do, who had no hands?" If the Board of Trade would only petition the Privy Council for the removal of Horsmanden, Justice Livingston, and Attorney General Kempe, all would again be quiet in the Province of New York! Similar suggestions were sent by Colden to the Earl of Halifax, then Secretary of State, who routed them to the Board of Trade.[22]

Two days after the Council refused to stay execution pending appeal of their decision to the Privy Council, Colden flew into a rage and berated his Council at great length. Most members of the Council refused to speak to him for weeks thereafter. William Smith, Jr., always the interested witness, wryly noted that undoubtedly both Colden and his councillors would write to the ministry to rally support for or against their position.[23]

By April of 1765 Colden was thoroughly distracted by the weight of public opinion against him, and he lapsed into silence despite increasing hostility in the press. When the lawyers began to publish what he deemed a licentious paper called *The Sentinel,* a weekly devoted to publicizing the appeals dispute, he reported it to the Board of Trade, but otherwise held his peace. In May he observed that, ". . . the Gentlemen of the Law seem to have placed Chief Stress of their cause on raising public Clamour, & therefore all endeavors to prevent it became fruitless."[24]

[22] *Ibid.,* 701-702; Halifax to Colden, Feb. 9, 1765, "Colden Papers, VII", NYHS *Collections,* LVI, 13. Governor Monckton on the same date, assured Colden that the matter would shortly be resolved, *ibid.,* pp. 11, 12. Halifax in his letter of Mar. 9, 1765, again assured Colden that the matter would soon be considered, *ibid.,* pp. 21, 22.

[23] Smith promptly reported Colden's outburst to Governor Monckton in London, Jan. 25, 1765, Smith, *Memoirs,* I, 28.

[24] Colden to Lords of Trade, Apr. 14, 1765, *Doc. Rel. Col. Hist. NY,* VII, 709; Colden to Halifax, Apr. 27, 1765, *ibid.,* 710; Colden to Monckton, May 3, 1765, "Colden Papers, VII", NYHS *Collections,* LVI, 43; for receipt of Privy Council decision in New York see Smith, *Appeals,* pp. 408-410. Klein, "Prelude . . .", *Wm&MQ,* XVII, 460; order of Supreme Court in regard to Waddel's power of attorney at Min. Sup. Ct. Jud., July 31, 1764-Aug. 2, 1766, pp. 327-334 [Oct. 22, 1765], N.Y.Co.Clk. HR, NYC.

Meanwhile in London, it had been decided to relieve Governor Monckton from his New York governorship so that he might be appointed to a more lucrative post at home. Sir Henry Moore was selected to replace him and his Commission began its passage through the seals. Some delay was experienced in drafting Sir Henry's instructions, undoubtedly because of the pendency of the *Forsey* v. *Cunningham* matter before the Privy Council. On July 26th, 1765 the Privy Council issued an order directing the New York Council to permit Cunningham's appeal, and this was duly transmitted to New York where it arrived on October 12th, 1765. Ostensibly Colden had been upheld by the Privy Council and it must have been a smug Lieutenant Governor who presented the order in council to his fellow members of the New York Council!

Obedient to the express instructions of the Crown, the New York Council reluctantly issued a formal demand upon the Supreme Court of Judicature, citing the Privy Council order and directing that Cunningham be permitted to take his appeal. At this point the Supreme Court of Judicature refused to take action because it claimed that Waddell's power of attorney, which had hitherto passed unchallenged, was defective.[25] On November 11th, this reply was given by the Justices before the Governor and Council. Clearly this action was taken for purposes of delay, and Colden, threatened by the Stamp Act rioters and burned in effigy on several occasions, was not likely to take prompt action. Even if he had, time was against him, for Sir Henry Moore arrived in New York City on November 12th, just one day after the Supreme Court justices defied Colden. Colden was superceded by the arrival of the Governor-in-Chief, and for all intents and purposes the controversy was over.

Two weeks after Sir Henry's arrival to take up the government of New York, an amended set of instructions arrived for Moore. Among the most significant alterations was the clause which limited appeals to the Governor and Council to those which were taken by writ of error. A petition by New York colonial agent Robert Clarke, which formed the basis for a representation by the Board of Trade to the Privy Council on

[25] Lords of Trade to King in Privy Council, June 20, 1765, *Doc.Rel.Col. Hist.NY*, VII, 745; Jeffrey Amherst to Colden, June 21, 1765, "Colden Papers, VII", NYHS *Collections*, LVI, 43.

September 24th, 1765, induced the Privy Council to reverse its decision of July 26th, and on the date of the Board of Trade's representation the amendment of Moore's instructions was issued to follow him across the seas to his troubled province of New York.[26] Thus ended the controversy of *Forsey* v. *Cunningham,* now better understood through the reappearance of George Harison's "Protest."

* * * * *

As is frequently the case with significant documents in legal history, the true value of George Harison's "Protest" is apparent only to one with some knowledge of the sources of early American law. In a day when law reports from American courts were non-existent, the student is hard-pressed to find any document that throws light on either the substantive or the procedural law of New York. Although it is well known that all motions were argued orally at the Saturday sittings of the Supreme Court of Judicature, the "Protest" is the only description of such a procedure that has come to light. Its value is of course, greatly enhanced by the constitutional significance of the case in which the motion was made.

Historians are indebted to Sir Thomas Phillips, the foremost private collector of Victorian England, for the survival of this manuscript. The "Protest" bears his cataloging marks, and the sale catalog of Sotheby, the London auctioneer, indicates that this manuscript was auctioned as part of the Phillips manuscripts sold on June 26, 1919. The price at that time was a mere £3 5*s*.[27] The New-York Historical Society purchased the "Protest" from a California collector, and was advised at that time that the manuscript had been acquired from an English source.

[26] For petition for rehearsing at Privy Council, see Smith, *Appeals* p. 408; representation of Board of Trade to Privy Council at *Doc.Rel.Col. Hist.NY,* VII, 762-764. Sir Henry Moore's arrival is recorded in *Calendar of Council Minutes* 1668-1783 (Albany: University of the State of New York, 1902), at p. 469. On Nov. 26, 1765 the notice of change of instructions was received by Moore, "Colden Papers, VII", NYHS *Collections,* LVI, 95. The New York Assembly on Dec. 15, 1765, condemned Colden's position in *Forsey* v. *Cunningham,* Smith, *Appeals,* p. 411.

[27] Catalog #478, June 26, 1919, p. 96. There is a notation on the reverse of the document that it was part of the "Phillippi M.S.S.", and that it was purchased on 26 June 1919 at the sale of the Phillippi M.S.S. Two numbers, 32985 and 478, presumably once used for cataloging purposes, appear on the reverse. The document is faced with Colden's certification, followed by Harison's "Protest", after which are included the three exhibits mentioned in the "Protest". All are fastened with a ribbon from which is appended the Great Seal of the Province of New York.

Precisely how the "Protest" was used in the litigation remains to be determined. The fact that it was certified by the Lieutenant Governor with the great seal of the Province indicates that it was intended for use outside of New York. Unfortunately there is no endorsement or notation on the document itself that is of any assistance in resolving this question. Professor Joseph H. Smith who has done the most thorough work in the manuscripts of the case gives reason to believe that papers other than the bare record were considered by the Privy Council, but he does not remember examining a copy of the "Protest".[28] Whether the "Protest" would have been considered in evidence is a matter of conjecture, but it seems likely that had it been so offered the tender would have been rejected as immaterial to the constitutional issue before the Privy Council. Had it been returned to counsel it might well have remained in private hands until it came into the collection of Sir Thomas Phillips. Now after two ocean voyages it has returned again to New York, and the New-York Historical Society is to be commended for its role in making this invaluable document available to scholars for the first time.

George Harison's "Protest"

By this Publick Instrument of Protest be it known and Made Manifest unto all to whom these Presents shall come, or may in any wise Concern, That on thursday the Twenty-fifth day of October in the Fifth year of the Reign of Our Sovereign Lord George the third by the Grace of God of Great Britain France and Ireland King Defender of the Faith &c and in the year of Our Lord one thousand Seven hundred and Sixty four: I George Harison Notary and Tabillion[29]

[28] See Smith, *Appeals,* p. 391, note 184, citing CO/5/1071, pp. 67-71. Professor Smith recently informed me that he was certain he did not see this "Protest" in his review of these documents. The "Protest" is filed in the Manuscript Division of the New-York Historical Society under the call number *Y-Oct. 29, 1764.

[29] The term "tabillion" is presumably from the French "tabellion," meaning a legal practitioner of inferior status. It is unknown to English or New York law. Only an attorney duly admitted by license of the Governor and by order of the Supreme Court could practice before the Supreme Court. Harison was, to my knowledge, not even admitted to practice in the inferior courts; he was a merchant and a partner in a brewery business, see Herbert A. Johnson, "John Jay: Colonial Lawyer." (Unpublished Ph.D. dissertation, Columbia University, 1965), pp. 200-203.

Publick, Lawfully Admitted, Sworn and Residing in the City of New York, in the Province of New York in America, was Called upon, by Mr. Robert Ross Waddell of this City Merchant (attorney in fact to Mr. Waddle Cuninghame late of the said City Merchant, but now beyond [*the*] Sea)[30] and Required to Attend him to the Supream Court of Judicature then Sitting at the City Hall of the said City, there to take down in writing all the Evidence that should be given in a Certain Cause that day to be tryed on an Action brought by Thomas Forsey against the said Waddle Cuninghame for an Assault Battery and wounding. Whereupon I the said Notary told him that I would Attend but that I could not possibly undertake to Commit the whole Evidence to writing as I did not write sufficiently fast, and therefore I Advised him to Employ Lambert Moore and James Emott, Esqrs. Notarys Publick, to attend for the same purpose, to which he replyed that he had engaged Mr. Emott, who would Attend, and he would also get Mr. Moore. Whereupon I the said Notary did accompany him the said Robert Ross Waddell to the City Hall of the said City where the Court being Opened, Present on the Bench the Hon[oura]ble Daniel Horsmanden, Esq. Chief Justice, David Jones Esqr. second Justice, William Smith Esqr. third Justice and Robert R. Livingston Esqr. Fourth Justice, Councill for the plaintiff were John Tabor Kemp Esqr. His Majesties Attorney General, John Morine Scott and Thomas Smith Esqrs., Councill for the Defendant were William Smith Jun[io]r Esqr. William Livingston Esqr. Whitehead Hicks and James Duane Esqrs.

The Cause Comeing on to be heard, I the said Notary Enquired of Mr. Waddell if his Notarys were ready. He told me that Lambert Moore had Just told him that he was very busy & would not come, and James Emott Appearing Seated himself and began to write down the Evidence, but very soon rose up and went Out of Court, thereupon Benjamin Kissam Esqr.[31] an Attorney of the said Court took up his pen and went on writeing what the Several Witnesses said upon the

[30] Apparently Cunningham had given bond and left for England sometime between the end of the criminal prosecution in January 1764 and October of the same year.

[31] Kissam's role in the case is somewhat remarkable. He had just completed trying another case on the trial calendar when *Forsey* v. *Cunningham* went to trial. However his participation in preparing an unofficial record can only be explained by the likelihood that he wanted to obtain a certain decision on the question of appeals being limited by writs of error. Another situation in which Kissam acted contrary to the desires of the entire Bench and Bar was his defence of the leaders of the 1766 rioters in Dutchess and Westchester counties, see Johnson, "John Jay", pp. 61-68.

Tryal, I the said Notary Continuing in the Court from the beginning to the End of the Tryal, which lasted about ten hours or a little More, the Councill on both sides having Sum[me]d up the Evidence, the Chief Justice gave the Charge to the Jury, Judge Livingston adding a few words.

A Constable being sworn to Keep them in the usual Manner the Court directed them to Seal up their Verdict if they Agreed soon. Then the Court Adjourned till the Next Morning, at ten o'the Clock, And he the said Robert Ross Waddell calling upon me the Next Morning told me that he heard the Jury had agreed upon their Verdict and found Fifteen hundred pounds Damages for the plaintiff besides Costs, and he told me that he was resolved to Appeal (upon his Majesties Instruction) to the Lieutenant Governor and Councill, and from them to the King and Councill, if the Damages found Exceeded the Sums Limited by the Instructions, for that he had Mr. Cuninghames positive Orders so to do,[32], and he must and would obey them. Therefore he desired me the said Notary to Attend in Court and hear his Application to Mr. Cunninghames Councill that they would be prepared to Move the Court for an Appeal, agreeable to the said Instructions, and I the said Notary Conceiving it my Duty to do every Act and thing that should be required of me as Notary Publick Did attend him to his said Councill, who, upon his Application to them to make such Motion, did Absolutely refuse to do it. And William Smith Jun[io]r, Esqr. did declare that he had told Mr. Cuninghame long before he had departed this Province that if he determined to Carry it to an Appeal, he would not be Concerned in the Cause, as it was a Measure he neither did, nor would Approve of.[33] Therefore he thought himself Honourably Acquited, and must Abandon the Cause. However the said Councill told the said Waddell that his Notary Might Move the Court, and did direct me the said Notary what to say.[34]

Then the Court being Met According to Adjournment, the Jury were Called and Gave their Verdict for the Plaintiff,

[32] This passage leaves little question that Cunningham had long before planned to challenge the traditional mode of procedure in regard to appeals.

[33] Smith's explanation was, "I had stipulated at the Commencement of the Suit ag[ains]t being concerned in that dangerous Measure . . . [of requesting an appeal on the facts] . . . I perswaded Livingston and Duane of Council with me to decline their Assistance also.", William Smith, *Historical Memoirs from 16 March 1763 to 9 July 1776,* William H. W. Sabine, ed., (2 vols., New York: Colburn & Tegg, 1956), I,24.

[34] This advice is not reflected in Smith's *Memoirs,* and well might he decline to mention such deception, for anyone familiar with the exclusive nature of the New York colonial Bar would anticipate the reaction to a Notary Public making a motion in the Supreme Court!

Fifteen hundred pounds and Costs, the Judges then upon the bench being the Chief Justice and Judge Jones. When I the said Notary Advanced Near the bench and Addressed the Court in the following words,

> May it please your honors, I am directed as a Notary Publick by Mr. Waddell Attorney to Mr. Cuninghame, to Move your honors (on a Matter that would have come more properly from his Councill but they have declined it, for Reasons which they are best able to give) that you will be pleased to Enter his Appeal from the Verdict and Judgement of this Court, to the Governor and Councill agreeable to the Kings Instructions, and he is ready to give Security Now in Court and I here tender your honors the Evidence taken on the Tryal by Banjamin Kissam Esqr. to be sent up in such Manner as your honors think proper.

Whereupon Mr. Scott, Councill for the Plaintiff rose up and said, that he was Surprised at the Motion, that I had no right to speak in that Court, and he hoped the Court would take Notice of it, to which I made no reply, and turned to the Court for their Answer.

When his honor the Chief Justice told me that he knew of no Appeals of that kind, that the Kings Instructions was to the Governor, and not to them, that I Had done very wrong in Speaking, but that the Court would Consider the Matter 'till tomorrow Morning. Whereupon I the said Notary did Offer the Evidence as before together with a Certified Copey of the said Instructions, and a bond ready to be Executed by Hugh Wallace, Jacob Walton, Theophilact Bache and William Kelly then attending in Court for that purpose, and Disired that the Motion I had made, might be entered upon the Minutes of Court, all which the said Court did Absolutely refuse and said further that they knew of No Appeals from them but by a writ of Error, which might be brought if the Defendant chose it.[35] To which I was directed to Answer that they meant to Appeal upon the Merits of the Cause and not by writ of Error, for that they did not Alledge there was Error. Whereupon I the said Notary went out of Court with the said Mr. Waddell, who Exprest great distress at his present Situation, being Void [*of*] Councill to Advise him what Measures to pursue in order to Obtain Relief.

And Saturday Morning he the said Waddell came to me again, and desired me to go with him and be a Witness to the Executing of a Certain bond which he then shewed to me, and

[35] Attorney William Smith records that, "The Chief Justice rejected the application as it is said with some Heat but I was not present.", Smith, *Memoirs*, I, 24.

he also shewed me a written paper Signed by himself in the form of a Motion or prayer to the Court, and Also a Certified Copey of his Majesties Instructions to His Governor of this Province, relating to Appeals,[36] all which he said he would lay before the Court, so soon as they Met, and desired my attendance in Court to Witness and Certifie their proceedings thereupon. And I the said Notary did go with him, and was present and did see Jacob Walton, Theophilact Bache, William Kelly and Hugh Wallace (all of them reputed Men of Character and fortune) Sign Seal and Deliver the said bond as their Act and Deed for the Uses therein Mentioned (A true Copey of which bond is hereunto annexed and numbered One, with my own hand).

And I did then Accompany the said Waddell to the City Hall, where the Court being Met According to Adjournment, Present on the Bench the Hon[oura]ble Daniel Horsmanden Esqr. Chief Justice, The Hon[oura]ble William Smith Esqr. third Justice and The Hon[oura]ble Robert R. Livingston Esqr. fourth Justice, when William Smith Jun[io]r Esqr. took Mr. Waddell and myself apart from the Court and told the same Waddell that if he Approved of it, He would Move the Court to set aside the Verdict on Account of the high Damages, which if the Court should come into, it might be the Means to prevent the Necessity of an Appeal, to which the said Waddell (Consented), and by Mr. Smiths direction sent for Mr. Duane, who coming into Court, did make a Motion to the Court to set aside the Verdict and grant a New Tryal and being Seconded in the same by Mr. Smith, it was Opposed by Mr. Scott, whereupon a Short Argument Ensued. The Motion was Overruled, and Mr. Scott moving for Judgement, the Court Ordered the same to be entered, and it was Accordingly Entered.[37]

The said Waddell then Delivered into the hands of the

[36] The critical instructions were those numbered 32 and 33, issued to Governor Robert Monckton on July 6, 1760, which deleted the words ". . . by writ of error" from the phrase ". . . appeals to the Governor and Council by writ of error . . .", "Protest". *Y-Oct. 29, 1764, New-York Historical Society.

[37] Smith, *Appeals,* p. 391, indicates that the Supreme Court was correct that English practice did not permit reduction of damages, but infers that they were wrong in assuming that a motion to set aside the verdict as excessive and grant a new trial was not proper. The "Protest" makes it clear that the motion was made, and overruled by the Court, but that no note was made of it in the minutes of the Court since it was not properly brought before the Court by a duly qualified counsellor of the Court. Horsmanden later stated that the atrocious nature of the assault and the damages caused, seemed to the Court adequate to support the jury verdict, "Colden Papers," VI, NYHS *Collections,* LV, 380.

Court the before mentioned original Bond together with the paper (a true Copey whereof is hereunto annexed and numbered two with my own hand) Signed by himself as Attorney to the said Waddle Cuninghame, and Also a Certified Copey of His Majesties Instructions to his Governor of this Province, relative to Appeals (a true Copey of which is also hereunto Annexed, Numbered Three with my own hand) praying their honors that the same might be rec[eive]d which the said Court did Absolutely refuse, but The Hon[oura]ble Justice Smith said he would read the Instructions, which was Opposed by Mr. Scott as being very improper, but the said Justice replyed that tho it was not proper yet he would read it for the Satisfaction of the partys, and did read the same Commenting thereupon, and Endeavouring to Convince the said Waddell that the Court would not admit of his Appeal in any Other form than by a writ of Error. And the said Waddell did then and there Move the said Court that this his Application might be made a Minute of Court which the said Court did refuse.

And the Chief Justice turning to me the said Notary told me, that the Court was Offended at my behaviour in Speaking the day before, but that they, believing I did not mean to Offend them, they should not resent it, and added that the Kings Instructions was to the Governor and not to them, that they were Judges of Law and not to be directed by any Instructions.[38]

Whereupon I Bowed to the Court most Respectfully and told them, that I had Appeared there in my Duty as a Notary Publick, that I was bound by my Oath as much as their honors were by theirs, that I had Spoken nothing of myself, and if I had acted improperly the Court should have forbid me to speak and I would have Ceased so to do immediately.

The said Robert Ross Waddell thus finding his principal the said Waddle Cuninghame, Abandoned by his Councill,[39]

[38] Smith, *Memoirs,* I, 24, says ". . . the Chief Justice [said] that he thought the Appl[i]c[ati]on Yesterday was very impertinent, and if he did not impute it to ingorance, he would have taken further Notice than meerly to reject it." The same source would indicate that it was Judge Livingston who observed that the King's Instructions bound the Governor and not the Supreme Court.

[39] Cunningham's attorney in fact was not left entirely without legal advice, for if Attorney William Smith can be trusted, he had employed ". . . one John Coghill Knapp a Villain transplanted for Fraud . . . into Virginia as he himself confessed to me last April, . . .", *ibidem*. Knapp, an English barrister, was the bane of the existence of the New York Bar. After an unsuccessful motion to be admitted to practice on the basis of his membership in the English Inns of Court, Knapp resorted to drawing deeds and wills, factoring the sale of slaves and advancing mortgage money. [see Johnson, "John Jay", pp. 49-51.] Such an ally was worse than another enemy!

Left in the Dark how to proceed properly in the Method to Obtain Releif against the Verdict, and Judgement of the said Court, and the whole Bench of Judges Averse to, and acting in Direct Opposition to His Majesties Royal Instructions whereby the Releif thereby intended is discouraged by the Ministers of Justice, in the highest Contempt of the Royal Prerogative, and to the Manifest Injury of His Majesties Good and Loyall Subjects the people of this Province and himself in particular, and Conceiving the same to be a Violent Step towards Shuting the Door of an Appeal to our Most Gracious Sovereign and his Most Honourable Privy Councill, He the said Robert Ross Waddell for his principal the said Waddle Cuninghame hath desired me the said Notary to Note and Testify Every Matter and thing herein before Contained, and to Protest against the said Councill for having so Abandoned their Clients Cause, and also against the Several Judges of the said Court for the Matters and things herein before Contained.

Therefore I the said Notary at the Request aforesaid, Have and by these presents Do Publickly and Solemnly Protest and Declare against them the Councill of the said Waddle Cuninghame, and also against the Judges of the said Supream Court for all Loss, Damages, Costs, prejudice and Injury that hath or shall happen, Arise Accrue or befall him the said Waddle Cuninghame for or by Reason his his said Councill so Abandoning his Cause, and also for or by reason of the Proceedings of the said Judges on the several Matters before Mentioned,

Thus Done and protested in the said City of New York this Twenty Seventh day of October in the year aforesaid,

In Faith and Testimony of the Truth of which, I the said Notary have hereunto Subscribed my Name and Affixed the Seal of my Office in the City of New York this 29th day of October A Dom. 1764.

George Harison
Not[ar]ius Publ[ic]us
/46/

English Statutes in Colonial New York

The extension of English law to the American Colonies is a matter that has long interested and vexed legal historians. Herbert Johnson examines the reception (i.e. the use and adoption) of English laws in New York, and suggests certain political significances thereof. Dr. Johnson, former editor of the Papers of John Marshall, is professor of history and law at the University of South Carolina.

ONE OF THE major problems facing historians of early American law is the determination of the extent to which English law applied in any given province at a particular time. While the requirement that the colonies have laws not repugnant to the common law of England[1] provided some conformity throughout the colonial period, there was substantial variation in the seventeenth century, not only between the colonies and the mother country, but also among the colonies themselves. With the increasing availability of English statutes and case reports during the eighteenth century, and the growing sophistication of the bar, there was a pronounced tendency to adhere to English legal norms.[2] The province of New York partook of this development, and while her experiences and actions do not necessarily provide a model for other jurisdictions, they tend to reenforce the theory that American colonial law was closest to the law of

1. See Joseph H. Smith, *Appeals to the Privy Council from the American Plantations* (New York, 1950), pp. 41–42, 51–53.

2. On the growth of the Bar, see Milton M. Klein, "The Rise of the New York Bar: The Legal Career of William Livingston," *William and Mary Quarterly*, 3d Ser., XV (1958), 334–358 at 335, and Felix Rackow, "The Right to Counsel: English and American Precedents," *Wm. & M. Qtly*., 3rd Ser., XI (1954), 3–27 at 13, 16, 17.

England in the years immediately before the outbreak of the American Revolution.

Throughout the eighteenth century and particularly in the decade immediately preceding the War for Independence, New York lawyers, legislators and judges were actively engaged in the extension of English law to the colony. At first the reception of English statutes was accomplished by usage, but as the colonial period drew to a close the New York General Assembly passed a number of acts designed to incorporate by reference a substantial group of Parliamentary statutes that dealt with such disparate subjects as real and personal property law, decedents' estates and wills, criminal law and procedure, and court administration. While these efforts in areas of private law do not have marked political or constitutional overtones, there were several other instances in which New York political leaders demanded rights under the law that were predicated upon rights held by subjects in England.

Those clashes have been noted by historians and are recognized as differences of opinion concerning the extension of English common law to the colonies–differences of opinion which brought the province into direct conflict with the imperial administration in Whitehall. For example, colonial demands for the grant of good behavior tenure to judges, followed by a sharp conflict over the inviolability of jury verdicts, were based upon demands for the protection of English laws in those areas.[3] Faced with gubernatorial and imperial challenges to New York institutions held to be based on hallowed English liberties, New York leaders resorted to English history and the practices of English courts to defend their court systems against the inroads of innovation and dependence upon the Crown.[4] Somewhat later, in

3. Milton M. Klein, "Prelude to Revolution in New York: Jury Trials and Judicial Tenure," *Wm. & M. Qtly.*, 3d Ser., XVII (1960), 439–462. New York's battle over judicial tenure, like that of most colonies other than New Jersey, dealt with the constitutional question of "good behavior" tenure. See Jerome J. Nadelhaft, "Politics and the Judicial Tenure Fight in Colonial New Jersey," *Wm. & M. Qtly.*, 3d Ser., XXVIII (1971), 46–63. In 1766 the Massachusetts attorney general refused to use informations in prosecutions of smugglers, claiming that such an extraordinary procedure was not sanctioned by English law. Oliver M. Dickerson, "Opinion of Attorney General Jonathan Sewall of Massachusetts in the Case of the *Lydia*," *Wm. & M & Qtly.*, 3d Ser., IV (1947), 499–504 at 504.

4. David S. Lovejoy, "Rights Imply Equality: The Case Against Admiralty Jurisdiction in America, 1764–1776," *Wm. & M. Qtly.*, 3d Ser., XVI (1959), 459–484.

justifying resistance to the quartering of British regulars in New York City residences, the General Assembly insisted that the English Mutiny Act should serve as an outer limit to the burdens that military necessity might force upon a civilian population.[5]

Since the line between private law and constitutional law in the Anglo-American legal systems is so narrow and obscure, it is possible that these two parallel tendencies—the statutory reception of English private law, and the use of English constitutional standards to protect New York legal and political institutions against Parliamentary dilution and executive innovation—were symptomatic of the basic underlying impulse toward revolution in provincial New York.

In eighteenth-century New York jurisprudence it was axiomatic that the common law of England and the statutes declaring the common law passed by Parliament prior to 1691, were applicable to New York and were part of the law of the province. In 1764 Chief Justice Daniel Horsmanden voiced the widespread feeling among the legal profession, that not only the statutes declaring the common law were included in New York law as of 1691, but also that all pre-1691 Parliamentary statutes that *altered* the common law had also been received.[6] At the time of his statement Horsmanden had both legal and political motivations in making this assertion, for he was debating the inviolability of jury verdicts in the face of Lieutenant Governor Cadwallader Colden's attempt to alter the traditional mode of appeal by writ of error. Yet as early as 1735 Sir John Randolph of Virginia had recognized the extraordinary tendency among New York lawyers to apply all of the statutory law of England enacted before 1691 to the province of New York.[7]

Adoption of the 1691 date permitted New York lawyers

5. The Assembly attempt to impose British limitations on the Parliamentary extension of the Mutiny Act to the colonies is noted in Carl L. Becker, *The History of Political Parties in the Province of New York, 1760–1776* (Madison, 1909), pp. 53–55; it is not discussed in the most thorough study of the Quartering Act in New York, Lee E. Olm, "The Mutiny Act for America: New York's Noncompliance," *New-York Historical Society Quarterly*, LVIII (1974), 188–214.

6. *The Report of An Action of Assault, Battery and Wounding Tried in the Supreme Court of Judicature for the Province of New-York, in the Term of October 1764 between Thomas Forsey . . . and Waddel Cunningham . . .* (New York, 1764), p. 4.

7. See the text of Sir John Randolph's letter printed in William Smith, *The History of the Province of New-York* (New York, 1830), I, 374–376.

THE

LAWS & ACTS

OF THE

General Assembly

FOR

Their Majesties Province

OF

NEW-YORK,

As they were Enacted in divers Sessions, the first of which began *April*, the 9th, *Annoq*; *Domini*, 1691.

At *New-York*,

Printed and Sold by *William Bradford*, Printer to their Majesties, King *William* & Queen *Mary*, 1694.

Title page of the first collected laws and acts of the province of New York, 1694. From Stokes, The Iconography of Manhattan Island.

to claim absorption into provincial law of a substantial body of legislation that did not specifically mention the colonies. It also reduced the confusion inherent in the legal precedents, such as they were, from the proprietary period, and permitted lawyers to cite pre-1691 "New York law" in English case reports and statute books. Perhaps Chief Justice Horsmanden and his associates in 1764 hoped that 1691 might serve the same function for New York as 1494 did for Ireland under the provisions of Poyning's law.[8] As Chief Justice Edward Coke had held in *Calvin's Case* (1608) and his *Fourth Institute*, when King John introduced the common law into Ireland in 1209, he granted the residents certain rights as Englishmen, and from then until 1494 the common law of England and the statutes passed prior to 1494 applied to Ireland.[9]

Contemporary New York legal opinion during the last quarter of the colonial period left little room for doubt concerning the determinative effect of the 1691 date. Yet two problems arise that cause historians to doubt the accuracy of Chief Justice Horsmanden's assertions. The most obvious is the fact that the first exercise of legislative authority took place in 1683 and 1684, rather than in 1691.[10] The laws passed at that earlier session, called the Dongan Laws, covered a variety of subjects and in some cases attempted to extend English statutes, such as the statute of frauds of 1676, to New York. However the disallowance of most of these laws, and the omission of the remainder from all statutory compilations printed during the colonial period, resulted in the deletion of these acts, for all practical purposes, from the law of the province. Either the 1683–84 laws were not in force in the province or, if they were technically part of New York law, they had been totally ignored by non-use during the colonial period.

The most serious problem in accepting the 1691 date as the significant year for the reception of English statutory law, is the clear evidence that all statutes passed by Parliament prior to that date were *not* in force in the province. This Chief Justice Horsmanden knew as did every competent

8. Poyning's Law, 10 Hen. 7, c.4 (1494) reasserted the requirement that statutes of the Irish Parliament receive approval from the English King in his Parliament before they would be valid. It also stipulated that the law of England as it existed in 1494 was to form part of the law of Ireland.

9. Coke, *The Fourth Part of the Institutes of the Laws*, England (London, 1797), pp. 283–86, 351; Calvin's Case, 7 Coke Reports 2a, 77 English Reports, Full Reprint (Exch. Ch., 1610). See also Smith, *Appeals to the Privy Council*, pp. xxx-xxxii, xlviii, lvi–lix, lxi.

10. The proprietary period was characterized by a complex and confusing court system, and the enactments of the 1683–84 assembly were not particularly helpful in remedying the situation since the province was shortly thereafter incorporated into the dominion of New England, and then passed through the disorderly transition of Leisler's rebellion. Herbert A. Johnson, "The Advent of Common Law in Colonial New York," in George A. Billias, ed., *Law and Authority in Colonial America* (Barre, 1964), pp. 74–87 at 85, 86.

lawyer practicing in colonial New York. At the same time, the 1691 date did not necessarily mean that English statutes passed after that date were not part of New York law. Frequently all or part of these later enactments were absorbed by usage into the common law of New York. Indeed the practice of law in the province must have been a quagmire for the unwary and inexperienced, and the amount of usage which governed the reception of English statutes into provincial law must have rendered clerkship training an absolute necessity for those who would succeed in practice. In his study of New York legal education Professor Paul Hamlin noted the distinct preference for clerkship training in New York,[11] and it is fairly clear that the lawyer so trained had distinct advantages over the barrister from the Inns of Court who knew little if anything about New York's reception of English statutes by usage.

Without the kind of clerkship training colonial New York lawyers received, today's legal historian is hard-pressed to ferret out examples of reception by usage in the fragmentary references in court records and lawyers' papers. Some of these peculiarities have already appeared in print. While editing the records of the Supreme Court of Judicature, Professor Hamlin and Mr. Charles E. Baker discovered contradictory holdings in the court concerning the applicability of the 1689 English Act of Toleration to the 1707 trial of minister Francis Mackemie.[12] They warn that:

11. Among the first generation of English barristers in New York not one achieved first rank, and after that early decade of the eighteenth century only one member of the Inns of Court achieved leadership at the colonial New York bar. On this evidence Paul M. Hamlin concluded that clerkship within the province was the most effective form of legal education. *Legal Education in Colonial New York* (New York, 1939), pp. 19–20; see also Lawrence H. Leder, "Robert Livingston's Sons: Preparation for Futurity," *New York History*, L (1969), 245–247, discussing the difficulties of a London-trained barrister in achieving a successful New York law practice.

12. Rev. Francis Mackemie, a dissenting Protestant minister, was indicted for preaching in New York without a license. At a pre-trial hearing he pleaded that the English act of toleration, 1 Wm & Mary, c. 18 (1689), was applicable in New York but the Crown lawyers argued to the contrary. At trial they reversed themselves and argued that the act of toleration had been extended to the province by virtue of the governor's instructions. The jury's general verdict of not guilty precluded an exposition of the law, but Mackemie's counsel had argued, "I take this Colony, as a Dominion of *England*, to be governed by, and subject to these three sorts of Laws: 1. The Common Law of *England*. 2. The express Statutes mentioning the Plantations, and such other as are for publick good, . . . 3. By the Laws of this

> Specifically what portion of the English common law and statute law was in force in [*colonial*] New York . . . [*can be determined*] by recourse to no general theory, or set of rules, but only by a painstaking examination of the record, case by case, from the earliest adjudications of the courts of the Province.[13]

Somewhat earlier, Professor Joseph H. Smith in his *Appeals to the Privy Council from the American Plantations* had observed that, ". . . colonial judicial records show a general and widespread practice of using applicable English statutes passed after colonization in which the dominions were not mentioned."[14]

The evidence would indicate that these legal historians are quite correct in their assessment, and at the same time it casts serious doubt upon the validity of the 1691 date as a basis for determining statutory reception of English laws into New York. Quite the contrary, it seems reasonably clear that the cutting edge of reception was by usage of the courts and not legislative adoption by colonial assemblies. Only as the colonial period drew to a close was there an effort in New York to recognize by statutes–that is acts of the General Assembly–that substantial body of English statutory material which had been brought into New York law by custom and usage since the early years of the eighteenth century.

One English statute received by usage into New York law was the Promissory Note Act of 1704, which authorized the assignability of notes in accordance with the law merchant.[15] This mercantile practice permitted transfer by endorsement, and allowed holders in due course to re-

---

Colony, and those are to be as near as may be agreeable to the Laws and Statutes of *England*, . . ." Paul M. Hamlin and Charles E. Baker, eds., *Supreme Court of Judicature of the Province of New York, 1691–1704* (3 vols.; New York, 1959), I, 405–407.

13. Ibid., p. 412.

14. Smith, *Appeals to the Privy Council*, pp. 486, 487, noting that the practice was particularly widespread in criminal matters. See also Smith's discussion in "The English Criminal Law in Early America," in *The English Legal System: Carryover to the Colonies* (Los Angeles, 1975), pp. 29–30, 41. A similar extension of English statutes and procedures is noted in Bradley Chapin, "Colonial and Revolutionary Origins of the American Law of Treason," *Wm. & M. Qtly.*, 3d Ser., XVII (1960), 3–34, at 5–7.

15. The English Promissory Note Act, 3 & 4 Anne, c. 8 (1704), and its reception by usage in New York by 1710 is discussed in Herbert A. Johnson, *The Law Merchant and Negotiable Instruments in Colonial New York, 1664–1730* (Chicago, 1963), pp. 35–36.

cover from the maker of the note without joining the original payee as a co-plaintiff. During the Dutch occupation of New York such assignments were valid according to the law merchant, and action might be brought by the assignee as well as the original party to the note. However English law at the time did not permit assignment and refused recovery in the common law courts. In 1684 New York's proprietary legislature passed an act permitting assignment and commencement of action by assignees, thereby anticipating the 1704 Parliamentary statute.[16]

However, as indicated, the acts of the 1683–1684 session are of doubtful validity in New York practice after 1691, and it seems safe to assume that the provincial law followed that of England and considered promissory notes non-transferrable by endorsement. The 1704 English statute was effective on May 1, 1705, and in 1710 the records of New York colonial courts show that legal actions observed the formula of the 1704 English act and referred to the "statute in such cases lately made." Yet it was not until 1773 that the New York General Assembly passed an act which, by a parallel provision to that of the 1704 English statute, provided for the assignability of promissory notes.[17]

An even more complicated situation arose concerning the reception into New York law of the 1676 English statute of frauds. Designed to prevent fraudulent practices in the making of contracts, the execution of wills and deeds, and certain other legal transactions, the English statute required written evidence of certain agreements or transactions before they could be enforced in the courts.[18] According to Chief Justice Horsmanden's rule of 1691, this statute should have been part of the law of the province of New York. Yet a cursory examination of the wills on file in the Prerogative Court of New York shows that real property might pass in title by a will in writing but without witnesses. Such a document would comply with the requirements of the 1540 English statute of wills, but not be valid under the 1676 English statute of frauds.[19] From this, one might assume that the 1676 statute

16. Ibid., pp. 28–35.

17. *The Colonial Laws of New York from the Year 1664 to the Revolution*, (5 vols.; Albany, 1894), V, 544–545 (Mar. 5, 1773). This source is hereafter cited *Colonial Laws, N.Y.*

18. 29 Car.2, c.3 (1676).

was not applicable in New York, but that was not entirely the case. The English statute of frauds laid down special requirements for the execution of oral, or nuncupative, wills, and New York's probate court was diligent in enforcing conformity with the precise requirements of that section.[20] Obviously there had been a partial reception of the 1676 English statute of frauds through usage, but certain sections had not been received, including the requirement for three or more witnesses to wills passing title to real property.

Another provision of the 1676 English statute of frauds is one familiar in American law at the present time—that agreements not to be performed within one year of the date of execution must be evidenced by an instrument in writing. In 1705 the New York Court of Chancery heard a suit on a contract in which the defendant asserted that since his contract was to be performed within a period that exceeded one year, it fell within the provisions of the statute of frauds. The Court overruled his plea. We must therefore assume that the judges held that in this situation the English statute of frauds did not apply in colonial New York.[21]

Even in such a vital matter as the statutory law governing the intestate inheritance of personal property, usage was the method utilized to bring into New York colonial law the rules of the 1670 English statute. The Duke's Laws of 1664, following New England Puritan formulae, provided for partible inheritance, or equal distribution among the children of the deceased, with the exception of the eldest son who was given a double share.[22] The English statute of distribution

19. The Act of Wills, Wards and Former Seisins, 32 Hen.8, c.1, sec. 2 (1540), and the applicable provisions of the 1676 statue of frauds are discussed in relation to New York wills in Herbert A. Johnson, "The Prerogative Court of New York, 1686–1776," *American Journal of Legal History*, XVII (1973), 110–111, 115–116.

20. Ibid., pp. 116–117. This selective reception was also true in Maryland during the years 1744–45. Smith, *Appeals to the Privy Council*, p. 483.

21. Benson v. Rose, 1705, is discussed in Johnson, "Prerogative Court," *AJLH*, XVII, 111.

22. Compare the English statute, 22 & 23 Car. 2, c. 10 (1670) with that of New York, *Colonial Laws, N.Y.*, I, 9–10. On the background of the Duke's Laws and its New England origin, see George L. Haskins and Samuel E. Ewing, "The Spread of Massachusetts Law in the Seventeenth Century," *University of Pennsylvania Law Review*, CVI (1957–58), 413–418, reprinted in David H. Flaherty, ed., *Essays in the History of Early American Law* (Chapel Hill, 1969), pp. 186–191; Morton Pennypacker, *The Duke's Laws: Their Antecedents, Implications and Importance*, in Paul M. Hamlin and Richard B. Morris, eds., *Anglo-American Legal History Series*, 1st Ser., No. 9, pp. 30–31.

of 1670, on the other hand, provided for an equal division of personal property among the intestate's surviving children. While the Duke's Laws originally applied only to Long Island and Westchester, the meagre evidence seems to indicate that they became the rule of decision throughout the province by 1670 and certainly by 1683.[23] We may then safely surmise that a system of partible inheritance and a double portion was accepted throughout New York by 1691.

On the other hand, commencing in 1754, the bonds posted by administrators of decedents' estates refer to the 1670 English statute as the rule governing the actions of New York administrators.[24] This ambiguous evidence indicates that at some time between 1691 and 1754 the intestate distribution statute enacted in England in 1670 was received into New York law through usage. It was not until 1774 that the 1670 English statute was enacted into law through parallel statutory provisions passed by the New York General Assembly.[25] Here the usage may have been one of long standing, and the elimination of the double portion for the eldest son may date from 1691.[26] Yet all that is clear from the meagre evidence is the fact that at least twenty years before the statutory adoption of the 1670 English statute of distribution, there had been reception by usage in provincial New York.

The slow and virtually imperceptible addition of English statutes to the body of New York law may have had a much larger impact than is currently believed, but it cannot be measured accurately until far more details concerning the substantive law of provincial New York are made available through monographic studies. On the other hand the scholarly work completed to the present time indicates a strong inclina-

23. Johnson, "The Advent of Common Law," in Billias, ed., *Law and Authority*, p. 85.

24. Johnson, "Prerogative Court," *AJLH*, XVII, 107–108. Possibly the litigation in Connecticut over partible inheritance of land may have persuaded New York to adopt English rules of intestate descent concerning personalty. See Charles M. Andrews, "The Influence of Colonial Conditions as Illustrated in the Connecticut Intestacy Laws," reprinted in Flaherty, ed., *Essays*, pp. 336–366.

25. *Colonial Laws, N.Y.*, V, 614 (Mar. 9, 1774).

26. The best discussion of partible inheritance and its origins is George L. Haskins, "The Beginning of Partible Inheritance in the American Colonies," *Yale Law Journal*, LI (1941–42), 1280–1315, reprinted in Flaherty, ed., *Essays*, pp. 204–244.

tion toward English law and procedures that was quite characteristic of New York's eighteenth-century legal history. In criminal procedure we have known of the introduction and widespread adoption of English practices early in the eighteenth century.[27] More recently it has been concluded that in regard to substantive criminal law, "the laws of England were put into effect almost across the board, at least for the more common offenses."[28] The Prerogative Court of New York was a remarkable copy of the English ecclesiastical court, except for its elimination of the more sophisticated and prolix methods of pleading and practice.[29] The tendency then, seems to have been inexorably in the direction of a system of laws and law courts remarkably similar to those of the mother country, and it is against that historical trend that we must assess the events in the decade immediately preceding the American Revolution.

Central to the history of law in New York in the prerevolutionary period is the General Assembly act passed on December 24, 1767,[30] which might have done much to clarify the earlier situation concerning English statutes received into New York law by usage only. It specifically mentioned thirty-one English Parliamentary enactments by their titles and the regnal years of their enactment, and "extended" their provisions to the province of New York. The preamble provides the rationale for this unusual procedure,

> Whereas divers Acts of Parliament passed since the Establishment of a Legislature in this Colony, have nevertheless been practised upon us extending to this Colony; tho' they are not declared in the said Acts to extend to the Plantations: and Sundry Acts have since been passed, which it would be expedient to extend to this Colony; And it being conducive to the common Weal, as well as agreeable to his Majesty's most gracious

27. Julius Goebel and T. Raymond Naughton explain that first English common law forms came into use, and then New York began a selective reproduction of English legal institutions. This was hastened by the arrival of able lawyers learned in the law of the mother country. *Law Enforcement in Colonial New York* (New York, 1944), pp. xxv–xxvi, 406–454, 558–602.

28. Smith, "English Criminal Law," in *English Legal System,* p. 30.

29. Johnson, "Prerogative Court," *AJLH,* XVII, 124 126–127, 128, 131–132, 141–142. In regard to the New York Court of Chancery see Julius Goebel, ed., *The Law Practice of Alexander Hamilton,* I (New York, 1964), 172–178.

30. *Colonial Laws, N.Y.,* V, 952–956.

Intentions: that the Laws of this Colony should conform as nearly as possible to the Laws of England; . . .[31]

The preamble further states that in order to remove doubts concerning the applicability of these and other statutes, the provisions were enacted into law.

While a legislative draftsman might have improved upon the phrase identifying the English acts as having been ". . . practised upon us extending to this Colony," the thrust of the words is obvious enough as a criticism of the lawyerly extension by usage concurred in by the New York colonial courts.[32] This is even more readily apparent when the 1767 New York act is examined in relation to the English statutes identified previously as having been received in whole or part, into the usages of New York provincial law. Thus, the 1767 act refers to the 1704 English promissory note act, the 1676 English statute of frauds concerning nuncupative wills, and the 1670 English statute of intestate distribution. Clearly the preamble sets forth with accuracy the need for a statutory "extension" of these English Parliamentary statutes that so long formed a part of New York provincial law by usage. If, as seems most likely, all of the English statutes mentioned in the 1767 legislation had already been received by usage, the act itself was merely declarative of the law of the province as it existed in 1767. On the other hand, if by chance some provisions covered English statutes not hitherto received by usage, it represented new law and an alteration of New York law in the direction of greater conformity with the statutory law of England.

If the 1767 reception act is accepted as a rough guide to English statutes that were extended by usage to provincial New York, we find that the practice was extensive and

31. Ibid., p. 952.

32. The 1768 General Assembly election was characterized by a "no-lawyers" platform, and a number of lawyers were rejected by the electorate. It was during the ensuing assembly that Judge Robert Livingston was declared ineligible for his assembly seat. On the election see Bernard Friedman, "The New York Assembly Elections of 1768 and 1769: The Disruption of Family Politics," *New York History*, XLVI (1965), 3–24, and Roger Champagne, "Family Politics versus Constitutional Principles: The New York Assembly Elections of 1768 and 1769," *Wm. & M. Qtly.*, XX (1963), 57–79, at 64–67. While popular resentment may have been reflected in this phrase, it is important to note that the 1767 act was passed by the lawyer-dominated General Assembly unseated in 1768.

intruded into all fields of law. Eight provisions may be classified as dealing with civil procedure, a particularly apt reception since the Supreme Court of Judicature had been established in 1691 with its powers defined by reference to the jurisdiction of the three common law courts at Westminster.[33] Six statutory extensions relate to matters of criminal law, a field in which Professor Goebel and Mr. Naughton, and more recently Professor Joseph H. Smith, have demonstrated a tendency to follow English models.[34] Three provisions deal with decedent's estates, an area in which New York practice seems to have been strongly influenced by English ecclesiastical court law and procedure.[35] And three others deal with real property law—which one may suspect was shaped by economic influences in colonial New York not dissimilar to those in England.[36] A brief statistical examination thus confirms the impression gained from the limited examples of "usage reception" mentioned above, that adoption of English Parliamentary statutes by usage was extremely common, and that it was not limited to any given field of law. On the other hand, the tendency toward adoption of English statutes was more pronounced in fields where provincial New York had attempted to reproduce English legal institutions. Reference to the common law courts in the General Assembly Act and later ordinances establishing the Supreme Court of Judicature, and the erection of the post-1686 probate system on an ecclesiastical court model, required English statutory reception in large measure if the transferral of these institutions to the New World was to result in effective court systems.

The 1767 reception act weakens any tendency to rely upon the 1691 date as the time before which English common law and statutes applied in the province. While twenty-eight of the thirty-one English statutes enumerated in the 1767 act were enacted after 1691, three had been part of English law prior

33. Hamlin & Baker, eds., *Supreme Court*, I, 67–77.

34. See notes 29, 30, above.

35. See notes 23, 24, 26, 31, above.

36. "By the time of the Revolutionary War, both the development of the colonies and the training of the legal profession had reached the point where it was but natural that the colonies would turn to their legal heritage [*from England*] for guidance." Felix Rackow, "The Right to Counsel: English and American Precedents," *Wm. & M. Qtly.*, 3d Ser., XI (1954), 3–27, at 13.

to that date, and hence, under Chief Justice Horsmanden's formula, would probably have been part of the law of New York. Yet the overarching intention of the 1767 New York act was clearly to insure the reception of English Parliamentary acts passed *after* 1691, and to regularize the law in all fields where usage had resulted in adoption prior to 1767.

The New York reception act would have done much toward eliminating the "hidden law" received through usage in colonial New York, although it may be premature to assume that all of the "usage receptions" had been enumerated in the reception act. Without careful scholarly research into each field it is impossible to evaluate the comprehensiveness of the statute nor its effectiveness in identifying English statutes received by usage in New York and incorporating them by express legislative mention into the statutory law of the province. Yet from the historical evidence we can form some idea of the intention of the New York General Assembly in passing the 1767 reception act.

Recognizing the variety of situations in which English law had been brought into provincial law by usages, the New York General Assembly sought to clarify the state of provincial law even while it demonstrated the conformity of New York law and practice to English standards. While such conformity was, in theory, required from each colony in North America either through its charter, its proprietary grant or its governor's commission, in practice the departures from English norms in substantive and adjective law were considerable. Having drawn closer to the English norm during the eighteenth century, New York chose to reveal her conformity through statutory recognition of the English law "practised upon" its people.

Whatever motives may have inspired the enactment of the 1767 reception act by the General Assembly, it was to have little direct impact upon the substantive law of New York since it was disallowed by the Privy Council in the name of the King when it was submitted to that body for review and approval. Characteristically, the reasons for the royal disallowance are ambiguous and obscure, but they leave some ground for surmising that the circumstances of the times and the constitutional ramifications of the act were responsible. The report of Richard Jackson, legal counsellor to the

Board of Trade, listed four reasons for recommending disallowance:

(1) No part of the laws introduced in New York by the terms of the act appears to be of public utility in the province,

(2) It was not fitting that the acts should be "thus adopted in Cumulo" without setting forth the terms of the statutes adopted,

(3) Such an accumulative act deprived the Crown and its governor "of the distinct approbation or disapprobation that is essential to the Constitution of the province, and to all similar constitutions . . ."

(4) A perusal of the act made it clear that introduction by this method would result in difficulties of construction, and some of these were such as ought not to be left to a court of justice to decide.[37]

The first objection is patently absurd, for not only had the enumerated English statutes been absorbed by usage into New York law, thereby evidencing their utility, but the very fact that the legislature took the time to identify these usages and incorporate them into the reception act indicates their importance to the province.

The second and third objections appear more convincing and more to the constitutional point. Cumulative adoption by date and title alone did limit the disallowance power of the Crown and veto power of the colonial governor, but on the other hand the Crown might veto *in toto*, as it did, and so might the colonial governor, who declined to do so. Yet neither disallowance nor veto would make any difference in the law as effective in New York; this reception act of 1767 was not formulating or receiving any law, it merely was ratifying and codifying prior reception through usage and custom. A veto or disallowance did not cancel the usage, but simply refused it statutory recognition.

Adoption of English statutes by date and title, however, did raise serious construction problems. First it implied that

37. James Munro, ed., *Acts of the Privy Council of England, Colonial Series*, (6 vols.; London, 1908–1912), V, 284–285, supplies the text of Jackson's report and the minute of the disallowance on Dec. 9, 1770. The Board of Trade received the New York legislation on May 6, 1768, and the New York reception act was tabled until advice could be obtained concerning the law officer of the Crown who should take it under consideration. On June 7, 1770 the Board considered several acts and, based on Jackson's reports, recommended to the King that several be disallowed. Presumably the 1767 reception act was among the statutes reported upon and subsequently disallowed. *Journal of the Commissioners for Trade and Plantations from January 1768 to December 1775* (London, 1937), pp. 25, 114–115, 191.

provincial law might absorb English Parliamentary statutes through usage, and the allowance of the 1767 statutes would give royal recognition to that practice, Furthermore the retrospective phraseology of the 1767 New York reception statute left it clear that these Parliamentary statutes might have been effective for an extended period of time prior to 1767 and that New York law was to that extent a product of Parliamentary legislation that had been enacted without mention of the dominions.

Was it too much to anticipate that such usage receptions of English Parliamentary statutes might be claimed to incorporate the English Bill of Rights and the English habeas corpus act of 1679, just as the provincial General Assembly a short time before had tried to engraft the Mutiny Act upon its interpretation of the Quartering Act? Left untrammelled, such an extension of English statutes to the American dominions might very well create an empire ruled not by the King's prerogative exercised in his Privy Council, but rather by the King in his Parliament at Westminster or the King in colonial assemblies sitting in his provincial capitals. Such a diminution of the royal prerogative was almost a century, and one revolution, away.

The fourth reason for disallowance is persuasive, if one is to assume that courts should not construe the terms of statutes. Whatever English practice may have been in that regard, it is clear that counselor Jackson again overlooked the declarative nature of the 1767 reception act. In merely identifying English statutes the reception act left unclear the date upon which those measures took effect in New York. Those statutes that dealt with civil procedure might receive constructions contrary to the interests of British mercantile creditors of New York residents. Those addressed to the statute of frauds might be construed to apply to certain nuncupative wills but not others. In short, the effective date of the reception would be unclear. Yet certainly that was no valid objection to the merits of the reception statute, for the recognition of the usage by New York's courts carried with it a customary usage establishing the time the practice was instituted.

Perhaps even more important to a consideration of the rationale of disallowance is the problem of the symmetry of imperial law. An English Parliamentary statute was construed by the courts of common law, the High Court of Chancery, the High Court of Admiralty, and ultimately by the House of Lords. Those constructions would presumably be binding upon all courts in the realm, but would they be treated as precedents in the Privy Council and made binding upon the empire? If an English statute were extended by title and date alone to a colonial possession, did the construction given to that statute in the English courts bind the colonial courts, or might they vary from the English norm? If so, was the English statute in force in the colony by virtue of colonial statutory acceptance or was it an act of the colonial legislature that drew upon English statutory material for its content, and incorporated the Parliamentary statute by reference?

On these points Jackson's reasoning is far from clear, and one is tempted to suspect that his analysis of the subject was not this extensive, but that he disliked the 1767 New York reception act because of an inherent sense that it disturbed the imperial formula—that there was a system of law for the realm, and one for each of the colonies in the King's dominions. Those systems could be made to interlock, and their rules could be exchanged, but only by the King's servants at Whitehall. Jackson's insistence, made official by the December 9, 1770 disallowance by the Privy Council, was that if New York's lawmakers wanted the benefit of English Parliamentary statutes, they would have to enact them into the law of New York without reference to the legislation in the mother country.[38]

After receiving notice of the disallowance, the New York General Assembly began to enact specific statutes which had the effect of incorporating into New York law the very same English statutes they had cited by title and date in 1767. The English statute of 1697 to prevent fraudulent and vexatious suits was copied almost verbatim in the General Assembly act of February 26, 1772.[39] The English statute of 1699 permitting posthumous children to inherit from their father despite failure to appoint trustees to protect contingent remainder interests was enacted in the General Assembly

38. As a practical matter this was precisely the course taken, and most of the English statutes mentioned in the 1767 reception act were passed as separate acts of the New York General Assembly from 1770 to 1775.

39. *Colonial Laws, N.Y.*, V, 287–291, enacting 8 & 9 Wm. 3, c. 11, secs. 1–8.

act of February 8, 1774.[40] We have already noted the 1773 enactment of the English promissory note act of 1704 and the enactment of the English statute on intestate estates in 1774.[41] The New York General Assembly seems to have been determined to witness very clearly the need of New York as a province to identify with the law and constitution of the mother country and to claim equality of treatment and rights with their fellow subjects within the realm.

Although increased conformity with English statutory law is the most significant trend that can be seen in the receptions of 1691 and 1767–1775, other aspects of these developments deserve comment. First and foremost, custom and usage formed the cutting edge of reception in colonial New York, at least as far as English statutes were concerned. This resulted in a complex and highly individualistic jurisprudence that lacked the qualities of certainty and simplicity that are essential to efficient administration of the law.

In 1691 and again in 1767 the vagueness of the customary law forced New York legislators to seek statutory ratification of prior receptions by usage. The 1691 reception served the dual purpose of clarifying and restating the law, and of accommodating the conflicting jurisdictions that plagued the proprietary province. Clearly the 1767 omnibus reception act served a similar purpose of ratification, but rather than unifying the administration of law and making general certain substantive rules of law, it seems to have served as a constitutional trial balloon, directed toward testing the reaction of Whitehall to a more general claim to the benefit of certain English statutes hitherto not extended to New York. The prompt and specific disallowance of the 1767 act on constitutional grounds eliminated the political potentialities of legal restatement, but the subsequent action by the General Assembly in passing the separate acts individually resulted in a similar restatement of New York law in regard to English statutes.

40. Ibid., V, 604–605, enacting 11 & 12 Wm. 3, c. 16, secs. 1, 2.

41. See discussion in notes 24–28 (intestate inheritance), and notes 17–19 (promissory notes). Another example is "An Act for the better advancement of justice," *Colonial Laws, N.Y.*, V, 537–543 (Mar. 8, 1773), parallelling the provisions of 4 Anne c. 16, secs. 1–5, 7–13, 17–23, 27 (1705), and referred to in the 1767 New York reception statute at *Colonial Laws, N.Y.*, V, 954.

The need for legislative action to regularize reception by usage is a situation that is perhaps not limited solely to the province of New York. Yet even if the phenomenon is considered in such a restricted geographical framework, it is clear that usage reception and the need for legislative ratification may have had widespread significance in the constitution and private law of the province. The law grew by the decisions of the courts and the practices of the people, yet such a mode of evolution created uncertainties that could only be resolved by statutory enactments which by their comprehensive nature touched every field of legal activity. While codification as such was not the purpose of the 1767 statute, it is obvious that the New York colonial experience with usage reception followed by statutory affirmance, was but one step removed from the revision of statutes that was to become common in post-Revolutionary America.

We may perhaps also conclude that the unique mode of statutory reception in New York provides us with additional insight into the function of the courts and legislature in developing positive law in colonial New York. In the courts the absence of printed reports and the uncertainty of oral recollections rendered the development of precedent almost impossible. Consequently the courts were governed by usages which might through the years rise to the level of precedent, yet not receive official sanction until embodied in legislative enactment. This heightened importance of the legislature could well have had significance for the Revolutionary generation which placed inordinate faith in legislative and representative government, and which for nearly three decades after the Revolution held the judiciary in suspicion and distrust.

The 1767 reception act provides valuable information concerning the state of private law in the province of New York and its relationship to Parliamentary statutes; on the other hand its disallowance may provide a key to the state of public law not only in New York but throughout the North American colonies of Great Britain. With the growing debate over the constitutional place of the colonies within the empire, and the rights of individual British subjects residing within those colonies, it is not unreasonable to assume that the 1770 disallowance was intended to emphasize the subordinate status of colonial subjects and the limited authority of their local legislatures. There was the growing likelihood that the increasing conformity of colonial law to English norms would eventually obliterate the constitutional distinctions which the British government sought to preserve between subjects residing within the realm on one hand, and Britishers residing in the colonies on the other. In the view of American colonials those distinctions appeared to have less and less validity as the eighteenth-century reception of English private law progressed. Viewed narrowly, the 1767 reception act appears to be a quest for certainty in private law and a release from the obscurity of reception by usage. Yet in the broader sense, the 1767 reception act and its disallowance are significant constitutional events in the history of colonial New York.

A Bibliography of American Colonial Legal History

Introduction

If historiography is the foster child of American colonial legal history, then bibliography must be its bastard. It would appear that the last attempt to publish a comprehensive bibliography was made by Professor Paul S. Reinsch in 1907, and the current submission may well be the last for another seventy years. There are several reasons for this neglect, one of which is that busy scholars would rather devote themselves to more elevating tasks than the preparation and typing of bibliographical entries. The dreary task is complicated by idiosyncracies of legal and historical bibliography that make accuracy a relative, rather than an absolute goal. Legal bibliographers are indifferent to a lawyer's need for details concerning "points of law." If he survives the drudgery of bibliographic search and preparation, and avoids the major pitfalls awaiting the unwary, the student who completes such a bibliography will be hard pressed to find a willing publisher. The unfortunate consequence is that those first venturing into colonial legal history were at a loss to orient themselves without extensive bibliographical research. While this did much to discourage the lethargic, it also contributed to the isolation of American colonial legal history from the mainstream of scholarship in early American history.

This bibliography is designed to guide its user into the surprisingly large amount of material currently available. It does not include manuscript sources, doctoral dissertations, or printed court records and statutes. To include such materials would vastly increase its size without a commensurate increment in usefulness. For the most part, students working on a given province will readily master the bibliography of printed primary sources, and doctoral dissertations of more recent vintage are readily accessible through *Dissertation Abstracts*.

Every effort was made to insure the inclusiveness of this bibliography. Frequently, *Writings in American History* entries, supplemented by the *American Historical Review* and *Recently Published Articles* duplicated entries also found in the *Index to Legal Periodicals. The Annual Survey of American Law*, published over the past four decades, provides another source to check completeness, and the compiler's own research and bibliography cards supply entries that otherwise would have been overlooked. Some materials are noted from nineteenth-century publications, but it should be recognized that most of those scholarly works are furtive. While many may be dismissed as popularistic, others rank as fine pieces of scholarship. Many are based upon primary sources subsequently lost through disaster or neglect. Even for the twentieth century it cannot safely be said that this bibliography is exhaustive or definitive. Bibliographical control in this important field is ultimately the responsibility of all scholars; the compiler looks forward to the suggestions and corrections that will undoubtedly emanate from his readers.

Searching for this bibliography was completed in June 1980; books reviewed in issues of the *American Historical Review* after that date are not included, nor are more recent articles in the *Index to Legal Periodicals* or the *Recently Published Articles* series. The 1885 date for the commencement of the *Index to Legal Periodicals* should be taken as the beginning date, with more thorough treatment to be expected after 1902. Of course, items that are known to the compiler but fall outside these dates, have been included.

Much can be said about the nature of work done in American colonial legal history by a review of this bibliography. Little surprise will be generated by the number of entries under constitutional law, criminal law and procedure, and civil procedure. Public law is a persistent theme of historical writing, and the nature of the primary sources makes procedural law more readily available to the investigator than the subjects covered in substantive law. Considering the amount of work now being devoted to family and women's history, it is surprising that domestic relations are not subject to more attention. Property law has been given more attention than most fields, but considering the centrality of real property to early American life, additional work seems to be needed. Indeed, there is a pressing need to move on to more thorough and thoughtful investigations in all the subject areas covered in this bibliography.

Less obvious in the completed bibliography is the sense of a surging interest in American colonial legal history in the past century. At the turn of the century, during the thirties, and again in the sixties, there was a revival of interest in this subject; it is almost as if thirty-year locusts produce a live generation of colonial legal historians three times in a century. The current phase of study shows evidence of more permanence. The establishment of the American Society for Legal History in 1956 (after an abortive American Legal History Society in the 1930s), provided an organizational framework encouraging professionalism in research and teaching. Coupled with the American Historical Association's Committee on the Littleton-Griswold Fund (now a joint AHA-ASLH Committee), the society provides support for American colonial legal history. Enthusiasm for American colonial legal history has been fanned by a more general interest in legal and constitutional history, both in law schools and history faculties. Gradually animosity and suspicion between legal scholars and professional historians have changed to cooperation and mutual respect. This bibliography would have been half its size had it appeared fifteen years ago, and the scope of its entries would have been far more modest than they are now.

Professor Reinsch would have been pleased with the product of the past seventy years, and the young men of the thirties who found their life's work in American colonial legal history deserve credit for transmitting their enthusiasm to the current generation of locusts.

Bibliography

GENERAL WORKS

Andrews, Charles M., ed. *Reports on the Laws of Connecticut by Francis Fane . . .* [1731] (New Haven: Tuttle, Moorehouse and Taylor Press, 1915).

Barton, Robert T., ed. *Virginia Colonial Decisions . . . The Reports by Sir John Randolph and by Edward Barradall . . . 1728-1741*, 2 vols. (Boston: Boston Book Co., 1909).

Billias, George A., ed. *Law and Authority in Colonial America* (Barre: Barre Publishers, 1965).

Billings, Warren M. Law and Culture in the Colonial Chesapeake Area, *Southern Studies*, 17 (1978), 333-348.

Boyer, Charles S. Jersey Justice in the Olden Days, *New Jersey Historical Society Proceedings*, New Series, 16 (1931), 257-284, 399-440.

Bradbury, Frank E. Law and Courts of the Massachusetts Bay Colony, *Bostonian Society Publications*, 10 (1913), 129-159.

Bryant, Samuel W. Rhode Island Justice—1772 Vintage, *Rhode Island History*, 26 (1957), 65-71.

Case, Bert Francis. Trials in Early Justice Courts, *Journal of American History*, 1 (1919), 284-288.

Chafee, Zechariah Jr. Colonial Courts and the Common Law, *Massachusetts Historical Society Proceedings*, 68 (1952), 132-159.

Chitwood, Oliver P. *Justice in Colonial Virginia* (Baltimore: Johns Hopkins Press, 1905); reprinted in *West Virginia Law Quarterly*, 32 (1926), 53-101, 192-225, 269-312.

Chumbley, George L. *Colonial Justice in Virginia* (Richmond: Dietz Press, 1938).

Clover, Ralph H. The Rule of Law in Colonial Massachusetts, *University of Pennsylvania Law Review*, 108 (1960), 1001-1036.

Commager, Henry Steele. The American Legal Tradition, *Cambridge Law Journal* 1 (1925), 233-239.

Curran, William J. The Struggle for Equity Jurisdiction in Massachusetts, *Boston University Law Review*, 31 (1951), 269-296.

Curtis, George B. The Colonial County Court, Social Forum and Legislative Precedent, Accomack County, Virginia 1633-1639, *Virginia Magazine of History and Biography*, 85 (1977), 274-288.

Cushing, John D. The Judiciary and Public Opinion in Revolutionary Massachusetts, in George A. Billias, ed., *Law and Authority in Colonial America* (Barre: Barre Publishers, 1965).

Davidson, Elizabeth. *The Establishment of the English Church in the Continental American Colonies* (Durham: Duke University Press, 1936).

Davis, John A. Blacks, Crime and American Culture, *Annals of the American Academy of Political Science*, 423 (1976), 89-98.

Deen, James. Patterns of Testation: Four Tidewater Counties in Colonial Virginia, *American Journal of Legal History*, 16 (1972), 154-176.

DeFuria, G. G. Administration of Justice in Delaware County before William Penn, *Pennsylvania Bar Association Quarterly*, 29 (1958), 216-224.

Dempsey, E. J. Law and Lawyers in American Colonial Days, *Nevada State Bar Journal*, 13 (1948), 190-193.

DePauw, Linda G. Land of the Unfree: Legal Limitations on Liberty in Pre-Revolutionary America, *Maryland Historical Magazine*, 68 (1973), 355-368.

Dewey, Frank L. New Light on the General Court of Colonial Virginia, *William and Mary Law Review*, 21 (1979), 1-14.

Ehrenzweig, Armin A. American Conflicts Law in Its Historical Perspective, *University of Pennsylvania Law Review*, 103 (1954), 133-156.

Ely, James W. Jr. Patterns of Statutory Enactment in South Carolina, 1720-1770, in Herbert A. Johnson, ed., *South Carolina Legal History* (Spartanburg: The Reprint Co., 1980).

Eno, Joel N. The First Court Trials in America, *Journal of American History*, 2, No. 1 (1907), 479-484; also in *Connecticut Magazine*, 9 (1907), 577-582.

Eschelman, H. Frank. The Constructive Genius of David Lloyd in Early Colonial Pennsylvania Legislation and Jurisprudence, 1686-1731, *Pennsylvania Bar Association Reports*, 16 (1910), 406-461.

Evans, Charles. Oaths of Allegiance in Colonial New England, *American Antiquarian Society Proceedings*, New Series, 31, Part 2 (1922), 377-438.

Farrell, John T., ed. *The Superior Court Diary of William Samuel Johnson, 1772-1773* (Washington: American Historical Association, 1942).

Faught, Albert S. Three Centuries of American Litigation, *Temple Law Review*, 13 (1939), 488-504.

Flippin, Percy S. *The Royal Government of Virginia, 1624-1775* (New York: Columbia University Press, 1919).

Friedman, Lawrence M. *A History of American Law* (New York: Simon and Schuster, 1973).

Gerwig, Robert. Colonial Georgia: Path to Self-Government, *Georgia State Bar Journal*, 12 (1976), 130-132.

Gill, Harold B. Jr., and Curtis, George M. III. Virginia's Colonial Probate Records and the Preconditions for Economic History, *Virginia Magazine of History and Biography*, 87 (1978), 68-73.

Goebel, Julius Jr. The Courts and the Law in Colonial New York, in Alexander C. Flick, ed., *History of the State of New York*, 3 (New York: Columbia University Press, 1933).

———. *History of the Supreme Court of the United States, Volume 1, Antecedents and Beginnings to 1801*, Paul A. Freund, ed. (New York: Macmillan Co., 1971).

Grinnell, Frank W. Legal History of Massachusetts from 1630 to 1953, *Massachusetts Law Quarterly*, 38 (1953), 5-132.

Hartog, Hendrik. The Public Law of a County Court: Judicial Government in Eighteenth Century Massachusetts, *American Journal of Legal History*, 20 (1976), 282-289.

Haskell, Thomas L. Litigation and Social Status in Seventeenth-Century New Haven, *Journal of Legal Studies*, 7 (1978), 219-241.

Haskins, George L. Codification of the Law in Colonial Massachusetts: A Study in Comparative Law, *Indiana Law Journal*, 30 (1954), 1-17.

______. *Law and Authority in Early Massachusetts* (New York: The Macmillan Co., 1960).

______. Law and Colonial Society, *American Quarterly*, 9 (1957), 354-364; reprinted in Flaherty, *Essays*, 41-52.

______. The Legal Heritage of Plymouth Colony, *University of Pennsylvania Law Review*, 110 (1962), 847-859.

______. Parliamentary Ideas and Ideals in the Representative Government of Early Massachusetts Bay Colony, *Publications of the Society of Colonial Wars in the Commonwealth of Pennsylvania*, No. 3, 1969 (Philadelphia: The Society, 1971).

______. Representative Government and the Bible Commonwealth in Early Massachusetts, *University of Akron Law Review*, 9 (1975), 207-222.

______, and Ewing, Samuel E. The Spread of Massachusetts Law in the Seventeenth Century, *University of Pennsylvania Law Review*, 106 (1958), 413-418; reprinted in Flaherty, *Essays*, 186-191.

Hilkey, Charles J. *Legal Development in Colonial Massachusetts 1630-1686* (New York: Columbia University Press, 1910).

Howe, Mark DeWolf, ed. *Readings in American Legal History* (Cambridge: Harvard University Press, 1949).

______, and Eaton, Jr., Louis F. The Supreme Judicial Power in the Colony of Massachusetts Bay, *New England Quarterly*, 20 (1947), 1-26.

______. Records of the Suffolk County (Mass.) Court, *New England Quarterly*, 7 (1934), 307-314.

Howe, Paul S. *The Religious and Legal Constitution of the Pilgrim State: The Facts of Early Pilgrim History* (Cape May, N.J.: A. R. Hand, 1923).

Howe, William Wirt. Roman and Civil Law in America, *Harvard Law Review*, 16 (1908), 342-358.

Hurst, James Willard. *The Growth of American Law: The Law Makers* (Boston: Little, Brown & Co., 1950).

Keasbey, Edward Q. Jersey Justice, *New Jersey Bar Association Yearbook 1919-1920*, pp. 39-61.

Kempin, Frederick G. *Legal History: Law and Social Change* (Englewood Cliffs: Prentice Hall, 1963).

Kibler, J. Luther. Early Colonial Government of Virginia, *Tyler's Quarterly Historical and General Magazine*, 31 (1950), 1-12; 32 (1951), 152-162, 262-274.

Konig, David T. Community Custom and the Common Law: Social Change and the Development of Land Law in Seventeenth Century Massachusetts, *American Journal of Legal History*, 18 (1974), 137-177.

______. *Law and Society in Puritan Massachusetts, Essex County, 1629-1692* (Chapel Hill: University of North Carolina Press, 1979).

Kropf, C. R. Colonial Satire and the Law, *Early American Literature*, 12 (1977-78), 234-242.

Law in Colonial New York: The Legal System of 1691, *Harvard Law Review*, 80 (1967), 1757-1772.

Lee, Carol F. Discretionary Justice in Early Massachusetts, *Essex Institute Historical Collections*, 112 (1976), 120-139.

Mars, David, and Kort, Fred. *Administration of Justice in Connecticut* (Storrs: Institute of Public Service, University of Connecticut, 1957).

Morris, Richard B. *Studies in the History of American Law* (New York: Columbia University Press, 1930).

Nelson, William E. *The Americanization of the Common Law: the Impact of Legal Change on Massachusetts Society, 1760-1830* (Cambridge: Harvard University Press, 1975).

Page, Edwin L. *Judicial Beginnings in New Hampshire, 1640-1700* (Concord: New Hampshire Historical Society, 1959).

Presser, Stephen B. An Introduction to the Legal History of Colonial New Jersey, *Rutgers-Camden Law Journal*, 7 (1976), 262-344.

———, and Zainaldin, Jamil S. *Cases and Materials on the Law and American History* (St. Paul: West Publishing Co., 1980).

Radin, Max. *Handbook of Anglo-American Legal History* (St. Paul; West Publishing Co., 1936).

———. The Rivalry of Common Law and Civil Law Ideas in the American Colonies, in *Law: A Century of Progress, 1835-1935*, 3 vols. (New York: New York University Press, 1937).

Reuschlein, Harold G. The Ante-taught Law Period in the United States, *Virginia Law Review*, 32 (1946), 955-979.

Rutman, Darrett B. The Mirror of Puritan Authority, in George A. Billias, ed., *Law and Authority in Colonial America* (Barre: Barre Publishers, 1965).

Shipton, Clifford K. The Locus of Authority in Colonial Massachusetts, in George A. Billias, ed., *Law and Authority in Colonial America* (Barre: Barre Publishers, 1965).

Singleton, Kathleen. The Grand Council of South Carolina, 1670-1690, *South Carolina Historical Association Proceedings*, 4th Annual Meeting (1934), 32-47.

Smith, Joseph H. *Cases and Materials on the Development of Legal Institutions* (St. Paul: West Publishing Co., 1965).

———. The Foundations of Law in Maryland, 1634-1715, in George A. Billias, ed., *Law and Authority in Colonial America* (Barre: Barre Publishers, 1965).

Swan, Bradford F. Frontier Justice in Newport—1652, *Rhode Island History*, 33 (1974), 3-7.

Turner, Eldon. A Functional Look at Law: Political Crisis, Values and Case Volume in Puritan Law, 1671-1680, *American Studies* (University of Kansas), 18 (1977), 71-86.

Warden, G. B. Law Reform in England and New England, 1620 to 1660, *William and Mary Quarterly*, 35 (1978), 668-690.

Washburne, Wilcomb E. Law and Authority in Colonial Virginia, in George A. Billias, ed., *Law and Authority in Colonial America* (Barre: Barre Press, 1965).

Willis, Hugh E. *Introduction to Anglo-American Law* (Bloomington: Indiana University Press, 1926).

Woodbine, George E. The Suffolk County Court, 1671-1680, *Yale Law Journal*, 43 (1936), 1036-1043; reprinted in Flaherty, *Essays*, 192-203.

Wroth, L. Kinvin and Zobel, Hiller B. Boston Massacre Trials, *American Bar Association Journal*, 55 (1969), 329-333.

______. *Legal Papers of John Adams*, 3 vols. (Cambridge: Harvard University Press, 1965).

Zobel, Hiller B. *The Boston Massacre* (New York: W. W. Norton & Co., 1970).

______. Law under Pressure: Boston, 1769-1771, in George A. Billias, ed., *Law and Authority in Colonial America* (Barre: Barre Publishers, 1965).

HISTORIOGRAPHY AND BIBLIOGRAPHY

Amos, Sir Maurice. A Plea for a History of American Law, *American Bar Association Journal*, 22 (1936), 757-759.

Beale, Joseph H. The Study of American Legal History, *West Virginia Law Quarterly*, 39 (1933), 95-103

Bibliographic Control and Guides to Historical Sources, *Law Library Journal*, 69 (1976), 347-368.

Billings, Warren M. English Legal Literature as a Source of Law and Legal Practice for Seventeenth-Century Virginia, *Virginia Magazine of History and Biography*, 87 (1979), 401-416.

Boorstin, Daniel J. Tradition and Method in Legal History, *Harvard Law Review*, 54 (1941), 426-436.

______. The Humane Study of Law, *Yale Law Journal*, 57 (1948), 960-975.

Boyer, Larry M. The Justice of the Peace in England and America from 1506 to 1776: A Bibliographic History, *Quarterly Journal of the Library of Congress*, 34 (1977), 315-326.

Bronner, Edwin B. The First Printing of Magna Charta in America, 1687, *American Journal of Legal History*, 7 (1963), 189-197.

Bryson, W. Hamilton. *Census of Law Books in Colonial Virginia* (Charlottesville: University Press of Virginia, 1978).

______. *The Virginia Law Reporters before 1880* (Charlottesville: University Press of Virginia, 1977).

Clemons, Harry, ed. Some Jefferson Manuscript Memoranda of Colonial Virginia Records, *Virginia Magazine of History and Biography*, 65 (1957), 154-168.

Dargan, Marion. *Crime and the Virginia Gazette, 1736-1775* (Albuquerque: University of New Mexico, 1934), University of New Mexico Bulletin, Sociological Series, Vol. 2, No. 1.

Durel, John W. New Hampshire County Court Records, *Historical New Hampshire*, 31 (1976), 164-175.

Flaherty, David H. An Approach to Legal History: Willard Hurst as Legal Historian, *American Journal of Legal History*, 14 (1970), 222-234.

______. An Introduction to Early American Legal History, in David H. Flaherty, ed., *Essays in the History of Early American Law* (Chapel Hill: University of North Carolina Press, 1969).

______. A Select Guide to the Manuscript Court Records of Colonial Virginia, *American Journal of Legal History*, 19 (1975), 112-137.

______. The Use of Early American Court Records in Historical Research, *Law Library Journal*, 69 (1976), 342-346.

Frank, John P. American Legal History: The Hurst Approach, *Journal of Legal Education*, 18 (1966), 395-410.

Friedrich, C. J. Law and History, *Vanderbilt Law Review*, 14 (1961), 1027-1048.

Fuller, Stephen M. Some Contemporary Approaches to the Study of Legal History and Jurisprudence, *Tulsa Law Journal*, 10 (1975), 576-582.

Gates, Paul W. Research in the History of American Land Tenure: A Review Article, *Agricultural History*, 28 (1954), 121-126.

Gersack, Dorothy H. Colonial, State and Federal Court Records, *American Archivist*, 36 (1973), 33-42.

Gordon, Robert W. J. Willard Hurst and the Common Law Tradition in American Legal Historiography, *Law and Society Review*, 10 (1976), 9-55.

———. Recent Trends in Legal Historiography, *Law Library Journal*, 69 (1976), 462-468.

Graff, Harvey J. A Reply [to Eric Monkkonen, "Systematic Criminal Justice History"], *Journal of Interdisciplinary History*, 9 (1979), 465-471.

Hamlin, Paul M. The History of American Law: Possibilities, Progress and Resources and Initial Requirements, *New York Law Forum*, 2 (1956), 76-96.

Haskins, George L. Court Records and History, *William and Mary Quarterly*, 5 (1948), 547-552.

Hilkey, Charles J. Unpublished Sources for Early American Legal History, *West Virginia Law Quarterly*, 40 (1934), 224-229.

Hogue, L. Lynn. The Sources of Trott's Grand Jury Charges, in Herbert A. Johnson, ed., *South Carolina Legal History* (Spartanburg: The Reprint Co., 1980).

Horwitz, Morton J. The Conservative Tradition in the Writing of American Legal History, *American Journal of Legal History*, 17 (1973), 275-294.

Howe, Mark DeWolf. Records of the Suffolk County Court, *New England Quarterly*, 7 (1934), 307-314.

Hurst, James Willard. Legal History: A Research Program, *Wisconsin Law Review, 1942*, pp. 323-333.

———. Old and New Dimensions of Research in United States Legal History, *American Journal of Legal History*, 23 (1979), 1-20.

———. The Uses of Law in Four "Colonial" States of the United States, *Wisconsin Law Review, 1945*, pp. 577-592.

James, Eldon R. Some Difficulties in the Way of a History of American Law, *Illinois Law Review*, 23 (1929), 683-688.

———. A List of Treatises Printed in the British Colonies and the American States before 1801, in *Harvard Legal Essays in Honor of Joseph R. Beale and Samuel Williston* (Cambridge: Harvard University Press, 1934).

Jeffrey, William Jr. Early New England Court Records, *Boston Public Library Quarterly*, 6 (1954), 160-184.

Johnson, Herbert A. American Colonial Legal History: A Historiographical Interpretation, in Alden T. Vaughan and George A. Billias, eds., *Perspectives on Early American History: Essays in Honor of Richard B. Morris* (New York: Harper & Row, 1973); reprinted herein at 3-34.

———. *Imported Eighteenth-Century Law Treatises in American Libraries, 1700-1799* (Knoxville: University of Tennessee Press, 1978).

Kammen, Michael G. Colonial Court Records and the Study of Early American History: A Bibliographic Review, *American Historical Review*, 70 (1965), 732-739.

Kocourek, Albert. Sources of Law in the United States of America and their Relation to Each Other, *American Bar Association Journal*, 18 (1932), 676-682.

Miller, George J. *The Printing of the Elizabethtown Bill in Chancery* [1747] (Perth Amboy: Board of Proprietors of the Eastern Division of New Jersey, 1942).

Moltke-Hansen, David. Newspapers in Colonial South Carolina Legal History, in Herbert A. Johnson, ed., *South Carolina Legal History* (Spartanburg: The Reprint Co., 1980).

Monkkonen, Eric. Systematic Criminal Justice History: Some Suggestions, *Journal of Interdisciplinary History*, 9 (1979), 451-464.

Morris, Richard B. Current Statesmen's Publication Program: An Appraisal from the Point of View of the Legal Historian, *American Journal of Legal History*, 11 (1967), 95-106.

______. The Sources of Early American Law: The Colonial Period, *West Virginia Law Quarterly*, 40 (1934), 212-213.

______. Early American Court Records: A Publication Program, *Anglo-American Legal History Series*, No. 4 (New York: New York University School of Law, 1941); also in *New York University Law Quarterly Review*, 18 (1941), 210-245.

Mullett, Charles F. The Value of Law to Historians, *Missouri Law Review*, 9 (1944), 144-164.

Murphy, Earl F. The Necessity of Policy Guides in Legal Historical Research, *Journal of Legal Education*, 12 (1959), 207-214.

McDowell, William L. Jr. Colonial and Early State Court Records in the South Carolina Archives, in Herbert A. Johnson, ed., *South Carolina Legal History* (Spartanburg: The Reprint Co., 1980).

Palmer, Benjamin W. The Historian and the Lawyer, *American Bar Association Journal*, 32 (1946), 530-536.

Parrish, Jenni. Law Books and Legal Publishing in America, 1760-1840, *Law Library Journal*, 72 (1979), 355-452.

Paxson, Frederick L. The Influence of Frontier Life on the Development of American Law, *Proceedings of the State Bar Association of Wisconsin for the Years 1919, 1920 and 1921* (Madison: Cantwell Print Co., 1921).

Philbrick, Francis S. Possibilities of American Legal History, *Law Library Journal*, 27 (1934), 191-213.

Pound, Roscoe. New Possibilities of Old Materials of American Legal History, *West Virginia Law Quarterly*, 40 (1934), 205-211.

Presser, Stephen B. Revising the Conservative Tradition: Towards a New American Legal History, *New York University Law Review*, 52 (1977), 700-725.

Reeves, Charles. Sources of South Carolina Legal History in the Atlanta Branch, Federal Archives and Records Center, in Herbert A. Johnson, ed., *South Carolina Legal History* (Spartanburg: The Reprint Co., 1980).

Reinsch, Paul S. English Common Law in the Early American Colonies, in *Select Essays in Anglo-American Legal History*, 3 vols. (Boston: Little, Brown & Co., 1907).

______. A Short Bibliography of American Colonial Law, in *Select Essays in Anglo-American Legal History*, 3 vols. (Boston: Little, Brown & Co., 1907).

Scafidel, Beverly. The Bibliography and Significance of Trott's Laws, in Herbert A. Johnson, ed., *South Carolina Legal History* (Spartanburg: The Reprint Co., 1980).

Shapiro, Martin, and Shapiro, Barbara. Interdisciplinary Aspects of American Legal History, *Journal of Interdisciplinary History*, 4 (1974), 611-626.

Stebbins, Howard L. Outline of Massachusetts Statute Law Publications, *Law Library Journal*, 20 (1927), 72-84.

Surrency, Erwin C., et al. Legal History and Rare Books, *Law Library Journal*, 59 (1966), 71-92.

Teachout, Peter R. Light in Ashes: The Problem of "Respect for the Rule of Law" in American Legal History, *New York University Law Review*, 53 (1978), 241-288.

Tushnet, Mark V. The Dialectics of Legal History, *Texas Law Review*, 57 (1979), 1295-1305.

———. Perspectives on the Development of American Law: A Critical Review of Friedman's "A History of American Law," *Wisconsin Law Review*, (1977), pp. 81-109.

Waters, James F. Brooklyn's Earliest Court Records, *American Journal of Legal History*, 2 (1958), 315-320.

Westfall, William. Law, Lessons and Learning in History, *Social Studies*, 67 (1976), 194-197.

Wiecek, William M. The Statutory Law of Slavery and Race in the Thirteen Mainland Colonies of British America, *William and Mary Quarterly*, 34 (1977), 258-280.

Wolf, Edwin 2d. The Disposal of the Library of William Byrd of Westover, *Proceedings of the American Antiquarian Society*, 68 (1958), 19-106.

———. The Library of Ralph Assheton: The Book Background of a Colonial Philadelphia Lawyer, *Papers of the Bibliographical Society of America*, 58 (1964), 345-379.

———. The Library of a Philadelphia Judge, 1708, *Pennsylvania Magazine of History and Biography*, 83 (1959), 180-191.

———. Historical Development of the American Lawyer's Library, *Law Library Journal*, 61 (1959), 440-450.

Wroth, L. Kinvin. Possible Kingdoms: The New England Town from the Perspective of Legal History, *American Journal of Legal History*, 15 (1971), 318-330.

Wyzanski, Charles Jr. History and Law, *University of Chicago Law Review*, 26 (1959), 237-244.

Zainaldin, Jamil S. The New Legal History: A Review Essay, *Northwestern University Law Review*, 73 (1978), 205-225.

Zobel, Hiller B. The Joys and Uses of Legal History, *Massachusetts Historical Society Proceedings*, 84 (1972), 53-70.

———. Lawyers' Papers as a Source of Legal History—Part I, Bridge of Words, 18th Century Lawyers and Papers, *Law Library Journal*, 69 (1976), 303-306.

RECEPTION

Andrews, Charles M. The Influence of Colonial Conditions as Illustrated in the Connecticut Intestacy Law, *Select Essays in Anglo-American Legal History*, 3 vols. (Boston: Little Brown & Co., 1907), 1: 431-463; reprinted in Flaherty, *Essays*, 336-366.

Baade, Hans W. The English Statute of Frauds in North Carolina: A Statute Spurned, *Duke Bar Journal*, 5 (1955), 16-25.

Brown, Elizabeth G. British Statutes in the Emergent Nations of North America, 1606-1949, *American Journal of Legal History*, 7 (1963), 95-136.

Chafee, Zechariah Jr. Colonial Courts and the Common Law, *Massachusetts Historical Society Proceedings*, 68 (1952), 132-159; reprinted in Flaherty, *Essays*, 53-82.

Clark, J. Murray. Why the "Lawes of Virginia." *Virginia Law Register*, New Series, 6 (1920), 81-100.

Dale, Richard C. The Adoption of the Common Law by the American Colonies, *American Law Register*, New Series, 21 (1882), 553-574.

Davis, Charles T. Some Thoughts on Early Colonial Development, *Massachusetts Historical Society Proceedings*, 64 (1932), 507-515.

Goebel, Julius Jr. King's Law and Local Custom in Seventeenth Century New England, *Columbia Law Review*, 31 (1931), 416-448; reprinted in Flaherty, *Essays*, 83-120.

______. *History of the Supreme Court of the United States, Volume 1, Antecedents and Beginnings to 1801*, Paul A. Freund, ed. (New York: Macmillan & Co., 1971).

Hall, Ford H. The Common Law: An Account of its Reception in the United States, *Vanderbilt Law Review*, 4 (1951), 791-823.

Hamilton, W. B. The Transmission of English Law to the Frontier of America, *South Atlantic Quarterly*, 67 (1968), 243-264.

Haskins, George L. The Beginnings of Partible Inheritance in the American Colonies, *Yale Law Journal*, 51 (1942), 1280-1315.

______. A Problem in the Reception of the Common Law in the Colonial Period, *University of Pennsylvania Law Review*, 97 (1949), 842-853.

Howe, Mark DeWolf. Migration of the Common Law: A Symposium—The United States of America, *Law Quarterly Review*, 76 (1960), 49-53.

______. The Sources of Law in Colonial Massachusetts, in George A. Billias, ed., *Law and Authority in Colonial America* (Barre: Barre Publishers, 1965).

______. The Process of Outlawry in New York: A Study of the Selective Reception of English Law, *Cornell Law Quarterly*, 23 (1938), 559-579; reprinted in Flaherty, *Essays*, 433-450.

Johnson, Herbert A. The Advent of Common Law in Colonial New York, in George A. Billias, ed., *Law and Authority in Colonial America* (Barre: Barre Publishers, 1965); reprinted herein at 37-54.

______. English Statutes in Colonial New York, *New York History*, 58 (1977), 277-296; reprinted herein at 193-212.

Kocourek, Albert. Factors in the Reception of Law. *Tulane Law Review*, 10 (1936), 209-230.

Lewis, Leon P. The Development of a Common Law System in Connecticut, *Connecticut Bar Journal*, 27 (1953), 419-427.

Maine's Reception of the Common Law, *Maine Law Review*, 30 (1979), 274-294.

Morris, Richard B. Massachusetts and the Common Law: The Declaration of 1646, *American Historical Review*, 31 (1926), 443-453; reprinted in Flaherty, *Essays*, 135-146.

Paxson, Frederick L. The Influence of Frontier Life on the Development of American Law, *Proceedings of the State Bar Association of Wisconsin for the Years 1919, 1920 and 1921* (Madison: Cantwell Print Co., 1921).

Pope, Herbert. The English Common Law in the United States, *Harvard Law Review*, 24 (1910), 6-30.

Pound, Roscoe. The Development of American Law and Its Deviation from English Law: Address, *Law Quarterly Review*, 67 (1951), 49-66.

______. The Pioneers and the Common Law, *West Virginia Law Quarterly*, 27 (1920), 1-19.

Reinsch, Paul S. English Common Law in the Early American Colonies, in *Select Essays in Anglo-American Legal History*, 3 vols. (Boston: Little, Brown & Co., 1907).

Reppy, Alison. The Slayer's Bounty—in New York, *New York University Law Review*, 20 (1945), 270-324.

Sioussat, St. George L. The Theory of Extension of English Statutes to the Plantations, *Select Essays in Anglo-American Legal History*, 3 vols. (Boston: Little, Brown & Co., 1907).

Smith, Joseph H. The English Criminal Law in Early America, in *The English Legal System: Carryover to the Colonies* (Los Angeles: University of California at Los Angeles, 1975).

Stern, William B. The Influence of Foreign Law on American Law, *Law Library Journal*, 33 (1940), 194-205.

Stoebuck, William B. Reception of English Common Law in the American Colonies, *William and Mary Law Review*, 10 (1968), 393-426.

Swindler, William F. The Advent of Common Law in America at Jamestown, *Commonwealth* (Va.) 26, No. 4 (1959), 23-24.

Zuckerman, Louis E. The Common Law of America, *American Law Review*, 53 (1919), 577-584.

ADMIRALTY

Andrews, William S. New York and Its Waters, *Cornell Law Quarterly*, 16 (1930), 1-18.

Bridwell, R. Randall. Mr. Nicholas Trott and the South Carolina Vice Admiralty Court: An Essay on Procedural Reform and Colonial Politics, *South Carolina Law Review*, 28 (1976), 181-218.

Carman, Ernest C. Sovereign Rights and Relations in the Control and Use of American Waters, *Southern California Law Review*, 2 (1929), 84-100; 3 (1930), 162-172, 266-319.

Clark, Dora M. The Impressment of Seamen in the American Colonies, in *Essays in Colonial History Presented to Charles McLean Andrews*. . . (New Haven: Yale University Press, 1931).

Crump, Helen J. *Colonial Admiralty Jurisdiction in the Seventeenth Century* (London: Longmans, Green & Co., 1931).

David, Harry P. The New York Law of the Foreshore at the Beginning of the Eighteenth Century, *Cornell Law Quarterly*, 11 (1926), 209-212.

Dow, George F. The Trial and Execution of Pirates Two Centuries Ago in New England, *Old-Time New England*, 14 (1923), 73-82.

Etting, Theodore M. *The Admiralty Jurisdiction in America* (Philadelphia: Rees Welsh & Co., 1879).

Harper, Lawrence A. *The English Navigation Laws* (New York: Columbia University Press, 1939).

Hart, Samuel. The Fundamental Orders and the Charter, *New Haven County Historical Society Papers*, 8 (1914), 238-254.

Hough, Charles M., ed. *Reports of Cases in the Vice Admiralty of the Province of New York and the Court of Admiralty of the State of New York* (New Haven: Yale University Press, 1925).

Jameson, J. Franklin, ed. *Privateering and Piracy in the Colonial Period: Illustrative Documents* (New York: Macmillan, 1923).

Johnson, Herbert A., and Syrett, David. Some Nice Sharp Quillets of the Customs Law: The *New York* Affair, 1763-1767, *William and Mary Quarterly*, 25 (1968), 432-451; reprinted herein at 105-124.

King, Joseph E. Judicial Flotsam in Massachusetts Bay, 1760-1765, *New England Quarterly*, 27 (1954), 366-381.

King, Stanley. Sand Dunes and Sea Law, *Duke's County (Mass.) Intelligencer*, 3 No. 1, (1961), 10-18.

Lovejoy, David S. Rights Imply Equality: The Case Against Admiralty Jurisdiction in America, *William and Mary Quarterly*, 16 (1959), 459-484.

Pares, Richard. *Colonial Blockade and Neutral Rights, 1739-1763* (Oxford: Clarendon Press, 1938).

Pennypacker, Morton. Captain Kidd, *New York History*, 26 (1944), 482-531.

Setaro, Franklyn C. The Formative Era of American Admiralty Law, *New York Law Forum*, 5 (1959), 9-44.

Smith, Maurice H. *The Writs of Assistance Case* (Berkeley: University of California Press, 1978).

Ubbelohde, Carl W. The Vice Admiralty Court of Royal North Carolina, 1729-1760, *North Carolina Historical Review*, 31 (1954), 517-528.

______. *The Vice Admiralty Courts and the American Revolution* (Chapel Hill: University of North Carolina Press, 1960).

Whittlesey, John J. *Law of the Seashore, Tidewaters and Great Ponds in Massachusetts and Maine* (Boston: The Murray Print Co., 1932).

Wroth, L. Kinvin. The Massachusetts Vice Admiralty Court and the Federal Admiralty Jurisdiction, *American Journal of Legal History*, 6 (1962), 250-268, 347-367.

BUSINESS ORGANIZATIONS

Baldwin, Simeon E. A History of the Law of Private Corporations in the Colonies and States, in *Select Essays in Anglo-American Legal History*, 3 vols. (Boston: Little, Brown & Co., 1907).

Davis, John S. *Essays on the Early History of American Corporations* (Princeton: Princeton University Press, 1959).

Ford, Worthington C., ed. Pickering v. Weston, 1623, *Massachusetts Historical Society Proceedings*, 54 (1922), 165-178.

Freeland, Fred. Merger and Consolidation of New York Business Corporations: History of Enabling Legislation, 1771-1956, *Fordham Law Review*, 25 (1956), 672-701.

Harbrecht, Paul P., and McCallin, Joseph A. The Corporation and the State in Anglo-American Law and Politics, *Journal of Public Law*, 10 (1961), 1-46.

Hartog, Hendrik. Because all the World was not New York City: Governance, Property Rights and the State in the Changing Definition of a Corporation, *Buffalo Law Review*, 28 (1979), 91-109.

Latham, Earl. The Body Politic of the Corporation, in Edward S. Mason, ed., *The Corporation in Modern Society* (Cambridge: Harvard University Press, 1959).

Livermore, Shaw. The Advent of Corporations in New York, *New York History*, 16 (1935), 286-298.

Semmes, Raphael, ed. Claiborne vs. Clobery, et al. in the High Court of Admiralty, *Maryland Historical Magazine*, 26 (1931), 381-404; 27 (1932), 17-28, 99-114, 191-214, 337-352; 28 (1933), 26-43, 172-195, 257-265.

Seymour, Edmund B. Jr. The Historical Development of the Common Law Conception of a Corporation, *American Law Register*, 51 (1903), 529-535.

CIVIL PROCEDURE

Arnold, Morris S. Historical Inquiry into the Right to Trial by Jury in Complex Civil Litigation, *University of Pennsylvania Law Review*, 128 (1980), 829-848.

Devlin, Patrick. Jury Trials of Complex Cases: English Practice at the Time of the Seventh Amendment, *Columbia Law Review*, 80 (1980), 59-88.

Ellefson, C. Ashley. The Writ of *Audita Querela* in Eighteenth Century Maryland, *Maryland Historical Magazine*, 59 (1964), 369-379.

Feer, Robert A. Imprisonment for Debt in Massachusetts before 1820, *Mississippi Valley Historical Review*, 48 (1961), 252-269.

Fisher, Sydney G. The Administration of Equity through Common Law Forms in Pennsylvania, in *Select Essays in Anglo-American Legal History*, 3 vols. (Boston: Little, Brown & Co., 1907).

Goodman, Leonard S. Mandamus in the Colonies, *American Journal of Legal History*, 1 (1957), 308-335; 2 (1958), 1-34, 129-147.

Harrison, Fairfax. Imprisonment for Debt in Colonial Virginia, *Virginia Magazine of History and Biography*, 25 (1927), 1-6.

Howe, Mark DeWolf. The Process of Outlawry in New York: A Study in the Selective Reception of English Law, *Cornell Law Quarterly*, 23 (1938), 559-579; reprinted in Flaherty, *Essays*, 433-450.

Johnson, Herbert A. Civil Procedure in John Jay's New York, *American Journal of Legal History*, 11 (1967), 69-80; reprinted herein at 159-170.

Karraker, Cyrus H. Deodands in Colonial Virginia and Maryland, *American Historical Review*, 37 (1932), 712-717.

Katz, Stanley N. The Politics of Law in Colonial America: Controversies over Chancery Courts and Equity Law in the Eighteenth Century, *Perspectives on American History*, 5 (1971), 257-286.

Levy, Nathan Jr. Mesne Process in the Early American Colonies, *Mississippi Law Journal*, 44 (1973), 671-691.

Millar, Robert W. Three American Ventures in Summary Civil Procedure [South Carolina, 1769], *Yale Law Journal*, 38 (1923), 193-224.

______. *Civil Procedure of the Trial Court in Historical Perspective* (New York: Law Center of New York University, 1952).

McCormick, JoAnne. Civil Procedure in the Camden Circuit Court, 1772-1790, in Herbert A. Johnson, ed., *South Carolina Legal History* (Spartanburg: The Reprint Co., 1980).

Nelson, William E. The Reform of Common Law Pleading in Massachusetts, 1760-1830: Adjudication as a Prelude to Legislation, *University of Pennsylvania Law Review*, 122 (1973), 93-136.

Newbold, David M. *Notes on the Introduction of Equity Jurisdiction into Maryland, 1634-1720* (Baltimore: M. Curlander, 1903).

Putnam, Harrington. The Early Administration of Equity in this Country, *Central Law Journal*, 90 (1920), 424-425.

Riesenfeld, Stefan A. Enforcement of Money Judgments in Early American History, *Michigan Law Review*, 71 (1973), 691-728.

______. Collection of Money Judgments in American Law—A Historical Inventory and Prospectus, *Iowa Law Review*, 42 (1957), 155-182.

Ryan, Edward L. Imprisonment for Debt—Its Origin and Repeal, *Virginia Magazine of History and Biography*, 42 (1934), 53-58.

Sedgwick, Arthur G., and Wait, Frederick S. The History of the Action of Ejectment in England and the United States, in *Select Essays in Anglo-American Legal History*, 3 vols. (Boston: Little, Brown & Co., 1907).

Taylor, H. Braughan. The Foreign Attachment Law and the Coming of the Revolution in North Carolina, *North Carolina Historical Review*, 52 (1975), 20-36.

Thayer, James Bradley. A Chapter in Legal History in Massachusetts (Witness competency), *Harvard Law Review*, 9 (1895), 1-12.

COMMERCIAL LAW AND CONTRACTS

Aiken, John R. New Netherlands Arbitration in the 17th Century, *Arbitration Journal*, 29 (1974), 145-160.

Bartolini, Anthony, and Picciotti, Anthony L. V. Compulsory Arbitration in Pennsylvania—Its Scope, Effect, Applications and Limitations in Montgomery and Delaware Counties, *Villanova Law Review*, 2 (1957), 529-542.

Beutel, Frederick K. Colonial Sources of the Negotiable Instruments Law in the United States, *Illinois Law Review*, 34 (1939), 137-150.

Dow, George F. Building Agreements in Seventeenth Century Massachusetts, *Old-Time New England*, 12 (1922), 135-139; 13 (1922), 28-32; 14 (1923), 131-134.

Jones, William C. An Inquiry into the Adjudication of Mercantile Disputes in Great Britain and the U.S., *University of Chicago Law Review*, 25 (1958), 445-464.

Kellock, Katharine A. London Merchants and the Pre-1776 American Debts, *Guildhall Studies in London History*, 1 (1974), 109-149.

Riddell, William R. The First Failure of a Boston Banker and Its Results, *Massachusetts Law Quarterly*, 18, No. 5 (1933), 85-87.

Watkins, Walter K. Three Contracts for Seventeenth Century Building Construction in Massachusetts, *Old-Time New England*, 12 (1920), 27-32.

CONSTITUTIONAL LAW

Adelman, David C. Strangers: Civil Rights of Jews in the Colony of Rhode Island, *Rhode Island Jewish Historical Notes*, 1 (1954), 104-118.

Andrews, Charles M. Royal Disallowance of Colonial Laws, *Proceedings of the American Antiquarian Society*, New Series, 24, Part 2 (1914), 342-362.

Andrews, Matthew P. Separation of Church and State in Maryland, *Catholic Historical Review*, 21 (1935), 164-176.

Arnold, Morris S. Historical Inquiry into the Right to Trial by Jury in Complex Civil Litigation, *University of Pennsylvania Law Review*, 128 (1980), 829-848.

Baninninga, Jerald L. James Otis on the Writs of Assistance, *Speech Monographs*, 27 (1960), 351-352.

Barnett, Lincoln. The Case of John Peter Zenger, *American Heritage*, 23 (1971), 33-41, 103-105.

Birch, John J. For Freedom of the Press [Zenger Trial], *Americana*, 34 (1940), 494-499.

Black, Barbara A. The Constitution of Empire: The Case for the Colonies, *University of Pennsylvania Law Review*, 124 (1976), 1157-1211.

Bowen, Clarence W. The Charter of Connecticut, *American Historical Association Annual Report, 1912*, pp. 107-111.

Bridwell, R. Randall. Nicholas Trott and the Proprietary Constitution, in Herbert A. Johnson, ed., *South Carolina Legal History* (Spartanburg: The Reprint Co., 1980).

Bronner, Edwin B. Penn's Charter of Property of 1701, *Pennsylvania History*, 24 (1957), 267-292.

Brydon, George M. The Antiecclesiastical Laws of Virginia, *Virginia Magazine of History and Biography*, 64 (1956), 259-285.

Buranelli, Vincent. Peter Zenger's Editor, *American Quarterly*, 7 (1955), 174-181.

______. The Myth of Anna Zenger, *William and Mary Quarterly*, 13 (1956), 157-168.

Byrns, Ruth K. Religious Tolerance in Colonial Maryland, *Catholic World*, 138 (1934), 694-700.

Caldwell, Robert G. The Settlement of Interstate Disputes, *American Journal of International Law*, 14 (1920), 38-69.

Carpenter, William S. The Separation of Powers in the Eighteenth Century, *American Political Science Review*, 22 (1928), 32-44.

The Case of the Pistole Fee: The Report of a Hearing of the Pistole Fee Dispute before the Privy Council, June 18, 1754, *Virginia Magazine of History and Biography*, 66 (1958), 399-422.

Chafee, Zechariah Jr. *Freedom of Speech* (New York: Harcourt Brace & Co., 1920).

Cheshire, Joseph B. The Fundamental Constitutions of Carolina, and Religious Liberty in the Province of North Carolina, *Historical Magazine of the Protestant Episcopal Church*, 1 (1932), 204-221.

Clark, Charles E. A Test of Religious Liberty: The Ministry Land Case in Narragansett, 1668-1752, *Journal of Church and State*, 11 (1969), 295-319.

Clark, J. Murray. The Relations between the British Dominion of Virginia and the Dominion of Canada, *Virginia Law Register*, New Series, 7 (1922), 641-656.

Clark, Michael D. Jonathan Boucher and the Toleration of Roman Catholics in Maryland, *Maryland Historical Magazine*, 71 (1976), 194-203.

Clarke, Mary P. Parliamentary Privilege in the American Colonies, in *Essays in Colonial History Presented to Charles McLean Andrews . . .* (New Haven: Yale University Press, 1931).

Conkin, Paul K. *Self-evident Truths: Being a Discourse on the Origins and Development of the First Principles of American Government—Popular Sovereignty, Natural Rights and Balance and Separation of Powers* (Bloomington: Indiana University Press, 1974).

Conley, Patrick J. Rhode Island Constitutional Development, 1636-1775: A Survey, *Rhode Island History*, 27 (1968), 74-96.

Connor, Henry G. The Constitutional Right to Trial by a Jury of the Vicinage, *University of Pennsylvania Law Review*, 57 (1909), 197-215.

Cook, Robert. Judicial Review and Legislative Power, in Herbert A. Johnson, ed., *South Carolina Legal History* (Spartanburg: The Reprint Co., 1980).

Corwin, Edward S. Franklin and the Constitution, *American Philosophical Society Proceedings*, 100 (1956), 283-288.

Crossman, Ralph L. The Legal and Journalistic Significance of the Trial of John Peter Zenger, *Rocky Mountain Law Review*, 10 (1938), 258-268.

Dargo, George. *Roots of the Republic: A New Perspective on Early American Constitutionalism* (New York: Praeger Publishers, 1974).

Davidson, Elizabeth. *The Establishment of the English Church in the Continental American Colonies* (Durham: Duke University Press, 1936).

DePauw, Linda G. Land of the Unfree: Legal Limitations on Liberty in Pre-Revolutionary America, *Maryland Historical Magazine*, 68 (1973), 355-368.

Dickerson, Oliver M. British Control of American Newspapers on the Eve of the Revolution, *New England Quarterly*, 24 (1951), 453-468.

Driscoll, John T. The Charter of Liberties and the New York Assembly of 1683, *United States Catholic Historical Records and Studies*, 4 (1903), 5-53.

Egerton, H. E. The Seventeenth and Eighteenth Century Privy Council and Its Relations with the Colonies, *Journal of Comparative Legislation*, 3rd Series, 7 (1925), 1-16.

Eldredge, Laurence H. *The Development of Freedom of the Press in Colonial America* (Philadelphia: Society of Colonial Wars in the Commonwealth of Pennsylvania, 1940).

Ervin, Spencer. The Establishment, Government and Functioning of the Church in Colonial Virginia, *Protestant Episcopal Church Historical Magazine*, 25 (1957), 65-110.

Flaherty, David H. *Privacy in Colonial New England* (Charlottesville: University Press of Virginia, 1972).

Frese, Joseph R. Early Parliamentary Legislation on Writs of Assistance, *Colonial Society of Massachusetts Proceedings*, 38 (1959), 318-359.

______. James Otis and Writs of Assistance, *New England Quarterly*, 30 (1957), 496-508.

Gaines, William H. Jr. Declarations of Unconstitutionality, *Virginia Cavalcade*, 6, No. 3 (1956), 42-47.

Gipson, Lawrence H. Massachusetts Bay and American Colonial Union, 1754, *American Antiquarian Society Proceedings*, 77 (1961), 63-92.

Glass, Albert S. Historical Aspects of Habeas Corpus, *St. John's Law Review*, 9 (1934), 55-70.

Greene, Jack P., ed. *The Nature of Colony Constitutions: Two Pamphlets on the Wilkes Fund Controversy in South Carolina* (Columbia: University of South Carolina Press, 1970).

______. South Carolina's Colonial Constitution: Two Proposals for Reform, *South Carolina Historical Magazine*, 62 (1961), 72-81.

Grey, Thomas C. Origins of the Unwritten Constitution: Fundamental Law in American Revolutionary Thought, *Stanford Law Review*, 30 (1978), 843-893.

Grinnell, Frank W. John Winthrop and the Constitutional Thinking of John Adams, *Massachusetts Historical Society Proceedings*, 63 (1931), 91-119.

Guernsey, Rocellus S. Religious Liberty in Colonial New York, *Magazine of History*, 19 (1914), 70-88.

Hadley, Arthur T. The Constitutional Position of Property in America, *Independent*, 69 (1908), 834-838.

Haffenden, Phillip S. The Crown and the Colonial Charters, 1675-1688, *William and Mary Quarterly*, 15 (1958), 452-465.

Hallam, Oscar. Judicial Power to Declare Legislative Acts Void, *American Law Review*, 48 (1914), 85-114, 225-273.

Hanley, Thomas O. *Their Rights and Liberties: The Beginnings of Religious and Political Freedom in Maryland* (Westminster: Newman Press, 1959).

Haskins, George L. Parliamentary Ideas and Ideals in the Representative Government of the Early Massachusetts Bay Colony, *Publications of the Society of Colonial Wars in the Commonwealth of Pennsylvania*, No. 3, 1969 (Philadelphia: The Society, 1971).

Hickman, Emily. Colonial Writs of Assistance, *New England Quarterly*, 5 (1932), 83-104.

Hill, A Shrady. The Parson's Cause, *Historical Magazine of the Protestant Episcopal Church*, 46 (1977), 5-35.

Hoffer, Peter C., and Hull, N. E. H. The First American Impeachments, *William and Mary Quarterly*, 35 (1978), 653-667.

———. Power and Precedent in the Creation of an American Impeachment Tradition: The Eighteenth Century Colonial Record, *William and Mary Quarterly*, 36 (1979), 51-77.

Holden, Benedict M. Jr. Freedom of Expression in Connecticut, *Connecticut Bar Journal*, 29 (1955), 240-249.

Hudson, Winthrop S. William Penn's *English Liberties:* Tract for Several Times, *William and Mary Quarterly*, 26 (1968), 578-595.

Huitt, Ralph K. The Constitutional Ideas of James Otis, *Kansas Law Review*, 2 (1953), 152-173.

Humphreys, R. A. The Rule of Law and the American Revolution, *Law Quarterly Review*, 53 (1937), 80-98.

Ingersoll, Edward. *The History and Law of the Writ of Habeas Corpus with an Essay on the Law of Grand Juries* (Philadelphia: T. K. and F. G. Collins, 1849).

Jennings, Francis. Thomas Penn's Loyalty Oath, *American Journal of Legal History*, 8 (1964), 303-313.

Jezierski, John V. Imperii in imperio: the 1754 Albany Plan of Union and the Origin of the American Revolution, *New England Quarterly*, 42 (1974), 18-35.

Johnson, Herbert A. George Harison's Protest: New Light on Forsey versus Cunningham, *New York History*, 50 (1969), 61-82; reprinted herein at 171-192.

Kahane, Dennis S. Colonial Origins of Our Free Press, *American Bar Association* Journal, 42 (1976), 202-206.

Kammen, Michael G. The Causes of the Maryland Revolution of 1689, *Maryland Historical Magazine*, 55 (1960), 293-333.

Katz, Stanley N. The Politics of Law in Colonial America: Controversies over Chancery Courts and Equity Law in the Eighteenth Century, *Perspectives in American History*, 5 (1971), 257-286.

———. Thomas Jefferson and the Right to Property in Revolutionary America, *Journal of Law and Economics*, 19 (1976), 437-630.

———. The Origins of Constitutional Thought, *Perspectives in American History*, 3 (1969), 474-490.

Keller, Arthur S., Lissitzyn, Oliver J., and Mann, Frederick J. *Creation of Rights of Sovereignty through Symbolic Acts, 1400-1800* (New York: Columbia University Press, 1938).

Kemmerer, Donald L. Judge's Good Behavior Tenure in Colonial New Jersey, *New Jersey Historical Society Proceedings*, 56 (1938), 18-30.

Kettner, James H. *The Development of American Citizenship, 1608-1870* (Chapel Hill: University of North Carolina Press, 1978).

Klein, Milton M. Prelude to Revolution in New York: Jury Trials and Judicial Tenure, *William and Mary Quarterly*, 17 (1960), 439-462.

Krugler, John D. Lord Baltimore. Roman Catholics and Toleration: Religious Policy in Maryland during the Early Catholic Years, 1634-1649, *Catholic Historical Review*, 65 (1979), 49-75.

Labaree, Leonard W. *Royal Government in America: A Study of the British Colonial System before 1783* (New Haven: Yale University Press, 1930).

______. *Royal Instructions to British Colonial Governors, 1670-1776*, 2 vols. (New York: Appleton and Century, 1935).

Leslie, William R. The Gaspee Affair: A Study of its Constitutional Significance, *Mississippi Valley Historical Review*, 39 (1952), 233-256.

Levy, Leonard W. *Legacy of Suppression: Freedom of Speech and Press in Early American History* (Cambridge: Harvard University Press, 1960).

______. *Origins of the Fifth Amendment: The Right Against Self-Incrimination* (New York: Oxford University Press, 1968).

______, and Leder, Lawrence H. Exotic Fruit: The Right Against Compulsory Self-Incrimination in Colonial New York, *William and Mary Quarterly*, 20 (1963), 1-21.

Lloyd, William H. Pylkington's Case and Its Successors, *University of Pennsylvania Law Review*, 59 (1920), 20-34.

Long, Joseph R. The Freedom of the Press, *Virginia Law Review*, 5 (1918), 223-246.

Lovejoy, David S. Equality and Empire: The New York Charter of Liberties, 1683, *William and Mary Quarterly*, 22 (1964), 493-515.

______. Rights Imply Equality: The Case Against the Admiralty Jurisdiction in America, *William and Mary Quarterly*, 16 (1959), 459-484.

Marshall, Peter. The British Empire and the American Revolution, *Huntington Library Quarterly*, 27 (1964), 135-145.

Matthews, Lois K. Benjamin Franklin's Plan for a Colonial Union, 1750-1775, *American Political Science Review*, 8 (1914), 393-412.

Merritt, Jesse. Thomas Dongan and the Charter of Liberties, *Nassau County Historical Journal*, 14 (1953), 99-105.

Moody, Robert E. A Reexamination of the Antecedents of the Massachusetts Bay Company's Charter of 1629, *Massachusetts Historical Society Proceedings*, 69 (1949), 56-80.

Morgan, Edmund M. The Privilege against Self-Incrimination, *Minnesota Law Review*, 34 (1949), 1-45.

Morgan, Gwenda. "The Privilege of Making Laws"; the Board of Trade, the Virginia Assembly and Legislative Power, 1748-1754, *Journal of American Studies*, 10 (1976), 1-15.

Morris, Richard B. Judicial Supremacy and the Inferior Courts in the American Colonies, *Political Science Quarterly*, 55 (1940), 429-434.

______. Freedom of Expression: Its Past and Its Future, *New York History*, 31 (1950), 115-135.

Mullett, Charles F. Medieval English Law and the American Revolution, *Virginia Law Review*, 20 (1934), 523-538.

McAninch, William S. Criminal Procedure and the South Carolina Jury Act of 1731, in Herbert A. Johnson, ed., *South Carolina Legal History* (Spartanburg: The Reprint Co., 1980).

McGovney, Dudley O. The British Privy Council's Power to Restrain the Legislatures of Colonial America: Power to Disallow Statutes, Power to Veto, *University of Pennsylvania Law Review*, 94 (1945), 59-93.

McKinney, Albert E. The Transition from Dutch to English Rule in New York, *American Historical Review*, 6 (1901), 693-724.

McKinley, Edward N. Religious Freedom in Maryland, *American Church Monthly*, 30 (1931), 50-57, 140-147.

McLaughlin, Andrew C. The Background of American Federalism, in *America and Britain* (New York: Dutton & Co., 1918).

______. *The Foundations of American Constitutionalism* (New York: New York University Press, 1932).

McLoughlin, William G. Isaac Backus and the Separation of Church and State in America, *American Historical Review*, 73 (1968), 1392-1413.

Nadelhaft, Jerome J. Politics and the Judicial Tenure Fight in Colonial New Jersey, *William and Mary Quarterly*, 28 (1971), 46-63.

Nelson, Harold L. Seditious Libel in Colonial America, *American Journal of Legal History*, 3 (1959), 160-172.

Nelson, William E. Eighteenth Century Background of John Marshall's Constitutional Jurisprudence, *Michigan Law Review*, 76 (1978), 893-960.

______. Legal Restraints of Power in Pre-Revolutionary America: Massachusetts as a Case Study, 1760-1775, *American Journal of Legal History*, 18 (1974), 1-32.

O'Connor, Thomas F. Religious Toleration in New York, 1664-1700, *New York History*, 17 (1936), 391-410.

Parker, Mattie Erma E. The First Fundamental Constitutions, *South Carolina Historical Magazine*, 71 (1970), 78-85.

Parkes, Henry B. Morals and Law Enforcement in Colonial New England, *New England Quarterly*, 5 (1932), 431-452.

Phillips, Hubert. *The Development of a Residential Qualification for Representation in Colonial Legislatures* (Cincinnati: Abingdon Press, 1921).

Pittman, R. Carter. The Colonial and Constitutional Privilege Against Self-Incrimination in America, *Virginia Law Review*, 21 (1935), 763-784.

______. Judicial Supremacy in America: Its Colonial and Constitutional History, *Georgia Bar Journal*, 16 (1953), 148-165.

Pole, J. R. *In Pursuit of Equality in American History* (Berkeley: University of California Press, 1978).

Potter, William W. Judicial Power in the United States, *Michigan Law Review*, 27 (1928), 1-22, 167-190; 28 (1929), 285-313.

Price, Warren C. Reflections on the Trial of John Peter Zenger, *Journalism Quarterly*, 32 (1955), 161-168.

Rackow, Felix. The Right to Counsel: Engish and American Precedents, *William and Mary Quarterly*, 11 (1954), 3-27.

Reid, John Phillip. *In a Rebellious Spirit: The Argument of Facts, the Liberty Riot, and the Coming of the American Revolution* (University Park: Pennsylvania State University Press, 1979).

______.In an Inherited Way: English Constitutional Rights, the Stamp Act Debates and the Coming of the Revolution, *Southern California Law Review*, 49 (1976), 1109-1129.

______. In Legitimate Stirps: The Concept of "Arbitrary," the Supremacy of Parliament and the Coming of the American Revolution, *Hofstra Law Review*, 5 (1977), 459-499.

______. In the First Line of Defense: The Colonial Charters, the Stamp Act Debate, and the Coming of the American Revolution, *New York University Law Review*, 51 (1976), 177-215.

______. In a Defensive Rage: The Uses of the Mob, the Justification in Law, and the Coming of the American Revolution, *New York University Law Review*, 49 (1974), 1043-1091.

______. "In our Contracted Sphere": The Constitutional Contract, the Stamp Act Crisis and the Coming of the American Revolution, *Columbia Law Review*, 76 (1976), 21-47.

______. In Accordance with Usage: The Authority of Custom, the Stamp Act Dispute, and the Coming of the American Revolution, *Fordham Law Review*, 45 (1976), 335-368.

Riddell, William R. Early Provincial Legislative Interference with Private Property, *Canadian Bar Review*, 11 (1933), 176-180.

______. The Powers of a Colonial Legislature in Impeachment and Contempt, *Royal Society of Canada Proceedings*, 3rd Series, 21, Sec. 2 (1930), 83-90.

______. Impeachment in England and English Colonies, *New York University Law Review*, 7 (1930), 702-708.

Robbins, Peggy. The Trial of Peter Zenger, *American History Illustrated*, 11 (1976), 9-17.

Ruchames, Louis. Race, Marriage and Abolition in Massachusetts, *Journal of Negro History*, 40 (1955), 250-273.

Russell, Elmer B. *The Review of American Colonial Legislation by the King in Council* (New York: Columbia University Press, 1915).

Salley, Alexander S. The Fundamental Constitutions of South Carolina, *South Carolina Historical Association Proceedings*, 4th Annual Meeting (1934), pp. 25-31.

Santos, Hubert J. Birth of a Liberal State: Connecticut's Fundamental Orders, *Connecticut Law Review*, 1 (1968), 386-400.

Schlesinger, Arthur M. Colonial Appeals to the Privy Council, *Political Science Quarterly*, 28 (1913), 279-297, 433-450.

Schuyler, Robert L. Working toward a Federal Domain, *Political Science Quarterly*, 28 (1913), 496-511.

Scott, Arthur P. The Constitutional Aspects of the "Parson's Cause," *Political Science Quarterly*, 31 (1916), 558-577.

Seiler, William H. The Church of England as the Established Church in Seventeenth Century Virginia, *Journal of Southern History*, 15 (1949), 478-508.

Shipton, Clifford K. James Otis and the Writs of Assistance, *Bostonian Society Proceedings*, (1961), pp. 17-25.

Smith, Glenn C. The Affair of the Pistole Fee, Virginia 1752-1755, *Virginia Magazine of History and Biography*, 48 (1940), 209-221.

______. The Parson's Cause, 1753-1765, *Tyler's Quarterly Historical and Genealogical Magazine*, 21 (1940), 140-171, 291-306.

Smith, John R. L. The Early Georgia Constitutions, *Georgia Bar Journal*, 17 (1954), 273-290.

Smith, Joseph H. Administrative Control of the Courts of the American Colonies, *Columbia Law Review*, 61 (1961), 1210-1253; reprinted in Flaherty, *Essays*, 281-335.

______. An Independent Judiciary: The Colonial Background, *University of Pennsylvania Law Review*, 124 (1976), 1104-1156.

______. *Appeals to the Privy Council from the Colonial Plantations* (New York: Columbia University Press, 1950).

Smith, Maurice H. *The Writs of Assistance Case* (Berkeley: University of California Press, 1978).

Speight, Harold E. B. The Case of John Peter Zenger—A Momentous Trial, *American-German Review*, 2, No. 1 (1935), 11-12, 52.

Spencer, Charles W. Colonial Wars and Constitutional Development in New York, *Society of Colonial Wars in the State of New York*, Publication 23 (1915), pp. 49-69.

Spindel, Donna J. Law and Disorder: The North Carolina Stamp Act Crisis, *North Carolina Historical Review*, 57 (1980), 1-16.

Steiner, Bernard C. Religious Freedom in Provincial Maryland, *American Historical Review*, 28 (1923), 258-259.

Stephenson, Gilbert T. Race Distinctions in American Law, *American Law Review*, 43 (1910), 29-52, 205-227, 354-381, 547-590, 695-758; also published, New York: D. Appleton, 1910.

Stumpf, Stuart O. Edward Randolph's Attack on Proprietary Government in South Carolina, *South Carolina Historical Magazine*, 79 (1978), 6-68.

Teachout, Peter R. Light in Ashes: The Problem of "Respect for the Rule of Law" in American Legal History, *New York University Law Review*, 53 (1978), 241-288.

Varga, Nicholas. The English Parliament's Authority over Virginia before the Restoration, *Virginia Magazine of History and Biography*, 62 (1954), 281-288.

Walker, Robert S. *The Constitutional and Legal Development of Habeas Corpus as the Writ of Liberty* (Stillwater: Oklahoma State University, 1960).

Ward, John M. British and American Constitutions: The American Experience, *Australian Journal of Political History*, 22 (1976), 347-366.

Washburne, George A. *Imperial Control of the Administration of Justice in the Thirteen American Colonies* (New York: Columbia University Press, 1923).

Weigle, Anna Jean. Anna Catherina Zenger and the Free Press, *D.A.R. Magazine*, 69 (1935), 726-729.

Welles, Edwin S. *The Origin of the Fundamental Orders* (Hartford: E.S. Welles, 1936).

Wiecek, William M. Somerset: Lord Mansfield and the Legitimacy of Slavery in the Anglo-American World, *University of Chicago Law Review*, 42 (1974), 86-146.

______. *The Sources of Antislavery Constitutionalism in America, 1760-1848* (Ithaca: Cornell University Press, 1977).

Wiener, Frederick B. *Civilians under Military Justice: The British Practice since 1689, Especially in North America* (Chicago: University of Chicago Press, 1967).

Wolford, Thorp L. The Laws and Liberties of 1648, *Boston University Law Review*, 28 (1948), 426-463; reprinted in Flaherty, *Essays*, 147-185.

Yankwich, Leon R. The Background of the American Bill of Rights, *Georgetown Law Journal*, 37 (1948), 1-28.

______. The Beginnings of Free Speech in America and Its Meaning Today, *Los Angeles Bar Association Bulletin*, 24 (1956), 360-361, 371-372, 374-376, 378.

Ziskind, Martha A. Judicial Tenure in the American Constitution: English and American Precedents, *1969 Supreme Court Review*, pp. 135-154.

Zollman, Carl. Religious Liberty in American Law, *Michigan Law Review*, 17 (1957), 355-377, 456-478.

COURTS

Bradbury, Frank E. Law and Courts of the Massachusetts Bay Colony, *Bostonian Society Publications*, 10 (1913), 129-159.

Brennan, Ellen E. The Massachusetts Council of the Magistrates, *New England Quarterly*, 4 (1931), 54-93.

Bronner, Edwin P., ed. Philadelphia County Court of Quarter Sessions and Common Pleas, 1695, *Pennsylvania Magazine of History and Biography*, 77 (1953), 457-480.

Bryant, James R. Office of Master in Chancery: Colonial Development, *American Bar Association Journal*, 40 (1954), 498-501, 503.

Byrd, Elbert Jr. *The Judicial Process in Maryland* (College Park: University of Maryland, 1961).

Curran, William J. The Struggle for Equity Jurisdiction in Massachusetts, *Boston University Law Review*, 31 (1951), 269-296.

Daly, Charles P. *Historical Sketch of the Judicial Tribunals of New York from 1623 to 1846* (New York: J. W. Amerman, 1855).

Dewey, Frank L. New Light on the General Court of Colonial Virginia, *William and Mary Law Review*, 21 (1979), 1-14.

Dolan, Paul. The Justice of the Peace System in Delaware, *Delaware Notes*, 29 (1956), 1-47.

Eastman, Frank M. *Courts and Lawyers of Philadelphia*, 3 vols. (New York: American Historical Society, 1922).

Ehrlich, Jessica K. "To Hear and Try All Causes Betwixt Man and Man": The Town Court of Newtown, 1659-1690, *New York History*, 59 (1978), 277-305.

Farrell, John T. The Early History of Rhode Island's Court System, *Rhode Island History*, 9 (1950), 65-71, 103-117; 10 (1951), 65-68, 80-85.

Ferguson, Isaac. County Courts in Virginia, 1700-1830, *North Carolina Historical Review*, 8 (1931), 14-40.

Flippin, Percy Scott. The Royal Government in Georgia, 1752-1776: VI: The Judicial System and Administration, *Georgia Historical Quarterly*, 10 (1926), 251-276.

Frank, John P. Historical Bases of the Federal Judiciary System, *Indiana Law Journal*, 23 (1948), 236-270.

Friendly, Henry J. The Historical Basis of Diversity Jurisdiction, *Harvard Law Review*, 41 (1928), 483-510.

Grinnell, Frank W. The Experimental Development of Early Massachusetts Courts, *Massachusetts Law Quarterly*, 1 (1915), 75-76.

Hammond, Harold E. The New York City Court of Common Pleas, *New York History*, 32 (1951), 275-295.

Hammond, John C. The Great and General Court of Massachusetts Bay Colony, *Massachusetts Bar Association Report*, 4 (1914), 42-63.

Hartog, Hendrik. The Public Law of a County Court: Judicial Government in Eighteenth Century Massachusetts, *American Journal of Legal History*, 20 (1976), 282-289.

Haskell, Thomas L. Litigation and Social Status in Seventeenth-Century New Haven, *Journal of Legal Studies*, 7 (1978), 219-241.

History of the New York Court of Common Pleas, *Albany Law Journal*, 5 (1872), 277-281.

A History of the Supreme Judicial Court of Massachusetts (Boston: Massachusetts Bar Association, 1942).

Johnson, Herbert A. The Prerogative Court of New York, 1686-1776, *American Journal of Legal History*, 18 (1973), 95-144; reprinted herein at 55-104.

Katz, Stanley N. The Politics of Law in Colonial America: Controversies over Chancery Courts and Equity Law in the Eighteenth Century, *Perspectives in American History*, 5 (1971), 257-286.

Kawashima, Yasuhide. Jurisdiction of the Colonial Courts over the Indians in Massachusetts 1689-1763, *New England Quarterly*, 42 (1969), 532-550.

Law in Colonial New York: The Legal System of 1691, *Harvard Law Review*, 80 (1967), 1757-1772.

Lloyd, William H. Jr. The Courts of Pennsylvania in the Eighteenth Century Prior to the Revolution, *University of Pennsylvania Law Review*, 56 (1908), 28-51.

______. The Courts of Pennsylvania Prior to 1701, *American Law Register*, 55 (1907), 529-567.

Maltbie, William M. The Courts and Constitutions of Connecticut, *Connecticut Bar Journal*, 9 (1935), 269-281.

______. Judicial Administration in Connecticut Colony before the Charter of 1662, *Connecticut Bar Journal*, 23 (1949), 147-158, 228-247.

Morris, Richard B. Judicial Supremacy and the Inferior Courts in the American Colonies, *Political Science Quarterly*, 55 (1940), 429-434.

McCain, Paul M. *The County Court in North Carolina before 1750 (Durham: Duke University Press, 1954).*

______. Magistrates' Courts in Early North Carolina, *North Carolina Historical Review*, 48 (1971), 23-30.

McCanna, Francis I. A Study of the History and Jurisdiction of Rhode Island Courts, *American Irish Historical Society Journal*, 22 (1923), 170-195.

MacDonald, Herbert S. An Obituary Notice of the Connecticut Justice of the Peace, *Connecticut Bar Journal*, 35 (1961), 411-431.

MacQueen, Edith E. The Commissary in Colonial Maryland, *Maryland Historical Magazine*, 25 (1930), 190-206.

Nelson, William. *The Law and Practice of New Jersey from Earliest Times Concerning the Probate of Wills, the Administration of Estates, the Protection of Orphans and Minors, and the Control of Their Estates; the Prerogative Court, the Ordinary and the Surrogates* (Paterson: Paterson History Club, 1909).

Newbold, David M. *Notes on the Introduction of Equity Jurisdiction into Maryland, 1634-1720* (Baltimore: M. Curlander, 1903).

Oliver, L. Stauffer. *The Origin of Pennsylvania's Present Day Courts in Early Colonial Times and a Famous Lawyer and the Zenger Trial* (Philadelphia: Society of Colonial Wars in the Commonwealth of Pennsylvania, 1939).

Parker, Herbert. *Courts and Lawyers of New England*, 4 vols. (New York: American Historical Society, 1931).

Rankin, Hugh F. The General Court of Colonial Virginia: Its Jurisdiction and Personnel, *Virginia Magazine of History and Biography*, 70 (1962), 142-153.

Reed, H. Clay, and Palermo, Joseph A. Justices of the Peace in Early Delaware, *Delaware History*, 14 (1971), 223-237.

Riddell, William R. Notes on the Pre-Revolutionary Judiciary in the English Colonies, *Canadian Bar Review*, 11 (1933), 317-324, 376-384.

Roeber, A. G. Authority, Law and Custom: The Rituals of Court Day in Tidewater Virginia, 1720-1750, *William and Mary Quarterly*, 38 (1980), 29-52.

Rugg, Arthur P. The General Court of Massachusetts, *Boston University Law Review*, 11 (1931), 1-21.

Russell, Evlyn B. An Overview of the Criminal Justice System of Hampshire County, 1677-1728, *Historical Journal of Western Massachusetts*, 5 (1977), 13-20.

Scott, Austin. The Ordinance for Establishing Courts in New Jersey, *New Jersey Law Journal*, 35 (1912), 170-174.

Scott, Henry W. *The Courts of the State of New York* (New York: Wilson Publishing Company, 1909).

Smith, Joseph H. Administrative Control of the Courts of the American Plantations, *Columbia Law Review*, 59 (1961), 1210-1253; reprinted in Flaherty, *Essays*, 281-335.

______.The Provinicial Court and the Laws of Maryland, 1675-1715, in Morris D. Forkosch, ed., *Essays on Legal History in Honor of Felix Frankfurter* (Indianapolis: Bobbs-Merrill, 1966).

______, and Hershkowitz, Leo. Courts of Equity in the Province of New York: The Cosby Controversy, 1732-1736, *American Journal of Legal History*, 16 (1972), 1-50.

______. *Appeals to the Privy Council from the Colonial Plantations* (New York: Columbia University Press, 1950).

Soffel, Sara M. The Early History of Our Courts, *Greater Pittsburgh*, 15, No. 11 (1934), 16-17.

Staples, Waller R. A History of the Old County Court System in Virginia, *Virginia State Bar Association Annual Report, 1895*, p. 127.

Surrency, Erwin C. The Development of the Appellate Function: The Pennsylvania Experiment, *American Journal of Legal History*, 22 (1976), 173-191.

______, ed. Directions for Holding Court in Colonial Georgia, *American Journal of Legal History*, 2 (1958), 321-325.

______. Evolution of an Urban Judicial System: The Philadelphia Story, 1683-1968, *American Journal of Legal History*, 18 (1974), 95-123.

______, ed. Report on Court Procedures in the Colonies, *American Journal of Legal History*, 9 (1965), 67-83, 167-178, 234-246.

______. Courts in the American Colonies, *American Journal of Legal History*, 11 (1967), 253-276, 347-376.

Townshend, Henry H. Judicial Administration in New Haven Colony before the Charter of 1662, *Connecticut Bar Journal*, 24 (1950), 210-234.

Vipperman, Carl J. The Justice of Revolution: The South Carolina Judicial System, 1721-1772, in Herbert A. Johnson, ed., *South Carolina Legal History*, (Spartanburg: The Reprint Co., 1980).

Vosburgh, Royden W. Surrogate's Courts and Records in the Colony and State of New York, 1664-1847, *New York State Historical Association Journal*, 3 (1922), 105-116.

Washington, Bushrod C. The Courts and Bar of Colonial Virginia, *Green Bag*, 12 (1900), 470-479.

Wilson, Solon D. Courts of Chancery in the American Colonies, in *Select Essays in Anglo-American Legal History*, 3 vols. (Boston: Little, Brown & Co., 1907).

Wingate, George A. The Surrogate's Court of the State of New York, Its Early History and Present Equitable Jurisdiction, *Brooklyn Law Review*, 2 (1933), 165-172.

Woodbine, George E. The Suffolk County Court, 1671-1680, *Yale Law Journal*, 43 (1936), 1036-1043; reprinted in Flaherty, *Essays*, 192-203.

Woodruff, Edwin H. Chancery in Massachusetts, *Boston University Law Review*, 9 (1929), 168-192.

Ziskind, Martha A. Judicial Tenure in the American Constitution: English and American Precendents, *1969 Supreme Court Review*, pp. 135-154.

CRIMINAL LAW

Barnes, Harry E. The Criminal Codes and Penal Institutions of Colonial Pennsylvania, *Friends' Historical Society Bulletin*, 11 (1922), 3-16, 68-84.

Fitzroy, Herbert K. The Punishment of Crime in Provincial Pennsylvania, *Pennsylvania Magazine of History and Biography*, 60 (1936), 242-269.

Flaherty, David H. Law and the Enforcement of Morals in Early America, *Perspectives on American History*, 5 (1971), 203-256.

Ford, Worthington C. A Pleading of William Leddra, 1659, *Massachusetts Historical Society Proceedings*, 61 (1928), 116-123.

Gillingham, Harold. *Counterfeiting in Colonial Pennsylvania* (New York: American Numismatic Society, 1939).

Gipson, Lawrence H. *Crime and Its Punishment in Provincial Pennsylvania: A Phase in the Social History of the Commonwealth* (Bethlehem: Lehigh University Institute of Research, 1935).

Greenberg, Douglas. *Crime and Law Enforcement in the Colony of New York* (Ithaca: Cornell University Press, 1976).

Greene, Evarts B. The Code of Honor in Colonial and Revolutionary Times, with Special Reference to New England, *Massachusetts Colonial Society Proceedings*, 26 (1927), 367-388.

Haskins, George L. The Capitall Lawes of New-England, *Harvard Law School Bulletin*, 7 (1956), 10.

______. Ecclesiastical Antecedents of Criminal Punishment in Early Massachusetts, *Massachusetts Historical Society Proceedings*, 42 (1960), 21-35.

______. Precedents in English Ecclesiastical Practice for Criminal Punishments in Early Massachusetts, in Morris D. Forkosch, ed., *Essays in Legal History in Honor of Felix Frankfurter* (Indianapolis: Bobbs-Merrill, 1966).

______. A Rule to Walk By, in Richard Quinney, ed., *Crime and Justice in Society* (Boston: Little, Brown & Co., 1969).

Kawashima, Yasuhide. Forced Conformity: Puritan Criminal Justice and Indians, *Kansas Law Review*, 25 (1977), 361-373.

Klein, Milton, M. Corruption in Colonial America, *South Atlantic Quarterly*, 78 (1979), 57-72.

Lane, Roger. Criminal Violence in America: The First Hundred Years, *Annals of the American Academy of Political Science*, 423 (1976), 1-13.

Maestro, Marcello T. Benjamin Franklin and the Penal Law, *Journal of the History of Ideas*, 36 (1975), 551-562.

______. *Voltaire and Beccaria as Reformers of Criminal Law* (New York: Columbia University Press, 1942).

McBratney, William H. The One Witness Rule in Massachusetts, *American Journal of Legal History*, 2 (1958), 155-160.

Naughton, T. Raymond. Criminal Law in Colonial New York, *New York History*, 14 (1933), 235-240.

Nelson, Harold L. Seditious Libel in Colonial America, *American Journal of Legal History*, 3 (1959), 160-172.

Nelson, William E. Emerging Notions of a Modern Criminal Law in the Revolutionary Era: An Historical Perspective, *New York University Law Review*, 42 (1967), 450-482.

Oaks, Robert F. "Things Fearful to Name": Sodomy and Buggery in Seventeenth-Century New England, *Journal of Social History*, 12 (1978), 268-281.

Parkes, Henry B. Morals and Law Enforcement in Colonial New England, *New England Quarterly*, 5 (1932), 431-452.

Prince, Walter F. The First Criminal Code of Virginia, *Annual Report of the American Historical Association, 1899*, 1, 311-363.

Reppy, Alison. The Spectre of Attainder of New York, *St. John's Law Review*, 23 (1948-49), 1-67, 243-290.

Riddell, William R. Witchcraft in Old New York, *Journal of Criminal Law*, 19 (1928), 252-258.

Scott, Arthur P. *Criminal Law in Colonial Virginia* (Chicago: University of Chicago Press, 1930).

Scott, Kenneth. *Counterfeiting in Colonial Connecticut* (New York: American Numismatic Society, 1957).

______. Counterfeiting in Colonial Maryland, *Maryland Historical Magazine*, 51 (1956), 81-100.

______. Counterfeiting in Colonial New Hampshire, *Historic New Hampshire*, 13 (1957), 3-38.

______. Counterfeiting in Colonial New Jersey, *New Jersey Historical Society Proceedings*, 75 (1957), 170-179.

______. *Counterfeiting in Colonial New York* (New York: American Numismatic Society, 1953).

———. Counterfeiting in Colonial North Carolina, *North Carolina Historical Review*, 34 (1957), 467-482.
———. *Counterfeiting in Colonial Pennsylvania* (New York: American Numismatic Society, 1955).
———. *Counterfeiting in Colonial Rhode Island* (Providence: Rhode Island Historical Society, 1960).
———. Counterfeiting in Colonial Virginia, *Virginia Magazine of History and Biography*, 61 (1953), 3-33.
———. Earliest Counterfeiting in New Jersey, *New Jersey Historical Society Proceedings*, 75 (1957), 18-34.
———. James Franklin on Counterfeiting, *American Numismatic Society Museum Notes*, 8 (1958), 217-220.
———. Some Counterfeiters of Provincial Currency, *South Carolina Historical Magazine*, 57 (1956), 14-22.
Semmes, Raphael. *Crime and Punishment in Early Maryland* (Baltimore: Johns Hopkins Press, 1937).
Sherman, Constance D. Curious Crimes in Colonial Newport County, *Rhode Island History*, 18 (1959), 116-118.
Smith, Joseph H. The English Criminal Law in Early America, in *The English Legal System: Carryover in the Colonies* (Los Angeles: University of California, Los Angeles, 1975).
Spindel, Donna J. Law and Disorder, The North Carolina Stamp Act Crisis, *North Carolina Historical Review*, 57 (1980), 1-16.
West, Edward H. Counterfeiting in Colonial Days, *Rhode Island Historical Society Collections*, 27 (1934), 50-53.
Williams, Jack K. *Vogues in Villainy: Crime and Retribution in Ante-bellum South Carolina* (Columbia: University of South Carolina Press, 1959).

CRIMINAL PROCEDURE

Blume, Alexander. Benefit of Clergy, *Brooklyn Bar Journal*, 5 (1954), 130-135.
Bosco, Ronald A. Lectures at the Pillory: The Early American Execution Sermon, *American Quarterly*, 30 (1978), 156-176.
Clarke, T. Wood. The Negro Plot of 1741, *New York History*, 26 (1944), 167-181.
Connor, Henry G. The Constitutional Right to Trial by a Jury of the Vicinage, *University of Pennsylvania Law Review*, 57 (1909), 197-215.
Cook, John D. New York Troika: Conflicting Roles of the Grand Jury, *Buffalo Law Review*, 11 (1961), 42-53.
Cross, Arthur L. Benefit of Clergy in the American Criminal Law, *Massachusetts Historical Society Proceedings*, 61 (1928), 154-181.
Dalzell, George W. *Benefit of Clergy in America and Related Matters* (Winston-Salem: J. F. Blair, 1955).
Dershowitz, Alan M. Criminal Sentencing in the United States: An Historical and Conceptual Overview, *Annals of the American Academy of Political Science*, 423 (1976), 117-132.
Fox, Sanford J. *Science and Justice: The Massachusetts Witchcraft Trials* (Baltimore: Johns Hopkins Press, 1968).
Goebel, Julius, Jr. and T. Raymond Naughton. *Law Enforcement in Colonial New York: A Study in Criminal Procedure (1664-1776)* (New York: Columbia University Press, 1944).

Greenberg, Douglas. *Crime and Law Enforcement in the Colony of New York* (Ithaca: Cornell University Press, 1976).

______. The Effectiveness of Law Enforcement in Eighteenth Century New York, *American Journal of Legal History*, 19 (1975), 173-207.

______. Patterns of Criminal Prosecution in Eighteenth Century New York, *New York History*, 56 (1975), 132-153.

Hardon, Henry W. Benefit of Clergy. *American Genealogist and New Haven Genealogical Magazine*, 10 (1934), 194-197.

Hesseltine, Norman F. Benefit of Clergy—A Historical Curiosity, *Massachusetts Law Quarterly*, 16 (1931), 73-77.

Hindus, Michael S. Black Justice under White Law: Criminal Prosecutions of Blacks In Antebellum South Carolina, *Journal of American History*, 63 (1976), 575-599.

______. Contours of Crime and Justice in Massachusetts and South Carolina 1767-1878, *American Journal of Legal History*, 21 (1977), 212-237.

______. The Sociology of Crime and Justice in South Carolina, in Herbert A. Johnson, ed., *South Carolina Legal History* (Spartanburg: The Reprint Co., 1980).

Howe, Mark DeWolf. The Process of Outlawry in New York: A Study in the Selective Reception of English Law, *Cornell Law Quarterly*, 23 (1938), 559-579; reprinted in Flaherty, *Essays*, 433-450.

Ingersoll, Edward. *The History and Law of the Writ of Habeas Corpus with an Essay on the Law of Grand Juries* (Philadelphia: T. K. and F. G. Collins, 1849).

Karraker, Cyrus H. Deodands in Colonial Virginia and Maryland, *American Historical Review*, 37 (1932), 712-717.

King, Ethel. The New York Negro Plot of 1741, *U.S. Catholic Historical Record*, 20 (1931), 173-180.

Lermack, Paul. Peace Bonds and Criminal Justice in Colonial Philadelphia, *Pennsylvania Magazine of History and Biography*, 100 (1976), 173-190.

______. The Law of Recognizances in Colonial Pennsylvania, *Temple Law Quarterly*, 50 (1977), 475-512.

McAninch, William S. Criminal Procedure and the South Carolina Jury Act of 1731, in Herbert A. Johnson, ed., *South Carolina Legal History* (Spartanburg: The Reprint Co., 1980).

Naughton, T. Raymond. Criminal Law in Colonial New York, *New York History*, 14 (1933), 235-240.

Rankin, Hugh F. Criminal Trial Proceedings in the General Court of Virginia, *Virginia Magazine of History and Biography*, 72 (1964), 50-74.

______. *Criminal Trial Proceedings in the General Court of Colonial Virginia* (Williamsburg: Colonial Williamsburg, 1965).

Reppy, Alison. The Spectre of Attainder in New York, *St. John's Law Review*, 23 (1948-49), 1-67, 243-290.

Riddell, William R. Judicial Execution by Burning at the Stake in New York, *American Bar Association Journal*, 15 (1929), 373-376.

Russell, Evlyn Belz. An Overview of the Criminal Justice System in Hampshire County, 1677-1729, *Historical Journal of Western Massachusetts*, 5 (1977), 13-20.

Salkin, Barry L. The Pardoning Power in Antebellum Pennsylvania, *Pennsylvania Magazine of History and Biography*, 100 (1976), 507-520.

Scott, Kenneth. The Liberties of the Kingston Gaol, *New-York Historical Society Quarterly*, 52 (1960), 275-283.

Semmes, Ralph. *Crime and Punishment in Early Maryland* (Baltimore: Johns Hopkins Press, 1937).

Sigler, Jay A. A History of Double Jeopardy, *American Journal of Legal History*, 7 (1963), 283-309.

Thayer, James Bradley. A Chapter in Legal History in Massachusetts (witness competency), *Harvard Law Review*, 9 (1895), 1-12.

Whyte, James H. Is the Grand Jury Necessary? *Virginia Law Review*, 45 (1959), 461-491.

Yackel, Peter G. Benefit of Clergy in Colonial Maryland, *Maryland Historical Magazine*, 69 (1974), 383-397.

Younger, Richard D. *The People's Panel: The Grand Jury in the United States, 1634-1941* (Providence: Brown University Press, 1963).

DEBTOR AND CREDITOR

Coleman, Peter J. *Debtors and Creditors in America: Insolvency, Imprisonment for Debt and Bankruptcy, 1607-1900* (Madison: State Historical Society of Wisconsin, 1974).

______. The Insolvent Debtor in Rhode Island, 1745-1828, *William and Mary Quarterly*, 22 (1965), 413-434.

Feer, Robert A. Imprisonment for Debt in Massachusetts before 1800, *Mississippi Valley Historical Review*, 48 (1961), 252-269.

Gipson, Lawrence H. Virginia Planter Debts before the American Revolution, *Virginia Magazine of History of Biography*, 69 (1961), 259-277.

Googins, Robert R. A Creditor's Right to Trust Income, *Connecticut Bar Journal*, 35 (1961), 256-266.

Riesenfeld, Stefan A. Collection of Money Judgments in American Law—A Historical Inventory and a Prospectus, *Iowa Law Review*, 42 (1957), 155-182.

______. Enforcement of Money Judgments in Early American History, *Michigan Law Review*, 71 (1973), 691-728.

Ryan, Edward L. Imprisonment for Debt—Its Origin and Repeal, *Virginia Magazine of History and Biography*, 42 (1934), 53-58.

Taylor, H. Braughan. The Foreign Attachment Law and the Coming of the Revolution in North Carolina, *North Carolina Historical Review*, 52 (1975), 20-36.

Thompson, Tommy R. Debtors, Creditors and the General Assembly in Colonial Maryland, *Maryland Historical Magazine*, 72 (1977), 59-77.

DOMESTIC RELATIONS

Blake, Nelson M. *The Road to Reno: A History of Divorce in the United States* (New York: Macmillan Co., 1962).

Cheshire, Joseph B. The Fundamental Constitutions of Carolina and Religious Liberty in the Province of North Carolina, *Historical Magazine of the Protestant Episcopal Church*, 1 (1932), 204-221.

Cobbledick, M. Robert. The Property Rights of Women in Puritan New England, in George P. Murdock, ed., *Studies in the Science of Society, presented to Albert Galloway Keller* . . . (New Haven: Yale University Press, 1937).

Cohn, Henry S. Connecticut's Divorce Mechanism: 1636-1966, *American Journal of Legal History*, 14 (1974), 35-54.

Cott, Nancy F. Divorce and the Changing Status of Women in Eighteenth Century Massachusetts, *William and Mary Quarterly*, 33 (1976), 586-614.

DePauw, Linda G. Women and the Law: The Colonial Period, *Human Rights*, 6 (1977), 107-113.

Douglas, James. *The Status of Women in New England and New France* (Kingston, Ontario: Jackson Press, 1912); also printed in *Queen's Quarterly*, 19 (1912), 359-374.

Flaherty, David H. *Privacy in Colonial New England* (Charlottesville: University Press of Virginia, 1972).

Fogarty, Gerald P. Slaves, Quakers and Catholic Marriage in Colonial Maryland, *Jurist*, 35 (1975), 142-161.

Friedman, Lee M. The First Breach of Promise Case in the United States—Koch v. Van Vorst, *Albany Law Journal*, 68 (1906), 179-180.

Frierson, J. Nelson. Divorce in South Carolina, *North Carolina Law Review*, 9 (1931), 265-282.

Hall, Fred S. Common Law Marriage in New York, *Columbia Law Review*, 30 (1930), 1-11.

Lawrence, Henry W. Puritan Scandals: Courtship, Marriage and Divorce, Three Centuries Ago, *Yankee*, 3, No. 12 (1937), 7-9, 29.

Meehan, Thomas R. "Not Made out of Levity," Evolution of Divorce in Early Pennsylvania, *Pennsylvania Magazine of History and Biography*, 92 (1968), 441-464.

Powell, Chilton L. Marriage in Early New England, *New England Quarterly*, 1 (1928), 323-334.

Riddell, William R. Legislative Divorce in Colonial Pennsylvania, *Pennsylvania Magazine of History and Biography*, 57 (1933), 175-180.

Rothenberg, Charles. Marriage, Morals and the Law in Colonial America, *New York Law Review*, 74 (1940), 393-398.

Ruchames, Louis. Race, Marriage and Abolition in Massachusetts, *Journal of Negro History*, 40 (1955), 250-273.

Semonche, John E. Common Law Marriage in North Carolina: A Study in Legal History, *American Journal of Legal History*, 9 (1965), 320-349.

Spaletta, Matteo. Divorce in Colonial New York, *New York Historical Society Quarterly*, 39 (1955), 422-440.

Weisberg, D. Kelly. "Under Great Temptations Heer": Women and Divorce in Puritan Massachusetts, *Feminist Studies*, 2 (1975), 183-194.

ECONOMIC REGULATION

Baird, Edward G. Business Regulation in Colonial Massachusetts, *Dakota Law Review*, 3 (1931), 227-256.

______. New Deal Laws in Colonial Days, *Connecticut Bar Journal*, 9 (1935), 187-201.

Bannister, Turpin C. Early Town Planning in New York State, *New York History*, 24 (1943), 185-195.

Bergstrom, E. Alexander. English Game Laws and Colonial Food Shortages, *New England Quarterly*, 12 (1939), 681-690.

Caldwell, Louis G. Early Legislation Regulating the Practice of Medicine, *Illinois Law Review*, 18 (1922), 225-244.

Dodd, Edwin Merrick Jr. The First Half Century of Statutory Regulation of Business Corporations in Massachusetts, in *Harvard Legal Essays written in Honor of Joseph Henry Beale and Samuel Williston* (Cambridge: Harvard University Press, 1934).

Eno, Joel N. Liquor Legislation in Connecticut Colony, *Journal of American History*, 7 (1913), 937-945.

Ezell, Stiles D. Regulation and Licensing of Physicians in New York, *New York State Journal of Medicine*, 56 (1957), 543-554.

Harbrecht, Paul P., and McCallin, Joseph A. The Corporation and the State in Anglo-American Law and Politics, *Journal of Public Law*, 10 (1961), 1-46.

Hayes, Raymond E. Business Regulation in Early Pennsylvania, *Temple Law Quarterly*, 10 (1936), 155-179.

Ingle, Edward. Regulating Physicians in Colonial Virginia, *Annals of Medical History*, 4 (1922), 248-250.

Jernegan, Marcus W. The Development of Poor Relief in Colonial Virginia, *Social Service Review*, 2 (1929), 1-9.

Jones, Franklin D. Historical Development of the Law of Business Competition, *Yale Law Journal*, 35 (1926), 905-938; 36 (1927), 42-55, 206-234, 351-383.

Klebaner, Benjamin J. Some Aspects of North Carolina Public Poor Relief, 1700-1860, *North Carolina Historical Review*, 31 (1954), 479-492.

Lund, Thomas A. Early American Wildlife Law, *New York University Law Review*, 51 (1976), 703-760.

Mackay, Howard. The Operation of the English Poor Law in Colonial Virginia, *Virginia Magazine of History and Biography*, 73 (1965), 29-40.

______. Social Welfare in Colonial Virginia: The Importance of the English Poor Laws, *Historical Magazine of the Protestant Episcopal Church*, 36 (1967), 357-382.

Morris, Richard B. *Government and Labor in Early America* (New York: Columbia University Press, 1944).

______, and Grossman, Jonathan. The Regulation of Wages in Early Massachusetts, *New England Quarterly*, 11 (1938), 470-500.

McCamic, Charles. Administration of Poor Relief in the Virginias, *West Virginia History*, 1 (1940), 171-191.

Nash, Gary B. Poverty and Poor Relief in Pre-Revolutionary Philadelphia, *William and Mary Quarterly*, 33 (1976), 3-30.

Public Poor Relief in Charleston, 1767, *South Carolina Historical Magazine*, 42 (1941), 83-86.

Risch, Erna. Encouragement of Immigration as Revealed in Colonial Legislation, *Virginia Magazine of History and Biography*, 45 (1937), 1-10.

Sable, J. T. Pennsylvania's Blue Laws: A Quaker Experiment in the Suppression of Spirit and Amusements, 1682-1740, *Journal of Sport History*, 1 (1974), 107-121.

Seyboldt, Robert E. Notes on the Regulation of the Practice of Medicine in Eighteenth Century Massachusetts, *New England Journal of Medicine*, 202 (1930), 1067-1068.

Sosin, Jack M. Imperial Regulation of Colonial Paper Money, 1764-1773, *Pennsylvania Magazine of History and Biography*, 88 (1964), 174-198.

Thistle, Raymond A. Jr. Rate Regulation of Common Carriers in Pennsylvania, *University of Pittsburgh Law Review*, 16 (1955), 124-167.

INDIANS

Berman, Howard R. Concept of Aboriginal Rights in the Early Legal History of the United States, *Buffalo Law Review*, 26 (1978), 637-667.

Grinde, Donald Jr. Native American Slavery in the Southern Colonies, *Indian Historian*, 10 (1977), 38-42.

Joyner, Christopher C. The Historical Status of the American Indians under International Law, *Indian Historian*, 11 (1978), 30-36.

Kawashima, Yasuhide. Forced Conformity: Puritan Criminal Justice and Indians, *Kansas Law Review*, 25 (1977), 361-373.

______. Jurisdiction of the Colonial Courts over the Indians in Massachusetts, 1689-1763, *New England Quarterly*, 42 (1969), 532-550.

______. Legal Origins of the Indian Reservation in Colonial Massachusetts, *American Journal of Legal History*, 13 (1969), 42-56.

Lauber, Almon W. *Indian Slavery in Colonial Times within the Present Limits of the United States* (New York: Columbia University Press, 1913).

Pedersen, Gilbert J. Early Title to Indian Reservations in Western New York, *Niagra Frontier*, 3 (1956), 5-12.

Robinson, W. Stitt. The Legal Status of the Indian in Colonial Virginia, *Virginia Magazine of History and Biography*, 61 (1953), 249-259.

Ronda, James P. Red and White at the Bench: Indians and the Law in Plymouth Colony, 1620-1691, *Essex Institute Historical Collections*, 110 (1974), 200-215.

Vaughan, Alden T. A Test of Puritan Justice, *New England Quarterly*, 38 (1965), 331-339.

Washburne, Wilcomb E. *Redman's Land/White Man's Law: A Study of the Past and Present Status of the American Indian* (New York: Charles Scribner's Sons, 1971).

Winston, Sanford. Indian Slavery in the Carolina Region, *Journal of Negro History*, 19 (1934), 431-440.

JURIES

Arnold, Morris S. Historical Inquiry into the Right to Trial by Jury in Complex Civil Litigation, *University of Pennsylvania Law Review*, 128 (1980), 829-848.

Connor, Henry G. The Constitutional Right to Trial by a Jury of the Vicinage, *University of Pennsylvania Law Review*, 57 (1909), 197-215.

Cook, John D. New York Troika: Conflicting Roles of the Grand Jury, *Buffalo Law Review*, 11 (1961), 42-53.

Devlin, Patrick. Jury Trial of Complex Cases: English Practice at the Time of the Seventh Amendment, *Columbia Law Review*, 80 (1980), 59-88.

The Grand Jury as an Investigatory Body, *Harvard Law Review*, 74 (1961), 590-605.

Howe, Mark DeWolf. Records of the Suffolk County Court, *New England Quarterly*, 7 (1934), 207-314.

Ingersoll, Edward. *The History and Law of the Writ of Habeas Corpus with an Essay on the Law of Grand Juries* (Philadelphia: T. K. and F. G. Collins, 1849).

Johnson, Herbert A. George Harison's Protest: New Light on Forsey versus Cunningham, *New York History*, 50 (1969), 61-82; reprinted herein at 171-192.

Jury Nullification in Historical Perspective: Massachusetts as a Case Study, *Suffolk University Law Review*, 12 (1978), 968-1011.

Klein, Milton M. Prelude to Revolution in New York: Jury Trials and Judicial Tenure, *William and Mary Quarterly*, 17 (1960), 439-462.

McAninch, William S. Criminal Procedure and the South Carolina Jury Act of 1731, in Herbert A. Johnson, ed., *South Carolina Legal History* (Spartanburg: The Reprint Co., 1980).

Nahun, Milton, and Schatz, Louis M. The Grand Jury in Connecticut, *Connecticut, Bar Journal*, 5 (1931), 111-121.

Whyte, James H. Is the Grand Jury Necessary? *Virginia Law Review*, 45 (1959), 461-491.

Younger, Richard D. *The People's Panel: The Grand Jury in the United States, 1634-1941* (Providence: Brown University Press, 1963).

JURISPRUDENCE

Buchanan, John G. Drumfire from the Pulpit: Natural Law in the Colonial Election Sermons of Massachusetts, *American Journal of Legal History*, 12 (1968), 232-244.

Buffinton, Arthur H. The Puritan View of War, *Colonial Society of Massachusetts Publications*, 28 (1935), 67-86.

Canty-Letsome, Rosezella. John Winthrop's Concept of Law in 17th Century New England, One Notion of Puritan Thinking, *Duquesne Law Review*, 16 (1977-78), 331-357.

Chase, Theodore. John Winthrop and the Doctrine of Judicial Immunity, *American Bar Association Journal*, 46 (1960), 602-608.

Chroust, Anton-Hermann. Blackstone Revisited, *University of Kansas City Law Review*, 17 (1949), 24-34.

Clover, Ralph H. The Rule of Law in Colonial Massachusetts, *University of Pennsylvania Law Review*, 108 (1960), 1001-1036.

Fellman, David. The European Background of Early American Ideas Concerning Property, *Temple Law Quarterly*, 14 (1940), 497-516.

______. Property in Colonial Political Theory, *Temple Law Quarterly*, 16 (1942), 388-406.

Riesenfeld, Stefan A. Law-making and Legislative Precedent in American Legal History, *Minnesota Law Review*, 33 (1948), 103-144.

Schuyler, Robert L. Working Toward a Federal Domain, *Political Science Quarterly*, 28 (1913), 496-511.

Scott, William B. *In Pursuit of Happiness: American Conceptions of Property from the Seventeenth to the Twentieth Century* (Bloomington: Indiana University Press, 1977).

Smith, Joseph H. New Light on the Doctrine of Judicial Precedent in Early America: 1607-1776, in John N. Hazard and Wenceslas J. Wagner, eds., *Legal Thought in the United States of America Under Contemporary Pressures* (Brussels: Establisements Emile Bruylant, 1970).

LABOR LAW

Haar, Charles M. White Indentured Servants in Colonial New York, *Americana*, 34 (1940), 370-392.

Heavner, Robert O. Indentured Servants: The Philadelphia Market, 1771-1773, *Journal of Economic History*, 38 (1978), 701-713.

Jernegan, Marcus W. *Laboring and Dependent Classes in Colonial America, 1607-1783* (Chicago: University of Chicago Press, 1931).

Jervey, Theodore D. The White Indented Servants of South Carolina, *South Carolina Historical Magazine*, 12 (1911), 163-171.

Margaret Patricia, Sister. White Servitude in the American Colonies, *American Catholic Historical Society Record*, 42 (1931), 12-54.

Mark, Irving. *Agrarian Conflicts in Colonial New York, 1711-1775* (New York: Columbia University Press, 1940).

Morris, Richard B. Government and Labor in Early America (New York: Columbia University Press, 1944).

McKee, Samuel. Indentured Servitude in Colonial New York, *New York State Historical Association Journal*, 12 (1931), 149-159.

______. *Labor in Colonial New York, 1664-1776* (New York: Columbia University Press, 1935).

A New Jersey Apprentice Indenture of 1680, *New Jersey Historical Society Proceedings*, New Series, 15 (1930), 269-270.

Smith, Warren B. *White Servitude in Colonial South Carolina* (Columbia: University of South Carolina Press, 1961).

Sutherland, Arthur E. The Tenantry of the New York Manors, *Cornell Law Quarterly*, 41 (1956), 620-639.

The Unemployed in Legal History, *U.S. Law Review*, 66 (1932), 139-145.

LEGAL PROFESSION

Alderman, Ernest H. The North Carolina Colonial Bar, *James Sprunt Historical Publications*, 13, No. 1 (1913), 33-56.

Alexander, Edward P. *A Revolutionary Conservative: James Duane* (New York: Columbia University Press, 1938).

Bedwell, C. E. A. American Middle Templars, *American Historical Review*, 25 (1920), 680-689.

______. The Middle Temple and America, *Landmark*, 1 (1919), 145-149.

Benson, Carville D. Notes on the Preparation of Conveyances by Laymen in the Colony of Maryland, *Maryland Historical Magazine*, 60 (1965), 425-438.

Biddle, Edward W. *The Courts and Bar of Cumberland County in the Eighteenth Century* (Carlisle: E. W. Biddle, 1914).

Blue, Fred O. Judge Nicholas Trott, *Bermuda Historical Quarterly*, 9 (1952), 285-294.

Bryson, W. Hamilton. The History of Legal Education in Virginia, *University of Richmond Law Review*, 14 (1979), 155-210.

______. *The Virginia Law Reporters before 1880* (Charlottesville: University Press of Virginia, 1977).

Canady, Hoyt P. Legal Education in Colonial South Carolina, in Herbert A. Johnson, ed., *South Carolina Legal History* (Spartanburg: The Reprint Co., 1980).

Chester, Alden. *Courts and Lawyers of New York*, 3 vols. (New York: American Historical Society, 1925).

Chroust, Anton-Hermann. Lawyers of New Jersey and the Stamp Act, *American Journal of Legal History*, 6 (1962), 286-297.

———. The Legal Profession in Colonial America, *Notre Dame Lawyer*, 33 (1957), 51-97, 250-379; 34 (1958), 44-64.

———. *The Rise of the Legal Profession in America, Vol. I, The Colonial Experience* (Norman: University of Oklahoma Press, 1965).

Coates, Albert. A Century of Legal Education, *North Carolina Law Review*, 24 (1946), 307-340.

Cochran, Richard E. Pennsylvania's Debt to the Inns of Court, in *Report of the 13th Meeting of the Pennsylvania Bar Association* (Philadelphia: Pennsylvania Bar Association, 1924).

Cockruft, Grace A. *The Public Life of George Chalmers* (New York: Columbia University Press, 1939).

Connor, Henry G. James Iredell: Lawyer, Statesman, Judge, 1751-1799, *University of Pennsylvania Law Review*, 60 (1912), 225-253.

Consalus, Charles E. Legal Education During the Colonial Period, 1663-1776, *Journal of Legal Education*, 29 (1978), 295-310.

Crary, Catherine S. The American Dream: John Tabor Kempe's Rise from Poverty to Riches, *William and Mary Quarterly*, 14 (1957), 176-195.

Dabney, William M. and Marion Dargan. *William Henry Drayton and the American Revolution* (Albuquerque: University of New Mexico Press, 1962).

David, Leon T. Councillors and the Law Officers in the Colonies in North America, *American University Law Review*, 12 (1963), 23-50.

Day, Alan F. Lawyers in Colonial Maryland, 1660-1715, *American Journal of Legal History*, 17 (1973), 145-165.

Dempsey, E. J. Law and Lawyers in American Colonial Days, *Nevada State Bar Journal*, 13 (1948), 190-193.

Dillon, Dorothy R. *The New York Triumvirate: A Study of the Legal and Political Careers of William Livingston, John Morin Scott and William Smith, Jr.* (New York: Columbia University Press, 1949).

Eastman, Frank M. *Courts and Lawyers of Philadelphia*, 3 vols. (New York: American Historical Society, 1922).

Eaton, Clement. A Mirror of the Southern Colonial Lawyer: The Fee Books of Patrick Henry, Thomas Jefferson and Waightstill Avery, *William and Mary Quarterly*, 8 (1951), 520-534.

Gawalt, Gerard W. Sources of Anti-Lawyer Sentiment in Massachusetts, 1740-1840, *American Journal of Legal History*, 14 (1970), 283-307.

———. Massachusetts Legal Education in Transition, 1766-1840, *American Journal of Legal History*, 17 (1973), 27-50.

Gnichtel, Frederick. Nathaniel Jones, Chief Justice of New Jersey, *New Jersey Law Journal*, 49 (1926), 117-122.

Goodman, Leonard S. Historic Role of the Oath of Admission, *American Journal of Legal History*, 11 (1967), 404-411.

Gordon, Armistead C. Some Lawyers in Colonial Virginia, in *Proceedings of the 32nd Annual Meeting, Virginia State Bar Association, 1921* (Richmond: Virginia State Bar Association 1921).

Grinnell, Frank W. Some Early Lawyers of Massachusetts and Their Present Influence in the Life of the Nation, *Report of the 26th Annual Meeting of the Maryland State Bar Association . . . 1921*, pp. 175-198; also printed in *Massachusetts Law Quarterly*, 7 (1922), appendix.

Hallam, Oscar. Early Courts and Lawyers, *Yale Law Journal*, 25 (1916), 386-395.

Hamilton, J. G. de Roulhac. Southern Members of the Inns of Court, *North Carolina Historical Review*, 10 (1933), 273-286.

Hamlin, Paul M. The First Grievance Committee in New York, *Anglo-American Legal History Series*, Paul M. Hamlin, ed., Series 1, No. 3 (New York: New York University School of Law, 1939).

______. *Legal Education in Colonial New York* (New York: New York University Law Quarterly Review, 1939).

______. New York's First Bar Association, *New York Law Forum*, 5 (1959), 348-367.

______. Peter van Schaack, *Columbia University Quarterly*, 24 (1932), 66-105.

Hemphill, John M. II. Edmund Randolph Assumes Thomas Jefferson's Practice, *Virginia Magazine of History and Biography*, 77 (1959), 170-171.

Hogue, L. Lynn. Nicholas Trott: Man of Law and Letters, *South Carolina Historical Magazine*, 76 (1975), 25-34.

Hughes, Robert M. The Historical Evolution of the Board of Law Examiners and Its Influence on Legal Education, *Massachusetts Bar Association Report*, 38 (1914), 846-863.

Hühner, Leon. Jews in the Legal and Medical Professions in America before 1800, *American Jewish Historical Society Proceedings*, 22 (1914), 147-165.

Jackson, Sydney W. Daniel Leonard, 1740-1829, *Bermuda Historical Quarterly*, 13 (1956), 136-145.

Johnson, Herbert A. John Jay: Lawyer in a Time of Transition, 1764-1775, *University of Pennsylvania Law Review*, 124 (1976), 1260-1292; reprinted herein at 125-157.

______. *John Jay: 1745-1829* (Albany: New York State Department of Education, 1970).

Jones, E. Alfred. *American Members of the Inns of Court* (London: St. Catherine Press, 1924).

Justices of the Peace of Colonial Virginia, 1757-1775 (Richmond: Davis Botton, 1922); also in *Virginia State Library Bulletin*, 14, Nos. 2, 3 (April, July, 1921).

Keasbey, Edward Q. *The Courts and Lawyers of New Jersey, 1661-1912*, 3 vols. (New York: Lewis Historical Publishing Co., 1912).

Klein, Milton M. From Community to Status: The Development of the Legal Profession in Colonial New York, *New York History*, 60 (1979), 133-156.

______. New York Lawyers and the Coming of the American Revolution, *New York History*, 55 (1974), 383-407.

______. The Rise of the New York Bar: The Legal Career of William Livingston, *William and Mary Quarterly*, 15 (1958), 334-358; reprinted in Flaherty, *Essays*, 392-417.

Kommers, Donald P. Reflections on Professor Chroust's *The Rise of the Legal Profession in America, American Journal of Legal History*, 10 (1966), 201-213.

Konkle, Buron A. David Lloyd, Penn's Great Lawmaker, *Pennsylvania History*, 4 (1937), 153-156.

Land, Aubrey C. *The Dulanys of Maryland* (Baltimore: Maryland Historical Society, 1955).

Ledbetter, Tommy R. The Early History of the Legal Profession, *Baylor Law Review*, 18 (1966), 380-393.

Macassey, Sir Lyndon. The Part Played by Members of the Inns of Court of England in the Formation of the United States, *American Bar Association Journal*, 17 (1931), 740-744.

Matthews, Nathan. The Results of the Prejudice Against Lawyers in Massachusetts in the Seventeenth Century, *Massachusetts Law Quarterly*, 13 (1927), 73-94.

Mays, David J. *Edmund Pendleton, 1721-1803*, 2 vols. (Cambridge: Harvard University Press, 1952).

Morris, Richard B. Legalism versus Revolutionary Doctrine in New England, *New England Quarterly*, 4 (1931), 195-215; reprinted in Flaherty, *Essays*, 418-432.

McKirdy, Charles R. Bar Divided: The Lawyers of Massachusetts and the American Revolution, *American Journal of Legal History*, 16 (1972), 205-214.

______. Before the Storm: The Working Lawyer in Pre-revolutionary Massachusetts, *Suffolk University Law Review*, 11 (1976), 46-60.

______. The Lawyer as Apprentice: Legal Education in Eighteenth Century Massachusetts, *Journal of Legal Education*, 28 (1976), 124-136.

Nolan, Dennis R. The Effect of the Revolution on the Bar: The Maryland Experience, *Vanderbilt Law Review*, 62 (1976), 969-999.

______. *Readings in the History of the American Legal Profession* (Charlottesville: Michie, Bobbs-Merrill, 1980).

O'Connor, John E. *William Paterson, Lawyer and Statesman, 1745-1806* (New Brunswick: Rutgers University Press, 1979).

Parker, Herbert. *Courts and Lawyers of New England*, 4 vols. (New York: American Historical Society, 1931).

Pound, Roscoe. The Legal Profession in America, *Notre Dame Lawyer*, 19 (1944), 334-354.

Reid, John P. A Lawyer Acquitted: John Adams and the Boston Massacre Trials, *American Journal of Legal History*, 18 (1974), 189-207.

Robinson, Conway. Of Lawyers in Virginia between 1704 and 1737, *Virginia Law Journal*, 1 (1877), 191-196.

Robinson, George W. *John Winthrop as Attorney: Extracts from Order Books of the Court of Wards and Liveries, 1627-1629* (Cambridge: G. W. Robinson, 1930).

Shipman, Arthur L. Connecticut's First Lawyer, *Connecticut Bar Journal*, 1 (1927), 110-123.

Smith, Joseph H. An Independent Judiciary: The Colonial Background, *University of Pennsylvania Law Review*, 124 (1976), 1104-1156.

Surrency, Erwin C. The Lawyer and the Revolution, *American Journal of Legal History*, 8 (1964), 125-135.

Trumbull, J. Hammond. A Sketch of the Life of Thomas Lechford, Esq., Lawyer, *Transactions of the American Antiquarian Society*, 7 (1885).

Van Tyne, Charles H. Lawyers and the American Revolution, *Law Times*, 163 (1927), 523-525.

Vipperman, Carl J. *The Rise of Rawlins Lowndes, 1721-1800* (Columbia: University of South Carolina Press, 1978).

Wakeling, Arthur. Victories of Great Lawyers—Andrew Hamilton, *Green Bag*, 23 (1911), 71-73.

Warren, Charles. *A History of the American Bar* (Boston: Little, Brown & Co., 1911).

Washington, Bushrod C. Court and Bar of Colonial Virginia, *Green Bag*, 12 (1900), 470-479.

Webber, Marvelle C. Origin and Uses of Bar Associations: Review of Much Interesting History Relating to the Legal Profession, Beginning with Colonial Times and Extending to the Present, *American Bar Association Journal*, 7 (1921), 297-300.

Wilcox, F. L. The South Carolina Bar, Past, Present and Future, *South Carolina Bar Association Proceedings*, 1926, pp. 102-120.

Wroth, L. Kinvin, and Zobel, Hiller B., eds., *The Legal Papers of John Adams*, 3 vols. (Cambridge: Harvard University Press, 1965).

LOCAL GOVERNMENT

Blawie, James, and Blawie, Marilyn. The Inherent Right to Local Self-Government in Connecticut, *Connecticut Bar Journal* 30 (1956), 231-252, 376-389.

Collier, James M. *County Government in New Jersey* (New Brunswick: Rutgers University Press, 1952).

Daniels, Bruce C. The Long Lasting Men of Local Government: Town Clerks in Colonial Connecticut, *Connecticut Historical Society Bulletin*, 41 (1976), 90-96.

______, ed. *Town and County: Essays on the Structure of Local Government in the American Colonies* (Middletown: Wesleyan University Press, 1978).

Davis, Harrison M. Local Government under the First Charter, *Essex Institute Historical Collections*, 66 (1930), 161-181.

Deutsch, Albert. The Sick Poor in Colonial Times, *American Historical Review*, 46 (1941), 560-579.

Faeth, Henry J. *The Connecticut County* (Storrs: Institute of Public Service, University of Connecticut, 1949).

Gray, Walter S. *County Government in Essex County, New Jersey* (Newark: Essex County Board of Chosen Freeholders, 1953).

Griffith, Ernest S. *History of American City Government: The Colonial Period* (New York: Oxford University Press, 1938).

Guess, William C. County Government in Colonial North Carolina, *James Sprunt Historical Publications*, 11 (1911), 5-39.

Holman, Allan W. Jr. Rights and Duties of Rural Landowners to the Erection and Maintenance of Partition Fences in Pennsylvania, *Dickinson Law Review*, 59 (1955), 266-270.

McBain, Howard L. The Legal Status of the American Colonial City, *Political Science Quarterly*, 40 (1925), 177-200.

McGovern, J. Raymond. Creation, Control and Supervision of Cities and Villages by the State, *Brooklyn Law Review*, 20 (1954), 158-171.

Nelson, William E. Legal Restraints of Power in Pre-Revolutionary America: Masschusetts as a Case Study, 1760-1775, *American Journal of Legal History*, 18 (1974), 1-32.

Riley, Edward M. The Town Acts of Colonial Virginia, *Journal of Southern History*, 16 (1950), 306-323.

Roeber, A. G. Authority, Law and Custom: The Rituals of Court Day in Tidewater Virginia, 1720 to 1750, *William and Mary Quarterly*, 38 (1980), 29-52.

Scudder, Harry J. The Formation of Civil Government in Suffolk County, in *Bicentennial: A History of Suffolk County* (Babylon: Suffolk County Board of Supervisors, 1885).

Seiler, William A. Land Processioning in Colonial Virginia, *William and Mary Quarterly*, 6 (1949), 416-436.

Seymann, Jerrold. *Colonial Charters, Patents, and Grants to the Communities Comprising the City of New York* (New York: Board of Statutory Consolidation of the City of New York, 1939).

Sly, John F. *Town Government in Massachusetts (1620-1930)* (Cambridge: Harvard University Press, 1930).

Teaford, Jon C. *The Municipal Revolution in America: Origins of Modern Urban Government, 1650-1825* (Chicago: University of Chicago Press, 1975).

Watson, Alan D. County Fiscal Policy in Colonial North Carolina, *North Carolina Historical Review*, 55 (1978), 284-305.

White, Philip L. Municipal Government Comes to Manhattan, *New-York Historical Society Quarterly*, 37 (1953), 146-157.

PROBATE

Andrew, Charles M. *The Connecticut Intestacy Law* (New Haven : Yale University Press, 1933); also in *Select Essays in Anglo-American Legal History*, 3 vols. (Boston: Little, Brown & Co., 1907); reprinted in Flaherty, *Essays*, 336-366.

Atkinson, Thomas E. The Development of the Massachusetts Probate System, *Michigan Law Review*, 42 (1943), 425-452.

Grattan, George G. IV. The Revocation of Wills by Subsequent Instrument, *Virginia Law Review*, 56 (1960), 373-389.

Guest, James W. The Court of Ordinary (South Carolina), *University of South Carolina Selden Society Yearbook*, 6 (1942), 40-46.

Haskins, George L. The Beginnings of Partible Inheritance in the American Colonies, *Yale Law Journal*, 51 (1942), 1280-1315.

Hoover, Lawrence H. Jr. Holographic Wills in Virginia: Problems at Probate, *Virginia Law Review*, 45 (1959), 613-628.

Hutton, A. J. White. The Probate of Wills in Pennsylvania, *Dickinson Law Review*, 54 (1954), 237-245.

Johnson, Herbert A. The Prerogative Court of New York, 1686-1776, *American Journal of Legal History*, 18 (1973), 95-144; reprinted herein at 55-104.

Limbaugh, Rush H. The Sources and Development of Probate Law, *Washington University Law Review*, 1956, pp. 419-447.

Nelson, William. *The Law and Practice of New Jersey from Earliest Times Concerning the Probate of Wills, the Administration of Estates, the Protection of Orphans and Minors, and the Control of Their Estates; the Prerogative Court, the Ordinary and the Surrogates* (Paterson: Paterson History Club, 1909).

Pitkin, Donald S. Partible Inheritance and the Open Fields, *Agricultural History*, 35 (1961), 65-69.

Reppy, Alison. The Slayer's Bounty—in New York, *New York University Law Review*, 20 (1945), 270-324.

Setaro, Franklyn C. The Surrogate's Court of New York: Its Antecedents, *New York Law Forum*, 2 (1956), 283-304.

Vosburgh, Royden W. Surrogate's Courts and Records in the Colony and State of New York, 1664-1847, *New York State Historical Association Journal*, 3 (1922), 105-116.

PROPERTY

Barker, Charles A. Property Rights in the Provincial System of Maryland: Proprietary Policy, *Journal of Southern History*, 2 (1936), 43-68.

______. Property Rights in the Provincial System of Maryland: Properietary Revenues, *Journal of Southern History*, 2 (1936), 211-232.

Barnes, Viola F. Land Tenure in English Colonial Charters of the Seventeenth Century, in *Essays in Colonial History Presented to Charles McLean Andrews* (New Haven: Yale University Press, 1931).

Beale, Joseph H. Jr. The Origin of the System of Recording Deeds in America, *Green Bag*, 19 (1907), 335-339.

Bigelow, Melville W. Memoranda of Traces of Primogeniture in *Massachusetts, Massachusetts Historical Society Proceedings*, 45 (1912), 34-35.

Bliss, Willard F. The Rise of Tenancy in Virginia, *Virginia Magazine of History and Biography*, 58 (1950), 427-441.

Bond, Beverly W. Jr. The Quit Rent in Maryland, *Maryland Historical Magazine*, 5 (1910), 350-365.

______. The Quit Rent System in the American Colonies, *American Historical Review*, 17 (1912), 495-516.

______. *The Quit Rent System in the American Colonies* (New Haven: Yale University Press, 1919).

Bugbee, Bruce W. *The Genesis of American Patent and Copyright Law* (Washington: Public Affairs Press, 1967).

Carroll, Kenneth L. The Court Inquires About a Ghost (entails and guardianship), *Maryland Historical Magazine*, 55 (1960), 28-43.

Cobbledick, M. Robert. The Property Rights of Women in Puritan New England, in George P. Murdock, ed., *Studies in the Science of Society, presented to Albert Galloway Keller*. . . (New Haven: Yale University Press, 1937).

Connolly, James C. Quit Rents in Colonial New Jersey, *Union County Historical Society Proceedings*, 1923, pp. 3-12.

______. Quit Rents in Colonial New Jersey as a Contributing Cause for the American Revolution, *New Jersey Historical Society Proceedings*, New Series, 7 (1922), 13-21.

DeLancey, Edward F. The Origin and History of Manors in New York and the County of Westchester, in J. Thomas Scharf, *History of Westchester County, New York*, 2 vols. (Philadelphia: L. E. Putnam & Co., 1886).

Dickinson, Josiah L. *The Fairfax Proprietary* (Front Royal: Warren Press, 1959).

Eno, Joel N. The English Manors of New York, *Journal of American History*, 16 (1922), 361-377.

Fellman, David. Property in Colonial Political Theory, *Temple Law Quarterly*, 16 (1942), 388-406.

______. The European Background of Early American Ideas Concerning Property, *Temple Law Quarterly*, 14 (1940), 497-516.

Fenning, Karl. The Origin of the Patent and Copyright Clause of the Constitution, *Georgetown Law Journal*, 17 (1929), 109-117.

Fitzgerald, William T. A. A Short History of the Origin and Development of Conveyancing, *New England Historical and Genealogical Record*, 65 (1911), 265-275.

Fitzpatrick, Benedict. Some New York Manors and Patents, *Americana*, 20 (1926), 316-348.

Flippin, Percy Scott. The Royal Government in Georgia, 1752-1776: V: The Land System, *Georgia Historical Quarterly*, 10 (1926), 1-25.

Fowler, Robert L. *History of the Law of Real Property in New York* (New York: Baker Co., 1895).

Fullerton, James N. Squatters and Titles to Land in Early Western Pennsylvania, *Western Pennsylvania Historical Magazine*, 6 (1923), 165-176.

Goebel, Julius Jr. Some Legal and Political Aspects of the Manors in New York, *Order of Colonial Lords of Manors in America Publications*, No. 19 (1928).

Granting of Land in Colonial South Carolina, *South Carolina Historical Magazine*, 77 (1976), 208-212.

Griffin, Ernest F. Manors, Grants and Great Patents, *Americana*, (1942).

Harris, Marshall D. *The Origin of the Land Tenure System in the United States* (Ames: Iowa State College Press, 1953).

Hartog, Hendrik. Because All the World Was Not New York City: Governance, Property Rights and the State in the Changing Definition of a Corporation, *Buffalo Law Review*, 28 (1979), 91-109.

Haskins, George L. The Beginnings of the Recording System in Massachusetts, *Boston University Law Review*, 21 (1941), 281-304.

______. Gavelkind and the Charter of Massachusetts Bay, *Transactions of the Colonial Society of Massachusetts*, 34 (1942), 483-498.

______. A Problem in the Reception of the Common Law in the Colonial Period [dower], *University of Pennsylvania Law Review*, 97 (1949), 842-853.

Holman, Allan W. Jr. Rights and Duties of Rural Landowners to the Erection and Maintenance of Partition Fences in Pennsylvania, *Dickinson Law Review*, 59 (1955), 266-270.

Howe, Mark DeWolf. The Recording of Deeds in the Colony of Massachusetts Bay, *Boston University Law Review*, 28 (1948), 1-6.

Keim, C. Ray. Primogeniture and Entail in Colonial Virginia, *William and Mary Quarterly*, 25 (1968), 545-586.

Konig, David T. Community Custom and the Common Law: Social Change and the Development of Land Law in Seventeenth Century Massachusetts, *American Journal of Legal History*, 18 (1974), 137-177.

Liversage, Vincent. *Land Tenure in the Colonies* (New York: Macmillan Co., 1945).

Livingston, John Henry. The Minor Manors of New York, *Order of Colonial Lords of Manors in America Publications*, No. 12 (1923).

Locke, William S. Escheat of Lands in Unknown Persons—Interpretation of an Ancient Statute, *Connecticut Bar Journal*, 19 (1955), 123-133.

Mark, Irving. *Agrarian Conflicts in Colonial New York, 1711-1775* (New York: Columbia University Press, 1940).

Mark, Irving, and Handlin, Oscar. Land Cases in Colonial New York, 1765-1767, The King v. William Prendergast, *New York University Law Quarterly Review*, 19 (1942), 165-194.

Melick, Harry C. W. *The Manor of Fordham and Its Founder* (New York: Fordham University Press, 1950).

Morgan, Lawrence N. Land Tenure in Proprietary North Carolina, *James Sprunt Historical Publications*, 12, No. 1 (1912), 41-63.

Morris, Richard B. Primogeniture and Entailed Estates in America, *Columbia Law Review*, 27 (1927), 24-71.

Morrison, Charles, Early Fairfax Land Grants and Leases along the South Branch of the Potomac, *West Virginia History*, 37 (1976), 1-22.

MacDonald, Norman. English Land Tenure on the North American Continent: A Summary, *Contributions to Canadian Economics*, 7 (1934), 21-44.

Nissenson, Samuel G. The Development of a Land Registration System in New York, *New York History*, 20 (1939), 16-42.

______. *The Patroon's Domain* (New York: Columbia University Press, 1937).

Pell, Howland. The Pell Manor, *Order of Colonial Lords of Manors in America Publications*, No. 5 (1917).

Pitkin, Donald S. Partible Inheritance and the Open Fields, *Agricultural History* 35 (1961), 65-69.

Prager, Frank D. A History of Intellectual Property from 1545 to 1787, *Journal of the Patent Office Society*, 26 (1944), 711-760.

Primogeniture in Rhode Island, *Rhode Island Historical Society Collections*, 31 (1938), 76-78.

Richardson, Hester D. *The Origin and Customs of English Manors, with an Account of Feudal Rights and Privileges in the American Colonies* (New York: H. D. Richardson, 1913).

Riddell, William R. Early Provincial Legislative Interference with Private Property, *Canadian Bar Review*, 11 (1933), 176-180.

Rife, Clarence W. Land Tenure in New Netherland, in *Essays in Colonial History Presented to Charles McLean Andrews* . . . (New Haven: Yale University Press, 1931).

Robertson, William. An Account of the Manner of Taking Up and Patenting Land in Virginia, *William and Mary Quarterly*, 2nd Series, 3 (1923), 137-142.

Rugg, Arthur P. A Famous Colonial Litigation: The Case between Richard Sherman and Capt. Robert Keayne (title to stray cow) *American Antiquarian Society Proceedings*, New Series, 30, Part 2 (1920), 217-250.

Scott, William B. *In Pursuit of Happiness: American Conceptions of Property from the Seventeenth to the Twentieth Century* (Bloomington: Indiana University Press, 1977).

Seiler, William A. Land Processioning in Colonial Virginia, *William and Mary Quarterly*, 6 (1949), 416-436.

Sutherland, Arthur E. The Tenantry of the New York Manors, *Cornell Law Quarterly*, 41 (1956), 620-639.

Watkins, Walter K. Three Contracts for Seventeenth Century Building Construction in Massachusetts, *Old-Time New England*, 12 (1920), 27-32.

Watson, Alan D. The Quit Rent System in Royal South Carolina, *William and Mary Quarterly*, 33 (1976), 183-211.

Wheeler, Charles B. *The Heathcote Manor of Scarsdale* (Baltimore: Williams & Wilkins Co., 1923).

Wightman, Ida M. The Mayhew Manor of Tisbury, *Order of Colonial Lords of Manors in America, Publications*, No. 10 (1921).

Zollman, Carl. The Development of the Law of Charities in the United States, *Columbia Law Review*, 14 (1919), 286-309.

PUBLIC OFFICERS

Boyd, Julian P. The Sheriff in Colonial North Carolina, *North Carolina Historical Review*, 5 (1928), 151-180.

Daniels, Bruce C. The Long Lasting Men of Local Government: Town Clerks in Colonial Connecticut, *Connecticut Historical Society Bulletin*, 41 (1976), 90-96.

Day, Benjamin M. A Historical Review of the Office of Sheriff in America, *Case and Comment*, 22 (1915), 232-236.

Karraker, Cyrus H. *The Seventeenth Century Sheriff, A Comparative Study of the Sheriff in England and the Chesapeake Colonies, 1607-1689* (Chapel Hill: University of North Carolina Press, 1930).

Kemmerer, Donald L. Judge's Good Behavior Tenure in Colonial New Jersey, *New Jersey Historical Society Proceedings*, 56 (1938), 18-30.

Riddell, William R. Powers of a Colonial Legislature in Impeachment and Contempt, *Royal Society of Canada Proceedings*, 3rd Series, 21, Sec. 2 (1932), 83-90.

______. Impeachment in England and the English Colonies, *New York University Law Review*, 7 (1930), 702-708.

Rugg, Arthur P. The Office of Attorney General, *Massachusetts Historical Society Proceedings*, 56 (1923), 171-173.

Warden, G. B. Office Holding and Officials in Boston, 1692-1775, *New England Historical and Genealogical Register*, 131 (1977), 267-290.

Watson, Alan D. The Appointment of Sheriffs in Colonial North Carolina: A Reconsideration, *North Carolina Historical Review*, 53 (1976), 385-398.

SLAVERY

Alpert, Jonathan L. The Origin of Slavery in the United States: The Maryland Precedent, *American Journal of Legal History*, 14 (1970), 189-221.

Clark, Ernest J. Jr. Aspects of the North Carolina Slave Code, 1715-1860, *North Carolina Historical Review*, 39 (1962), 148-164.

Clarke, T. Wood. The Negro Plot of 1741, *New York History*, 26 (1944), 167-181.

Cobb, Herschel P. Old Slave Laws of Georgia, *Case and Comment*, 23 (1916), 7-10.

Crawford, Paul. A Footnote on the Courts for the Trial of Negroes in Colonial Connecticut, *Journal of Black Studies*, 5 (1974), 167-174.

Davis, John A. Blacks, Crime and American Culture, *Annals of the American Academy of Political Science*, 423 (1976), 89-98.

Fogarty, Gerald P. Slaves, Quakers and Catholic Marriage in Colonial Maryland, *Jurist*, 35 (1975), 142-161.

Greene, Lorenzo T. Slave-holding in New England and Its Awakening, *Journal of Negro History*, 13 (1928), 492-533.

Grinde, Donald Jr. Native American Slavery in the Southern Colonies, *Indian Historian*, 10 (1977), 38-42.

Guild, June P. *Black Laws of Virginia* (Richmond: Whittet & Sheeperson, 1936).

Hindus, Michael S. Black Justice under White Law: Criminal Prosecutions of Blacks in Antebellum South Carolina, *Journal of American History*, 63 (1976), 575-599.

Hoffert, Sylvia. The "One Great Evil" [miscegenation], *American History Illustrated*, 12 (1977), 37-41.

Jernegan, Marcus. A Forgotten Slavery of Colonial Days, *Harper's*, 127 (1913), 745-751.

Johnson, Whittington B. The Origin and Nature of African Slavery in Seventeenth Century Maryland, *Maryland Historical Magazine*, 73 (1978), 236-245.

King, Ethel. The New York Negro Plot of 1741, *U.S. Catholic Historical Record*, 20 (1931), 173-180.

Lauber, Almon W. *Indian Slavery in Colonial Times within the Present Limits of the United States* (New York: Columbia University Press, 1913).

Menard, Russell. From Servants to Slaves: The Transformation of the Chesapeake Labor System, *Southern Studies*, 14 (1977), 355-390.

Nordstrom, Carl. The New York Slave Code, *Afro-American New York Life and History*, 4 (1980), 7-25.

Palmer, Paul C. Servant and Slave: The Evolution of the Legal Status of the Negro Laborer in Colonial Virginia, *South Atlantic Quarterly*, 65 (1966), 355-370.

Riddell, William R. The Slave in Early New York, *Journal of Negro History*, 13 (1928), 53-86.

Ruchames, Louis. Race, Marriage and Abolition in Massachusetts, *Journal of Negro History*, 40 (1955), 250-273.

Scott, Kenneth. The Slave Insurrection in New York in 1712, *New-York Historical Society Quarterly*, 45 (1961), 43-74.

Sirmans, M. Eugene. The Legal Status of the Slave in South Carolina, 1670-1740, *Journal of Southern History*, 28 (1962), 402-473.

Slotkin, Richard. Narratives of Negro Crime in New England, 1675-1800, *American Quarterly*, 25 (1973), 3-31.

Szasz, Ferenc M. The New York Slave Revolt of 1741: A Reexamination, *New York History*, 48 (1967), 215-230.

Turner, Edward R. Slavery in Colonial Pennsylvania, *Pennsylvania Magazine of History and Biography*, 35 (1911), 141-151.

Wiecek, William M. Somerset: Lord Mansfield and the Legitimacy of Slavery in the Anglo-American World, *University of Chicago Law Review*, 42 (1974), 86-146.

______. *The Sources of Antislavery Constitutionalism in America, 1760-1848* (Ithaca: Cornell University Press, 1977).

Winston, Sanford. Indian Slavery in the Carolina Region, *Journal of Negro History*, 19 (1934), 431-440.

STATUTES

Andrews, Charles M. The Royal Disallowance, *American Antiquarian Society Proceedings*, New Series, 24, Part 2 (1914), 342-362.

Billings, Warren M., ed. Some Acts Not in Hening's Statutes: The Acts of Assembly, April 1652, November 1652 and July 1653, *Virginia Magazine of History and Biography*, 83 (1975), 22-76.

Brown, Elizabeth G. British Statutes in the Emergent Nations of North America, 1606-1949, *American Journal of Legal History*, 7 (1963), 95-136.

Calder, Isabel. John Cotton's "Moses His Judicials," *Colonial Society of Massachusetts Publications*, 28 (1935), 86-94.

Clark, J. Murray. Why the "Lawes of Virginia," *Virginia Law Register*, New Series, 6 (1920), 81-100.

Edmunds, John H. Massachusetts Laws of 1660, *Colonial Society of Massachusetts Publications*, 27 (1932), 194-197.

Fitzpatrick, John T. Revisions and Compilations of the Laws of New York, *Law Library Journal*, 11 (1919), 21-31.

Fitzroy, Herbert W. K. Richard Cosby Goes to Court, 1683-1697: Some Realities of Colonial Legislation, *Pennsylvania Magazine of History and Biography*, 62 (1938), 12-19.

Gay, Frederick L. Remarks in Communicating the Capitall Lawes of New England, London, 1643, *Colonial Society of Massachusetts Publications*, 17 (1915), 116-118.

Goodwin, William A. R. Laws Relating to the Early Colonial Church in Virginia, *Protestant Episcopal Church Historical Magazine*, 3 (1934), 34-37, 96-110.

Haskins, George L. Codification of the Law in Colonial Massachusetts: A Study in Comparative Law, *Indiana Law Journal*, 30 (1954), 1-17.

Korey, Marie E. Some Notes on Colonial New York Laws, *American Antiquarian Society Proceedings*, 88, Part 1 (1978), 90-102.

Kukla, Jon. Some Acts Not in Hening's Statutes: The Acts of Assembly, October 1660, *Virginia Magazine of History and Biography*, 83 (1975), 77-97.

Matthews, Albert. The Printing of the Capital Laws in 1642, *Colonial Society of Massachusetts Publications*, 27 (1932), 112-115.

Norwood, Leslie E. Colony Ordinance of 1641-47 and Its Effect on Maine Law, *Peabody Law Review*, 3 (1939), 77-83.

Pennypacker, Morton. The Duke's Laws: Their Antecedents, Implications and Importance, in Richard B. Morris and Paul M. Hamlin, eds., *Anglo-American Legal History Series*, No. 9 (1944).

Riesenfeld, Stefan A. Law-making and Legislative Precedent in American Legal History, *Minnesota Law Review*, 33 (1948), 103-144.

Riley, Edward M. The Town Acts of Colonial Virginia, *Journal of Southern History*, 16 (1950), 306-323.

Root, W. T. The Massachusetts Book of Laws of 1648, *Iowa Law Review*, 15 (1931), 179-185.

Shelton, Thomas W. Why the "Lawes of Virginia," *Central Law Journal*, 91 (1920), 262-263.

Surrency, Erwin C. Revision of Colonial Laws, *American Journal of Legal History*, 9 (1965), 189-205.

TORTS

Bowler, Clara A. Carted Whores and White Shrouded Apologies: Slander in the County Courts of Seventeenth-Century Virginia, *Virginia Magazine of History and Biography*, 85 (1977), 411-426.

Chase, Theodore. John Winthrop and the Doctrine of Judicial Immunity, *American Bar Association Journal*, 46 (1960), 602-608.

Greene, Evarts B. The Code of Honor in Colonial and Revolutionary Times, with Special Reference to New England, *Massachusetts Historical Society Proceedings*, 26 (1927), 367-388.

Karraker, Cyrus H. Deodands in Colonial Virginia and Maryland, *American Historical Review*, 37 (1932), 712-717.

Scott, Kenneth. The Ducking of Anne Dougel, *New York Folklore Quarterly*, 15 (1959), 28-35.

TREASON

Chapin, Bradley. *The American Law of Treason: Revolutionary and Early National Origins* (Seattle: University of Washington Press, 1964).

______. The American Revolution as Lese Majesty, *Pennsylvania Magazine of History and Biography*, 79 (1955), 310-330.

______. Colonial and Revolutionary Origins of the American Law of Treason, *William and Mary Quarterly*, 17 (1960), 3-21.

Connor, Elizabeth. Treason on the Sassafras, *Maryland Historical Magazine*, 51 (1956), 154-158.

Hurst, James Willard. English Sources of the American Law of Treason, *Wisconsin Law Review*, 1945, pp. 315-356.

______. The Historic Background of the Treason Clause of the United States Constitution, *Federal Bar Journal*, 6 (1945), 305-313.

______. Treason in the United States, *Harvard Law Review*, 58 (1944-45), 226-246.

Leder, Lawrence H., ed. Records of the Trials of Jacob Leisler and His Associates, *New-York Historical Society Quarterly*, 36 (1952), 430-457.

Wakeling, Arthur. The Trial of Leisler for High Treason, *Green Bag*, 23 (1911), 287-291.

Index

About the Author

HERBERT A. JOHNSON, past president of the American Society for Legal History, is Professor of History and Law at the University of South Carolina in Columbia. His earlier works include *John Jay, 1745-1829* and *The Papers of John Marshall.*

www.ingramcontent.com/pod-product-compliance
Lightning Source LLC
LaVergne TN
LVHW011752200926
848484LV00003B/683